A New Edition of

Health and Safety for You

Wellness from Webster/McGraw-Hill

Health and Safety for You has it all. This new edition, revised to keep pace with the fast-changing field of health, was designed with teachers and students in mind. Here are some highlights:

An Active Approach to Wellness

The wellness orientation of health begins in the first chapter (page 2) and continues throughout the book—both motivation and information help teenagers make positive health decisions for today and for the long term.

Current Health Topics

Today's serious health concerns are all here—stress (page 52), cancer prevention (page 154), sexually transmitted diseases (page 312), nutrition (page 320), smoking (page 258), alcohol abuse (page 269), drug abuse (page 280), and the aging process (page 114).

Solid Content

The foundation of effective health education is solid content on body systems. Unit 5 (beginning on page 164) treats all these important areas.

Self-Care and Emergencies

The latest in practical health information is covered—emergency procedures and other self-care aspects of health and wellness, including CPR (page 398), first aid (page 387), the Heimlich maneuver (page 406), poisoning (page 389), and being a health consumer (page 421).

Solid Educational Features

Each chapter is reinforced with strong features to support learning. The Preface on page v describes them all.

A Teacher's Resource Notebook

The Teacher's Resource Notebook contains wall posters and reproducible student activity and resource sheets, anatomical drawings, vocabulary sheets as well as chapter and unit tests.

Health and Safety for You

Seventh Edition

School Division/McGraw-Hill Book Company

New York   St. Louis   San Francisco   Dallas   Oklahoma City   Atlanta

Editor-in-Chief: Martha O'Neill
Project Editor: Howard N. Portnoy
Editing Supervisor: Maureen Meehan
Production Supervisor: Salvador Gonzales

Cover Design: Paddy St. J. Bareham
Cover Photography: Lawrence Migdale
Text Design: A Good Thing, Inc.
Art Direction: Rosemary O'Connell
Design Supervision: Clint Anglin
Photo Editing Manager: Suzanne V. Skloot
Photo Research Editors: Buff Rosenthal, Safra Nimrod

This book was set in 11 pt. Baskerville by J & L Graphics, Inc.

Diehl, Laton: *Health and Safety for You*, 1957 Edition
Copyright renewed 1985 by Antoni M. Diehl, Annabelle Diehl Bush, Frank W. Finn

Library of Congress Cataloging-in-Publication Data

Tsumura, Ted K.
    Health and safety for you.

    Tsumura's name appeared first in previous ed.
    Includes index.
    Summary: An introduction to anatomy, physiology,
mental and physical health, preventive medicine,
environment and heredity, safety, drugs, nutrition,
human sexuality, and health careers.
    1. Health—Juvenile literature. [1. Health]
I. Jones, Lorraine Henke. II. Bonekemper, Thomas W.
III. Title. [DNLM: 1. Accident Prevention—popular
works. 2. Health. 3. Physiology—popular works.
4. Preventive Medicine—popular works. QT 215 T8824h]
RA777.T77 1986   613   86-5195

ISBN 0-07-065386-0

Send all inquiries to:
GLENCOE DIVISION
Macmillan/McGraw-Hill
15319 Chatsworth Street
P.O. Box 9609
Mission Hills, CA 91346-9609

The Authors

Lorraine Henke Jones is assistant professor of nursing at Ball State University. Formerly a health-education specialist for Prince George's County Public Schools in Maryland, she holds a master's degree in both nursing and health education. The recipient of numerous honors in her field, Professor Jones has written articles for health education and nursing journals and has coauthored health and safety programs for the American National Red Cross and the Agency for Instructional Television.

Ted K. Tsumura teaches health/physiology at Overland High School in Aurora, Colorado. He holds a doctorate in health education and was named Colorado Teacher of the Year in 1976. He is a member of several professional educational organizations, including the Schoolsite Task Force Committee of the Colorado Heart Association. Dr. Tsumura has coauthored a genetics textbook and is director-at-large of the National Association of Biology Teachers.

Thomas W. Bonekemper is assistant professor of medicine at Hahnemann University in Philadelphia. He has taught health education at the secondary level and is a diplomate of the American Board of Internal Medicine. As a physician, Dr. Bonekemper has a special interest in patient education and preventive medicine.

Consultants

Robert C. Ascher
Supervisor of Health
Newport News, Virginia

Mary Joyce Baker
Irving High School
Irving, Texas

Patricia L. Barnett
Coordinator of Health
Clayton, Georgia
County Schools

Dona Gail Boatman
Memorial High School
Joplin, Missouri

Larry Brain, M.D.
Psychiatric Institute of
Washington
Washington, D.C.

Dorothy Brooks
Bailey Junior High School/
Arlington Independent School
Arlington, Texas

Pat Davis
Hutcheson Junior High School/
Arlington Independent School
Arlington, Texas

Ted Dickie
Plano, Texas

Roberta L. Duyff
Nutrition Education Consultant
St. Louis County, Missouri

Pamela Erwin
Assistant Director of Athletics
Hurst-Euless-Bedford
Independent School District
Bedford, Texas

Alan Foodman, M.D.
Sarasota Palms Hospital
Sarasota, Florida

Wendy L. Harrison, Ed.D.
Dundalk Community College
Baltimore, Maryland

John G. McKay, Jr.
Executive Director
Texans' War on Drugs
Austin, Texas

John Meeks, M.D.
Psychiatric Institute of
Montgomery County
Rockville, Maryland

Stephen Meister, M.D.
Department of Pediatrics
Columbia Presbyterian
University Medical Center
New York, New York

Horace E. Morgan
Western Hills High School
Fort Worth, Texas

Judie Smith
Educational Coordinator
Suicide Crisis Center
Dallas, Texas

Charlotte Sorrel
L.V. Berkner High School/
Richardson Independent
School District
Richardson, Texas

David Warner
Chairman
Texas Diabetes Council
Austin, Texas

Preface

Health and Wellness with a Comprehensive Scope

HEALTH AND SAFETY FOR YOU is a comprehensive textbook that will help you to learn about *total health*—physical, mental, and social well-being. Its focus is on *wellness* and *preventive health and safety measures*. It encourages you, the student, to choose responsible health behaviors right now to improve and safeguard your health.

Features

☐ *Solid content* with current, simple, direct explanations that allow you to make intelligent decisions about health behavior. You will learn how your body works, how to prevent disease, and how and where to get treatment if necessary.

☐ *Readable text* has many subject headings that organize the content for you and allow easy reference.

☐ *Colorful photographs and illustrations* bring the text to life. They show how your body works and help you to learn by letting you see facts and ideas for yourself.

☐ *Easy-to-read captions* focus your attention on the important ideas in each chapter. They help you to understand the more complex information.

☐ *Learning objectives* at the beginning of each chapter guide your learning. They alert you to the key concepts within each chapter.

☐ *Effective chapter summaries* in the form of Main Ideas and Key Words allow you to review and evaluate what you have learned. Important key words are defined in the glossary. Pronunciations are included.

☐ *Discussion* of the latest health topics and of research is encouraged in the periodic chapter feature called Something to Think About.

☐ *Active learning* is stimulated in the section called Apply Your Knowledge. This section engages you in independent research, class experiments, interviewing, and community participation.

☐ *Information on the latest health career opportunities* offers you the chance to consider a future in the field of health service.

Contents

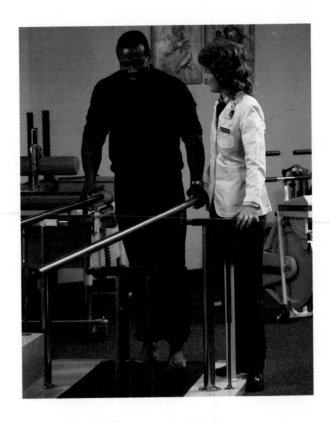

Unit 1
Active
Body

Chapter 1

Health and Wellness

After reading this chapter, you will be able to:

- ☐ Explain the World Health Organization's definition of health.
- ☐ Describe how our health goals have changed since the beginning of the century.
- ☐ Give examples of wellness behavior.
- ☐ Explain the relationship between attitude and good health.
- ☐ Take an inventory of your own health and wellness.

"A-OK"
"In the pink"
"Fit as a fiddle"
"Right as rain"
"Sound as a dollar"
"Healthy as a horse"

These people aren't talking about space shots or color or music or weather or money or animals. They're talking about their good health.

Are you a healthy person? There are a lot of different ways to express the idea of good health and probably as many ideas about what health means. One of the most important things you will learn in this book is what your own health means to you.

Health

Let's look at one definition of health. The World Health Organization defines **health** as "A state of complete physical, mental, and social well-being, and not merely the absence of disease or infirmity."

Physical well-being

During this century, the leading causes of death changed in the United States and in other developed countries. In 1900, at the beginning of the century, the leading causes of death were pneumonia, influenza, and tuberculosis. These are diseases caused by bacteria and viruses. They are known as **communicable diseases** because they can spread when conditions are favorable for bacteria and viruses to grow.

Medical research in the twentieth century found a way to prevent and control these diseases. New sanitation laws and better drugs meant that people could avoid these illnesses or be cured of them. By 1979, more than three-fourths of the way through the century, the leading causes of death were different. People were more free of communicable diseases. They lived a longer time and were now becoming victims of noninfectious diseases: heart attacks, cancer, high blood pressure, and strokes. Most evidence shows that these diseases are *not* spread by bacteria and viruses. They are diseases that often occur later in life. And they are influenced by a lifetime of day-to-day health habits. This has led to new ideas about what health means. The term **wellness** is often used to describe a broader view of good health. Wellness includes not only physical well-being but also emotional, social, and intellectual fitness.

Through this decade and into the 1990s, medical researchers will be finding new ways to control some of these noncontagious killer diseases. More important, many people are now taking steps to prevent these diseases.

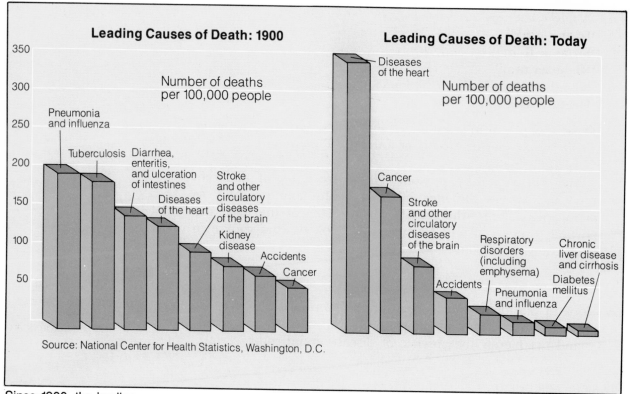

Leading Causes of Death: 1900

350
300
250
200
150
100
50

Number of deaths per 100,000 people

Pneumonia and influenza

Tuberculosis

Diarrhea, enteritis, and ulceration of intestines

Diseases of the heart

Stroke and other circulatory diseases of the brain

Kidney disease

Accidents

Cancer

Leading Causes of Death: Today

Number of deaths per 100,000 people

Diseases of the heart

Cancer

Stroke and other circulatory diseases of the brain

Accidents

Respiratory disorders (including emphysema)

Pneumonia and influenza

Diabetes mellitus

Chronic liver disease and cirrhosis

Source: National Center for Health Statistics, Washington, D.C.

Since 1900, the leading causes of death have changed. People are now more free of diseases that are spread by bacteria and viruses.

Mental and social well-being

When was the last time you felt good about yourself? Can you really enjoy another person? Are you able to handle normal disappointments? The answers to these and similar questions have to do with your mental and social well-being.

In the first part of the twentieth century, people had just begun serious research into the behavioral sciences of psychology and sociology. By the time of the World Health definition, health professionals and the public were taking psychological and sociological findings seriously. It seemed as if mental and social ills could be successfully prevented and treated. Well-being also could be called a state of mind, not just a state of the body.

Of course, mental health and physical health are closely connected. Can you experience mental and social well-being during a painful ear infection? Is your attitude about yourself any different during a period in your life when you have acne?

Or can you experience physical well-being when you are constantly undergoing mental or social tension—involved in an ongoing battle with someone who plays an important role in your life, for example? When you think about it, it is almost impossible to separate mental and social health from physical health.

Can you predict how healthy you will be in the year 2050? Do you know how healthy you will be when you reach 35? Can you tell how healthy you will be next year or even a week from now?

While you cannot predict the future with certainty, you can get an idea of what your chances are for good health. Is there a new, miracle method of diagnosis to tell you this? No. You can tell yourself by reviewing your own day-to-day health habits. If the health habits you practice *right now* are positive ones, you have a better chance of avoiding or postponing illness and injury. The U.S. Public Health Service believes in prevention. In 1979, the Surgeon General issued a report titled *Healthy People*. The report said that Americans are healthier now than they have ever been and that each one of us is responsible for our own health. The report established health goals. Many of the goals for healthy adolescents and young adults are in areas you will read about in *HEALTH AND SAFETY FOR YOU*.

Safety belts can help decrease your chances of being seriously injured in an automobile accident.

Good health in later life depends in part on your health behavior right now.

It seems so simple. Why doesn't everyone practice positive health habits? Medical research has linked lung cancer and heart disease to cigarette smoking. Why don't people stop smoking? Safety belts can prevent needless deaths during an automobile accident. And yet many people did not use seat belts until state laws made them mandatory. Care of teeth is another example. Flossing your teeth is an important habit, and yet many people don't take the time to clean their teeth thoroughly.

Flossing your teeth is part of a positive wellness program.

More than 25 years ago, the United States Public Health Service tried to find out why people do or do not adopt positive health measures. They found that people will take such measures if:

1. They see the health problem as one that has a good chance of affecting them.
2. They think that there would be serious consequences if the problem did affect them.
3. They believe there is a course of action that can reduce the threat.
4. They believe this course of action is reasonable.*

In other words, if you are convinced that:

- it is possible for you to have caries, or gum disease;
- it is possible for the dental problems to result in loss of teeth or need for painful surgery to the mouth area;
- flossing can remove plaque build-up and reduce caries;
- flossing is really not such a chore;

then you will probably get into the habit of flossing on a regular basis.

Health attitudes

You know, of course, that not everyone takes positive health measures. People's information, lack of information, and attitudes vary a great deal. Suppose that you interview five people. You tell each person that he or she is 25 pounds overweight. You also tell each person that overweight increases the chances of heart disease. Then you ask each person the four questions that decide wellness behavior. Their responses are on page 8. Take a look at them now.

Excuses for lack of wellness behavior

What does each person seem to be saying? If you look closely at these interviews, you will see some common excuses for not taking positive health measures:

- Ray believes it is all a matter of fate. He thinks there is nothing he can do to prevent disease and death.
- Anne feels she is too young to be concerned. She can't imagine a time when her health will show the effects of her long-term health habits.
- Cheryl thinks this is all someone else's problem. *She* doesn't have to worry about heart disease.

*Adapted from "What Research in Motivation Suggests for Public Health," by Irwin M. Rosenstock, in the *American Journal of Public Health*.

Question	Do you think you have a chance of having heart disease?	Do you think having heart disease would be serious?	Do you think there is anything you can do about your weight to lower the risk of heart disease?	If there is something you can do, do you think it is reasonable?
Ray	Probably. My grandparents were both overweight, and they both died of heart disease.	Yes. It seems like it could be serious—even fatal.	Probably not. Fat people and thin people get heart disease. There are many factors. Who can tell for sure?	If your time is up, you go. Dieting is hard, and it might not make any difference.
Anne	I'm only 20. I can't imagine having a heart attack. It doesn't seem possible.	Very serious. You would have to do something about overweight if you ever got heart disease.	Look, I'll cross that bridge when I come to it. I'm only 20!	It's not reasonable to live in the future. You have to live in the present.
Cheryl	I'm not so worried about heart disease. I read that women don't get heart diseases as often as men do.	Heart disease is serious for those people who get it.	I don't think my weight has anything to do with my own risk of heart disease. That's a problem men have. (End of interview.)	
Max	Yes. I guess my chances of heart disease are increased by overweight.	It all depends. People recover from heart disease. I have a friend who had three heart attacks. So he takes it easy.	I can drop these extra pounds.	I want to lose some weight, but not because of heart disease. I'd like to lose it because I think I'd be more attractive if I were 25 pounds slimmer.
Sue	Yes. Overweight is a risk factor for the heart.	Yes. Heart disease is a leading cause of death in the United States.	I could lose weight.	I probably won't. I hate to diet. I can't stick to a diet long enough to lose 25 pounds.

- Max might take some positive measures—but for his own reasons. He is not so concerned about heart disease.
- Sue finds the positive measures too difficult.

What do you think of each person's responses? What part do information and attitude play in these answers?

Wellness inventory

As a textbook, *HEALTH AND SAFETY FOR YOU* can provide you with information about your body: how it is constructed and how it functions. It can give you guidelines for good health. It can explore the meanings of mental and social well-being. It can give you insights into new developments in health and medicine.

But by itself, *HEALTH AND SAFETY FOR YOU* cannot make you a healthier person. It will be up to you to take information you learn from this text and apply it to your own health behaviors. Remember, you are responsible ultimately for your own health.

But before you decide on your health behaviors, you will need to know where you stand. The following inventory can help you take stock of your present well-being—physical, mental, and social.

Try this fitness test. Sit and slowly reach for your toes. If you can reach about 2½ inches beyond your toes, you are fairly flexible.

Part 1: Physical well-being

1. Are you physically fit?

    Physical fitness can be measured. In Chapter 3, you will participate in a fitness test. But before you move on, read the following questions. (If you have an injury or your doctor has advised you not to participate in any physical activity, tell your teacher.)

    Sit on the floor with your legs out straight and your feet flexed. Slowly reach for your toes. If you can reach 2½ inches beyond your toes, you are fairly flexible. If you can go beyond 6½ inches, you are very flexible. How did you do? Most students range between 2 inches and 6 inches.

2. Are you feeding your body the required nutrients? Think of everything you ate yesterday. Did you:

    - eat or drink at least four servings from the milk and cheese group—yogurt, milk, and cheese?
    - eat at least four servings of fruits and vegetables that are a good source of vitamins A or C?
    - eat at least four servings of bread and cereal products?
    - eat at least two servings of meat, poultry, fish, or beans?
    - avoid junk foods?

3. Have you had your blood pressure taken within the last year?
4. Do you know if there are any substances that cause you to have contact dermatitis (redness and swelling of the skin)?
5. Do you brush and floss your teeth every day?
6. Do you know what symptoms would make you suspect that you had a sexually transmitted (venereal) disease?
7. How often do you take over-the-counter medications (decongestants, antacids, pain relievers, and so forth)?
8. Do you have a record of your inoculations? Do you know if you are still protected by these inoculations?

Continued

9. How many hours of sleep do you average at night?
10. Do you routinely do warm-up exercises before strenuous physical activity?
11. Do you know the first thing to do if you are burned?
12. Do you wear a safety belt while driving or riding in an automobile?
13. Do you know the warning signals of cancer?
14. Do you know how good your vision is?
15. Do you know how to spot medical quackery?

Part II: Mental and social well-being

16. Which need seems to cause you the most conflict, your need for dependence or your need for independence?
17. How do you fulfill your need to create?
18. Do you have sudden changes of mood for no clear reason?
19. Do you have a social relationship that you find satisfying?
20. How do you react when you deal with people who are different from you?
21. Name one goal that you have achieved.
22. Name three goals that you have set for yourself for the future.
23. Do you feel good about being the sex you are?
24. How do you relax when you are feeling the effects of stress?
25. Under what conditions would you seek professional help? Where would you go to find it?

Key Words

health   communicable diseases   wellness

Main Ideas

- Health goals have changed greatly since the beginning of the century.
- Positive health habits can help you to stay healthy throughout your lifetime. These habits are part of a program of wellness.

Understand the Reading

1. What is the World Health Organization's definition of health?
2. What were the leading causes of death at the beginning of this century? What are the leading causes now?
3. What is wellness?
4. What are the four circumstances under which people will take positive health action?
5. What are some of the excuses people give for not taking positive measures?

Chapter 2
Basis of Movement

After reading this chapter, you will be able to:

- [ ] Identify the four types of joints that connect the bones of the human skeleton.
- [ ] Identify the three types of muscles that make movement possible.
- [ ] Describe the jobs of the two different-colored fibers that make up every muscle.
- [ ] Explain what causes muscle aches and how to treat them.
- [ ] Tell how to prevent muscle soreness caused by exercising.

After her skiing accident, Michiko had to wear a long plaster cast on her broken arm. For the six weeks the cast was on, she felt no pain. But once the bone had mended and the doctor had removed the cast, Michiko was surprised to find that her arm had become skinny. The slightest movement caused her extreme discomfort. Michiko feared at first that something was terribly wrong.

But the doctor reassured her. Lack of movement, he explained, causes muscles to weaken. Movement, in other words, is the natural state for our bodies. The physically active body continues to form new bone tissue and to tone and strengthen the muscles.

The skeletal system

Have you ever heard the expression "dry as a bone"? Actually, the bones in the body are not dry at all. On the contrary, they are living tissue, and they need blood and nourishment, just as the other tissues of the body do.

You know that bones support the body and that muscles are attached to them. But did you know that most of the cells of the blood are formed inside the bone? A hollow area inside each bone contains special tissue called **bone marrow**. Red bone marrow produces red blood cells and three types of white blood cells. It also produces platelets that aid in the clotting of blood. Red bone marrow is found in all the bones of young children and in the pelvic bones, breastbone, ribs, and backbone of adults.

The bones protect vital organs, such as the brain, heart, lungs, and spinal cord. Calcium and phosphorus are two of the minerals in bone that make it hard and strong. Calcium is also important for other vital functions in the body. It helps muscles to contract, blood to clot, and nerves to carry impulses.

You are supported and protected by 206 bones. They differ greatly in size and shape. Bones are connected to one another by tough, fibrous tissues called **ligaments**. The place where two or more bones are connected is called a **joint**. The ends of the bones in a joint are surrounded by **synovial fluid**. This fluid is like a lubricant and lets the ends of the bones move freely. When there is injury to a joint, such as an ankle or knee, too much fluid may be produced. This causes swelling and pain.

There are many types of joints in the skeleton.

Hinge joints permit back-and-forth movement. The joints of the fingers, knees, and elbows are hinge joints.

Ball-and-socket joints allow movement in all directions. The rounded end of the upper arm bone (humerus) rotates in the socket made by the shoulder girdle. The hip joint is also a ball-and-socket joint.

Gliding joints let the flat surface of one bone slide on the flat surface of another. These joints are found between movable vertebrae, such as those in the backbone. Gliding joints let a person bend the back from side to side and forward and backward. Bones of the wrist also form a gliding joint.

Pivot joints allow a pivotal type of turning movement. This kind of movement is more limited than that of the ball-and-socket joints. The joint between the first two vertebrae is a pivot joint. It allows the head to turn from side to side and to move up and down. A pivot joint allows you to turn a doorknob or use a screwdriver.

Bone replaces cartilage as children grow.

Cartilage is a kind of connective tissue that is softer than bone. A baby's skeleton has a great deal of cartilage. As a child grows, most of this cartilage is replaced by bone cells and calcium salts. Lack of calcium or vitamin D in a person's diet during infancy may cause a disease called rickets. The bones of a person with rickets are soft and often deformed. Such deformities may be bowed legs or enlarged joints.

The bones of young people in their teens are harder than babies' bones. And yet teenagers' bones are still not as hard as the bones of adults. Most of the skeleton in adults is made of bone. But cartilage is found in the ears, the lower part of the nose, and the respiratory tract. The disks between the vertebrae and the ends of long bones are also made of cartilage. This cartilage cushions and protects the end of the bone.

While a bone is being formed, tiny blood vessels called capillaries reach every part of the bone. Calcium salts harden the bone tissue, but tiny canals that contain blood vessels remain. Because of these small canals in the bones, there is a constant exchange of minerals between bone and blood. In this way, bone structure changes slowly all through life. If a bone breaks, bone cells in the area begin to build new bone tissues.

Ball-and-socket Joint

Hinge Joint

Pivot Joint

Gliding Joint

Hinge Joints

Red and white blood cells are made inside the bone.

Shaft of Bone

Compact Bone   Epiphysis   Spongy Bone   Marrow   Blood Vessel

The more bones are used, the stronger they become.

The early astronauts returned to earth with bones that had weakened. This weakening was due to weightlessness in space. In zero gravity, the muscles did not stimulate the bones. So the bones became weaker through a loss of calcium, or **decalcification**. Do you know what would happen to your leg if it were in a cast and not able to move for months? Fortunately, a walking cast lets you put stress on a broken bone and helps the bone heal faster.

Some interesting points about the skeleton

The human skull is made up of the 8 flat bones of the **cranium** and the 14 bones of the face. The cranium holds the delicate human brain. A person's brain is not fully grown at birth. It can continue to grow because the 8 cranial bones are not joined together when the baby is born. The spaces between the bones are called **sutures.** The sutures let the baby's skull become smaller during its passage through the mother's narrow pelvic opening at birth. All the sutures usually close between the fifth and sixth month after birth. But if the sutures close too early, the brain cannot grow and the child will be mentally retarded. This is called a **microcephalic** condition (*micro* = small/*cephalic* = headed).

A liquid called cerebrospinal fluid helps to protect the brain and spinal cord by acting as a cushion against blows to the head. But if this fluid becomes trapped inside the brain, the pressure will grow and cause the brain to push outward. This creates what is called a **hydro-cephalic** condition (*hydro* = water/*cephalic* = headed). The sutures may remain open because of the extra pressure.

Skeletal difference between females and males

One major difference between a male skeleton and a female skeleton can be seen in the pelvic region. The female pelvis is wider and shallower. While the opening in the male pelvis is triangular, the opening in the female pelvis is almost oval. The special features of the female pelvis are important for childbearing.

Is there an advantage to having arches in the foot?

Humans are the only animals with arches. Do you run faster, jump higher, or land more gracefully with arches? The answer to this question is no. However, since you have arches, your body weight is spread evenly over the foot. Arches also provide the necessary support for the foot to be used as a lever when you stand on your toes. And after you jump, arches help absorb the shock when you land. The curved arch of the foot also protects blood vessels and nerves.

Many women undergo very noticeable changes in their posture when they reach late middle age. Some of them develop humps in the spine or experience shortened stature. Fractures of the hip become more common. These changes are a result of **osteoporosis**, a condition in which the bones gradually weaken and become more brittle.

For a long time, researchers believed that women were doomed to suffer the effects of osteoporosis. But recent research has shown otherwise. Osteoporosis can be made less severe or prevented altogether by increasing the amount of calcium taken in the teen years. Foods rich in calcium, such as milk products, green leafy vegetables, sardines, and canned salmon, should be a regular part of a teenage girl's diet.

Something to think about

Osteoporosis

Ligaments and muscles support the bones that form the foot's crosswise and lengthwise arches. To keep these arches from falling, a condition called flatfoot, it is important to exercise the muscles that support them. People who spend many hours standing should be aware of this problem.

Is arthritis common only to older people?

Arthritis is a condition that causes the joints to swell and become painful. One form, called "stress," or traumatic, arthritis, is common to young people. Young athletes often injure or irritate the same joint over and over again. They may find that the bones of the injured joint become thicker. The joint may become more and more painful and harder to move.

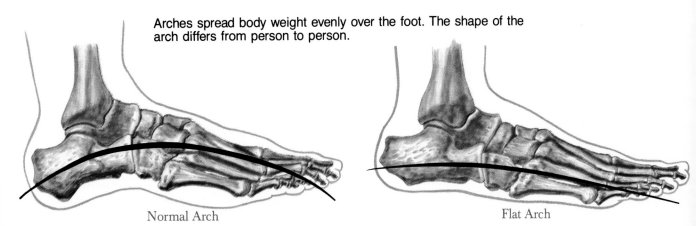

Arches spread body weight evenly over the foot. The shape of the arch differs from person to person.

Normal Arch

Flat Arch

There are many other types of arthritis. The most common form is a "wear-and-tear" disease that chiefly affects older people. Another form, called rheumatoid arthritis, is the most severe kind. It usually strikes people between 20 and 50 years of age. Even children can get a form of the disease known as juvenile rheumatoid arthritis. Gout is a type of arthritis that mainly affects men.

People who have arthritis should be under the care of a physician. Physicians cannot cure all forms of arthritis. In fact, they do not know for sure what causes it. But doctors can prescribe drugs that bring some relief. Heat, massage, and other forms of physical therapy may help to lessen swelling, ease pain, and prevent crippling. Unfortunately, many arthritis sufferers fall victim to quacks who claim they can bring about "cures."

Muscles in motion

Before you buy a car, it is a good idea to test-drive it. You should be interested in its total performance. You will want to check the brakes, gears, and accelerating power. After the test drive, you may look at the parts under the hood to see how they fit together. Then, in case of a breakdown, you might know what to do.

In the next chapter, you will study the performance of your body. You will stretch, pull, and jump to test your motor functions. Now it is important for you to know something about the body parts that permit such action, just in case something goes wrong.

There are over 600 muscles that move different parts of your body. Winking, chewing, breathing, and walking are just a few of the many movements that depend on muscles. Some muscles are made up of over 200,000 cells. Other muscles are small, having only a few hundred muscle cells. Muscle cells are long and can contract. They are also known as muscle fibers.

Each muscle is surrounded by blood vessels, nerves, and connective tissue. Many muscle fibers are grouped together by connective tissue to form a **fasciculus**. Many fasciculi form a muscle bundle, which works as a single muscle. The connective tissue that holds the muscle fibers together is usually longer than the fiber. This tissue extends to form the **tendon**. The tendon attaches the muscle to the bone.

The nerve that attaches to a muscle causes the muscle to contract. When a muscle contracts, it becomes shorter and thicker. The two ends of the muscle draw closer together. During muscle contraction, energy is given off as work and heat. When a muscle is not contracted, it is relaxed.

Muscles never totally relax, even when a person is asleep. This slight, constant contraction of muscles is called muscle tone. A healthy muscle feels firm because of its tone. A muscle with poor tone feels soft and flabby. Good muscle tone helps the posture. It also aids in circulation, in digestion, and in the elimination of wastes from the digestive tract. Good muscle tone is an important key to performance in sports and in

Ligaments connect bones to joints. Tendons connect muscles to bones.

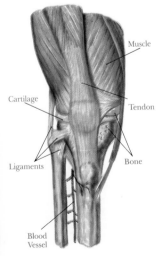

Muscle

Cartilage

Tendon

Ligaments

Bone

Blood Vessel

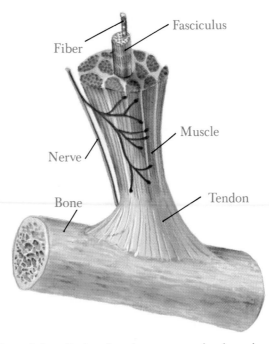

Tiny groups of muscle fibers form a muscle bundle.

many other forms of physical activity. It is also important in keeping your body healthy.

There are three types of muscles.

Voluntary muscles are those skeletal muscles whose movement a person can control. They are also called striated muscles because they look striped, or striated, when seen under a microscope.

Involuntary muscles are the smooth muscles in the walls of the blood vessels, stomach, intestines, and other hollow tubes of the body. A person cannot consciously control them. They are also called smooth muscles because they have no striations. The smooth involuntary muscles are very strong, but they contract slowly. The nerves that attach to smooth muscles come from the part of the nervous system that controls involuntary action.

Cardiac muscle, or the heart muscle, looks very much like striated muscle under a microscope. Its fibers seem to be woven together. However, it is an involuntary muscle. Nerve impulses to the heart muscle may speed up or slow down its rate of contraction. During exercise, the heart muscle contracts faster and with more force than when the body is at rest.

General health and such emotions as excitement and worry affect the tone of all muscles—voluntary and involuntary.

Some interesting points about muscles

When we eat the meat of a chicken, cow, or pig, we are eating the muscles of these animals. In some animals, such as chickens and turkeys,

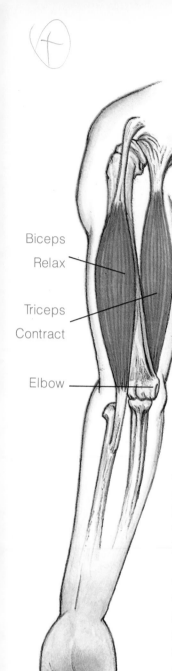

Biceps
Relax

Triceps
Contract

Elbow

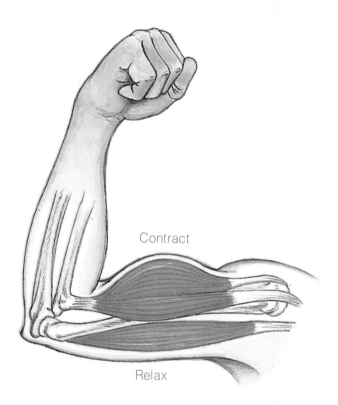

Contract

Relax

Many muscles work
in pairs to produce
movement. When one
contracts, the other
relaxes.

we have a choice of eating white or dark meat. Scientists have found that white and dark meat are different colors because the dark meat has more of a red-colored protein called **myoglobin**. This protein is very much like the hemoglobin that gives red blood cells their color. Myoglobin stores oxygen in muscle cells for use during exercise.

In the body, muscles are a mixture of red and white fibers. If you were to examine a muscle, it would be hard to see the color difference with the naked eye. It has been estimated that the calf muscle has about 50 percent red and 50 percent white fibers. Not only do muscles have different amounts of myoglobin, but the nerve cells leading to the muscles are also different. Red muscle has a nerve that is small in diameter. This nerve is slow in carrying nerve impulses. But it is always carrying impulses, even when the muscle is at rest. White muscle has a nerve that is large and fast in carrying impulses but not as active when the muscle is at rest.

Muscles also differ in the jobs they do. When you run 100 meters or lift, push, or pull heavy objects, the white muscle is in action. But the white muscle, though powerful, cannot continue to exert force. It lacks endurance and will tire quickly. The red muscle has more staying power because it is always being stimulated by nerves. It helps you to keep good posture and to move gracefully. It will endure cross-country or long-distance running.

The shoulder and arm muscles of a weight lifter are large because the diameter of each white muscle fiber increases with exercise. The

Gymnast Mary Lou Retton performs a routine that requires both strength and flexibility.

red muscle fiber of a long-distance runner does not change in size. However, there are more blood vessels, myoglobin, and chemicals to give the runner continuous energy. With the increased blood flow, oxygen and nutrients can reach the red fibers more quickly and efficiently. This increases muscular endurance. Thus, white muscle gives you the burst of energy needed for powerful, short movements. But red muscle provides support and is useful for activities that need endurance. When you exercise, try to strengthen both red and white muscle. (Refer to Chapter 3 for information on developing the muscles.)

Red muscles are important for endurance. White muscles are used for power movements that involve strength.

Aching muscles often come from too much stretching or from overusing muscles that are rarely used.

Women and girls cannot develop the kind of large, strong muscles seen in males. For that type of muscle growth, a male hormone called testosterone is needed. Most females do not have much testosterone in their bodies. Exercise will simply help to strengthen and tone their white muscle fibers and to make their red muscle fibers more efficient.

Sometimes an increase in muscle size is desirable. Large, strong muscles can be an advantage in such sports as football, wrestling, and gymnastics. It is not possible to grow new muscles where there were none before. But if the size of muscle cells is enlarged, the tissue will become larger. It may seem as if you have grown new muscles, but you have only enlarged the muscle cells you already had.

What causes muscle aches?

Almost everyone has had aching muscles at one time or another. The most common causes of aching muscles are strains, too much stretching, or overuse of muscles that have not been used regularly. If you have not played volleyball for a season and then join a volleyball tournament, your neck muscles may feel sore and stiff the next day.

Whenever your muscles have been conditioned for a special kind of exercise, the body produces greater amounts of a substance called **lactic acid.** Lactic acid is normally produced by contracting muscles. However, if the muscles are more active than usual or if you change exercise and use different muscles, the lactic-acid level increases. The buildup of lactic acid and other waste materials irritates the muscles. This is felt as muscle soreness.

How do you prevent muscle soreness?

To prevent soreness, a proper warm-up of the muscles is necessary. No matter how flexible you are, if the muscles are not warmed up before vigorous exercise, you may become sore. The purpose of a warm-up for a car engine is to let the working parts get enough lubrication. This prevents friction between parts. The same is true of the body. During your warm-up, the temperature of the body fluids and muscles will rise slightly. This will increase the need for chemicals that produce energy in the muscles. Warm-ups may vary with the type of activities involved. But it is a good idea to warm up as many parts of the body as possible.

Types of warm-ups

Warm-ups can be divided into two types, general and specific. General warm-ups are not related to the sport or activity in which you will be taking part. They include calisthenics that let you slowly stretch the muscles, tendons, and ligaments all over the body. Specific warm-ups are closely related to the activity you will take part in. If the sport is volleyball, the specific warm-up should include the correct movements of the arms, the follow-through with the head, and other movements used in the game.

Both types of warm-ups allow the muscles to adapt to new physical demands. They also prepare the heart and blood vessels for vigorous action. Unfortunately, the heart is not 100 percent efficient. If it were, you could begin an activity without any warm-up, and your heart would be able to increase the volume of blood at once.

The amount of warm-up needed will vary with the person, the temperature, and the type of activity. Some people are very flexible and have no difficulty with stretching exercises. Others are stiff. Also, the body will take longer to warm up on cold days. (In Chapter 3, you will learn more about the correct methods of stretching.)

General warm-ups prepare the muscles, blood vessels, and heart for increased action.

Why you yawn

Human beings yawn for the same reason cats and dogs do. A yawn helps circulate the blood carrying oxygen to the head. The next time you feel sleepy in a classroom, stretch your arms and your neck muscles, and you may avoid yawning.

What is a hernia?

When any organ is pushed through the wall around it, the condition is called a **hernia**, or rupture. The most common hernia occurs when a part of the intestine is pushed through the wall of the abdomen. In men, there are two weak areas in this muscular wall in the groin. This is where most hernias occur. The navel is another place where many hernias occur. The muscles of the abdomen may be weakened, and strain may cause the intestine to push through the weak area.

A hernia should receive medical attention at once. The loop of intestine that is pushed out in a hernia must be returned permanently to the abdominal cavity. It is important to stop interference with the blood supply to that part of the digestive tract. It is also important to let food pass through the injured part of the intestine. Keeping the muscles of the abdomen in good condition will help prevent hernias.

Key Words

arthritis	gliding joints	ligaments
ball-and-socket joints	hernia	microcephalic
	hinge joints	myoglobin
bone marrow	hydrocephalic	osteoporosis
cardiac muscle	involuntary muscles	pivot joints
cartilage		sutures
cranium	joint	synovial fluid
decalcification	lactic acid	tendon
fasciculus		voluntary muscles

Main Ideas

- Bones are living tissue and have important jobs, such as blood formation, support, movement, and protection.
- The ends of bones are held together by ligaments and are protected by cartilage.
- Bones need physical stimulation in order to stay strong.
- At birth, the bones of the cranium are separated by spaces called sutures. The sutures later close up.
- Skeletal muscles are under voluntary control. Smooth muscles and the heart muscle are not under voluntary control.
- The color of muscle depends on myoglobin. The color also indicates what job the muscle does.

Continued

- General and specific warm-ups are important not only for skeletal muscles but also for the blood vessels and heart.
- Muscles can develop weak spots, which internal organs can push through. This is called a rupture, or hernia.

1. Why is the skeleton called a living organ?
2. Give three reasons why calcium is important for the body.
3. What is the function of synovial fluid? Where is synovial fluid found?
4. Explain the difference between a ligament and a tendon.
5. List the four major kinds of joints and describe the movement of each.
6. Describe how cartilage is slowly replaced by bone. Is all cartilage replaced? Explain.
7. What is the advantage of having sutures at birth? When do the sutures close?
8. What is the major difference between male and female skeletons?
9. Are there any advantages to having arches in the foot?
10. Explain how flatfoot can occur.
11. How many forms of arthritis are there? Can all forms be cured? Explain.
12. What is another name for involuntary muscles? How do they differ from voluntary muscles?
13. How would a sprinter's thigh muscle compare in size with a long-distance runner's?
14. Why is it important to strengthen both red and white muscles?
15. What is the difference between general and specific warm-ups?

1. Interview players on your school's football, track, basketball, and swimming teams. Determine what kinds of specific and general warm-ups athletes in each of these sports do. Note the similarities and differences between the various types of warm-ups. Sum these up in a report to your class.
2. Try to find a book in your library that describes the muscular system of an animal. (If you are unsuccessful, try to speak with a veterinarian.) Make a list of differences between the muscles of the animal and those of a human being. In particular, note differences in muscle shape and length. Based on what you have learned in this chapter, discuss with your classmates possible reasons for these differences.

Chapter 3

Fitness:

Sports and Recreation

After reading this chapter, you will be able to:

- ☐ Describe the correct methods for warming up for physical exercise and athletic competition.
- ☐ Name the factors that determine physical fitness.
- ☐ List the parts of an effective conditioning program for athletes.
- ☐ Recognize the causes of sports injuries and explain how to prevent them.

How often should you exercise? Studies conducted by NASA scientists show that if you do not exercise your body regularly, your muscles will lose up to one-fifth of their maximal muscle strength for every three days you do not exercise. That's why it is so important to find a physical activity you really like. If you enjoy the exercise, you are more likely to do it at least the three days a week you need to maintain muscle strength. Lack of movement is unnatural for the human body. Without exercise, the nervous, digestive, circulatory, skeletal, and respiratory systems are also affected.

Your body is made for movement. The greatest value of exercise is that it helps to tone the muscles and strengthen the heart. If you understand what happens to your body when you exercise, you should be able to choose the activities that are best for you.

The importance of exercising

Warming up the engine

While you are asleep, most of your muscles are flexed, or bent, rather than extended. When you are sitting at your desk, your knee, hip, and elbow joints are usually flexed. If your muscles remain in a flexed position for a long time, they can temporarily shorten and become tighter. Thus, when you get up in the morning or stand after sitting for a long time, your body may be stiff and sluggish.

Before you do any fast-paced activities, it is always best to warm up. General and specific warm-ups are recommended for sports and recreational events. But even when you wake up in the morning, simple stretching movements can make you feel good.

Proper stretching is an important first step in many exercises.

The correct method of stretching

Stretching exercises should be done slowly. The purpose of stretching is not only to lengthen the muscles but also to lengthen the tendons and connective tissue. The tendon, which is actually an extension of the connective tissue that wraps around the muscle fibers, is plastic, like putty. When it is stretched, it does not snap back. If stretching is done correctly, the muscle fiber should lengthen up to a point and then relax while the tendon continues to stretch. The expression "no pain . . . no gain" does not apply during stretching. Learn the following rules for stretching:

1. Stretch slowly, and hold the stretch for a minimum of 60 seconds.
2. Stretch slowly to the point of tightness. Don't stretch to the point of producing pain. Pain means injury, and injury means loss of flexibility.
3. Don't bounce. Vigorous movements cause muscle fibers to contract and tighten.
4. A good stretch will be effective for approximately 3 hours. Warm up just before and after an activity.

Different physical abilities among athletes

Karen and Sandy are both good athletes. They both enjoy competitive sports and recreational activities. Karen is flexible, agile, and well coordinated. She also has good equilibrium, or balance. Sandy is fast and strong and has great physical endurance. From the description of Karen and Sandy, can you decide who is the balance-beam star and who is the low-hurdle champ? Actually, both of these sports call for many of the same strengths. But some of Karen's and Sandy's strong points differ.

Total **physical fitness** is based on all of these factors: flexibility, coordination, equilibrium, agility, speed, strength, and endurance.

Flexibility is the ability to move the joints of the body easily and smoothly when you bend, twist, and stretch. The more flexible you are, the more easily you can move in and out of various positions without injury.

Coordination means that your entire body is working smoothly. When you play tennis and your eyes follow the ball across the net, you may already be moving where you think the ball will be returned. When you first try to dribble a soccer ball with your feet, you might not do it with grace and ease. But your coordination usually improves with practice.

Equilibrium is the ability to balance yourself easily if your body begins to sway or lean in one direction. Expert ice skaters can spin

Benefits Derived through Various Sports and Recreational Activities

	Flexibility	Coordination	Equilibrium	Agility	Speed	Strength	Endurance
Badminton	√	√		√	√		√
Ballet	√	√	√	√	√	√	√
Baseball		√		√	√		
Basketball		√	√	√	√		√
Bicycling					√		√
Bowling			√				
Boxing		√		√	√	√	√
Calisthenics	√	√	√	√			√
Canoeing						√	√
Diving	√	√		√			
Fencing		√	√	√	√		√
Figure skating	√	√		√	√		
Fishing		√					
Football				√	√		√
Frisbee	√	√		√			
Golf		√					
Gymnastics	√	√	√			√	
Handball		√			√		√
Hiking							√
Hockey		√	√	√	√		
Horseback riding			√				
Jogging							√
Judo	√			√	√	√	
Jumping rope		√		√			√
Karate	√	√		√	√		√
Lacrosse		√					√
Mountain climbing	√		√				√
Pool/Billiards		√					
Racquetball	√	√		√	√		√
Rowing						√	√
Scuba diving		√	√				√
Skateboarding	√	√	√	√			
Skiing	√	√					√
Soccer	√	√		√	√		√
Softball		√			√		
Square dancing		√		√			
Swimming		√				√	√
Table tennis		√		√	√		√
Tennis		√		√	√		√
Track and field					√		√
Volleyball	√			√	√		√
Waterskiing			√				
Weight training						√	
Wrestling	√			√	√	√	√
Yoga	√		√				

around 30 or more times at a blurring speed, and they are able to balance themselves during and after spinning. Bowlers, discus throwers, and gymnasts also need good equilibrium to perform gracefully and well.

Speed is the measure of how fast the body parts can move. In order to run a 100-meter dash or to chase a tennis ball, you need speed. The legs, the arms, and other parts of the body can all move with speed.

Agility means that you can react quickly with fast, sure movements. Springing to your feet and dodging easily from side to side are examples of being agile.

Strength means being able to use the power of the muscles to lift, push, jump, or pull. Developing strong muscles also strengthens tendons, ligaments, and bones. You are less likely to be injured when your body is strong.

Endurance is the most important factor in a physically fit body. It is the ability of the body to stand up to stress for long periods of time. Your body may be flexible, agile, speedy, strong, and well-coordinated. But you can still be physically unfit if you lack endurance. Muscles need oxygen. Oxygen is carried by the red blood cells that give nourishment to all parts of the body. You don't need much strength to move your arms through the water while swimming. But you do need endurance to swim the length of the pool six times. If you keep doing the same activity over a period of time, new blood vessels will be formed. These newly formed blood vessels will carry more nutrients and oxygen to the small muscle fibers that make up the larger muscle bundle. Thus, the more you swim, the better your muscles can endure long periods of movement.

It is your heart that chiefly determines your endurance. The heart itself is a muscle and has to be strong. How can you check to find out how much work your heart is doing? While you are in your chair, press the first two fingers of one hand at either side of your neck just under the jaw. Find the pulse. (Do not use your thumb; it has a pulse of its own.) Count the number of beats for 10 seconds. Then multiply that number by 6. This is your heart rate per minute.

When you exercise actively, your body needs more oxygen. So your heart muscle increases its rate of beating. This supplies the extra oxygen to the body muscles. Activities that call for endurance help to strengthen your heart and improve your lung capacity. The sooner your heart returns to its normal resting rate after exercise, the better your endurance. Your breathing should return to normal within 10 minutes after you finish exercising.

Researchers have found that when young people exercise, their hearts should beat about 150 to 175 times per minute. If your heart rate does not reach 150 beats per minute while you are bowling, it might be wise to take on another sport as well. The heart can become stronger and work more efficiently only if you apply some degree of stress. After

Your pulse rate tells how much work your heart is doing.

heavy exercise, such as a one-on-one basketball game, check your pulse for 30 seconds. Then multiply the number of beats by 2 to get your pulse rate per minute. If this rate is over 175, you might be overdoing the exercise. There has been too much stress, and you need to rest.

Getting enough exercise

Don't be a once-a-week jogger or a weekend superstar. You should exercise at least 3 days a week or once every other day. Regular exercise improves your endurance. If your exercise raises your heart rate to 150 beats per minute, 15 to 20 minutes of activity per day will be enough. If your heart rate is less than 150, you need to put in more days or longer hours of exercise.

When you exercise, your heart pumps more blood into circulation with each heartbeat than it does when you rest. This puts greater pressure on the walls of the arteries carrying the blood. Thus your blood pressure is increased. Blood usually travels at the rate of 55 feet per minute in the large arteries. But during vigorous exercise, the blood in the large arteries may travel at the rate of 450 feet per minute.

What is your "fitness quotient"? To find out, perform each of the tasks described below. Then compare your scores with those of your classmates. Are there any areas in which you need work?

Your fitness quotient

PART 1: FLEXIBILITY

Task: Stand with your feet together, and bend down slowly. Touch your toes without bending your knees. Do not bounce up and down. Now start over in the same position, and bend down slowly again. This time, however, touch the floor with your fingers. Bend down a third time, and try to touch the floor with your knuckles. On the fourth bend, attempt to touch your palms to the floor.

Your score: touched toes—1 point; touched floor—2 points; touched knuckles to floor—3 points; touched palms to floor—4 points

PART 2: COORDINATION

Task: Stand about 6 feet from a flat wall. Using your right hand, toss a tennis ball underhand against a flat wall. Catch the ball with your left hand, and quickly toss it back. Then catch it with your right hand. Continue to do this for 30 seconds. Keep count of the number of times you catch the ball. (Important: The clock should continue running, even if you drop the ball.)

Your score: 25 catches—1 point; 28 catches—2 points; 32 catches—3 points; 35 catches—4 points

PART 3: EQUILIBRIUM

Task: Stand on your toes with your heels together. Close your eyes, and hold your arms straight out in front of you. Stay in this position

Flexibility (*top*), coordination (*bottom*)

for as long as you can without shifting your feet or opening your eyes. Have a friend time you.

Your score: up to 15 seconds—1 point; up to 20 seconds—2 points; up to 25 seconds—3 points; 30 seconds or more—4 points

PART 4: SPEED

Task: In your classroom, draw a circle on the chalkboard approximately 10 inches above your head. Stand 10 inches from the board, and face sideways. Spread your legs approximately 2 feet apart. Begin by touching the circle with the hand closest to the board. Then reach over and touch the foot farthest from the board. Repeat the action 10 times while a friend times you.

Your score: 11 seconds or more—1 point; 10 seconds—2 points; 9 seconds—3 points; 8 seconds or less—4 points

PART 5: AGILITY

Task: Draw a line on the floor. Stand to one side of it. As quickly as you can, jump sideways back and forth over the line. Keep your feet together. Have a friend time you for 1 minute. Keep track of the number of times your feet touch the floor.

Your score: 145 times—1 point; 160 times—2 points; 175 times—3 points; 185 times—4 points

PART 6: STRENGTH

Task: Measure your height in inches. From a line on the floor, mark off a distance equal to your height. Stand behind the line. Bend your knees, swing your arms backward, and then jump. Measure the length of your jump.

Your score: own height—1 point; own height plus 2 in.—2 points; own height plus 4 in.—3 points; own height plus 6 in. or more—4 points

Equilibrium (*top*),
speed (*center, bottom*)

PART 7: ENDURANCE

Task: Use a sturdy chair or bench. Step up and down 30 times per minute for each of 3 minutes. When 3 minutes are up, sit down and quickly find your pulse. (See page 28 for instructions on how to take your pulse.)

Your score: 120–125—1 point; 95–115—2 points; 85–90—3 points; 75–80—4 points

Once you have completed all seven tasks, use the following scale to determine your fitness quotient:

Points	Rating
22–28	excellent
15–21	very good
11–14	good
7–10	need work

Water and salt requirement during exercise

Exercise usually makes a person perspire. The body can lose large amounts of water and salt through perspiration. These losses must be replaced, or cramps and nausea may result. On a warm day, a football player may lose as much as 10 pounds during a game. But the player may regain the lost weight by the following morning simply by drinking water. On a day when water is lost from the body through perspiration and is not replaced, the average amount of urine excreted is less. This urine is likely to be darker than usual. Water can also be lost through the kidneys and from the surface of the lungs.

If you are taking part in vigorous physical activities, your body may need water even if you are not thirsty. In fact, a large amount of water is lost through the skin even when you are not perspiring. In low humidity when the air is dry, water loss from the skin and breathing organs is high. Also, drinking certain fluids that contain caffeine or alcohol can cause the body to lose water faster. You can prevent heat cramp, heat exhaustion, and heatstroke by drinking plenty of water before and during physical activity.

Remember the following rules about water and salt replacement:

- Avoid fluids containing caffeine or alcohol. (They cause you to lose water too quickly.)
- Avoid sugared drinks. (Water is absorbed too slowly.)
- Don't take salt tablets or eat salty foods. (Water is taken away from the bloodstream and muscles. A few extra shakes of salt on your daily food are sufficient during hot weather.)
- It is not necessary to drink commercially prepared electrolyte solutions. (It is cheaper and just as effective to drink a solution of 1 tablespoon of salt to 1 gallon of water.)

Do you have to "work up a sweat" to benefit?

Don't assume that sweating means you have reached your peak of exercise. Sweating is simply a way of lowering your body temperature, which can rise as much as 7° to 10° Fahrenheit during a workout on a hot day. Also, sweating does not remove waste products from your pores, reduce your weight, or promote fitness.

A conditioning program is important for athletes.

Conditioning, or training, is a program of exercise, rest, and eating that athletes follow to get and stay in top physical condition. In conditioning, exercise must be regular. It should also be increased slowly from day to day. How exercise affects a person's muscles, digestion, circulation, and sleep will show what that individual is able to do. Then, after the person has reached a level of maximum performance, the

Agility (*top*), strength (*center*), endurance (*bottom*)

Your body may need water even when you are not thirsty. Drink water before and during physical activities.

daily amount of exercise at that level should be kept up. Conditioning also includes regular periods for sleep and relaxation. A person in training needs the same kinds of foods that any healthy person does.

Aging and exercise

As people get older, they sometimes forget the importance of activity and exercise. They forget that the condition of the circulatory system is directly related to the amount and kind of exercise they get.

For a time, British doctors were puzzled by the fact that bus drivers in London had a higher rate of heart attacks than bus conductors. When the doctors looked for reasons, they found that the bus drivers got little exercise. The bus conductors moved about as they went up and down the steps of the double-decker buses to collect tickets. Most people need more exercise than they get, especially older people who spend most of their time indoors. A good exercise program and proper diet will help prevent heart attacks and problems with blood circulation.

The kind of exercise you do is not important. Swimming is just as good as stickball, and stickball is just as good as jogging. What matters is that you enjoy the exercise and keep doing it. Walking is an excellent way to exercise. You will use the same amount of calories whether you walk or jog a mile.

When you are young, you may enjoy strenuous sports, such as basketball and football. But as you reach middle age, your heart and blood vessels will change. Then vigorous exercise may not always be wise. It can cause serious damage, especially if you have not been exercising regularly. Therefore, in addition to sports that you can enjoy in your youth, it is good to learn some "lifetime sport" you can continue to do. Bowling, golfing, cycling, hiking, jogging, and swimming are good lifetime sports. They give you pleasure and also improve your health.

Eating and exercise

Eating just before or after exercising may cause stomach pains. For an hour or two after you eat, a greater flow of blood is needed in your digestive tract. If you exercise soon after eating, digestion is interrupted. The extra supply of blood is taken away to fill the needs of the skeletal muscles. Something similar happens if you eat just after exercising. Then the extra supply of blood cannot be moved quickly away from the skeletal muscles to the stomach and intestines. In either case, stomach pains may result.

Knowing your limitations

Most people need regular exercise in reasonable amounts. But before any person takes part in heavy physical work or exercise, a physician should check the condition of the heart. Most high schools and colleges require that all students have a physical exam to find out if they are in condition to join in physical-activity programs. Most schools also require medical supervision of sports events.

A person should feel refreshed, rather than fatigued, just after exercise and for several hours afterward. If the person feels exhausted, weak, or shaky, overexercising may be the problem.

Too much of a good thing?

How much exercise is too much? Some people have gotten so caught up in fitness that they go too far. The potential for physical injury and mental "burnout" are very real when you force your body to perform beyond its normal capabilities. If *some* exercise is good, *more* does not necessarily mean better.

The human body is a wonderful and delicate machine. You already know that being physically active helps you maintain proper weight, muscle tone, and physical strength. You look, feel, and work better. Unfortunately, there are many people who ignore the pains in their knees, ankles, and other parts of the body. They work out compulsively. There is no advantage in going beyond the fitness level.

In fact, there are real disadvantages. Researchers are finding, for example, that women who run over 20 miles per week can increase the risk of osteoporosis. Strenuous exercise can cause a decrease in body fat and interruption of the menstrual cycle. This causes low estrogen production, which can lead to bone degeneration. In men and women, the increase in stress arthritis, muscle tears, foot injuries, and other permanent injuries related to the "fitness boom" are also of concern to many physicians. Fitness, like the other parts of wellness, means using good common sense.

Know your limits. The right amount of exercise makes you feel better, not worse.

The use of anabolic **steroids**, or synthetic male hormones, to improve athletic performance is very dangerous. The greatest concern is the link between steroids and liver cancer. Other effects in men include decrease in the size of the testes, impotence, and stunted growth. Women who use steroids experience liver damage, increased facial hair, lowering of the voice, and menstrual irregularities. Steroids may give a person a small competitive edge. However, the high risk of destroying the body, which took time to grow and develop for competition, is too great. True athletes will win by their own courage and talent.

The truth about steroids

Injuries to the muscle and soft tissue are common among young people who take part in physical activities or active sports. **Muscle lameness** is a condition that occurs when you overuse your muscles. It is similar to muscle soreness. But muscle soreness is caused by a buildup of waste products (lactic acid). Muscle lameness occurs when there is tearing of tiny muscle fibers that have been forced to contract under a heavy load

What you should know about sports injuries

or force. Since the muscle tissue is injured, the pain and stiffness may last for three to four days.

To prevent muscle lameness, it is a good idea to exercise with barbells or with weights strapped to the body or legs. Gradually increasing the weight will help to condition the muscles for the forceful movements needed in many sports. This kind of exercise is called weight training.

Very light exercise, gentle stretching, and heat, ointment, or light massage will help to speed up healing for muscle lameness. Resting the muscles for three to four days will also help.

A **pulled muscle** causes pain so severe that exercise cannot be continued. In a pulled muscle, a large muscle bundle or a tendon that attaches muscle to bone may have torn or separated from the attachment points. Since the blood vessels of the muscle bundle are damaged, immediate treatment by a physician may be needed. Again, lack of warm-up and too much force exerted on a cold muscle are the major causes of a pulled muscle. A pulled muscle can be healed only by resting it.

Certain kinds of muscle pulls are common to certain sports. In most cases, the injury occurs where there has been a fast and forceful movement. For example, the biceps and triceps of the upper arm are important muscles for throwing. So if you are a baseball pitcher, these muscles are the most likely to be injured. If you are a tennis player, your calf muscles may be injured. The calf muscles are attached to the Achilles tendon, which is in turn attached to the heel bone. These muscles give you the power to pull up your heels when you serve and to position yourself for the return. If you are a sprinter, you may injure the hamstring muscles at the back of the thigh.

CAUTION: Sports and recreational activities may be hazardous to your health.

A **charley horse** is the result of a hard blow (contusion) to the front part of the thigh. The muscle, blood vessels, nerves, and other soft tissues are damaged. For a charley horse, use treatments that stop internal bleeding as much as possible. Put ice or a cold pack on the injured area. The cold will cause the blood vessels to narrow, which will lessen the bleeding. If you apply pressure to the area, the blood vessels will be squeezed. Therefore, less blood will flow around the injured area. Raising the thigh will also decrease the blood flow through the arteries. This will increase the blood flow in the veins that lead away from the injury.

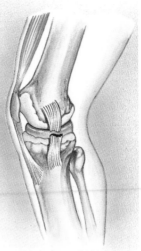

Dislocated Knee

Don't move a person who has suffered a dislocation. Call a doctor at once.

You should rest the injured leg as much as possible. Keep it in a horizontal position. If your charley horse is very bad, you should contact your doctor for further treatment. For a mild injury, heat can be applied to the area after two or three days. The heat will improve circulation and will help speed the healing. If you are involved in any contact sport, you could get a charley horse. Even football players with protective padding can get very bad muscle injuries.

Muscle cramps usually occur in muscles that must carry weight, such as the calf, hip, or thigh muscles. Cramps sometimes occur in a tired muscle during sleep or in a muscle that has been working very hard. Sometimes cramps are caused by a light blow or strain on a tired muscle. In a normal muscle bundle, some of the fibers are resting and some are contracting. However, during a cramp, almost all of the muscle fibers are contracting at the same time.

Stretching the muscle within the normal range of movement may help the cramping. Applying firm pressure while gently massaging the area may also help. The best way to avoid muscle cramps is to warm up properly and to drink enough fluids before and after exercise. Wearing protective clothing whenever possible may also prevent injury.

Sprains and **dislocations** are problems that affect the joints. The joint between two bones may receive a sudden, forceful blow called a trauma. Also, if stress is put on a joint by twisting, stretching, or pounding, the ligament that joins the bones can weaken, tear, or be cut. These injuries are called sprains.

If you are wearing shoes with high heels and step off a curb, you could twist your ankle. When an ankle is sprained, blood vessels usually break and swelling takes place. Many athletes will sprain an ankle at one time or another. If the sprain is very bad, an X ray should be taken to make sure that no bones are broken.

Wrap the sprained area tightly to help close broken blood vessels. Then put on a cold pack every half hour. Keep it on for about 20 minutes at a time. This will slow the circulation. Don't leave the cold pack on too long. If you do, the joints could become stiff and painful. Prop the leg up for better circulation of fluids away from the injury. Then when the swelling lessens 24 to 48 hours later, use heat on the injured area. The blood vessels will enlarge and carry more nourishment to the tissue. They will also help remove injured tissue from the sprained area.

Bones are held together at the joints by ligaments, tendons, and muscles. But if enough force is applied, a bone may be pushed out of its socket. This painful injury is called a dislocation. Don't move the injured area. And allow no one but a doctor to treat the dislocation. There are many blood vessels, soft tissues, and nerves connected to the joint. So if you think your thumb is dislocated, for example, never have a friend or coach pull it "back into place."

Shinsplints is a lower-leg pain that is sometimes felt by athletes who run on hard surfaces. It can happen to you if you run cross-country, on a track, or even down the street. It can also occur if you play tennis or basketball. What causes shinsplints? There are two theories. Both theories state that the main cause of shinsplints is the partial separation of the muscle from its bone attachment.

One way to avoid shinsplints is to strengthen any weak muscles before you run. You should also try to avoid running on hard surfaces during warm-up and early training. Make sure that your shoes fit well. Wear an extra pair of socks to help absorb the shock. Most important, learn the correct way to jog or run, and always warm up, even if your muscles are toned and strong.

Should you develop shinsplints, immediate treatment by your doctor is very important. The swelling must be stopped. The injured muscle needs long periods of rest. Since shinsplints is painful, you should know how to avoid or prevent it.

Shinsplints can be a problem for athletes who run on hard surfaces.

agility	equilibrium	pulled muscle
charley horse	flexibility	shinsplints
conditioning	muscle cramps	speed
coordination	muscle lameness	sprains
dislocations	physical fitness	steroids
endurance		strength

- The muscles are made for movement. When they don't move, they become weaker.
- It is important to warm up the muscles before exercise or sports.
- Total physical fitness is based on flexibility, coordination, equilibrium, agility, strength, speed, and endurance.
- Water lost during exercise must be replaced.
- Conditioning is important for athletes.
- It is important to know your limitations when exercising.
- Proper training can help prevent muscle injuries.

1. Discuss the correct method of stretching.
2. What are the differences between flexibility, agility, and speed?
3. List some sports that call for a great deal of coordination.
4. Why is it important to drink plenty of water before and during vigorous physical exercise?
5. What makes up a conditioning program?
6. Why should exercise be avoided just before and after eating?
7. Explain the differences between muscle lameness and muscle cramps.
8. How does a cold pack help a charley horse or a sprained ankle? Why should you prop up the injured area?
9. What is the difference between a sprain and a dislocation?
10. Explain how shinsplints can be prevented.

1. Select a professional sport, such as boxing, baseball, or football. Find out as much as you can about the sort of conditioning a player of that sport undergoes. A good place to find this information is your local library. Write a report on your findings.
2. Take your pulse for 1 minute before you get out of bed in the morning. Then, sit up and take your pulse again. Next, stand and take your pulse a third time. Record the differences in pulse rate. Compare your three pulse rates with those of classmates. Discuss possible reasons for any variations.

Unit 2

Under-standing Yourself

Chapter 4
Emotional Needs and Maturity

After reading this chapter, you will be able to:

- ☐ Define emotional needs and identify the five basic types.
- ☐ Define personality and identify the main influences on an individual's personality.
- ☐ Recognize the importance of understanding your feelings and developing self-confidence.
- ☐ Explain what a responsible decision is.
- ☐ Explain how to be a fair judge of your personality and that of others.

One day you feel fine. The next day you feel unhappy. Sometimes you have a sudden shift of mood for no apparent reason. You even find yourself on occasion asking, "Who am I?" Feelings are important—they are yours. The way you learn to deal with your feelings will play a part in the adult you become.

People have basic **emotional needs**, just as they have basic physical needs. Emotional needs must be satisfied if a person is to enjoy life and feel a sense of security. People who cannot satisfy their emotional needs may feel frustrated, lonely, or insecure. They may feel that they don't have a purpose or a worthwhile place in life.

Unmet emotional needs can make a person very unhappy or even emotionally sick. Disturbed emotions can sometimes lead to physical illness. This happens when feelings are "transferred," or unconsciously given, to the body. The result may be aches, pains, or other physical problems. It is important to understand the causes of disturbed emotions or feelings. These problems almost always can be traced back to unmet emotional needs.

Love

The need to give and receive love and affection is very strong in all human beings. This need exists from the beginning to the end of life. Newborn babies respond to being held and cuddled, while children show a strong need to exchange affection with family and friends. Adolescents have basically the same needs as children. But they also need the additional reassurance of belonging to a group. Young adults expand their need for loving relationships through dating, seeking a long-term partner, or planning and caring for a family. Adults need to go on giving and receiving love and maintaining loving relationships. The need for love does not stop as a person grows older. Elderly adults continue to need loving relationships with people of all ages. Meeting this need is thought to add years to a person's life. Because love involves a commitment to the happiness, security, and well-being of the loved one, a person has feelings of contentment and satisfaction in giving and receiving love.

A positive self-concept

Everyone needs to have a positive self-concept. **Self-concept** is a term used to describe how a person views herself or himself. People with a positive self-concept understand and accept their personalities, abilities, and shortcomings.

Having a positive self-concept includes having self-respect—a feeling of personal worth. Receiving respect from others is important, but holding yourself in high esteem is even more important. It takes hard and serious thought to know who you are and what you want to be. It takes courage to learn to be yourself and to let your words and actions reflect the person you are. You alone are responsible for forming your personal identity.

During the high school years, you will probably depend on your parents to satisfy many of your physical needs, such as food, clothing, and shelter. At the same time, however, you are learning to become an independent person. More and more, you think and act for yourself and make your own decisions. Your needs for dependence and independence may cause problems between you and your parents. Sometimes you may accept your dependence on them. But you may reject that dependence when it conflicts with your growing need for personal self-esteem. Through both conflicts and positive experiences, you will gain the judgment that will help you make choices as an independent person.

Personal achievement

Everyone has a strong need to succeed at something. For example, a child may receive emotional satisfaction from completing a jigsaw puzzle or coloring a picture book. A young adult may feel satisfaction upon graduating from high school, finding a job, or being accepted by a college. Some people are "A" students, and some are athletes. Some achieve success in the fine arts, music, or theater. Others develop their abilities in such fields as business, education, social work, law, industrial arts, or medicine.

It is important for you to discover the areas in which you can feel a sense of achievement. One way you can find out a great deal about your own strengths is through taking aptitude tests. Another way is by talking to counselors or other adults who have special training in helping others to know themselves better. Or you can simply try new activities to see what you enjoy. Knowing your strongest points and how they can be put to use will help you to achieve.

The need to create

The need to create is probably one of the strongest emotional needs. Children satisfy this need by drawing, playing "make-believe," or building models, for example. Young people may paint, sew, play musical instruments, work imaginatively in a craft, or write poems or stories. Young adults may even build full-sized boats or remodel cars. Coming up with a new solution to a problem is also a way of being creative.

Making a home and a family of one's own is a common way to satisfy the need to create. Dating is an early expression of this need. For most people, dating and getting to know people of the opposite sex are preparations for choosing a long-term partner. In exploring close per-

The need for love does not stop as a person gets older. Older adults need loving relationships with people of all ages.

sonal relationships, you discover the character and traits you like best in others. You are learning to build a meaningful relationship, and this is a creative act. At the same time, you will also be satisfying your need for love and a sense of belonging.

Philosophy of life

Everyone needs to have a purpose in life. Your philosophy of life includes your standards, your sense of values, and your idea of the direction in which you are growing. Even small children, in their own way, need to have a personal plan for living.

Your plan for living is likely to change and grow as you change and grow. But it is important that your philosophy of life fit you and also fit the world in which you live. Take the time to think about your philosophy of life. Your plan will help you with many of the day-to-day decisions you have to make. Your philosophy may be affected by many things: family customs or standards, religion, ideas you have read, experiences you have had, and personal beliefs.

Mature personality

What is personality? To people who study human behavior, **personality** means the total person: the thinking, acting, and feeling self that reacts to the world. Your individual traits make your personality different from anyone else's.

Development of personality

The family is one of the most important influences on personality. A child's first lessons in behavior and emotions are learned from parents. By the time a child is 5 years old, patterns of behavior and ways of reacting to different situations have already developed.

From the age of 5 until about the age of 12, role models, especially parent models, are very important. Family relationships have a great impact on the kind of adult a child will become. If parents understand and accept their child, there is a very good chance that the child will develop a healthy personality. On the other hand, if parents often reject or punish a child without good reason, the child may grow up always expecting to be rejected or punished. The child may then become unsure and uncomfortable when relating to others.

During adolescence, family relationships continue to influence the growing personality. Adolescents feel a strong inner drive for freedom and independence. Their increased knowledge and exposure to other values lead them to question previously accepted values and advice from parents. This is often a difficult stage. The way a teenager and his or her parents handle the conflicts and strains of this period will greatly affect the young person's ability to form a mature personality.

Finding out what you are like is a major step toward maturity.

Developing maturity

Maturity means full development. Maturity is not necessarily a characteristic of adulthood. Some adults are not mature in their actions and attitudes. And some high school students, and even younger people, show maturity in their behavior. Mature behavior is behavior that is appropriate for a person's age and stage of development. In general, maturity means having realistic goals, making wise decisions, practicing self-control, and accepting responsibility for one's behavior.

Developing maturity in the teen years

The teenage years are an important stage in the process of maturing. For many, this is a difficult and confusing time. It is normal for young people to alternate many times between behaving maturely and behaving immaturely at this stage. Adulthood holds the promise of greater freedom, but it demands greater responsibility, too.

"What am I like?" "What will I become?" Discovering the makeup of your personality and setting your life on course are major steps toward maturity. The options offered to teenagers can be upsetting. As one teenager summed it up, "When I began to realize all the decisions I had to make, I really got scared." The transition from childhood to adulthood is rarely a smooth process for anyone.

Understanding your feelings

Why is belonging to a group important to most teenagers?

Do you have sudden changes of mood for no clear reason? Do you feel impatient or in a hurry without knowing why? Are you easily bored by

things you used to enjoy? These feelings can be expected during the teen years. You will probably have feelings like these again. But you may never again have as many different, strong, and confusing feelings as those you have during your teens.

Some of the causes of such feelings are physical. The hormones bringing about physical changes at this time also affect your feelings and attitudes. These changes take place at a fast rate. They can cause troublesome changes in your mood and in your feeling of well-being.

A big change is also taking place in your relationships with people. You are in the middle of building a different kind of relationship with those around you, especially with your parents. At times, you or your parents or all three of you may feel worried and tense about your new role. For example, you may be expected to take on more responsibility. At the same time, you are expected to continue to accept the rules that your parents have made. Such double messages result in conflicts. Being more aware of the reasons why you feel as you do will enable you to handle your feelings better.

You are also learning new ways of relating to people your own age. In addition, relationships change quickly during adolescence because teenagers themselves are changing so quickly. For most people at this age, the need to belong makes relationships with other teenagers seem to be the most important part of life. Being accepted can make you feel very happy. Being rejected can cause real pain.

Overcoming shyness

Shyness is a word used to describe the feelings, thoughts, and physical behaviors that inhibit a person in forming some relationships. When a person says, "I'm shy," the person usually thinks of himself or herself as different from or inferior to other people. The person consequently feels awkward around others. Some people describe feeling as if they were "on stage" and others were judging their performance. They are reluctant to approach people, avoid smiling at people they don't know, consciously or unconsciously avoid eye contact with others, and lack social skills in general.

How does one overcome shyness? Shyness, experts say, is a learned way of behaving. This means that a shy way of behaving can be unlearned. The negative thoughts and feelings that result in shyness can be changed, and a positive attitude can be developed. People sometimes have the mistaken notion that they have to make comments that are unique, entertaining, or profound to have a good conversation. But the most important factor in conversation is to be a good listener. Listening doesn't mean just keeping quiet—it is a way of responding to another person's comments that shows you care about what the person is saying. A good listener pays attention to what the other person feels is important and enjoys talking about. Asking questions about the other person's hobbies, favorite sports, job, or friends is usually a good idea.

Shyness can be unlearned. A first step is to be a good listener.

Also, it is important to learn how to relax, to maintain eye contact with people, and to smile. Practicing these behaviors when talking to friends or relatives can be helpful in relieving shyness. The more often you behave this way, the easier it becomes.

Developing self-confidence

Self-confidence—feeling secure in yourself—is a very valuable trait. It is one of the "prizes" of maturity. Like maturity itself, self-confidence is often earned through experience.

It is normal to think that others are more sure of themselves than you are. Your own doubts and insecurities seem much greater to you than anyone else's. But the fact is, everyone has self-doubts. How many times have you heard a friend say, "I was too embarrassed to ask" or "I just didn't have the nerve to try"? Many young people feel uncertain and fear failure. So they don't risk talking to people they want to get to know. They don't try out for the band, the school play, a team sport, or a job they would like to have. They may never find out what they have to offer. Remember that risking failure also means risking success. It is important to learn how to handle feelings of being unworthy and insecure. Sometimes these feelings can serve to make people try to better themselves.

There are many ways to increase your self-confidence. First, understand yourself. Know what your abilities are, and learn how to make

A Guide For Making Responsible Decisions

Use available resources. Ask yourself, "Where can I get some worthwhile help in making this decision?" This may mean talking over your feelings with a friend, parent, or counselor. Friends may seem the easiest choices for help, but they may be struggling with questions just like yours. Reading a book, going to a meeting, or having information mailed to you are also ways to get help.

Explore the choices. In your mind or on paper, list all of your possible choices. Many times people do not consider all the options they have.

Think about the results. Think about each of your possible choices. Consider what might happen as a result of your decision. Then be sure you are willing to accept the consequences of your actions.

the most of them. Then, from time to time, stop and think about yourself. Are you fulfilling your needs and goals? Are you using your abilities fully? Next, use your energy to work on strengths rather than to worry about weaknesses. The more you build up your strengths, the more confidence you will have. Finally, check up on your inner appearance—your inner self—as often as you check up on your outward appearance. Remember the times when you like what you see.

Making responsible decisions

More and more often, you think and act for yourself. You are learning to make your own decisions, which is necessary. In the future, you will have to decide about such things as education, career, marriage, a place to live, and a personal lifestyle. For now, you must make decisions about school, social life, and family.

A **responsible decision** is one that is based upon personal standards and that causes the least possible harm to you or others. But knowing what a responsible decision is may not always be enough. You may have to choose among several possible choices.

It is a good idea to have a set of steps to follow when making decisions. With a plan of action, you will be more likely to make a responsible long-term decision or a good day-to-day decision.

Expect that some of your decisions will be better than others. Everyone makes mistakes from time to time. When you do make the wrong choice, try not to spend too much time feeling sorry about it. Instead, learn to profit from mistakes.

Remember that many people are willing to help you with both long-term decisions and day-to-day situations that you have to handle. In addition to parents, teachers, school counselors, doctors, and clergy, free counseling services and telephone "hot lines" are available in almost every community. These services have been set up to help you in case you need them.

Personality Trait Checklist
1. I feel comfortable about myself.
☐ I am not overcome by my emotions of fear, anger, love, jealousy, guilt, or worry.   ☐ I can take life's disappointments as they come.   ☐ I have a tolerant, easygoing attitude toward myself as well as toward others.   ☐ I can laugh at myself.   ☐ I neither think too much nor too little of my abilities.   ☐ I feel able to deal with most situations in my life without help.   ☐ I do my everyday tasks without complaining.   ☐ I enjoy spending some time alone in building or creating something, reading, or just thinking.   ☐ I have developed a philosophy of life and a standard of values.
2. I feel comfortable with other people.
☐ I am able to show a real and friendly interest in others.   ☐ I have personal relationships that are satisfying and lasting.   ☐ I like and trust my friends, and I can be sure that they like and trust me.   ☐ I respect the many differences I find among people.   ☐ I do not take advantage of others, nor do I allow others to take advantage of me.   ☐ I feel that I am part of a group.   ☐ I feel a sense of responsibility to my neighbors and to all people of the world.
3. I can meet the demands of life.
☐ I do something about my problems as they happen.   ☐ I accept my responsibilities toward myself and other people, whether they are my friends or not.   ☐ I shape my environment whenever possible. I adjust to it whenever necessary.   ☐ I make plans for the future and hope to reach my goals.   ☐ I welcome new experiences and new ideas.   ☐ I make use of my abilities and set realistic goals for myself.   ☐ I put my best effort into whatever I do, and I get satisfaction from doing it.
*Adapted from *Mental Health Is 1, 2, 3*   (New York: National Association for Mental Health)

Looking at your personality

To rate your personality, you must first try to measure yourself according to your own values. Do you measure up to the standards you set for yourself? Then, try to see yourself as others see you. How do you think

Do you measure up to your own standards for yourself?

you appear to others? Make a list of your desirable and undesirable traits.

After doing this, you can work to correct your weaknesses and to build up your strengths. You might like to check your personality traits against the checklist on page 48. Each item is thought to be a desirable trait. Answer as honestly as you can.

Looking at others

Your feelings about another person are usually a response to personality. When you vote, when you choose a friend, or when you seek a life companion, you will be acting on your judgment of personality.

There are many ways to build self-confidence. Learn how to make the most of your skills and talents.

Mistakes to Avoid in Rating Others' Personalities
Drawing a conclusion from only one event. The new girl who did not return your greeting on her first day in class may not be a snob. She was probably nervous. Or perhaps she simply did not hear you. Give her a chance before you decide.
Placing too much value on surface traits. Sometimes young people make the mistake of thinking that someone has a good personality because the person is good-looking or dances well.
Using a "personality test" from a magazine or newspaper. These tests are very limited. They usually reveal only a small part of the personality. However, carefully prepared tests given by a trained psychologist can often help in judging certain aspects of personality.
Stereotyping. People often expect others to have a certain kind of personality because of their body type, nationality, religion, or race. This kind of "prejudging," which we call stereotyping or prejudice, leads to many false ideas and wrong judgments. Remember that people are individuals. Personality is the whole person in relation to his or her environment. You can't tell what a person is like until you get to know that person.

To rate someone else's personality traits, use the traits suggested for measuring your own personality. Does the person feel comfortable about herself or himself? Does the person meet the demands of life? You must watch an individual in many different situations to learn how the person behaves.

Your opinion of someone else's personality should be based on all you can know. You should consider background, aims, desires, and the means used to reach personal goals. In rating another person's personality, try to avoid the kinds of mistakes in judgment that are outlined in the chart above.

Your hopes and expectations in relationships with other people should be reasonable. Relationships with other people (including friends) are always mixtures of happiness and disappointment. Good friends accept this fact. Many times, you and your friends will have different views and may argue. To remain friends, you have to accept and respect the personality of the other person. This acceptance is a sign of mature behavior.

Key Words

emotional needs	**personality**	**self-concept**
maturity	**responsible decision**	**shyness**

Main Ideas

- Emotional needs must be satisfied if a person is to enjoy life and feel a sense of security.
- Among the most important emotional needs are giving and receiving love, having a positive self-concept, succeeding at something, creating, and having a personal philosophy of life.
- The process of building a new relationship with one's parents during the teenage years often leads to conflict and tension.
- Maturity involves understanding your feelings, developing confidence, and making responsible decisions.
- Shyness is a learned way of behaving and can be unlearned.
- An important part of mature behavior is the ability to accept and respect the personalities of others.

Understand the Reading

1. List five important emotional needs described in this chapter.
2. Describe what can happen—both emotionally and physically—to a person whose emotional needs are not met.
3. Explain the importance of having a positive self-concept.
4. List three ways you can discover activities in which you are most likely to experience personal achievement.
5. What is maturity? What is mature behavior?
6. What are the physical and social reasons why teenagers sometimes experience rapid mood changes?
7. Name several ways that a person might overcome shyness.
8. How does taking risks increase self-confidence?
9. What are the three steps you can follow in making a responsible decision?
10. List four errors to avoid in rating other people's personalities.

Apply Your Knowledge

1. Think of a person who is famous for work in a creative field—dance, music, painting, writing, theater, and so forth. Find information about the person in an encyclopedia or reference book for the arts. Try to determine if any facet of that person's personality is obvious in his or her work. Be as creative as you can in your assessment. In a brief report to the class, discuss the relationship between the individual's art and personality.
2. Read a novel that deals with a teenager growing up before the twentieth century. (Your local or school librarian should be able to help you find such a book.) Make notes on influences that helped shape the person's developing philosophy of life. Write a report on this in a composition for class. Discuss the presence or absence of these influences in your own life.

Chapter 5

Living with Stress

After reading this chapter, you will be able to:

☐ Identify three types of situations that create a stress response in the body.

☐ Recognize the harmful effects of stress on the various systems of the body.

☐ Identify and explain four useful ways of coping with stress.

How well are you able to handle the events that occur in your life? Why is it that some people are able to cope with an experience that would overwhelm someone else?

One famous American faced many difficult situations in his lifetime. Many people believe that his successful handling of many crises added a great deal to his strength of character and his later success.

His mother died in 1818 when he was nine years old. In 1828, his sister died. In 1832, he lost his first job and was defeated for the state legislature. In 1833, he failed in business. In 1835, a girlfriend died. In 1838, four years after being elected to his state's legislature, he was defeated for speaker of the state house of representatives. In 1843 and again in 1844, he was defeated for nomination to the United States Congress.

Elected to Congress in 1847, he did not seek reelection in 1848 because he knew he was too unpopular to win. In 1849, he was rejected for land officer. In 1854, he was defeated for the United States Senate. In 1856, he was defeated for the nomination for Vice President. In 1858, he was again defeated for the United States Senate. Several years later, one of his three sons died. Finally, though, in 1860 he was elected President of the United States.

His name was Abraham Lincoln.

The stress response

Human beings face their problems and challenges in the mind. However, the mind does not operate alone. It works closely with the physical processes of the body. While you don't expect your stomach to solve a problem or to feel excited, you might pass the problem or excitement to your stomach. The effect on the human body of physical and mental demands and pressures may be thought of as **stress**.

The stress response is the body's way of reacting to any demand made on it. The stress response is a kind of alarm. The body can produce a stress reaction in response to a crisis, to everyday situations, and to change.

Stress—a response to crisis

Imagine this: A prehistoric woman is sitting outside her cave enjoying the afternoon sunlight. Suddenly, from the corner of her eye, she sees the shadow of a mountain lion crouched close to the ground. Instantly, her body reacts. Her heart beats quickly and her blood pressure rises. Hormones that aid muscle performance flood into her bloodstream. She starts to breathe rapidly to take in more oxygen. Digestion is stopped at once so that all her body energy can be used to fight off the attack or to flee from it.

The woman has experienced a stress reaction. Her body processes spring into action, ready for fight or flight. This stress response helped our ancestors to survive in dangerous environments.

Thousands of years later, the stress response is the same for people who are reacting to a danger signal. For example, you are walking towards home late at night. The street is completely empty. You hear footsteps behind you and look over your shoulder. Three large figures are following you. You walk faster, and the footsteps quicken, too. You turn sharply at the next corner, and the figures follow you more closely now. Your home is a mile away, so you walk rapidly to the door of the nearest house and ring the bell. No answer. No one is at home. The figures move to the doorstep where you are standing. At this point, your body would be experiencing the same stress reaction that occurred in your ancestors' bodies when they were threatened. Your body systems would be all set to fight or to flee.

Physical dangers are not the only demands that people face today. Your life is far more complicated than that of the cave dweller who was enjoying the sunshine. Suppose that you have a tough math course. To keep up, you should be doing the homework problems every night. But you never seem to understand the problems well enough to do the homework. Class is also confusing. As a result, your grade on the last test was terrible. Today, you walk into the classroom, and the teacher asks the class to put away their books. She is going to give a "pop" quiz.

Your body probably reacts with a surge of activity. Your pulse rate and breathing rate increase. Hormones rush into the bloodstream. Your temperature rises and you begin to perspire. Physically, you experience a stress reaction. Your body is all prepared to fight or to flee—but you can't. There is no physical danger from the math teacher or from a paper-and-pencil quiz. Besides, the rules of classroom behavior do not permit you to rush from the room.

What happens when the body experiences a stress reaction and then cannot use the physical responses that result? In the case of the math quiz, the body will absorb this quick surge of energy. In a very short time, the body will adjust to the stress situation and return to normal. If the demand made on the body by the stress was very strong, you might later experience a physical reaction like indigestion or a headache.

Something that makes a demand on the body is known as a **stressor**. The mountain lion, the three figures, and the quiz are all stressors. In these examples, each of the stressors is part of a crisis situation.

Stress—a response to everyday situations

The math course itself can also be a stressor. Each time you go to class or try to do your homework, you might experience low-level stress reactions. If your poor performance in math continues, you might experience unnoticeable stress symptoms even when you are not consciously thinking about the course. These low-level stress reactions are caused by worrying about math. They result in ongoing bodily changes that you probably don't notice—at first.

Everyone's life has some stress. In day-to-day situations, the body can handle normal stress. Even when stress continues, the body will react by demanding physical and mental rest. After rest, it is again ready to take on stress.

In fact, a certain amount of stress is necessary. The right amount for you depends on your individual physical and mental makeup. Alicia, for example, is always on the go. She participates in all sorts of clubs and organizations in school. Out of school, she competes year-round in sailing races. Keeping up with all her activities requires her to handle a great deal of physical and mental stress.

Mike, on the other hand, is more easygoing. He is not lazy at all. He spends time with his friends, works part-time at a record store, and keeps up with schoolwork. However, he would not be comfortable with Alicia's schedule. To him, that much stress would be harmful. This is sometimes called **distress**. His body and mind would begin to demand rest. Eventually, his body and mind would refuse to function properly until he got rest.

Both Alicia and Mike give their top performances when the stress in their lives is at the best level for each of them. Too little stress can be as undesirable as distress. Many older people in the United States find themselves in situations where they have too little stress in their lives. Low performance levels and physical and mental illness can be the result of too little stress.

Stress is your body's way of reacting to demands made on it.

A certain amount of stress is needed to help you achieve.

Stress—a response to change

Life changes are powerful stressors. When a baby changes from eating liquid foods to eating solid foods, the baby changes its way of eating. When a child enters school, the child must adjust to the fact that many of the needs of the group come first. In adolescence, young people must begin to develop adult attitudes and ideas about responsibility. They must learn to behave in a mature way. Falling in love, getting married, and becoming a parent are other examples of changes that involve new stresses in living.

In the mid-1960s, Dr. Thomas Holmes and Dr. Richard Rahe developed The Social Readjustment Rating Scale. This scale is based on the idea that even a happy event can create stress if a lot of change is necessary. The scale was made after surveying hundreds of adults. People who took part in the survey were asked how much stress they experienced in adjusting to a change in life events. The life events were ranked according to how much adjustment each event required. Dr. Holmes found that people who had to adapt to a great deal of change in a given year were very likely to become ill as a result of the stress. The greater the amount of stress, the more serious the illness was likely to be.

Since that time, similar life-event scales have been developed for people of different ages. The Youth Adaptation Rating Scale on page 57 was created by having adolescents identify stressful events in their lives. The events are ranked in descending order—from most stressful to least

Youth Adaptation Rating Scale

Rank	Life Event	Rank	Life Event
1	Death of a parent/guardian	29	Starting to perform (speeches, presentations, musical performances)
2	Death of a boy/girl friend/close friend		
3	Death of a close family member	30	Getting a bad report card
4	Getting someone pregnant/getting pregnant	31	Problems developed with teachers/employers
5	Going to jail/reform school	32	Getting a ticket or other minor problems with the law
6	Getting beat up by parents		
7	Getting caught using drugs	33	Breaking up with boy/girl friend
8	Getting V.D.	34	Getting a bad haircut
9	Getting attacked/raped/beat up	35	Graduation
10	Parents getting a divorce/separation	36	Moving out of the house
11	Starting to use drugs	37	Pet dies
12	Getting a major illness/injury/car accident	38	Taking the driver's license test
		39	Going on first date/starting to date
13	Not getting promoted to next grade	40	Getting glasses
14	Caught cheating or lying repeatedly	41	Losing or gaining weight
15	Getting married	42	Trying to get a job/job interview
16	Going into debt	43	Family member moving out
17	Getting expelled/suspended	44	Referral to the principal's office
18	Pressure to take drugs	45	Arguments with peers/brothers/sisters
19	Being stereotyped/discriminated against/having bad rumors spread about you		
		46	Getting acne/warts
		47	Getting a new addition to the family
20	Fights with parents	48	Getting braces
21	Moving to a different town/school/making new friends	49	Making a team (drill, athletic, debate)
		50	Fad pressure
22	Falling in love	51	Going on a diet
23	Making career decisions (college, majors, training, etc.)	52	First day of school
		53	Going to the dentist/doctor
24	Becoming religious or giving up religion	54	Getting an award, office, etc.
25	Getting fired from a job	55	Getting a car
26	Getting pressure about having sex	56	Starting to go to weekend parties/rock concerts
27	Taking finals/SAT test		
28	Trouble getting a date when it was not a problem before	57	Getting a minor illness (cold, flu, etc.)
		58	Changing exercise habits

From *Journal of School Health*, Vol. 54, No. 5, © May 1984, American School Health Association
Sue Beall and Gayle Schmidt, "Development of a Youth Adaptation Rating Scale"

stressful. The death of a parent or guardian is ranked as being the most stressful event. Changing exercise habits is ranked as the least stressful event. You may agree with some of the ratings. You may disagree with others. Think about the reasons why a certain ranking might not be the same for all people. How would the ranking be different for you?

Is stress harmful?

You probably have felt the effects of unrelieved stress in the form of stomachache, headache, diarrhea, or indigestion. In your body's attempt to adjust to stress, you may have found that your mouth became dry, you became depressed or irritable, or you lost your appetite or started to eat uncontrollably. These are common stress symptoms.

Researchers have found that ongoing stress can have a very serious effect on the body. New research is underway to find out to what degree long-term stress is responsible for damage to and diseases of major body systems. The chart below gives examples of the effect stress is known to have on major body systems. In addition, stress is a factor in a wide variety of other health problems, including diabetes, skin conditions, immune disorders, and even cancer.

Coping with stress

Self-esteem, philosophy of life, relationships with others, and successful handling of past difficult situations affect one's ability to cope well. Each event in life brings a unique chance for emotional growth. Failures, as well as successes, offer the potential for positive growth. Growth depends on how a situation is viewed and handled.

How do you keep your stress level at the proper point—the point where you perform best as an active individual but avoid the harmful effects of stress?

Keep your body working for you, not against you. A healthy body makes you better able to adapt to the normal stresses of everyday life. It also helps you to weather the stresses caused by life changes. You

Something to think about

Is stress something that is "all in your head"? Consider . . .

Major Body System	Conditions Caused or Made Worse by Unrelieved Stress
Cardiovascular system	heart attack, high blood pressure, migraine headache
Digestive System	ulcers, colitis, constipation, diarrhea
Nervous system	insomnia, nervousness, memory problems, depression
Respiratory system	hyperventilation, asthma, increase in colds and other infections
Skeletal-muscular system	backache, arthritis, being "accident-prone"

probably already know the guidelines for maintaining the good health of your body. They are the simple rules that you have learned at home and in school for most of your life: eat a well-balanced diet, get enough sleep, and exercise regularly. You may get tired of hearing them. They may seem too familiar or too "goody-goody." But the fact is that these simple health practices keep you alive and functioning.

Know how to judge a situation. Some situations can and must be changed. Some situations should be left alone. Judgments about when to act and when to let something pass are usually made on the basis of experience. You can evaluate the experience you are having by looking closely at your actions and the actions of others.

For instance, suppose you eat lunch with Fred. Every once in a while, Fred gets loud and rowdy. It seems funny to you at first, but then it becomes hard to take. Fortunately, you like Fred for a number of reasons, and his loud behavior doesn't happen that often. But today is "one of those days," and by lunchtime you're tired of it. Fred is causing you some stress. You have had a polite discussion once before about your reaction to his loudness. But Fred hasn't changed much as a result. Here is what you could do:

- Yell at Fred. You feel like doing this.
- Sit there and take it. You don't feel like doing this, but you think it might be wise.
- Finish your lunch and go to the library. Tell Fred you feel like being by yourself.

The reality of the situation is that you like Fred and want to be his friend despite his occasional outbursts. He hasn't changed his behavior and isn't likely to. Yelling will create more stress because it will make you worry about hurting your friendship. Sitting and fuming will let the stress reactions build up in you. Simply removing yourself until things become more calm is a realistic way of handling the situation. Tomorrow Fred will have quieted down again.

Try to spot stress and plan for it. If you know that a stressful situation will soon occur, it will help to be prepared. Suppose you are afraid to give speeches and you have an oral report due next week. You know all about the stress reaction that you will experience when you stand in front of the class. You can:

- Prepare your report thoroughly, put it on note cards, and practice it in front of the mirror and in front of your family or friends.
- Get yourself ready to speak a week in advance by asking a question or making a comment in class whenever possible. (You'll get used to hearing your own voice speak out loud.)

The ability to make quick judgments under stress is a part of many jobs.

- Admit that giving oral reports is stressful for you. Tell yourself that you are *allowed* to experience stress at first. Realize that your body is simply reacting and that the same body can adapt.
- Ask yourself how you might turn off your **flight response** and turn on your **fight response**. Create positive images in your mind of how you will use the energy from your stress reaction to "get into" and deliver the speech. Good public speakers know how to use the physical readiness caused by stress to improve their performances.

Sometimes stress is hard to spot. There are times when you feel the stress symptoms before you understand the cause of the stress. You should see a doctor about any physical symptoms that become too annoying or seem more serious than usual.

Learn something about relaxation.   What makes you relax? Is it a soft sofa and a good book? An hour of jogging? A chance to sit and daydream? A phone conversation with a friend?

The word *relaxation* reminds many people of the word *play*. Sometimes people use this association to dismiss their need to relax: "I can't relax today. I have too much to do." Relaxation can be enjoyable, but that does not mean that it is unnecessary.

When you relax the muscles in the body, you slow down the body's processes. When you use the muscles in the body forcefully, you reduce built-up body tension. Both of these acts provide physical and mental relief. From what you know about stress, you can see that relaxation can help prevent physical symptoms from building up. Relaxation helps you to stay healthy.

You may have noticed that relaxing after a stressful day feels even more refreshing than relaxing after a day when your stress load was low. After a stressful situation, the relief you provide to your body feels particularly good. Can you think of some time when this has been true for you?

Some people find it difficult to relax. These people are often the ones who need relaxation the most to handle high levels of stress. Relaxation is like any other physical activity the body performs—it improves with practice. By regularly giving your body a relaxation break, you will notice an improvement in your day-to-day performance. You will also notice that your ability to adapt to sudden stress reactions increases.

These are only a few ways to cope with stress. You might have found that other ways work best for you. The important thing is to find a way to cope. You can't avoid all stress—and you would not want to. But you can learn how to handle the expected stress in your life and how to avoid unnecessary stress. This will make it easier for your body to adapt to those stresses that you don't expect. By learning to cope with problems and pressures, you can keep your body from becoming ill or damaged by the effects of constant, unrelieved stress. Developing this ability to cope needs to be part of your wellness program.

Your body needs to relax for physical and mental relief. Relaxation helps you stay healthy.

Key Words

Main Ideas

- Stress is the effect of both physical and mental demands on the body.
- The body produces a stress reaction in response to a crisis, everyday situations, and change.
- Ongoing stress can lead to a variety of health problems, many of them serious.
- Methods for coping with stress include keeping healthy, dealing realistically with everyday situations, trying to plan for stressful situations, and relaxing.

Understand the Reading

1. What is stress? What is a stressor?
2. What are the three kinds of situations that produce a stress response in the body?
3. What happens to the body when you are faced with a crisis?
4. Name four typical life changes that often result in stress.
5. According to The Youth Adaptation Rating Scale, what is the most stressful event in a teenager's life? The least stressful event?
6. Name five physical symptoms that may result from unrelieved stress.
7. What are some health problems that have been linked to ongoing stress?
8. What are four ways of coping with stress?
9. List three ways in which you can "keep your body working for you" to lower ongoing stress.
10. What happens to your body physically when you relax?

Apply Your Knowledge

1. In a science encyclopedia or similar reference book, locate the name Dr. Hans Selye. Learn about the original research that Dr. Selye did and the concept that he was responsible for developing. Describe the doctor's work in a report to the class.
2. Do some research on biofeedback. (You will want to start with Chapter 33 of this book, which discusses the concept briefly.) Through your research, determine the types of problems biofeedback has been used to treat and how successful it has been. Report on this phenomenon to the class. Describe in your own words the kind of connection between body and mind that this technique implies.

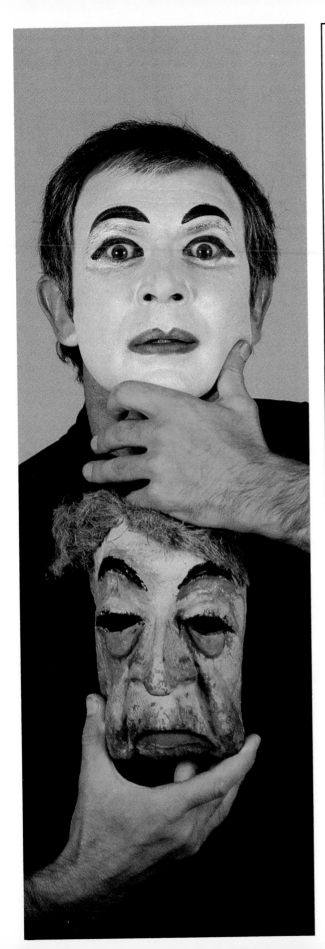

Chapter 6
Emotions and Mental Health

After reading this chapter, you will be able to:

☐ Define anger and discuss positive and negative ways of dealing with it.

☐ Describe the various types of defense mechanisms people use to satisfy emotional needs.

☐ Explain the differences among fear, anxiety, and guilt.

☐ Describe the causes of depression and outline ways of handling it.

☐ Identify the causes of suicide and discuss how to deal with someone who appears suicidal.

☐ Describe the kinds and causes of mental illness and discuss treatment available for people with mental problems.

I was so lonely that I felt I was in prison. I thought about talking to Mr. Sawyer, who was like a friend to his students. But I was afraid he wouldn't have time for me. Finally, I got up the nerve. I started talking to Mr. Sawyer, and then the words just poured out. With his help, my parents and I found a doctor that we've been seeing. Lately, I've started realizing that life doesn't have to feel like prison. I'm finally free.

—(*a 17-year-old currently undergoing psychotherapy for depression*)

Anger and hostility

Everyone is capable of becoming angry or hostile. At an early age, you begin to learn how to control these strong emotions. As you grow older, you learn when and how to put anger to use. For example, you may have allowed your grades to fall, so you do not get a reward you want, such as being listed on the honor roll. Your anger with yourself may make you work much harder to improve your grades.

Even anger toward others can be constructive. Suppose a classmate were left out of certain activities because the person was of a different race or had a handicap. Your anger may cause you to take a strong stand for what you believe is fair. Your action may persuade others to change their behavior.

Constructive ways to deal with anger

Anger and hostility may build up in anyone. Many kinds of small conflicts and frustrations may cause this to happen. If it happens to you, you can usually get rid of hostile feelings by talking about the problem with someone who is not involved. It is sometimes not really a good idea to talk over the matter too soon with the person you are angry with. More anger, not less, may result. Sometimes, too, you may not feel like talking about the problem, or you may not be able to find the right person to talk to. It may be possible to relieve the hostility in another way. One good way is to work off the anger in very demanding physical activity. Physical action will use the extra energy that builds up when you get angry. Then you will be able to think more clearly about why you felt the anger and how you can handle the situation that made you angry.

Later, if you talk about your feelings with the person who made you angry, remember to attack the issue, not the person. In other words, don't name-call or make nasty remarks. They get in the way and make it hard for the other person to understand the reasons why you got angry and the behavior you expect in the future. Uncontrolled remarks have a way of creating more situations that are also out of your control. In the following two examples, who do you think makes the point best?

Physical exercise is not only fun. It is also a good way to use the extra energy that builds up when you get angry.

First teenager to younger sister: "You stupid brat! You scratched my new record. You're always doing rotten things! You can never listen to any of my records again."

Second teenager to younger sister: "I'm very angry. You scratched my new record, and I was really looking forward to listening to it. Next time, ask *me* to put the records on the turntable."

Poor ways to deal with anger

Many ways of getting rid of hostility and anger are **antisocial**. That is, they work against other people, groups, or society. For example, Sal is "touchy" and gets into arguments easily. If you could read his mind, you would discover that he feels a need for more friends—a group to belong to. But for some reason, Sal thinks that this goal cannot be reached, and he has stopped trying. Frustration and loneliness cause him to be disagreeable and hostile toward the very people he wants as friends.

Rule-breaking is a hostile act. Rules help you learn what is expected of you. Breaking a rule usually results in unwanted consequences. A student who breaks rules and upsets classes may be getting rid of anger. The emotion may have been the result of failure to achieve in school. Two things may help. First, the person can look for an area in which she or he can do well. Doing well in any area will increase positive feelings of self-worth. Second, the student can look for acceptable ways to relieve the built-up anger. Taking part in sports or talking out angry feelings can help.

It is not always wrong to challenge rules. Questioning—and even rebelling against—some rules is part of growing up. Intelligent challenging of rules you do not agree with takes courage. Conforming to or following rules because "everybody else is doing it" is easy.

Most criminal and delinquent acts are antisocial acts against a person, a group, or society as a whole. There is no single cause of such behavior. But anger and hostility are often the reasons behind law-breaking acts.

Defense mechanisms

People sometimes use **defense mechanisms** to satisfy emotional needs. A defense mechanism helps someone relieve or avoid the pain of emotional conflict. It helps people "save face" in their own eyes and in the eyes of others. Everyone uses defense mechanisms as a way of dealing with conflicts. Difficulties occur when defense mechanisms are overused and are substituted for more direct ways of dealing with problems. This can lead to severe emotional problems requiring professional treatment. Several different kinds of defense mechanisms are explained below.

Rationalization is inventing an explanation for a failure or mistake that actually has other causes. People are often not aware they are rationalizing. Rationalization can easily become a habit. It helps preserve self-respect for a time. But it is a way of sidestepping a problem and shifting the blame onto someone or something else. Only by learning to face failure honestly can a person work to overcome the failure and succeed.

Compensation is trying to provide substitutes for real or imagined shortcomings. Compensation can result in successful actions. For example, a person with too much stage fright to try out for the school play may apply for the job of assistant director—and get it. Sometimes, however, a person covers up a shortcoming with unacceptable behavior. A child who is physically smaller than others of the same age may unconsciously try to seem bigger and more important by bragging about his or her experiences.

What defense mechanism might this person be using?

Negativism is always saying no to the suggestions or instructions of others. Instead of attacking a problem directly, a negative person may do nothing or may do the opposite of what is suggested. The negativist refuses to try, perhaps out of fear of failure. He or she passes up the chance to gain recognition or a sense of personal worth.

Identification consists of taking on the qualities or characteristics of another person. Sometimes, for example, people mentally link themselves with a character in a film or television play. They experience what the character experiences and feel and think as the character feels and thinks. Sometimes identification is a way of fulfilling a wish. A person may wish to be just like someone else. Identification is easy to see in fans who act or dress just like the sports star or entertainer they most admire. Occasional use of identification may help a person to satisfy a need for a role model. If used too much, this mechanism may cause a person to live in a dream world. In extreme cases, this pattern can be corrected only with special professional help.

Daydreaming is similar to identification. In daydreaming, a person substitutes a dream world for the real one. Daydreaming can be a normal and sometimes useful part of a creative life. But the daydreamer must recognize the difference between the fantasy world and real life. Some inventions and artistic masterpieces are the result of daydreams. Creative ideas, make-believe thoughts, or dreams can be acted upon and turned into real products or works of art.

Escape is running away when real or imagined defeat seems certain. When some people think they cannot face or solve a problem, they try to avoid it. A person who behaves in this way will gain little self-respect until the problem is faced in a direct way. There are several different escape mechanisms. *Repression* is an unconscious method of escape. A person pushes unwanted conflicts out of awareness. The person is usually unaware that there is any problem at all. *Suppression* is a conscious process of ignoring or avoiding an emotion. It is like closing the door to a room where something unpleasant is happening. *Regression* is living and behaving like a child. A person who does not have the courage or resources to face and solve a problem directly will sometimes go backward to a dependent position. This person may become more dependent, rather than less, on parents or others for support and for satisfaction of needs.

Conversion takes place when a mental conflict is turned into a physical symptom. For example, a student who fears that he or she will not know what to say on a date may become so ill that it is impossible to go out. The pains and physical symptoms are real, not imagined. But the cause of the physical symptoms is mental conflict. *Projection* is blaming others for a person's own unacceptable motives or faults. It involves refusing to take responsibility for what has happened or what is felt or thought. (Example: You say about a new student in class, "I feel uncomfortable with him because he always wants to show me up," when in fact you are the one who has competitive and unfriendly feelings toward *him*.)

Fear

Everyone has felt fear of one kind or another. Feeling afraid is normal. It helps a person get ready for what may happen next. There are two general types of fear—fear of the unknown and fear of the known.

Fear of the unknown

Almost everyone has at some time felt afraid of the unknown. Unexplained things may seem to threaten our safety or well-being. For example, a child may be very fearful of the loud noises at a fireworks display. But an older person knows that the explosions are under control.

To get rid of fears of the unknown, you should look more closely at them. Then, when the unknown becomes known, you can decide whether or not your fear is reasonable. Having an open mind also helps you to overcome fears of the unknown or unfamiliar. If you are willing to consider new ideas, you will find that the unknown can sometimes turn out to be exciting.

Fear of the known

Fears of the known can be either useful or harmful. Reasonable fears can prepare you to act. If you wake up in the middle of the night and smell smoke, you are wise to be fearful. You will check out the source of the smoke and perhaps avoid a tragedy.

Fear of thunder, on the other hand, is an unreasonable fear. Light and electricity (lightning) travel much faster than sound (thunder). When you hear thunder, lightning has already flashed. The danger is over. The damage, if any, has already been done.

It is hard for many people to tell the difference between reasonable and unreasonable fears. Learning the difference is an important part of growing.

Anxiety

Anxiety, or worry, is a sense of uneasiness and distress about the future. Anxiety, like fear, can be unreasonable. Some worries, however, are reasonable and useful. For example, if you worry about failing a test, you may begin to study. Anxiety in this case has a positive result.

Guilt

Everyone has values, or ideas of what is right or wrong. You have a clear conscience when you do what you believe is right, and you have a guilty conscience when you have done something you believe is wrong. Guilt feelings can be constructive when they help you live up to your values. But if strong feelings of guilt last for a long time, they can lead to serious emotional disturbance. Extreme guilt feelings are a good reason to seek help from those who are professionally trained.

The term **depression** is used to refer to several distinct conditions. Depression can refer to a mood that most people experience at one time or another. They may say they feel "blue" or "down" because of a disappointment, failure, or frustrating experience. Depression can also refer to feelings of sadness and helplessness, inability to experience pleasure, loss of energy, and bodily complaints. These symptoms are short-lived, but are more intense than the normal range of ups and downs. Finally, depression can refer to a very serious emotional problem. Symptoms of this last form of depression include changes in appetite and sleep habits, loss of energy, feelings of pessimism and hopelessness, and thoughts of death and suicide.

Causes of depression

The causes of depression are not completely understood. Mental health experts say that depression has many different sources. Some of these include life history, psychological makeup, and hereditary factors. Recent studies have shown that some depression may be biochemical in nature. These cases have their origins inside the person rather than in some environmental influence. Other mental health experts suggest some kinds of depression may be caused by allergies. They have observed cases in which household cleaning products or foods, such as sugar, seem to be at the root of the problem.

Some specific factors are known to bring on depression, especially in teenagers. These include low self-esteem, lack of self-confidence, feelings of guilt or powerlessness, loneliness, pressure, personal loss, and attachment to peer group to the exclusion of parental attachment.

Recognizing depression and understanding its causes are important.

Dealing with depression

Some adolescents attempt to deny depression or respond to it in ways that are harmful to themselves and others. Some types of behavior that may be caused by depression are poor academic performance, truancy, delinquency, alcohol and drug abuse, sexual promiscuity, and running away. It is not always possible to prevent depression from occurring. But being aware of the reasons for depression and being able to recognize it are two important steps in preventing a serious depressive mood from setting in. Other important steps in preventing and coping with depression are:

- Keeping a balance between being involved with peers and remaining close to parents.
- Making more or new friends.
- Making better use of existing social relationships.
- Being involved in a constructive activity or project.
- Not setting unrealistic or unreachable goals.

If depression continues for too long a time, it is important to seek help. An understanding teacher, counselor, school nurse, or doctor can sometimes help a young person overcome depression. These people may also know about other sources of help. Deep and long-lasting depression can have serious consequences.

Suicide

Sometimes the emotional pain of depression becomes too much to bear. An individual may feel that life is no longer worth living. The only solution that seems acceptable to a person in that state of mind is **suicide**, the act of intentionally killing oneself.

Suicide is a leading cause of death among young people between the ages of 15 and 24. Teenagers who attempt suicide often feel worthless, hopeless, and overwhelmed. The most frequently encountered situations that bring about these feelings are loss of an important relationship (usually with a boyfriend, girlfriend, or parent); being under the influence of a drug; and conflicts with parents or problems at school or elsewhere that seem unsolvable.

According to a government report, some people appear to be especially prone to suicide because of "stress overload." Whether or not stress becomes a problem for a person, however, depends on a combination of things. A person's feelings of stress and his or her reaction to it may change with time, circumstance, and environmental factors.

Clues that a serious problem exists

It is normal for young people to be depressed at times or to experience feelings of loneliness or of being overwhelmed. At one time or another, many people think about suicide as a possible solution. But these thoughts should pass quickly as the person realizes there are better ways to solve the problem. It is cause for concern when depression lasts and the person is not getting help.

What are some clues that a person might be a likely candidate for suicide? Mental health experts suggest the following:

It is vital to let a friend with emotional troubles know that you care.

- Withdrawing socially.
- Daredevil behavior.
- Extreme ups and downs in mood.
- Giving away treasured possessions.
- Previous threat or attempt to commit suicide.
- Change in work or school performance.
- Talking, reading, or writing (letters, stories, or poems) about death.
- Increase in smoking.
- Increased use of alcohol or other drugs.
- Extreme desire to punish oneself or another person.

Suicide: Facts and Fables

Fable: People who talk about suicide don't commit suicide.

Fact: Of any ten persons who will kill themselves, eight have given definite warnings of their suicidal intentions.

Fable: Suicide happens without warning.

Fact: Studies reveal that suicidal people give many clues and warnings regarding their suicidal intentions.

Fable: Suicidal people are fully intent on dying.

Fact: Most suicidal people are undecided about living or dying, and they "gamble with death," leaving it to others to save them. Almost no one commits suicide without letting others know how he or she is feeling.

Fable: Once suicidal, a person is suicidal forever.

Fact: Individuals who wish to kill themselves feel "suicidal" only for a limited period of time.

Fable: Improvement following a suicidal crisis means that the suicidal risk is over.

Fact: Most suicides occur within about 3 months following the beginning of "improvement" when the individual has the energy to put morbid thoughts and feelings into effect.

Fable: Suicide strikes much more often among the rich—or, conversely, it occurs almost exclusively among the poor.

Fact: Suicide is neither a rich person's nor a poor person's disease. Suicide is very "democratic" and is represented proportionately among all levels of society.

Fable: All suicidal individuals are mentally ill, and suicide is always the act of a psychotic person.

Fact: Studies of hundreds of genuine suicide notes indicate that although the suicidal person is extremely unhappy, he or she is not necessarily mentally ill.

Something to think about

Adapted from *Some Facts about Suicide* by E. S. Shneidman and N. L. Farberow, Washington, D.C., PHS Publication No. 852, U.S. Government Printing Office.

- Change in eating and sleeping habits.
- Low self-esteem.
- Inability to concentrate or make decisions.

How you can help

If you suspect that a friend might be thinking about suicide, there are some things you can do to help. A teenager who is contemplating suicide often thinks that no one cares or understands what he or she is going through. You can help prevent this feeling of isolation by following these suggestions.

To begin with, listen. Even if you cannot solve your friend's problem, listening will let your friend know that his or her well-being is important to you. If you think you recognize a warning sign, don't panic. Remaining calm yourself is one of the ways you can help. However, do take seriously any warning signs you see. If you think your friend is suicidal, do not hesitate to take the action steps described here.

Second, be supportive. It is a mistake to call someone's problems or feelings unimportant. It is also a mistake not to take suicide threats seriously.

Third, talk. Depending upon the situation, you might remind the person that the depressed feelings will pass. Emphasize the fact that there are alternatives to this act. Tell the person that as long as he or she is alive, there is a chance the problem can be solved. Point out that once suicide is chosen, the act cannot be undone.

Last, take action. Try to get the person to come with you to a counselor, his or her parents, your parents, a doctor, an emergency room, or any adult who can provide help. By going with your friend, you are making sure the person gets help. You are also showing that you care. Even if your friend won't come with you, don't carry the load alone. Tell someone that you think your friend might harm himself or herself and that you need help.

There are also things that you should not do when you suspect a friend is suicidal. First, do not allow yourself to be sworn to secrecy. If your friend asks you to promise not to tell anyone, do not agree to keep a suicide plan secret. Second, do not dare your friend to commit suicide. That reverse psychology simply doesn't work—it does not tell your friend that you care what happens. Finally, do not be judgmental and tell your friend that he or she has no right to feel depressed or that the problem really is not that bad. Just accept the fact that your friend is in trouble and needs understanding.

Is suicide always preventable?

Most people who are suicidal do not want to die. They simply want the emotional turmoil and the despair to go away. Life does not seem worth living to them at that moment. Thus, many suicidal people make an attempt to let others know how they feel, even though the warning signs may go unheeded. It is important for all of us to remember that emotional crises do pass and that, even in the most extreme crises, solutions exist.

Once a suicide has occurred, family and close friends may dwell on what they should have done to prevent it. These feelings need to be openly explored, preferably with a professional. The time spent can be brief, but it is very important. If this is not done, feelings of guilt are likely to linger for a long time.

The natural question that arises is, "Could we have done something to prevent it?" Thinking back, it can be easy to say a suicide could have been prevented. Such an after-the-fact judgment, however, may not reflect the true situation. Some people who are planning suicide are very good at covering up their intentions. Some can be so determined that there is no stopping them. Even experienced professionals can be fooled. Suicide can be prevented in many instances, but there are situations in which the best efforts fail. Ultimately, the responsibility for choosing life or death belongs to the suicidal person, not to the family or friend.

Mental illness

About one-fifth of all the hospital patients in the United States are people who are mentally ill. Many more people not in hospitals have mental or emotional disturbances severe enough to make their relationships with other people very difficult.

By learning about mental and emotional illnesses and their causes, you can better understand the principles of good mental health. Knowing about mental illness will also help you understand people who are undergoing treatment for mental or emotional disorders.

Causes of mental illness

The causes of mental illness may be physical, emotional, or both. Some are the result of changes in brain chemistry or in other parts of the nervous system. These changes may be caused by disease, injury, or age. Mental illnesses may also be caused by changes in physical and chemical balances within the body. Still other mental disorders seem to have no physical cause. Such disorders are usually thought to result from the failure to satisfy emotional needs or to recover from emotional shock.

Degrees of mental illness

It is not always easy to know when a person is mentally ill. The behavior of a disturbed person often appears to be much like the behavior of a normal person. All people get upset from time to time and occasionally lose control over their emotions. In general, however, mentally healthy people are able to face the realities of life and behave in a way to get the greatest satisfaction. Mentally ill people use some of the same methods that normal people do to solve problems. But they may use them at the wrong time or carry them to extremes. And their goals are often unrealistic.

One common sign of mental disturbance is an inability to get along with other people. All of us find it hard at times to get along with others. This is normal. But for emotionally or mentally disturbed persons, it may be hard most or all of the time. It is not always easy to tell whether the difficulty is normal or is the symptom of a more serious disturbance. The changes from normal behavior to severe mental illness are not exact.

Kinds of mental illness

Most mental illnesses fall into three major categories: neurosis, psychosis, and psychosomatic disorder.

Neurosis is a mental disorder characterized by poor development of skills used to meet basic emotional needs. These poorly developed skills make relating to others more difficult. They also make the person more vulnerable to emotional shocks, such as losing a job or the sudden loss of a loved one.

One common type of neurotic illness is excessive fear or anxiety. Often the person cannot explain the fear. It is not unusual for a child to be afraid of the dark, but it is abnormal for an adult to experience this fear. Darkness may not be the cause of the fear. It may be that a deeply repressed fear is the real cause—a fear that the person is not aware of or cannot openly discuss.

Sometimes anxiety is unconsciously changed into physical disability. For example, an athlete's extreme worry about a pole-vault contest might result in leg paralysis. If no physical cause were present, the vaulter would be said to suffer from physical conversion of a mental anxiety. The person would not be conscious of this conversion.

Psychosis is a mental disorder in which a person is out of touch with reality at least part of the time. Because the person cannot adjust to the real world, he or she makes up a new world. The dream world may be a world filled with great anxiety. Or it may be a place where the person is a hero. But these feelings have no relation to real situations. Psychotics are usually not conscious of their behavior. They cannot tell the difference between the dream world and the real world.

Psychoses are sometimes caused by physical damage to the brain. These are called organic psychoses. Brain tumors, syphilis, and alcohol or other drugs can cause this kind of psychosis.

Psychosomatic disorders are physical problems caused by emotional or psychological factors. Physicians believe that some cases of heart trouble, stomach ulcers, constipation, diarrhea, skin disorders, and other physical disorders are caused or made worse by mental and emotional disturbances. Psychosomatic disorders are real. The physical effects are just as damaging as the effects that result from physical illness.

Even people with good mental health sometimes need help with an emotional problem.

Treating mental health problems

A person who is qualified to treat emotional and mental health problems is called a therapist. Two kinds of specialists who are qualified to treat mental and emotional disturbances are **psychiatrists** and **clinical psychologists**. A psychiatrist is a physician with a specialty in treating mental disorders. Because a psychiatrist is a medical doctor, he or she may prescribe medication to treat the mental problem. A clinical psychologist is a person trained in both the theories and techniques of treatment of psychological problems. In most cases, the individual has a doctoral degree in psychology.

Mental health specialists use several different kinds of **therapy**, or treatment, to help people. The kind of therapy used depends upon the individual client.

Psychotherapy is a treatment of mental and emotional disturbances that involves talking with the client. Psychotherapy is a slow process of learning about oneself. Working together, the client and therapist search for reasons for the abnormal feelings and behavior. The client expresses his or her feelings, dreams, and thoughts to the therapist. In time, better ways of meeting emotional needs are learned, and the person is able to live more happily and fully.

Psychotherapy can also be used with families or groups. Sometimes it is helpful for the therapist to work with an entire family as a unit. In **family therapy**, the therapist usually works with individual family members at some times and the family unit at other times. The goal is to help each member of the family understand his or her effect upon the other members and upon the unit as a whole.

Group therapy is practiced by a therapist with several clients at the same time. The group members usually have emotional problems that are somewhat alike. Some people find that group therapy works better than individual therapy. One advantage is seeing that other people have emotional problems, too. Another advantage is learning from others in the group. Group members see how certain ways of communication can add to or decrease emotional instability.

Psychoanalysis is a special kind of psychotherapy. A psychoanalyst works with a person intensely over a long period of time. The goal of this type of treatment is to help the person thoroughly understand his or her psychological makeup.

In **drug therapy**, tranquilizers, antidepressants, or stimulants are used to treat mental health problems. Drugs cannot cure a mental illness, but can help to relieve symptoms and provide a sense of control for some clients whose lives would otherwise be more seriously disrupted.

A self-check on your mental health

One definition of mental health is the ability to face the facts of life and achieve the greatest possible satisfaction. Below are some characteristics of the mentally healthy person. Using this list as a guide, do a self-check on your mental health. Make a note of those areas in which you think you need to improve. Think of ways you can make changes.

The Mentally Healthy Person

1. Accepts problems and conflicts and works through them to a satisfactory end.
2. Is able to love and to accept the love of others. Finds satisfaction in human relationships.
3. Can work and play cooperatively in give-and-take relationships.
4. Uses defense mechanisms when effective, but does not depend upon them to solve all problems.
5. Has a standard of values that guides actions.
6. Is able to change or adjust behavior when necessary, but only if moral standards are maintained.
7. Has developed a philosophy of life that meets the demands of society, satisfies personal dreams and goals, and is within his or her capabilities.
8. Can control anger and hostility, as well as other emotions, and has learned harmless ways of getting rid of hostility.
9. Develops creative interests and abilities so that satisfaction can be found in doing things well.
10. Is ready to accept responsibility for feelings and actions.

Key Words

antisocial	drug therapy	psychoanalysis
anxiety	family therapy	psychosis
clinical	group therapy	psychosomatic
psychologists	neurosis	disorders
defense	psychiatrists	psychotherapy
mechanisms		suicide
depression		therapy

- Anger is a natural emotion that can be used constructively.
- People use the various types of defense mechanisms to satisfy emotional needs.
- Fear, anxiety, and guilt can all be used constructively.
- The term *depression* covers a variety of conditions, ranging from a negative mood to a serious emotional problem. Serious depressions need to be treated before they get out of hand.
- Suicide is a serious problem among teenagers. Clues that a person is considering suicide exist, and ways of preventing a suicide are available.
- Neurosis, psychosis, and psychosomatic disorders are three major kinds of mental illness. A variety of treatments for mental problems is available.

1. What are some good ways of getting rid of anger?
2. What is the purpose of a defense mechanism? How is it sometimes helpful? When can it cause a severe emotional disturbance?
3. How can fear of the known be useful?
4. What can you do about situations that produce guilt feelings? Give an example.
5. Describe two different types of depression.
6. What are some ways of preventing a depressive mood from setting in?
7. List three clues that indicate a person might be thinking about suicide.
8. What are three ways you might help a friend who is thinking about suicide?
9. What is the difference between psychotherapy and psychoanalysis?
10. List five traits of a mentally healthy person.

1. Plan a debate among members of your class on this statement: It is more important to treat some criminals for their mental illnesses than to imprison them. For the debate, find out how treatment of criminals has been improved and what further improvements are hoped for. Decide on your own point of view about the treatment of criminals, and be prepared to defend it.
2. Research the subject of occupational therapy as a tool in the treatment of the mentally ill. A first step in your research would be to contact the American Occupational Therapy Association, 600 Executive Boulevard, Suite 200, Rockville, MD 20852. Be prepared to report your findings to the class.

Unit 3
The Life Cycle

Chapter 7

Human Reproduction

After reading this chapter, you will be able to:

☐ Name and explain the functions of the various parts of the male and female reproductive systems.

☐ Describe the process by which a life begins.

☐ Describe the birth process.

☐ Explain the precautions that need to be taken in prenatal care.

☐ Describe what individuals need to know in order to be good parents.

All human babies are formed by the joining of two cells. One cell comes from the mother, and one comes from the father. The mother's egg cell, or *ovum*, is very small. It can hardly be seen by the human eye. The father's *sperm* cell is even smaller. It can be seen only through a microscope.

Sperm are made in two glands in the male called *testes*, or testicles. Ova (the plural of ovum) are made in two glands in the female called *ovaries*.

Puberty is the stage of life during which a person's reproductive system begins to work. For boys, puberty is the period when the testes begin to make sperm. For most boys, this is the period between the ages of 12 and 15. The outward sign of puberty is the development of **secondary sexual characteristics**. A boy's voice gets deeper, and hair begins to grow on the face, under the arms, and in the genital area. Arm, leg, and chest muscles become stronger and harder. A boy's skin becomes thicker and tougher, and his shoulders get wider. The development of these male sexual characteristics is controlled by a substance called **testosterone**. Testosterone is the male sex hormone made by the testes.

The male reproductive system

Testes

The testes are formed in the abdomen. Shortly before birth, they usually move downward into a pouch of skin and connective tissue that hangs outside the body. This pouch is called the **scrotum**. In some cases, one or both testes do not move into the scrotum until after birth. Sometimes a doctor's help is needed to bring the testes into the scrotum.

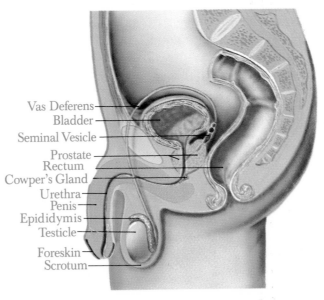

At puberty, the testes of the male begin to make sperm.

Vas Deferens
Bladder
Seminal Vesicle
Prostate
Rectum
Cowper's Gland
Urethra
Penis
Epididymis
Testicle
Foreskin
Scrotum

As each testis passes through the lower wall of the abdomen, the passageway usually closes behind it. If the passageway does not close, a hernia, or tear, may occur at this spot later in life. Such a hernia may be seen as a swelling in the groin that develops after lifting something heavy. Or it may feel like pressure from inside the abdomen. This kind of hernia can be fixed surgically without serious risk.

Sperm

Sperm are shaped somewhat like tadpoles. Each sperm has a head that contains a nucleus. The sperm also has a tail that waves back and forth, which makes the sperm move.

Sperm are made in tiny tubes in the testes called seminiferous tubules. Uncoiled, this network of tubes would be more than a mile long. After the sperm are made, they pass into the **epididymis**. This is a comma-shaped structure found on the back side of the testes. Here the sperm develop further. Then, helped by a wavelike movement, they pass into an inner duct called the **vas deferens**. This duct connects with the urethra, which opens to the outside of the body. The urethra is also the passage from the bladder to the outside of the body. But it does not carry urine and sperm at the same time.

The sperm are carried in the secretions of special glands: the seminal vesicles, the prostate gland, and Cowper's glands. The seminal vesicles produce a fluid that mixes with the sperm. This fluid, along with the sperm in it, is called **semen**. The semen picks up other substances from the prostate gland at the neck of the bladder and from Cowper's glands just below the prostate.

Semen is a thick, whitish fluid. Millions of sperm cells are carried in semen. Sperm and semen sometimes pass out of the body during sleep. This is called a nocturnal emission, or wet dream. It is a normal event.

The urethra passes through the **penis**, the outside reproductive organ of the male. The penis is a tubular organ made of spongy tissue containing many small blood vessels. When the blood vessels contain only a little blood, the penis is soft. When they are filled with blood, it becomes larger and stiff, or erect. At birth, the head of the penis, called the glans, is covered by a fold of tissue called the foreskin. Often the foreskin is removed shortly after birth. The removal is called circumcision. This may be done for religious or health reasons.

The female reproductive system

For girls, puberty is the time when the ovaries begin to release ova. For most girls, this is the period between the ages of 11 and 14. Secondary sexual characteristics appear as outward signs of puberty. The breasts develop, the hips get broader, and other parts of the body become more rounded. Hair begins to grow under the arms and in the genital area. The girl's skin becomes softer and smoother. **Estrogen** is one of the

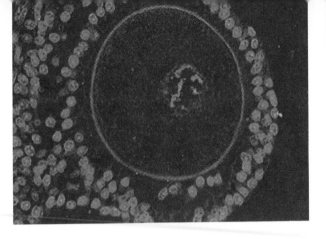
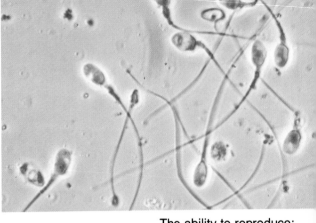

female sex hormones. It is made by the ovaries and causes the female secondary sexual characteristics to develop.

Ovaries

The ovaries are located in the lower part of the abdomen. All of the egg cells, or ova, are present in the ovaries at birth. Beginning at puberty, the ova mature and are released by the ovaries. Usually, only one ovum matures and is released each month.

The monthly release, ejection, and movement of a mature ovum from the ovary is called **ovulation**. Ovulation occurs at about the same time every month. It usually continues on a monthly basis for about 30 or 40 years. **Menopause** is the time when the ovaries stop releasing ova. The menopause usually occurs when a woman is around 50 years of age. In addition to estrogen, the ovaries also release the hormone **progesterone**. This hormone is mainly responsible for the beginning of menstruation.

At puberty, the ovaries of the female begin to release ova that have been present since birth.

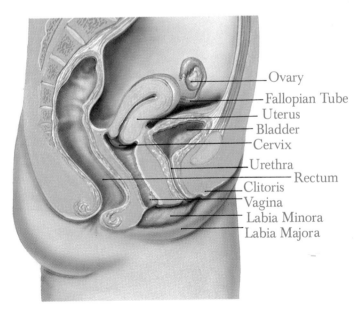

- Ovary
- Fallopian Tube
- Uterus
- Bladder
- Cervix
- Urethra
- Rectum
- Clitoris
- Vagina
- Labia Minora
- Labia Majora

Ova

An ovum is round and cannot move by itself. Gravity and gentle suction move it from the ovary to the open end of one of the oviducts, or **fallopian tubes**. A fallopian tube carries the ovum to the **uterus**, or womb. The uterus is a muscular organ shaped something like a pear. It is about 3 inches long and 2 inches wide at the top. The uterus narrows down to the **cervix**, or neck of the womb. The cervix is about ½ to 1 inch in diameter.

Menstruation

The uterus is in the middle part of the abdomen. Its spongy lining is called the **endometrium**. This lining has many small blood vessels. Ten days to two weeks after ovulation, the blood vessels in the endometrium break down if there is no pregnancy. The lining then comes away from the walls of the uterus. Along with the disintegrated ovum, the lining is passed out of the body through the **vagina**. The vagina is the tube that connects the uterus to the outside of the body. The loss of the endometrium is known as **menstruation**. Menstruation usually takes place once each month and may last from 3 to 7 days. Right after menstruation, the uterus begins to form a new lining.

The cycles of ovulation and menstruation take about 28 days. But they do not begin at the same time. Ovulation usually takes place 14 days before menstruation begins.

The endometrium during the four stages of the menstrual cycle: (a)rest stage at time of ovulation, (b)premenstrual stage, (c)during menstruation, (d)beginning to grow again after menstruation.

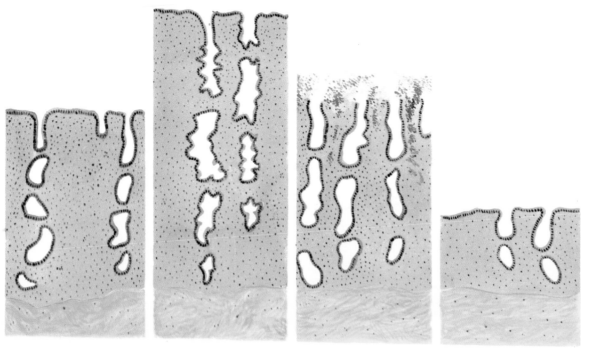

The external female genital organs include the labia minora, the labia majora, and the clitoris. The labia minora are two small folds of skin that cover the openings to the vagina and urethra. The labia majora are two larger folds of skin that cover the labia minora. The clitoris is a small, very sensitive organ just above the urinary opening. The term *vulva* is used to indicate all of the outer female sex organs.

The menstrual cycle is regulated by the female sex hormones estrogen and progesterone. Since hormones affect the whole body, including the brain, it is not surprising that many women experience mood changes or other psychological effects of menstruation. These effects are most likely to occur just before the menstrual flow begins. Research has shown that some women perform better than usual during their premenstrual days. Other studies have identified a condition known as **premenstrual syndrome (PMS)**. The symptoms of PMS are difficult to pin down because they are not the same for all women. PMS can involve physical discomforts, such as headache, constipation, or abdominal swelling. It can also include such psychological discomforts as feelings of irritability or depression. At the present time, no one can say exactly what PMS is or how to treat it. The advice of experts is to be aware that it exists and is due to biological events occurring in the body. If the discomforts get in the way of normal activities, a woman should seek medical help.

Toxic shock syndrome

In 1980, a life-threatening condition called **toxic shock syndrome (TSS)** was found to be associated with tampons, a form of internal menstrual protection. Researchers also recognized other links to the onset of TSS and even diagnosed cases of the disease in men. The symptoms of the disease include sudden high fever, vomiting, diarrhea, and dizziness. It occurs mainly in women under 30, although it can occur in women of any age.

Scientists believe that TSS requires the presence of *Staphylococcus aureus*, a bacterium that commonly exists on the skin. Some forms of the bacterium give off a toxin (poison) that gets into the body, probably through the bloodstream. While tampons themselves have not been found to be the direct cause of TSS, the majority of reported cases have been among tampon users.

While occurrences of TSS are rare—the syndrome affects about 1 woman in 10,000 each year—TSS is very serious. Because the symptoms of TSS are similar to flu symptoms, victims often do not seek treatment. This is a mistake. A few deaths from TSS have been reported, and other very serious health problems have occurred in TSS victims. If TSS symptoms occur during a menstrual period, the woman should remove the tampon if one is being used and seek medical attention right away.

The beginning of life

Semen can be discharged, or ejaculated, into the vagina. The millions of sperm that are in the semen move through the vagina toward the uterus. The sperm continue through the uterus to the fallopian tubes.

Fertilization, or **conception**, can occur only when an ovum and a sperm join. An ovum can be fertilized for only a few days after ovulation. If no sperm is present during those few days, fertilization cannot take place. If there is an ovum in one of the fallopian tubes, it is likely that it will be joined by a sperm. When this happens, changes take place in the cell membranes of the fertilized ovum that prevent other sperm from joining the cell.

Immediately after fertilization, rapid cell division of the fertilized ovum takes place. The fertilized ovum, called a **zygote**, moves down the fallopian tube to the uterus, where the **embryo** will grow. Embryo is the term used for the developing cluster of cells during these early stages. The blood vessels in the endometrium have a rich supply of blood to support growth.

Once an embryo has started to grow in the uterus, ova are not released for the next 9 months. This is the amount of time needed for the development of a baby. During this period, the endometrium does not break down. Menstruation does not occur again until after the baby is born.

Cell division

After the ovum and sperm join together, the zygote divides into 2 cells. Then each of these cells divides to make 4 cells. Cell division continues, making 8 cells, 16 cells, 32 cells, 64 cells, and so on. In this way, a

Sperm travel up through the uterus and into the fallopian tubes.

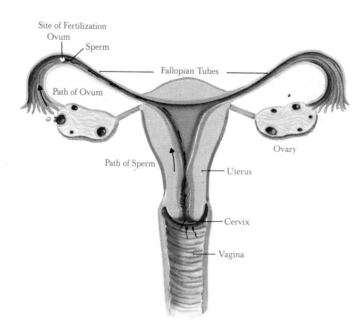

86

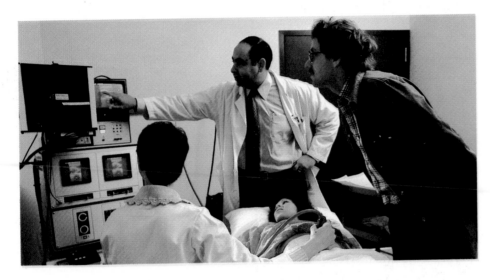

A pregnant woman needs good medical care from the beginning of pregnancy.

great number of cells are formed. The dividing process is rapid and becomes more complex with each division.

Cell differentiation

Cells of many different shapes are formed. Some are flat, while others grow long and are spindle-shaped. Some are six-sided, while others are irregular in shape. The many kinds of cells have different jobs in the human body. Each cell will join with others like it to form parts of the body. The flat cells will become skin cells, and the spindle-shaped cells will become muscle cells. The six-sided cells will become liver cells, and the irregular cells will form bone. This process is called **cell differentiation**.

As the cells grow, the embryo lengthens. A bulge appears on one end. Little buds form near the top and bottom. The bulge becomes the head, and the buds become arms and legs. After the second month, the embryo is more than 1 inch long. The torso, head, eyes, nose, mouth, arms, and legs have begun to form. The embryo is now called a **fetus**.

Needs of the fetus

As the fetus grows in size, the uterus enlarges. The walls of the uterus stretch so that there is enough room for growth. More of the space inside the mother's abdomen is taken up by the uterus. Other organs are then pushed aside, and the abdomen sticks out.

The needs of the growing fetus are the same as those of other living beings. It must have oxygen, water, and other nutrients. The organ that supplies these needs is the **placenta**. It forms along the wall of the uterus and is joined to the fetus by the **umbilical cord**. Through the

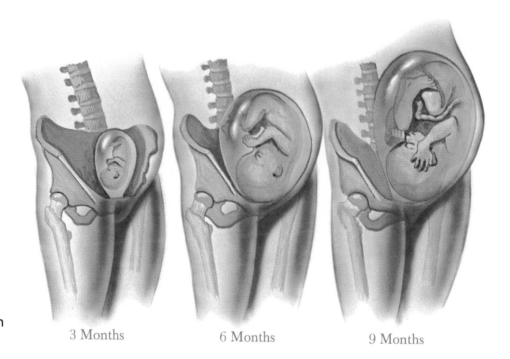

3 Months   6 Months   9 Months

placenta and the umbilical cord, oxygen and nutrients pass from the mother's blood into the blood of the fetus. Also, waste products from the fetus pass into the mother's blood to be given off by her body.

Birth

A baby usually grows and develops inside the uterus for about 9 months. In some cases, however, pregnancy lasts longer than 9 months. In other cases, babies are born before they reach their full development. Then they are premature and usually weigh less than 5 pounds at birth. With extra care during the first few weeks of life, many premature babies survive. A birth that takes place before the fetus has developed enough to live is called a **miscarriage**.

Labor

When the fetus is a fully developed baby, the muscles in the walls of the uterus begin to contract. This puts pressure on the baby inside the uterus. At first, the contractions are mild. As time goes on, the contractions become stronger and occur more often. This forces the baby down into the lower part of the uterus. Such contractions are painful and are called labor pains. The lower uterus and the birth canal stretch as the pressure from the contractions pushes the baby along. Labor is the period of time from the start of the contractions until the baby is completely out of the birth canal.

In the birth of a woman's first baby, the muscles of the uterus may be hard to stretch. Labor may last longer than it does in the birth of the second or third child.

Birth process

A baby is usually born headfirst. The head is the largest and heaviest part of the fetus. It moves to the lower part of the uterus many weeks before birth. The baby's head helps to dilate, or enlarge, the lower part of the uterus and the vagina.

Sometimes a breech birth occurs. In a breech birth, the baby is not born headfirst. Instead, the feet or buttocks are at the lower end of the uterus. Skillful effort and more time are needed to deliver babies who are in a breech position. Breech births occur in less than 4 percent of all births.

When normal birth is not possible, the doctor can remove the baby by surgery. An opening is made in the mother's abdominal wall and uterus, and the baby is lifted out. This is called a cesarean section. Cesarean sections are becoming more common today. New equipment helps the doctor to decide when the birth process is becoming too difficult and is causing harm to the mother or child.

Completion of birth

The umbilical cord connecting the baby to the placenta stays attached during birth. The doctor puts a clamp around the cord and cuts it soon after the baby is born. The baby is now ready to carry on life processes outside the mother's body. Within a few days, only the navel, or **umbilicus**, is left to mark the point where the umbilical cord was attached.

After the birth of the baby, the uterus continues to contract. These contractions push the placenta out of the mother's body. At this stage, the placenta is called the afterbirth. During the next 6 weeks, the uterus contracts until it is back to normal size. After a period of rest, the endometrium begins to grow again. The ovaries release an ovum, and the menstrual cycle starts again.

Feeding the baby

In the later months of pregnancy, hormones in the mother's blood cause the breasts, or mammary glands, to develop. These glands enlarge. Shortly after the birth, they begin to produce milk. It is natural and usually desirable for a mother to breast-feed a baby. If the mother cannot breast-feed, the child is fed cow's milk, the milk of other animals, or specially prepared formulas.

Multiple births

A multiple birth is one in which more than one baby is born. The possibility of multiple births is thought to be:

twins:	1 in 90 births
triplets:	1 in 8,000 births
quadruplets:	1 in 500,000 births
quintuplets:	1 in 54 million births

There are two kinds of twins, identical and fraternal. Identical twins are of the same sex. Such characteristics as color of hair and eyes, facial features, and size are the same. Not all fraternal twins are of the same sex. They are no more alike than ordinary brothers and sisters are.

Identical twins

Identical twins begin as one fertilized ovum. At one of the very early stages of cell division, something causes the cluster of cells to separate into two clusters. Then each set continues to divide. In this way, two embryos develop. Because both develop from the same ovum and sperm, they have the same genes. If another complete separation occurs early in the cell division, identical triplets will be born. More separations are rare but could lead to four or more identical babies. When more than one embryo develops from a single fertilized ovum, all are attached to one placenta. However, each embryo has a separate umbilical cord.

Identical twins whose bodies are joined together are called conjoined twins. Conjoined twins may be joined at any area of the body. The joining is the result of an incomplete separation of the cells during the

Fraternal twins (*left*) grow from two separate fertilized eggs. Identical twins (*right*) grow from the same egg.

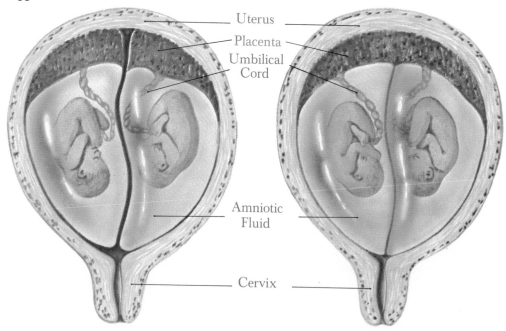

Uterus

Placenta

Umbilical Cord

Amniotic Fluid

Cervix

Quintuplets occur only once in every 54 million births.

early stages of cell division. The joined place may include only skin and muscle. Or it may involve many tissues or vital organs. Conjoined twins can sometimes be separated by surgery. In other cases, separation is not possible.

Fraternal twins

Occasionally, an ovary releases two ova at or very near the same time. Both ovaries can also release an ovum at the same time instead of alternating, which is usual. If both ova are fertilized by sperm, normal development follows. This leads to the birth of fraternal twins. Each twin develops from a separate sperm and ovum. If three or more ova are released and each is fertilized by a sperm, three or more babies will be born at the same time. They are fraternal because each develops from a different ovum and sperm. Each will have a separate placenta and umbilical cord.

Prenatal care

It is important for a woman who might be pregnant to find out as soon as possible whether or not she is carrying a child. This is necessary so that the baby can get the best possible start in life. It is also important for the mother's health. The medical care given to a pregnant woman is called **prenatal** (before-birth) **care**.

Pregnancy testing

An early sign of pregnancy is missing an expected menstrual period. Other signs that may mean pregnancy include enlarged breasts, nausea, frequent urination, tiredness, and a need for more sleep.

When a menstrual period is 2 weeks late, a woman should have a pregnancy test. This test is simple and inexpensive. Chemicals are added to a sample of the woman's urine. The mixture indicates whether the woman is pregnant. This test can be done in a doctor's office, a hospital, a clinic, or at home. (A woman using the home test might want to have the results checked by a qualified specialist.) Someone who is not sure about how much the test costs or where it is available can telephone the local public health department. Information is also available from "hot lines." Most communities have set up centers that offer special, and often free, health services.

Nutrition

An expectant mother should begin to follow a doctor's advice about diet, vitamins, and exercise as soon as possible. During pregnancy, the developing baby depends on its mother for all its needs. The mother's health is therefore very important to the baby. Children born to poorly nourished mothers usually weigh less. They are also more likely than other children to be born with serious health problems.

An expectant mother should eat plenty of nourishing foods, especially proteins. All of the baby's organs and tissues are made from digested foods absorbed from the mother's blood. An expectant mother needs to drink extra milk for calcium and vitamin D. This will give the baby strong bones and teeth. Pregnancy is a time to eat as many natural foods as possible. Pregnant women should avoid processed foods and should stay away from fast-food restaurants. These foods often have many additives and limited nutritional value. If a woman already has good eating habits, following a nutritious diet during pregnancy is easy. But getting the needed nutrients will take a special effort for those women who often eat at fast-food restaurants or who eat mostly junk foods.

Disease and drugs

The mother-to-be should avoid being around people with communicable diseases. Some illnesses that are not serious for a grown woman may do great damage to a fetus during the first 3 months of pregnancy. German measles (rubella) is one such disease. A pregnant woman should take the best possible care of herself and contact a physician if she does become ill.

Any time a pregnant woman takes a drug or medication without a physician's supervision, she may be harming the unborn child. The list of drugs that may be harmful to a fetus gets longer every year. Even some drugs that were once prescribed by doctors for pregnant women have since been found to cause harm to the unborn baby.

Some of the drugs that carry a warning label have been found to be dangerous when taken at any time during pregnancy. Some seem to be dangerous only when taken during the early part of pregnancy. This is when the embryo is developing. Other drugs seem to be more harmful to the fetus when taken later in pregnancy. Some medications are thought to be safe when taken in small amounts but harmful when taken in large amounts. An expectant mother should not use any drugs except with her doctor's advice.

A pregnant woman who is addicted to hard drugs, such as heroin, runs a very high risk of seriously harming her unborn baby. Women who are drug addicts often give birth to babies who are addicted. Such babies may suffer withdrawal symptoms after birth. To avoid drug-related problems, an expectant mother who is addicted to drugs needs special treatment during pregnancy. Medical treatment and counseling have helped many expectant mothers to decrease or end their need for drugs. Birth defects that are the result of disease, drugs, or damage during pregnancy are called congenital defects.

Cigarettes and alcoholic beverages

Nicotine and alcohol are poisons that might harm growing tissues. Nicotine and alcohol are absorbed into the blood and can pass through

WHY START A LIFE UNDER A CLOUD?

Smoking is harmful to your baby's health. Quit for both of you. For help call your American Cancer Society.

the placenta into a baby's body. Studies have shown that smoking increases the risk of miscarriage, lowers birth weight, and raises the baby's chances of complications at delivery. Since 1985, cigarette manufacturers have been required to place a warning label four times per year on all cigarette packages and advertising.

A pregnant woman who regularly drinks a large amount of alcohol or who drinks too much from time to time also runs a high risk of harming her unborn baby. Research has found that a very serious group of birth defects called **fetal alcohol syndrome (FAS)** can occur (see Chapter 21). Babies with FAS show a combination of such symptoms as mental retardation, heart defects, and facial and other outer deformities. Babies of heavy drinkers also have more common health problems. These include low birth weight, crankiness, and sometimes alcohol addiction along with withdrawal symptoms. The exact amounts of nicotine and alcohol that may be harmful are not known.

Special problems

Special help is sometimes needed in handling a pregnancy. How much help is needed depends on many factors. These include the physical and emotional health of the expectant mother, whether or not the pregnancy was planned by both parents, the age of the parents, their relationship, their economic situation, and their plans for the future. In teenage pregnancy, most or all of the above factors often present a problem. For example, teenagers run a high risk of having physical problems during pregnancy. They also have a greater-than-average risk of having a baby with health problems. This includes birth defects. The younger the teenager, the greater the risk.

It is not unusual for a teenager who learns that she is pregnant to feel overwhelmed by the situation. According to present information, pregnancy is one of the main reasons why young people run away. Running away usually makes things worse for everyone involved. Teenagers can normally get more help from their parents than they realize. After the initial shock, most parents want to help. Free counseling and other professional services are also available in most communities.

Special problems also exist for women who become pregnant after the age of 35. As a female grows older, so do the ova. Because the eggs are older, they are more likely to divide incorrectly. This can result in a baby born with Down's syndrome (see Chapter 10). Most doctors offer special prenatal care to older women, which includes tests to determine the presence of genetic disease.

Research is underway to determine the extent to which occupational (on-the-job) exposure to chemicals, radiation, or other materials is responsible for abnormal births. It is important for pregnant women to be aware of their environment at all times and to take precautions to protect the unborn baby.

Whether or not to be a parent and when to be a parent are important decisions to make. What you decide will affect you and the people around you. If you become a parent, your decisions will also affect the child. Some people willingly give up their right to make these personal decisions. That is, they let someone else make the decision for them, or they let things happen by chance. But doesn't it seem sensible to make such important decisions only after careful consideration and planning?

The fact that a person is biologically capable of being a parent does not mean that she or he is ready to be a good parent. Sometimes a child is conceived and brought into the world by people who are not prepared to be parents or who have no wish to be parents. When this happens, many serious problems are likely to occur for both the parents and the child. On the other hand, when two people plan and look forward to the birth of their baby, parenthood can be the beginning of some of life's most rewarding experiences.

Two requirements for being a good parent

Maturity. Raising children takes time and patience. It often means giving up the freedom to do what you want to do when you want to do it. That kind of giving can be very stressful. The more mature you are, the better able you'll be to cope with such common stresses of parenthood as money problems, childhood illnesses, and discipline.

Personality. Your success at being a parent will also be influenced by your personality. Certain interests and traits make some people better suited for parenthood. One study found that successful parents usually have a sense of humor, flexibility, consistency, patience, and optimism. Other parts of your personality—your goals, how you feel about yourself, and your willingness to assume responsibility—also influence your role as a parent.

Parenthood can be one of life's greatest rewards. Still, being a good parent takes work.

95

Parents can make a big difference in their children's growth and development. How much they are able to help their children grow and learn depends upon their parenting skills. Children have many needs, both emotional and physical. At the top of the list is the need for love and a sense of security. The responsibility for fulfilling these needs is the parents'.

A good parent will also develop a positive but realistic view of his or her child. Expecting too much from a child in activities such as sports and school will only frustrate the child. But children need their parents to set limits. A parent who gives his or her child anything the child wants may be doing more damage than good.

Many of the skills involved in parenting can be learned "on the job." But learning some skills ahead of time will make parenting easier and give the parent more confidence. Parents-to-be can strengthen their parenting skills through parenting-education classes and workshops. Courses in parenting are offered by local chapters of the Red Cross and in some prenatal clinics at hospitals and health departments. These courses usually allow the parents-to-be to "act out" the role of mother and father and to hear the views and concerns of others in the same situation. Some high schools offer parenting classes for young people who want to be parents in the future.

Parenthood is a tough job. But the opportunity exists for tomorrow's parents and children to be happier and healthier than ever before. It can happen if teenagers—tomorrow's parents—take advantage of the choices they have and the information that is now available.

Key Words

cell differentiation	miscarriage	secondary sexual characteristics
cervix	ovaries	
conception	ovulation	semen
embryo	ovum	sperm
endometrium	penis	testes
epididymis	placenta	testosterone
estrogen	premenstrual syndrome (PMS)	toxic shock syndrome (TSS)
fallopian tubes		
fetal alcohol syndrome (FAS)	prenatal care	umbilical cord
	progesterone	umbilicus
fetus	puberty	uterus
menopause	scrotum	vagina
menstruation		vas deferens
		zygote

- The male reproductive system produces sperm. The female reproductive system produces ova.
- Life begins when a sperm and ovum join. This is followed by cell division and cell differentiation.
- The birth of a human being is divided into several stages: labor, the birth process, and completion of birth.
- Twins that come from a single ovum are identical; twins that come from separate ova are fraternal.
- Prenatal care is important to the development of a healthy baby.
- Parenthood is a challenging and rewarding experience.

1. Describe the path sperm take from the testes to the outside of the body.
2. Describe the process of menstruation.
3. What is toxic shock syndrome? What are its symptoms?
4. What is conception? Where does it take place?
5. What is cell division? How is it different from cell differentiation?
6. How does a fetus obtain oxygen, water, and other nutrients?
7. Describe the birth process.
8. What is the difference between identical and fraternal twins?
9. What effects can cigarette smoking have on an unborn baby?
10. Name three parenting skills.

1. A form of childbirth that has become popular in some parts of the country over the past few years is midwifery. This is not a new custom, but one that reaches back into earlier periods of history. Use library research or contact the American Red Cross to find out what you can about midwifery. Learn what kinds of individuals can become midwives and the nature of the training they undergo. Tell what you have learned about this "new" practice in a report to the class.
2. Speak with a professional at the neonatal nursery of a hospital. Ask about the special needs of children born prematurely. Determine, in particular, (1) what defines a premature baby, (2) why premature babies often need to stay in incubators, and (3) the different types of arrangements hospitals make to enable parents of premature children to spend time with their newborn. Report to the class on your findings.
3. Through library research in encyclopedias of science, learn about Ignatz Semelweiss. Discover how this man's dedication accidentally resulted in a monumental medical breakthrough.

Chapter 8
Personal Growth and Family

After reading this chapter, you will be able to:

☐ Name the different types of family unit.
☐ Describe the responsibilities of the members of the family group.
☐ Explain the responsibilities of dating.
☐ Identify sensible reasons for getting married; describe a successful marriage.

☐ Identify the types of abuse that can occur within a family and what help is available for families in crisis.

"Families are America's most precious resource and most important institution. Families have the most fundamental, powerful, and lasting influence on our lives. The strength of our families is the key determinant of the health and well-being of our nation, of our communities, and of our lives as individuals."

—White House Conference on Families

Family relationships

The family is the basic unit of society. But there are many different kinds of families. Some families have two parents, while others have one. Some families include grandparents or other relatives in the family unit.

Two words that sociologists (students of family and group relationships) have traditionally used to describe families are *nuclear* and *extended*. A nuclear family consists of one set of parents or a single parent and the children of the parents. An extended family consists of several nuclear families—parents, grandparents, children, aunts, uncles, and cousins. In the decades of the 1970s and 1980s, sociologists have begun to speak of a new family unit, the **extended nuclear family**. Because of a rise in the number of divorces and remarriages in this country, children often have more than one set of parents and brothers and sisters. Living arrangements have changed as well. Children can live with some members of their extended nuclear family at one time and with the others at other times.

No matter what the family structure, the members of the family affect one another emotionally, socially, and economically. For example, when you are feeling really happy, the other members of your family probably know it. If you earn your own spending money, you may help the family budget. Sometimes you are not aware of the impact that you have on other family members. You may also not always realize the effect they have on you. But relationships within the family have a great deal to do with your moods, decisions, and ability to get along with other people.

Roles within the family

Every day, each of us plays many different roles. We behave differently in each role. Typical roles for a teenager might include those of child, student, friend, member of a group or team, baby-sitter, and newspaper deliverer.

It is often necessary to change roles in a matter of seconds. Sometimes you even have to play two roles at the same time. At home, for example, you may be a daughter or son to one family member and a sister or brother to another. At school, a classmate may see you as a friend, while a teacher sees you as a student. Each of these people expects different

It is important for family members to understand and accept their family roles.

behavior from you. So it is no surprise that you sometimes respond in a way that is not appropriate. There will also be times when you do not feel like playing a certain role at all. But the more roles you can handle, the more sure of yourself you are likely to be as you become an adult.

When a person plays a role inappropriately, problems are likely to result. For example, suppose a parent asks a teenager to be home by a certain time. The teenager does not feel like playing the child role and snaps, "I'm sixteen and old enough to take care of myself. Leave me alone." Of course, it is true that a 16-year-old is able to accept a great deal of responsibility. But does such an answer to one's parent achieve anything? How do you think the parent should respond? This leads to a larger question. What is an acceptable relationship between a parent and a teenage child?

It is important for family members to understand and accept their family roles. As you mature, it becomes easier to change from one role to another when it is necessary. You also gain self-control so that you can play a role even if you don't feel like it. The role-playing skills you learn within the family are important, for you will continue to play many roles all through your life.

Responsibilities within the family

Each member of a family has responsibilities that fit his or her age, abilities, and relationship to others in the family. Parents are responsible for giving the kind of care that will help their child grow into a physically, emotionally, and socially healthy person. Children need to know that their parents will always try to care for them and protect them. They need to feel that their parents will continue to love them even if they misbehave. When children do misbehave, it is very important for parents to show that they dislike the bad behavior, not the child.

Parents should have reasonable hopes and expectations for their children. They also need to be able and willing to help their child learn how to make good decisions. It is especially important for parents to realize how their own behavior can affect their children. Often, neither parents nor children are aware of the many ways in which the parents serve as models for the children.

Children must try to be sensitive to the needs of others in the family—their brothers and sisters, as well as their parents. They must remember that every member of the family, and not only their parents, is responsible for contributing to the well-being of the family unit.

Activities within the family

When is the last time you suggested an activity that involved all the members of the family? Naturally, each member of the family has different personal interests. And teenagers often want to spend their free time in peer-group activities with their friends. But family members can enjoy doing some things together. Eating meals together or sharing simple tasks around the home may give them a chance to share thoughts and feelings. If you take the time to let your family know how things are going with you, you will make it easier for them to understand you.

Communication within the family

The quality of communication within the family is important. Communication is the way in which facts, ideas, and feelings are exchanged. It affects relationships within and outside the family.

For a young person, family life can be the training ground for learning to communicate well. There is a great tendency for each of us to become overly emotional when talking about things that are very important to us. It takes practice to learn how to "keep cool" during this kind of discussion. It is hard to think clearly when feeling a strong emotion. It is also hard to concentrate on what is being said when someone (or worse, more than one person) is showing a strong emotion such as anger. Can you remember watching a very emotional discussion? Did you find it hard to concentrate on *what* the people were saying because of *how* they were saying it? Families can be very emotional groups of people. You learn how to handle your emotions within your family.

It is not realistic to hope for total harmony in the family. Some disagreements are likely to occur in any group of human beings. Conflicts within a family are to be expected. Such conflicts may be about important matters, such as money, religion, choice of friends, drinking, or drugs. But conflicts often arise over small things, such as what television program to watch or the length of time spent on the telephone. If the people involved are willing to talk about the problem and to listen to

Take time to plan things that all the members of your family can do together.

different points of view, many conflicts can be settled. But if family members waste time and energy in simply being angry with each other or ignoring each other's interests and welfare, serious family problems can develop.

A mature person will try hard to keep the lines of communication open within the family. Often another family member can help, but sometimes someone outside the family is needed. In the past few years, many special counseling services have been set up to help teenagers and parents who are having a difficult time with family life. People trained to help solve family problems include ministers, priests, rabbis, psychiatrists, psychologists, and social workers. Most communities offer free family counseling services for those unable to pay.

Dating

Dating is a widespread practice among high school students. Whether or not you date, the fact that so many people do has an effect on your life, your relationships with others, and your feelings about yourself.

Why date?

Young people have different reasons for deciding to date. Some teenagers say that they date to have fun and because their friends are dating. Others say that they date because they have romantic feelings for another person. Still others say that they are beginning to think about choosing a marriage partner. But some teenagers do not date at all. Some are more interested in other things. Others feel that they just aren't ready. The age at which dating actually begins does differ widely.

Dating practices

There are many different kinds of dating arrangements. These arrangements are related to a person's physical, emotional, and social development. Cultural customs and peer-group practices also affect dating patterns.

When young people first begin to date, they often take part in group activities. Parties, dances, and other social events offer them chances to be together in a relaxed and casual way. Being part of a group can help a young person feel more comfortable with members of the other sex. For this reason, many young people also enjoy double-dating with friends. Having a friend of the same sex present helps some teenagers feel more at ease. A date in which both people pay their own way can also help to ease financial and social pressure. This can also help create a more natural and relaxed atmosphere.

"Going steady," "going with" someone, or "steady dating" are ways of talking about an exclusive one-to-one dating arrangement. There are many different reasons for having such an arrangement. One of the reasons usually given is the security of always knowing that you have a date for social events. Other reasons include freedom from competition for dates and the dependable companionship that comes from a steady relationship. But there are disadvantages, too. Going steady may limit your chances to get to know many different people. It may also be difficult to "get back into circulation" if the steady relationship ends.

People begin to date at different ages and for different reasons.

Responsible dating

Mature teenagers accept and respect the responsibilities that come with dating. Their responsibility toward their parents includes letting the parents know where they plan to go and when they plan to get home. They are also responsible for getting home at the agreed-upon time. It is the parents' responsibility to make fair rules and set reasonable limits for their children's dating practices. If you and your parents don't agree on the limits, it can be helpful to talk about the reasons for the disagreement. Even if you don't reach an agreement, talking over the problem will help you understand each other's viewpoint.

Your sense of responsibility is very important in dating. How much thoughtfulness and respect you show for your dating partner shows how mature you are.

As you mature, changes take place both in your body and in your mind. Your attitudes and behavior change in many aspects of your life. Among the most important of these changes are the changes in **sexuality**. As you reach puberty, you become aware of sexual desire and the emotions that come with it. You may wonder what is normal, what is abnormal, what is acceptable, and what is unacceptable.

Sexual attitudes and behaviors

Boys and girls share the responsibility for their sexual behavior. If you have a special affection for another person, it is easy to get carried away by your feelings. A physical attraction can be very strong. Think ahead about sensible limits to set in expressing affection. This will help you stay out of situations that could lead to uncomfortable feelings, unwanted pregnancy, or other serious problems. It is hard to make sound decisions on the spur of the moment. In the end, it is up to you to decide about sexual activity on a date.

Peer pressure

Friends who try to talk you into doing something that you are not sure you want to do are taking away some of your personal freedom. You need to be free to find out who you are before making decisions that may have a lifelong effect. Peer pressure can lower your standards while increasing feelings of inadequacy. Many young people are not aware of peer pressure while it is being applied. Looking back, they can spot it.

Sexual behavior

As more is learned about the causes of behavior, there is a greater willingness to talk about and understand different kinds of sexual behavior. One kind of behavior that is widely discussed today is **homosexuality**. This word comes from the Greek root *homo*, meaning "same."

Being able to resist peer pressure is an important part of growing up.

Homosexuality is sexual attraction toward members of one's own sex. There are both male and female homosexuals. Some homosexuals feel little or no sexual attraction toward members of the other sex. Others are **bisexual**. The root *bi* means "two." Bisexuals can be attracted to members of both sexes.

A person who is attracted to members of the other sex is called **heterosexual**. This word comes from the Greek root *hetero*, meaning "opposite." Heterosexuality is the normal and accepted condition. Today, some believe that homosexuality is related to psychological confusion early in life about male and female roles. Some homosexuals who have a strong desire to change their sexual behavior have done so through psychotherapy.

It should be noted that there is a difference between being a homosexual and being curious about or attracted to the same sex for a limited period of time. Childhood and adolescent homosexual attractions are common among both boys and girls. In most cases, these feelings are eventually replaced by heterosexual attractions.

Antisocial sexual behavior

Sex linked with behavior that is harmful to someone else is totally unacceptable. People who commit sexual offenses are emotionally disturbed or mentally ill. They are also breaking the law. Growing public awareness about these criminal behaviors has led to new efforts to prevent them from happening. New and more helpful ways are also being found to treat the victims of sex-linked crime. You will read more about sexual assault in Chapter 30.

Marriage

A sound marriage is a strong foundation for a happy family life. Because of available knowledge and resources, the chances for having a successful marriage today should be greater than ever. But statistics show that there is also a very great likelihood that a marriage will end in divorce or separation. What are the ingredients of a successful marriage?

Preparation for marriage

"Getting married" said one young person "is all that I've ever dreamed of doing." The first question is—why? What hopes does that person have? Are the hopes realistic? Does the person's intended partner know and share them? In fact, is the individual ready for marriage at all? These are just a few of the questions to be answered before getting married.

Marriage can be a rewarding experience. It can result in a special sense of belonging and fulfillment. But it is also a demanding relationship, even for people who are fully mature. When you make a commitment to another person, you are promising that you can be counted on. However, during the teen years, a young person's feelings and behaviors are likely to be less steady, settled, and predictable than they will be later in life.

Early marriage is seldom a dream come true. It usually means giving up comforts, conveniences, personal freedom, and sometimes educational opportunities. It also demands taking on responsibilities that most people are not emotionally or financially ready to accept. For these reasons, a high proportion of marriages of people who are between the ages of 15 and 19 end in divorce or separation.

Knowing whether to get married or when to get married is mainly a matter of self-examination. Because an early marriage is likely to present special problems, it is very important for a young couple to think carefully about their readiness for marriage. Both partners should be sure they understand and accept each other's habits, interests, religious beliefs, philosophies, and lifestyles. In addition, a young couple can discuss questions such as the following to determine their readiness for marriage.

- Have we both learned acceptable ways of meeting our physical and emotional needs?
- Have we planned a way for each of us to get the education necessary to realize our individual potentials?
- Have we planned a way to share the work and costs of maintaining a home?
- Are we able to afford the things that we think are important? Do we agree on what these things are?
- Would we be able to afford these things if we had to support a child?
- Do we have the same general goals in life?

Marriage is more than just a joyous ceremony. Whether to get married, and when, are important questions.

A successful marriage

Marriage is an ongoing process. There is no one point or time at which a person can say, "I have a successful marriage. The task is complete." Marriage is a relationship that grows and changes over the years, just as the people who are married change and grow. Naturally, if a couple are well prepared for marriage, it will be easier for them to make their marriage work. But all marriages have strengths and weaknesses. The marriages that succeed are the ones that build on the strengths and shore up the weaknesses. It takes practice. Learning to recognize a problem and being willing to work on it are two keys to marital success.

Sometimes a problem is all too easy to recognize. An event, such as a serious illness, a long period of unemployment, a death in the family, or the birth of a handicapped child, creates a situation that cannot be ignored. Learning to accept the challenges that life presents can be a painful part of the growth process in marriage. At such times, a couple's

Part of what makes a marriage successful is helping each other.

attitudes become very important. If they believe that a good answer can be found, then they will probably succeed in overcoming the difficulty. Today, there are also many community resources available to help couples with special problems.

Divorce

Nobody enters marriage expecting to be divorced. But statistics show that divorce is a common occurrence in this country.

A divorce affects all members of a family. It can be a painful experience for everyone involved. A divorce can result in financial problems, child-custody disputes, changes in former friendships, and emotional problems. People often find themselves trying to deal with feelings of loneliness, guilt, and anger. The single most dominant feeling is usually one of failure.

What effect does divorce have on children? The initial response that most children have is one of distress. Younger children are apt to blame themselves for a divorce. Adolescents are more likely to have feelings of anger and sometimes shame. Children often fantasize that the parents will get together again, and some even take measures to try to make this happen.

In spite of the negative effects of divorce, however, most children adjust. The more love and support they receive from both parents, the easier it is for them. The friendlier the parents are toward each other, the less difficult divorce is for the children. Couples who separate should have as a goal that there be a minimum amount of destructiveness to themselves and their children. If the situation is too difficult to handle, they should seek professional counseling. With time and effort, a sense of stability and harmony can be restored for everyone involved.

Family planning

The birth of a baby is an important event. Many lives are touched when a baby is born. Just how the lives of the people involved are affected depends a great deal on whether or not the baby's birth was planned.

Scientific research has made family planning easier and safer. Today, it is possible to prevent or postpone pregnancy in a way that is in keeping with a person's religious beliefs, physical and emotional health, and financial situation. It is also possible to improve the likelihood of pregnancy if a child is wanted.

Contraception is one form of birth control. Contraception literally means the prevention of conception. A method is used to prevent the union of a sperm and an egg so that no pregnancy takes place. There are many different methods of contraception. Some methods include the use of a medication. Others involve the use of a mechanical device. Medications and devices that prevent conception are called **contraceptives.** Some contraceptives are reliable, and others are not. In addition, some religions allow only certain methods of family planning and disapprove of other means.

A person trying to make a decision about contraception should think carefully about the matter. A doctor, hospital clinic, or family planning center can provide correct information and counseling. Such services are often available free of charge. Information is given in a private, confidential way.

Family planning also includes the decision to adopt children. Couples who are not able to have children or who had previously decided not to often adopt children. Couples who already have children sometimes also choose to adopt. In some cases, a single person is allowed to adopt a child. Adoption agencies help people find a child who will benefit from becoming a member of their family.

Family planning makes it possible for parents to give their children economic advantages, as well as more individual attention. Family planning also helps to slow down population growth. As the world's population increases, the need for food, energy, and other resources becomes greater. Some of these vital resources are limited. So family planning can affect not only the future of a family, but also the quality of life in the world.

Abortion is different from contraception. Abortion means the ending of a pregnancy. If an abortion is performed by a qualified physician, the health risk for the woman is small. But an abortion performed by an unqualified person or one performed by the pregnant woman herself is very dangerous to the woman's health and life. An abortion is a serious matter. Other factors, such as the psychological effects, should be carefully considered before any decision is made.

A father beats his 2-year-old son so badly that the child has to be taken to the hospital. The parents try to hide the real cause of the injuries. They tell the doctor that the child has accidentally fallen down a flight of stairs.

A 26-year-old married woman is very withdrawn and inhibited. Once again, she phones her friends to make an excuse for not being at an event that she had planned to attend with them. Why? Because she does not want her friends to see the swollen left eye and new bruise on her cheek. Her husband beat her the evening before—not a new experience for this young wife.

Family violence is a very real problem in our society. Studies show that one in every four families experiences violence as a regular occurrence. Several million American children between the ages of 13 and 17 assault their parents each year. Besides kicking, punching, and biting, over 100,000 siblings attack each other with knives and guns every year.

Why would people treat a member of their own family this way? This is a question to which we are just beginning to find answers. Research has disclosed that the most common form of violence within a family occurs between brothers and sisters. An argument over which TV show to watch is likely to lead to violence in families where this type of behavior is tolerated.

The pressures of life and anger can cause a person to lose control and strike out without thinking. In cases of abuse, both the abuser and the victim need help.

Parent abuse

Parents interviewed about abusive behavior from their children usually describe a pattern of verbal abuse that began at a young age and led to physical attack by the time the child was in the midteens. The attack was usually triggered by the parent's not giving or permitting something that the child wanted. Most often the parents reacted with feelings of guilt or shame for not being able to handle their own child. They did not report the child to the authorities. In many cases, the child was as confused as the parents. For example, often the child was raised in a home where violence in some form occurred regularly. The child therefore considered this to be normal behavior. Other young abusers were under the influence of alcohol or another drug at the time of the incident. Still others may be examples of what many experts are currently studying: the influence of frequent exposure to violence on television and in the movies.

Abuse of the elderly

Another form of mistreatment that occurs in some homes is the abuse of older relatives. **Abuse of the elderly** includes neglect, isolation, verbal abuse, or overmedication to keep the elderly person from "being a problem." This happens especially in situations where family members feel burdened or resentful at having to care for an elderly relative.

Spouse abuse

Spouse abuse is the mistreatment of a spouse by his or her mate. Women are more likely to be physically abused. Men are more likely to be abused emotionally than physically.

Violent episodes may be triggered by disagreements over money, alcohol or drug abuse, children, or housekeeping. Often the abuser has unreasonable expectations about the roles of husband and wife. Abusers may be unable to fulfill responsibilities or live up to their image of the person they would like to be. Frustration, shame, and guilt may surface in the form of hurting their spouse.

Child abuse

Child abuse is the mistreatment or neglect of a child by a parent, guardian, or other family member. Child abuse is especially dangerous because children are usually unable to escape or to report the problem.

Some of the common factors known to contribute to child abuse are parental immaturity, unreasonable expectations by the parent, lack of "parenting" knowledge, and economic hardship. A parent, for example, may not understand a child's capabilities and limitations and may think

Many major cities sponsor groups to fight the evil of child abuse.

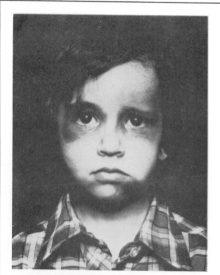

YOU REALLY SHOULD GET TO KNOW THE PERSON WHO DID THIS.

Parents who abuse their children are desperate people in need of help.

SCAN/NEW YORK trains volunteers to work with parents in their homes, providing support to deal with their problems. If you think you have the courage to match your convictions, send us this form to learn about volunteering.

SCAN/NEW YORK
We can beat child abuse.

the child is misbehaving. Or a parent may blame a child for financial problems or take out economic frustrations on the child.

Another reason for child abuse is that the parent often does not know the difference between discipline and abuse. Studies have shown that many such parents were themselves brought up in homes where child beating was common. These parents have expressed the belief that, "I can discipline my child any way that I want to. After all, it's my child!" Many child abusers look on a child as a possession or an annoyance, not as a human being with needs and rights.

Child sexual abuse

Child sexual abuse is sexual contact with a child by an adult or older child. By being aware that this is a widespread problem and being alert to it, you may be able to help prevent or stop child sexual abuse. Here are the facts:

- Children at risk for sexual abuse may be girls or boys of almost any age.
- Sexual abuse of children can occur anywhere—at home, at school, in the park, in public rest rooms, or in deserted lots.
- Abuses are most often committed by someone the child knows—a family member, relative, baby-sitter, or neighbor.
- The abuser may be male or female, although most are male.
- The abuse of the child is usually repeated unless someone does something to keep it from occurring again.

If the abuse remains undiscovered and the victims do not get help, they may develop problems. Among these are inability to trust others, withdrawal from peers in an effort to keep the incident secret, and contracting a disease. Symptoms of emotional harm may not be evident for years. Lack of treatment makes the victims more likely to become sexual abusers themselves.

Help for the family in crisis

In cases of abuse, both the victim and the abuser need help. There are many sources of help, and many of the services are free or inexpensive. These services can usually be found in the yellow pages of the telephone book under "Social Service Organizations," "Mental Health Services," or "Crisis Intervention." It is important for troubled families to recognize the seriousness of a problem and to get help. It is also important for others to be concerned about domestic violence and to take positive action to prevent and eliminate it.

Help for the abuser

Studies show that most people who abuse a family member are not mentally ill. The abusive person's behavior is normal most of the time.

Most often, the cause of the abuse is that the abuser feels extremely frustrated or angry at the moment. If the potential victim's behavior is annoying, the abuser strikes out impulsively. The reason for abuse often is that the abuser is under a great deal of stress. The person cannot cope with a difficult situation, so the helpless family member becomes the victim.

Until recently, few attempts were made to rehabilitate abusive parents, who obviously need help. Now there is treatment whose goal is to make it possible for family members to be reunited. Many kinds of programs exist to provide therapy for abusive parents. One such program is Parents Anonymous, which operates like Alcoholics Anonymous. Abusive parents voluntarily take part in group therapy. They learn how to help themselves and each other. The parents are able to call other members of the group when they feel frustrated and desperate. Talking about their feelings reduces the chance that the child will become the victim of the parent's emotions.

With the help of a professional counselor, abusive spouses can learn to express anger in a way that is not destructive. Couples can be helped to learn that no one deserves emotional or physical abuse, regardless of the circumstances.

Help for the victim

The needs of the victim of family abuse vary from case to case. Often a person needs emergency help. Some communities have set up 24-hour telephone hot lines to provide counseling and information on other sources of help. In emergencies, there are shelters (short-term lodging) where women can go with their children. Other sources of help include family and social service agencies, mental health centers, clergy and religious groups, and support groups of others who have been abused.

Child abuse, in particular, is a complicated problem. Each of us has the responsibility to report a suspected case of child abuse to the authorities at once. To this end, most states have "good samaritan" laws, which protect informers in child-abuse cases from legal threats. If suspected abuse is reported without delay, lives and family relationships can be saved. But the real solution to the problem is prevention. The more young people learn about good parenting, the less likely it is that future children will suffer abuse and neglect.

Key Words

abortion	contraception	heterosexual
abuse of the elderly	contraceptives	homosexuality
bisexual	extended	parent abuse
child abuse	nuclear family	sexuality
		spouse abuse

- The two traditional family units are the nuclear family and the extended family. Students of family relationships have recently identified a third type—the extended nuclear family.
- Each member of a family has responsibilities that depend on age, capabilities, and relationship to other family members.
- A mature person accepts the responsibilities of dating.
- People should think carefully about their readiness for marriage before getting married.
- Scientific research has made family planning safer and easier.
- Abuse is a problem that affects all family members. Abusers are sometimes children, parents, or spouses.
- Help for the family in crisis is available.

1. What is a nuclear family? An extended family? An extended nuclear family?
2. What are three reasons given by teenagers for dating? What are two of the limitations of "going steady"?
3. What is peer pressure?
4. Explain some of the responsibilities that come with dating.
5. List four questions a person considering marriage should ask.
6. What are three problems that can lead to a troubled marriage?
7. What kinds of problems can divorce result in?
8. Explain some of the advantages of family planning.
9. What are some of the causes of spouse abuse? Of child abuse?
10. Are people who behave abusively within the family mentally ill? Explain.

1. Marriage ceremonies differ from culture to culture. With the aid of a librarian, research the subject of marriage in different societies around the world. Determine, in particular, differences in the types of ceremonies, in the rituals that surround the ceremony, and in the individuals who perform the marriages. You might be surprised by some of the facts you uncover. Report your findings to the class.
2. Write a report entitled "Three Hundred Years of American Families." In the report, detail changes that have occurred in family life in this country from colonial times through the present. Be as specific as possible. Try to account for changes in day-to-day life that might have had some bearing on differences in the way members of a family group relate to each other. As research tools, try to use a colonial writer's diary and novels that depict family life in the eighteenth and nineteenth centuries.

113

Chapter 9
Growing Old

After reading this chapter, you will be able to:

☐ Explain biological aging and describe various theories on why it occurs.

☐ Identify common physical signs of aging.

☐ Identify the physical, mental, and social problems that face the aging.

☐ Explain how individuals can age gracefully.

☐ List the five emotional stages of dying.

☐ List the four stages of grief.

To many people, the thought of growing old is a depressing one. To them, aging means slowing down, both physically and mentally. It is unfortunate that so many have this view. Old age can be a highly rewarding time of life, especially for those who have maintained their spiritual and physical fitness. You can set the tone now for your later years.

What aging means

What you consider to be "old" often depends on how old you are. A 2-year-old may think that a 16-year-old is old. Many 16-year-olds think that people over 40 are old. Whatever age you think of as the beginning of old age, remember that aging is a subtle, gradual, and lifelong process. Each individual ages differently. Even within an individual, different body systems age at different rates.

Biological aging

As the body grows older, there is a decline in the amount of energy and an increased inability to perform activities it was once able to do. The degree of change in a person is that person's **biological age**.

There are many theories about how and why biological aging occurs. The cellular theory suggests that there is a limit to how often cells are able to divide and create new cells. According to this theory, cells have a definite life span. The autoimmune theory claims that aging occurs because the body's immune system begins to "backfire." The immune system, which ordinarily prevents foreign substances from infecting the body, begins in old age to see the body itself as an "enemy" and attacks it. Another theory, the defective-DNA theory, holds that errors begin to occur late in life in the body's DNA, or structural blueprint. Once this blueprint changes, the cells can no longer function normally. Still another theory is that there is an accumulation of harmful material. The body stores harmful material, such as waste products, which prevents the cells from functioning properly.

Physical signs of aging

John, age 35, had been an athlete all his life. In school, he had been on the soccer and track teams. As an adult, he continued his interest in sports by playing tennis several evenings each week.

Lately, after particularly long and vigorous tennis matches, John had been feeling tired. His leg muscles ached some, and his back hurt. John was worried that something was wrong. What was happening was quite natural, though. John was aging. His muscles had begun to lose a little of their elasticity. By the next day, he usually felt normal again. But John would never be as spry as he had been during the earlier part of his life.

Many aging individuals manage to feel younger by keeping physically and emotionally fit.

Loss of muscle elasticity is only one body change that comes with aging. Other signs of aging that are commonplace are thinning and graying of the hair and loss of moisture in the skin. The internal systems of the body change as well. The digestive and circulatory systems (see Unit V) no longer work as efficiently as they once did. All the senses—vision, hearing, taste, smell, and touch—become less acute.

Concerns about the physical signs of aging can be seen in the many products advertised to slow down or hide a person's age. These products include beauty creams, hair dyes, and liquids that cover or bleach age spots. Use of these products is fine when they are used in moderation and as part of a general program to remain healthy and fit. A healthful attitude is, after all, what keeps people feeling vigorous longer.

Problems of aging

It is a myth that most elderly people in America are very sick or disabled and living in nursing homes. In fact, the large majority of people past the age of 65 are healthy and able to lead independent lives. It is true, however, that certain problems arise as people get older.

Health problems

The risk of chronic (ongoing) disease increases with age. In addition to the signs of aging mentioned above, a fair percentage of elderly people have arthritis. Arthritis is a painful disease of the joints that makes movement more difficult. Hypertension, or abnormally high blood pressure, is also common. Among the life-threatening ailments, heart disease—the leading cause of death—is nearly seven times more com-

Causes of Death by Age Group*

Cause	65–74 years	75–84 years	85 years and over
Heart disease	1,175.8	2,850.3	7,458.8
Cancer	814.8	1,221.8	1,575.3
Accidents	54.3	108.2	273.3
Stroke	206.3	715.6	2,126.8
Pneumonia, flu	52.5	209.3	845.8
Suicide	16.2	18.6	17.7
Chronic liver disease	42.4	31.0	20.7
Diabetes	61.9	127.7	217.2
Atherosclerosis	21.4	112.1	608.7

*Per populations of 100,000 in a recent year

Pablo Picasso, the famous painter and sculptor, continued to work throughout his long life.

mon in people over 85 than it is in people between 65 and 74. The chart on page 116 shows some of the more common chronic diseases and how they affect different age groups.

Mental decline

Does getting old mean losing the power to think clearly? According to **gerontologists**, experts who study aging and the aged, the answer is a clear no. It is true, however, that the more the mind is used earlier in life, the better it works later on. The same is true of memory and the ability to use the mind creatively. Older people are still able to learn and remember, provided they have made good use of their minds throughout their lives.

There are, nevertheless, some diseases associated with aging that affect the normal working of the mind. In **multi-infarct dementia**, a series of minor strokes causes damage to brain tissue. Normal brain activities, including reasoning and remembering, are interrupted. Another disease that causes mental decline in the elderly is **Alzheimer's disease**. It is named for the German doctor who first described it in 1906. The exact cause of Alzheimer's disease is not yet fully known. Recent laboratory procedures have shown that changes in the nerve cells of the brain's outer layer damage the brain. Some scientists think these changes may be related to environment or to genetic background.

Taking up a hobby adds purpose to the lives of many retired individuals.

Other problems of the aging that are usually related to memory are often grouped together under the term **senility**. Senile people are forgetful and confused. They frequently undergo changes in behavior and personality. Not all memory lapses in old age, however, are signs of senility. Slight confusion or occasional forgetfulness may be the result of stress, poor nutrition, or the side effect of a medication.

Social problems

One of the most difficult changes for many elderly people to adjust to is a change in daily life. Old age usually means retirement from a job or career. The end of work leaves many elderly people feeling less important and uncertain of what to do with all the time on their hands. An organization like **SCORE**, which attempts to place retired executives in positions where their skills and experience can help younger generations of workers, is one solution. Other elderly people are able to cultivate hobbies and newly discovered interests that help make constructive use of their time.

A more serious problem that confronts the elderly is the death of friends or a spouse (husband or wife). The death of a spouse is particularly difficult. The loss of close friends and loved ones leaves the elderly person feeling alone and depressed. Some older people are able to overcome this depression by finding new friends who share similar losses. Others are sometimes invited to move in with the family of a grown son or daughter. This, too, helps reduce some of the pain of the loss.

Old people are often seen to be helpless and fragile. This leads to yet another problem—that of personal physical attack. Old people are often targets of street crimes, such as mugging and purse snatching. Individuals who commit such crimes rely on the fact that their victims are usually weak and cannot react or move very quickly.

In spite of the real problems the elderly are faced with, many people grow old gracefully. What makes the difference? People who have followed a program of wellness for most of their lives are healthier and happier in their later years. Individuals, for example, who have exercised regularly, eaten well, and avoided smoking and prolonged exposure to the sun are more likely to have healthier lungs, hearts, and skin.

Benefits come also to those who have developed a bright mental outlook. A positive self-image and an ability to deal effectively with stress enable people to adjust more readily to the changes that naturally occur in later years. These people look forward to leading not merely long lives but fulfilled lives. It is the quality of life, rather than the quantity, that is important to them.

A quality life in the later years includes not only good health but a fair amount of recreation and fun. The elderly continue to need loving relationships with people of all ages. They also need to be able to continue to contribute to the well-being of others. When this occurs, everyone benefits.

Many people have made their greatest contributions after middle age. Clara Hale, acclaimed as a "true American hero" in the President's 1985

Aging gracefully

Recreation and companionship are two ingredients of graceful aging.

119

State of the Union address, is one such example. Fifteen years before, this 80-year-old turned her Harlem home into the nation's only residential center for the care of drug-addicted infants. Officials of other cities and even some foreign countries have approached "Mommy Hale" about helping to solve a problem she sadly admits is worldwide.

Something to think about

The Graying of America

Older people are beginning to outnumber younger people in the population of the United States. This line graph shows the changes in six age groups between the years 1960 and 2000. Note that the number of people aged 65 and over doubles between 1960 and 2000. By the mid-1960s, the 65-and-over group outnumbers the group under 5. In the late 1970s, they exceed the group 5-to-11 years old. And in the mid-1980s, they shoot ahead of the teenagers. In the larger groups of the adult population, those aged 40 to 64 will outnumber those aged 20 to 39 by the late 1990s.

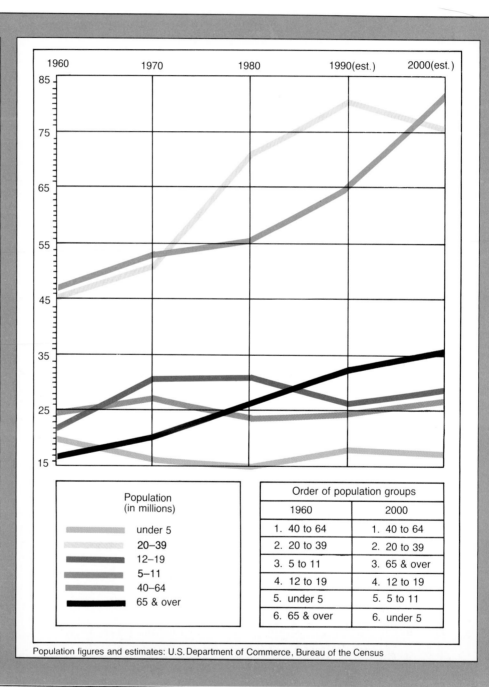

Population (in millions)

- under 5
- 20–39
- 12–19
- 5–11
- 40–64
- 65 & over

Order of population groups	
1960	2000
1. 40 to 64	1. 40 to 64
2. 20 to 39	2. 20 to 39
3. 5 to 11	3. 65 & over
4. 12 to 19	4. 12 to 19
5. under 5	5. 5 to 11
6. 65 & over	6. under 5

Population figures and estimates: U.S. Department of Commerce, Bureau of the Census

Organizations for the elderly

With the rise in the number of older people, the number of organizations to serve and represent them has also increased. The Gray Panthers and the American Association of Retired Persons are just two of the active political groups working for the rights of the elderly. Their lobbying has helped enact legislation that permits druggists to fill prescriptions for older people with generic (store-brand) drugs instead of higher-priced, brand-name drugs. Such action to help the elderly has been aided by the growth of community centers and other programs for the aging. Many of these programs are a part of the **Older Americans Act (OAA)**. Under this act, the states receive federal funds to be used by agencies to help the aging. Important programs created through the OAA are home health services, home-repair and chore services, legal aid, and recreational activities at senior centers.

The best news is that the American public is becoming more aware not only of the growing number of older people and their needs but also of their special qualities. Older people have a special perspective on life based on experience. One sign of maturity is to have overcome the anxiety about growing old and to have begun to plan for the exciting possibilities of the later years. The motto of this new attitude about aging is, "Grow old with me, the best is yet to be."

Death and dying

Human beings are the only creatures on earth who know early in life that someday they will die. Although this fact is something that the healthy person does not think about all the time, each of us has to live with the reality of our own death and accept the idea. Each of us also has to prepare for the possibility of dealing with the death of someone close to us. Learning to deal with these difficult and painful ideas becomes slightly easier when we understand something about the nature of death and dying.

Definitions of death

In the past, a person was considered dead when he or she stopped breathing and the heart stopped beating. However, special medical equipment became available that could keep the heart and lungs working in people who would otherwise be dead. It then became necessary to consider another definition of death. In 1968, a committee of the Harvard Medical School presented a new definition based on the concept of brain death. They stated that a person could be considered dead if the following four conditions were present: the person was in a permanent coma, had no movement or breathing without a mechanical respirator, had no reflexes, and had a flat electroencephalogram (no brain waves). This definition is now widely accepted in the United States, and some states have written it into law.

Dr. Elisabeth Kübler-Ross has conducted many workshops on the subject of death and dying.

The stages of dying

If most people could choose how they would die, they would choose to do so peacefully, while they were sleeping. But this is not always how death occurs. Death sometimes follows a long battle with a disease. People who suffer from such diseases and who know that their lives are coming to an end are said to be **terminally ill**.

Elisabeth Kübler-Ross, a physician specializing in psychiatry, interviewed many people with terminal illnesses. She wrote a book called *On Death and Dying*, which summarized her findings about the emotions people experience when told they are dying. In her book, Dr. Kübler-Ross identifies five stages that she saw in the people she interviewed. Not all patients experienced each stage, and the length of time spent at a stage differed from patient to patient. Nevertheless, the five stages have been accepted by other experts in the study of terminal illness as typical.

Stage 1: Denial and shock. When patients are told that they will soon die, many go into temporary shock. Often they react by saying, "No, that's not possible" or "It can't be me." Some will go from one doctor to another, hoping that at least one will make a different diagnosis.

Stage 2: Anger and bitterness. When patients finally accept the fact that they will die, they enter the second stage. The patients are usually angry with everyone. The doctor, nurse, family member, or friend will be the target of the patients' anger. They ask the question, "Why me?" The patients try to hide behind masks because they are not sure how they should react to the terminal illness. After the rage is over, they enter the third stage.

Stage 3: Bargaining and compromise. During this stage, the patients try in many ways to extend life. Some will look for a doctor who has a miracle cure. Others will attend religious services more often to make promises that they will be better people. In as many ways as possible, they attempt to prevent death or at least to postpone it for a while longer. But finally, the patients realize that they have no control over death.

Stage 4: Depression and sorrow. By now, the dying patients are showing more signs of tiring. The disease has spread to many parts of the body, or a vital organ is not working properly. The realization that they will not be able to fulfill promises and goals brings on depression. The fact that they will lose many friends and loved ones becomes unbearable.

Stage 5: Acceptance and peace. The final stage is one of understanding. The dying patients accept their illness and are at peace with the world. They prefer to be in a quiet environment, and visitors are generally limited to several close relatives and friends.

Studies have revealed that most terminally ill people want to know the truth about their condition. Some people can sense that they are dying, even if they are not told. It is especially helpful to these people to be able to discuss their feelings about death with people who do not feel uncomfortable listening.

Another issue the patient and family must deal with is where the dying person will spend the final days. Should the person be in a hospital? In a nursing home? At home? A choice that is becoming more common among the terminally ill can be found in the **hospice** movement. The term *hospice* refers to the care facility and to the care itself. In a hospice setting, the dying patient receives care in homelike surroundings (sometimes the patient's actual home) by specially trained medical personnel. The aim of the hospice is to provide the patient with an atmosphere in which death can be faced with dignity. The dying person has more control over his or her care, and support is offered to both the patient and family.

Grief

When someone we care about or love dies, we have many reactions to the loss. These reactions fall under the general heading of **grief**. The particular form grief takes depends on a variety of factors, including the way in which the deceased died and the emotional makeup of the grieving person. In general, the more a death affects the day-to-day affairs of those left behind, the greater the grief tends to be.

As with the five stages of dying, experts recognize four stages of grief. These stages are roughly parallel to the stages of dying. As with dying, they differ from person to person.

Stage 1: Numbness. At first, there is no feeling at all. Those in the earliest stages of grief are similar to people in physical shock. They are in a state of emotional shutdown. If they feel anything at all, it is an emptiness. This stage of grief is strongest when the death of the loved one was rather sudden or surprising.

Stage 2: Yearning. After a time, the survivors begin to feel a terrible hole in their lives, a gap that was formerly filled by the presence of the loved one. They ache. They wish that the person hadn't been taken from them and that he or she could come back, if only for a moment.

Stage 3: Despair. The reality that the lost one won't be returning finally settles in on those grieving. Their sorrow becomes quieter and more thoughtful.

Stage 4: Rebuilding. The survivors are finally able to pick up the pieces of their lives and move on. They have not forgotten the one they grieve for. Rather, their emotional wounds have begun to heal, and they feel ready to return to the affairs of daily life.

Love and tolerance of others are qualities that enrich our lives.

There is no "correct" length of time to grieve, just as there is no way of measuring the pain of the loss for each survivor. For most people, grief lessens over time. Each person recovers from the loss at a rate that is right for her or him.

Life is for living

Although a knowledge of the life cycle of humans is very important, we must focus our attention on the part of the life cycle called the "here and now." Rather than live a daily struggle against the end of life, we can use our knowledge of death to enrich the present. Knowing that tomorrow may be our last day can motivate us to see to it that some growth takes place within us now. Tolerance and love of others are just a few of the qualities that enrich all experience. As we learn to value such qualities, life becomes more meaningful and lasting in value. After biological death, the influence we have had on our families, friends, and the world can continue.

Key Words

Alzheimer's disease	hospice	Older Americans Act (OAA)
biological age	multi-infarct dementia	SCORE
gerontologists		senility
grief		terminally ill

- Many theories have been offered to explain biological aging. These include the cellular theory, the autoimmune theory, the defective-DNA theory, and the harmful-material theory.
- A number of physical signs accompany aging.
- The aging face certain health problems, some mental decline, and social problems.
- A person can age gracefully by following a life of wellness goals.
- Experts have identified five common stages that the dying person experiences.
- Individuals who have lost a loved one experience four stages of grief.

Understand the Reading

1. What is biological aging? What are four theories scientists use to explain it?
2. List some of the physical changes that occur in human beings as they age.
3. How can old people slow down the decline of their minds?
4. What is senility? What are some other causes of memory lapse?
5. What are three social problems faced by the elderly?
6. Name four things an individual can do that will help him or her age gracefully.
7. List two programs under the Older Americans Act (OAA).
8. According to the Harvard Medical School, what are the four conditions that determine death?
9. What are the five stages of dying?
10. What are the four stages of grieving?

Apply Your Knowledge

1. Arrange to have a gerontologist (doctor who treats the elderly) speak to your class. Various members of the class should think of original questions that can be posed to the specialist. Ask, in particular, what new problems have arisen among the elderly over the last several generations. With the doctor's guidance, try to isolate possible causes of these new problems.
2. In the library, locate more information on one of the theories of biological aging mentioned on page 115. Learn the names of the individuals who claim responsibility for the theory, and read why they believe their theory to be superior to the others that have been advanced. Summarize what you have learned in class. Compare your findings with those of classmates who have investigated other theories of aging.
3. Read up on a celebrated artist, composer, or performer who lived to be quite old and continued to produce throughout life. Determine how that individual managed to remain intellectually alert. Discuss your findings with the class.

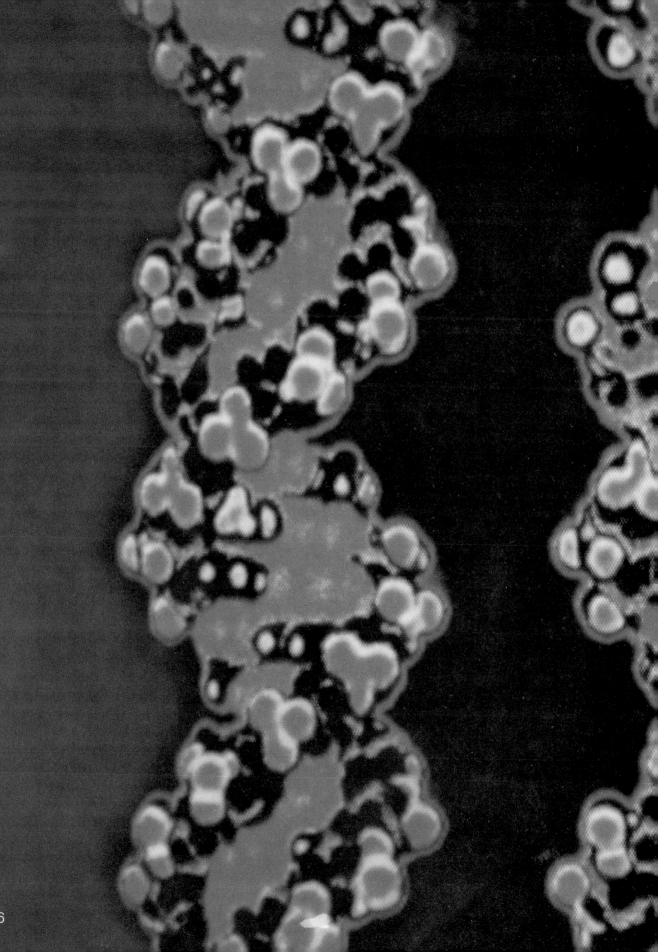

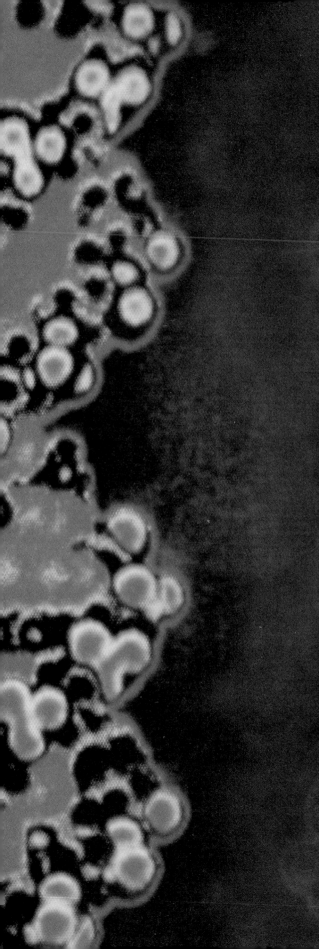

Unit 4
Environment and Heredity

Chapter 10

Generation to Generation

After reading this chapter, you will be able to:

- [ ] Describe the structure of DNA.
- [ ] Explain how traits are passed along from one generation to the next.
- [ ] Explain how hereditary disorders can be predicted and tested.
- [ ] Explain the differences between recessive inheritance, dominant inheritance, and sex-linked inheritance.
- [ ] Recognize the importance of genetic research.

In the nineteenth century, an Austrian monk named Gregor Mendel noticed that some of the pea plants in his garden had wrinkled stems and that some had smooth stems. Continuing to observe the plants over several generations, Mendel found that these characteristics were repeated in predictable patterns. What Mendel had discovered in plants is seen today when adults look at a small child and say things like, "he's got his mother's eyes" or "she's got her father's hair." In other words, certain characteristics—such as height and facial appearance in people and wrinkling in plant stems—are passed along from one generation to the next. These characteristics are said to be *inherited*.

What are genes?

Heredity is the passing of traits or characteristics from parents to children. This process is carried out using complex structures called **genes**. Genes are the blueprint of the body. You have thousands of different genes neatly arranged on paired structures called **chromosomes**. There are 46 chromosomes inside the nuclei of almost every cell in the body. Only mature red blood cells without nuclei have no chromosomes. The sperm and egg cells have one-half the total number, or 23 chromosomes. Although your characteristics depend upon your genes, your environment can greatly affect what you can become.

DNA: The "atom" of life

Genes are portions of a large molecule called deoxyribonucleic acid, or **DNA**. Since all living things are composed of DNA, it is sometimes thought of as the atom, or essential unit, of life. In 1953, Dr. James Watson and Dr. Francis Crick found that their model of DNA looked like a spiral staircase or a twisted ladder. The "sides" of the ladder are long strands of DNA twisted around each other. The "rungs" of the ladder are made of chemical compounds called bases. The bases are found along the ladder in a special order. This order is a list of instructions that tells every cell in the body what to do. It is the blueprint talked about earlier called the **genetic code**.

DNA instructs the cell. DNA causes the production of new cells. It also tells the cell to make proteins for its growth and development. Proteins are made of substances called **amino acids**. To make a certain protein, the right amino acids must be joined together in the right order. The arrangement of the DNA bases decides the order in which the amino acids are joined. When the amino acids are in the right order, they make the protein that the body needs.

DNA contains the master plan for forming all protein. Skin, hair, muscles, and other body tissues are made up mostly of proteins. Proteins also control the body's activities. For example, hemoglobin, the oxygen-carrying substance in red blood cells, is a protein. Antibodies, the body's infection fighters, are proteins. Enzymes are proteins, and so are hormones. Without the DNA code to specify the order of amino acids, the body could not make proteins correctly.

Recombinant DNA

In the relatively recent past, scientists learned how to introduce a short piece of DNA from one strain of organism into the DNA of another. The result is **recombinant DNA**. The process is called gene splicing. With the assistance of gene splicing, bacteria can be used to help us.

To aid diabetics, a gene responsible for making insulin in rats would be spliced into the DNA of a bacterium. As the bacterium reproduced, the second generation of bacteria would inherit the insulin-producing gene. Since bacteria reproduce rapidly, many insulin-producing colonies could be formed. Since diabetes is caused by a shortage of insulin, this would be a great aid to diabetics.

Similar applications of gene splicing, or recombinant DNA, could be used in beneficial programs such as the creating of oil-eating bacteria to clean up oil slicks in the ocean.

Genes at work

Genes work in pairs to develop each characteristic. One gene in each pair comes from one of the parents. The other comes from the other parent. Sometimes the two genes may not "agree" on what a characteristic will be. Then the **trait**, or characteristic, is decided by the **dominant gene**. When this happens, the other gene, the **recessive gene**, does not work.

Everyone has a pair of genes that decide eye color. Suppose that a person has one gene for blue eyes and one gene for brown eyes. This person will have brown eyes, because the gene for brown eyes is dominant, and the gene for blue eyes is recessive. A person with two genes for brown eyes will also have brown eyes. A person with blue eyes must have two genes for blue eyes. If one gene had been for brown eyes, the person would have had brown eyes.

If you know the parents' genes for eye color, you can predict the eye colors of their children. For example, suppose one parent has two genes for brown eyes. Suppose the other parent has two genes for blue eyes. Each child inherits one eye-color gene from each parent. Each child can then have only one possible combination of eye-color genes: one blue and one brown. In this case, each child will have brown eyes.

Let's take a more complicated example. Suppose that each parent has one gene for blue eyes and one for brown eyes. A child has equal chances of inheriting a gene for blue eyes or a gene for brown eyes from its father. It also may inherit either a gene for blue eyes or one

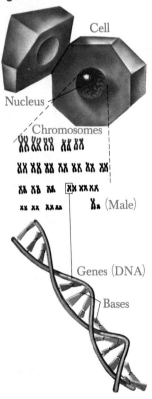

The nucleus of every cell contains chromosomes, which are made up of genes.

Cell

Nucleus

Chromosomes

(Male)

Genes (DNA)

Bases

for brown eyes from its mother. What are the possible pairs of eye-color genes the child could inherit?

Although genes are responsible for eye color, the amount of pigment (coloring), called **melanin**, may differ from one person to another. Blue eyes have little pigment. As pigment increases, the iris can become green, hazel, or brown. Some babies born with blue eyes may gradually develop more melanin in the front layer of the iris. Thus, their eyes may darken as they grow.

Sex is determined by chromosomes X and Y.

You have already learned that 46 chromosomes are found in the nucleus of each cell. Two of the 46 chromosomes are sex chromosomes. If you are a female, you have the sex chromosomes known as *XX*. If you are a male, you have the chromosomes *XY*.

Before fertilization, every egg cell has one X chromosome. The sperm, however, can have either one X or one Y chromosome. If the egg is fertilized by a sperm carrying an X chromosome, the baby will be a female with *XX* chromosomes. If the egg is fertilized by a sperm carrying a Y chromosome, the baby will be a boy with *XY* chromosomes. Thus, it is the father's sperm that determines the sex of the child.

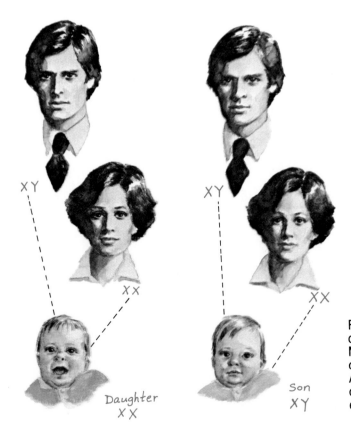

Females have sex chromosomes *XX*. Males have sex chromosomes *XY*. A baby inherits one chromosome from each parent.

131

Genetics in medicine

Brian and Jill Greene's first child seemed normal at birth. But by his first birthday, there were symptoms that showed he was mentally retarded and physically abnormal. The Greenes gave much tender loving care to this child. They also wanted very much to have a normal, healthy child. But they did not want to risk another pregnancy that might bring them a second retarded child. Financially and emotionally, the responsibility of raising two retarded children would be more than they could bear. Finally, they went to their family doctor. Their doctor suggested that they talk to a **medical geneticist**.

The Greenes had their second child. The baby was normal, as predicted by the medical geneticist. Brian and Jill had received good counseling from a specialist in genetics.

Genetic counseling

The study of heredity is called **genetics**. A knowledge of genetics has helped scientists understand many problems in medicine. Many diseases, for example, are hereditary. Some of these diseases show up at birth, causing birth defects. Other hereditary disorders, like those listed in the chart, show up later in life.

The role of the medical geneticist is not an easy one. When a disease is caused by a chromosome or a gene, there is always a chance that it will appear in a family. The medical geneticist begins counseling by examining the affected child and others in the family. A family health history, called a **family pedigree**, can be an important key in unlocking the mystery of the disease.

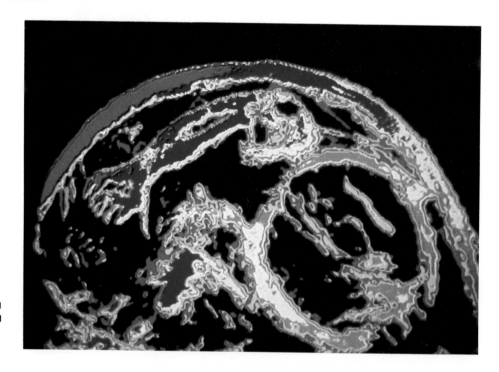

Ultrasound images can be used to locate birth defects at the prenatal stage.

Disorder	Description	When Appears Generally
Cystic Fibrosis	Abnormality of mucous and sweat glands	birth to 6 months
Tay-Sachs Disease	Brain damage resulting in death	birth to 6 months
Sickle-Cell Anemia	Blood disorder	from 6 months on
Duchenne Muscular Dystrophy	Gradual weakening and total loss of use of muscles	2 to 4 years
Wilson's Disease	Degenerative disease affecting the liver and eyes	8 to 20 years
Glaucoma	Disease of the eye	from late 30s on
Huntington's Disease	Gradual degeneration of nervous system resulting in death	from late 30s on

Some hereditary disorders occurring after birth

There are over 2,165 genetic disorders listed by medical geneticists. With the help of computers and a knowledge of mathematical probabilities, the medical geneticist helps the family understand all the facts about their genetic problem.

Can genetic disorders be prevented?

There is no way to prevent genetic disorders. But there are tests that can be given to **carriers**. Carriers are people who do not have the disease themselves but do have the genes or chromosomes that might cause their children to be born with the disease or defect. The tests given to people who might be carriers are simple—two drops of blood are taken from the person's finger.

Prenatal (before-birth) tests, such as **amniocentesis**, can be performed in order to find possible defects caused by chromosome error. Amniocentesis is done after the fourteenth week of pregnancy. Amniotic fluid is the fluid that surrounds the fetus in the uterus. A small amount of this fluid is removed with a special needle placed through the walls of the mother's abdomen and uterus into the amniotic cavity. The fluid has cells from the fetus. Using a complex method, the chromosomes of a cell are stained and photographed. The photograph is enlarged, and the chromosome images are cut out like paper dolls. Next, they are arranged according to size. If a defect in a chromosome is found, the medical geneticist and the parents can lessen the damage through fast

Amniocentesis is a test performed before birth to see if the unborn child has damaged, missing, or extra chromosomes.

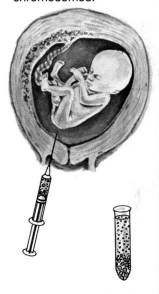

133

action at or before birth. When amniocentesis is done by medical experts, it has very little risk for mother or unborn child. However, not all birth defects can be found through prenatal testing.

Sickle-cell trait

Rosalyn volunteered to be tested for genetic disorders during a health fair held at her school. Several days later, a genetic counselor called Rosalyn to the nurse's office. The counselor explained the results of the test to her. Rosalyn was told that she was a carrier of a sickle-cell gene. This condition is called **sickle-cell trait**. Sickle-cell trait is not a disease. It means that the carrier has inherited a sickle hemoglobin (red blood cell) from one parent and a normal hemoglobin from the other. The normal hemoglobin stops the cells in the body from growing into the sickle shape.

Sickle-cell trait does not usually produce symptoms. But in rare cases, people with this trait may have problems at very high altitudes. Others may sometimes have blood in their urine.

If sickle-cell trait is not a disease, why should people be concerned? Sickle-cell trait is important because the condition is inherited. A person who has a sickle-cell gene may pass it on to his or her children. For example, suppose a parent has one sickle-cell gene and one normal gene. The other parent has two normal genes. Their child has a 50 percent chance of having sickle-cell trait. Suppose each parent has one sickle-cell gene and one normal gene. The child will have a 25 percent chance of being normal, a 50 percent chance of having sickle-cell trait, and a 25 percent chance of having sickle-cell anemia.

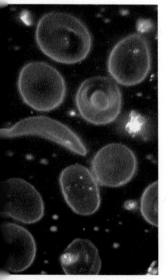

Normal red blood cells are round in shape. The red blood cells of someone with sickle-cell anemia are longer and bent.

Sickle-cell anemia

If a person inherits sickle-cell hemoglobin from both parents, the condition is called **sickle-cell anemia**. A person with sickle-cell anemia may experience any of a variety of symptoms, including slowed growth, strokes, poor vision or blindness, and slow-to-heal leg ulcers. Sufferers of the disease will also often be prone to serious infection and need blood transfusions.

Many geneticists think that the sickle-cell gene may have been a helpful mutation. A **mutation** is a change in a gene. If the mutation takes place in a sperm or an egg, it may be passed on to a child. Some mutations may be harmful, but others are believed to be useful. The sickle-cell gene may have been a useful gene. Scientific evidence shows that a person who has the gene is more resistant to malaria than a person who does not have the gene. The gene for sickle-cell anemia is much more common in parts of the world where malaria is widespread. In these areas, more people die of malaria who do not have the gene for sickle-cell trait. In parts of Africa where malaria is common, 40 percent of the black population carries the gene. In the United States, where malaria is not common, only about 10 percent of the black population has the gene.

Lethal genes

Geneticists define **lethal genes** as genes that lead to death. **Tay-Sachs disease** is fatal brain damage found mostly in infants of East European Jewish ancestry. The lethal genes cause complete mental breakdown, blindness, muscular weakness, and eventually death. A person with Tay-Sachs disease is missing one enzyme. This enzyme prevents an important chemical process from taking place.

The spread of Tay-Sachs disease can be prevented by testing for carriers. Geneticists can measure the enzyme levels in blood to find out if a person is a carrier.

Cystic fibrosis

One person in twenty-five is a carrier of **cystic fibrosis**, an inherited disorder of children. It is the most common genetic disease affecting the white population of the United States. The disease affects the mucous and sweat glands. It causes the mucous gland to secrete a thick and sticky mucus rather than a free-flowing secretion. The thick mucus blocks different pathways of the body, such as the pancreas, trachea, and digestive tract. Breathing becomes very difficult when the mucus clogs the body's air sacs. The disease can be found early by checking the amount of salt in the perspiration of a patient.

What is recessive inheritance?

Sickle-cell anemia, Tay-Sachs, cystic fibrosis, and 943 other genetic diseases have one thing in common. They all involve **recessive inheritance**. This means that two defective genes are needed to cause the disease. Both parents of the affected child may seem normal, but both parents carry the same defective gene. The child who receives the harmful gene from both parents will inherit the birth defect.

When both parents are carriers of a recessive trait, each of their children will have a 25 percent chance of inheriting the disease. But each child born to the couple will also have a 25 percent chance of not inheriting the gene. And each child will have a 50-50 chance of inheriting only one defective gene. A child with one defective gene will become a carrier of the recessive trait.

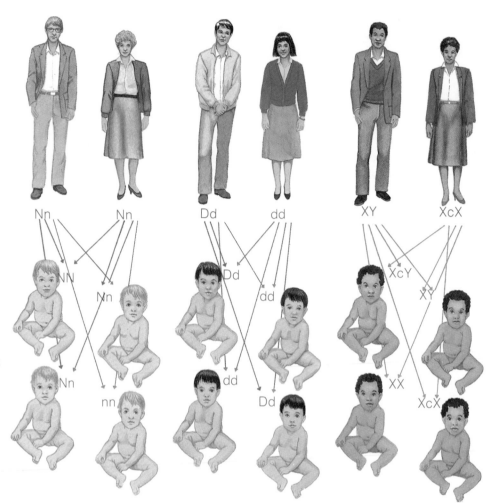

With recessive inheritance, two genes are needed to cause a trait to appear (*left*). With dominant inheritance, only one gene is needed (*middle*). With sex-linked inheritance, the gene causing the trait is usually carried on an *X* chromosome (*right*).

What is dominant inheritance?

Over 1,200 diseases involve **dominant inheritance**. This means that only one defective gene is needed to cause the disease. Glaucoma (a disease of the eye), Huntington's disease (breakdown of the nervous system), polydactylism (extra fingers and toes), and achondroplasia (a form of dwarfism) are diseases caused by a dominant trait. The risk for a child with a parent having such a disease is 50-50. And there is also a 50-50 chance that the child will not receive the abnormal gene. If the parent has two defective genes, then all children born will inherit one defective gene and be affected. Luckily, the chance of a person having two defective genes is very rare.

What is sex-linked inheritance?

Genes causing color blindness, hemophilia, and close to 200 other disorders are carried on the sex chromosome *X*. Normal females have two X chromosomes. Normal males have one X and one Y chromosome. In most cases of **sex-linked inheritance**, the mother carries the defective gene on one of her X chromosomes. Since her second X chromosome is normal, she is protected from the disorder. But each son born to her will have a 50-50 chance of inheriting the defective gene. If the son inherits the defective gene on the X chromosome, he will automatically show the disorder because he does not have another X chromosome that is normal. His Y chromosome will not protect him.

The daughters born to a carrier mother will have a 50-50 chance of being carriers themselves. In turn, they may possibly pass the disorder on to their sons.

The "extra" chromosome

Down's syndrome, or trisomy 21, is the most common and best known of the chromosome errors. This disease is not caused by a gene, but by an entire chromosome. Children with Down's syndrome have an extra chromosome. Symptoms include mental retardation, poor muscle tone, a large and protruding tongue, short and broad hands, and folding eyelids that give the eyes a slanted look.

The age of the mother seems to be an important factor in Down's syndrome. The risk of having a child with Down's syndrome is 1 in 3,000 if the mother is less than 29 years of age. It increases to 1 in 280 for mothers between the ages of 35 and 39, and the risk becomes 1 in 70 after age 40.

Almost all children with Down's syndrome have 47 chromosomes instead of the normal 46. Researchers think that the extra chromosome is caused by poor splitting of the chromosome during cell division. Unlike the sperm cells of the male, which are continually being made, all egg cells are formed and present in the female at birth. As the female grows older, so do the egg cells. Because the eggs are older, their chromosomes are more likely to divide incorrectly. And one egg cell may get an extra strand.

Color blindness is a sex-linked trait. In the most common kind of color blindness, red and green are hard to tell apart.

Poor muscle tone, one of the symptoms of Down's syndrome, can be improved through exercise.

137

Skin color is a
multifactorial inheritance.

What is multifactorial inheritance?

Not all traits are inherited dominantly, recessively, or through sex-linked chromosomes. Some characteristics are determined by more than one set of genes. Traits that are influenced by genes and the environment or that seem to "run in the family" or have many variables come under the category of **multifactorial** (many factors) **inheritance**. The vast list of traits that have multifactorial origins includes skin color, height, intelligence, diabetes, cleft palate, eye color, spinal bifida, weight, blood pressure, nose shape, lung capacity, fingerprints, and some forms of cancer.

There is no way to predict accurately the chances of a particular trait appearing in an individual, since traits cannot be categorized strictly in terms of either genetics or environment. For example, skin color is determined by melanin. Many genes are involved in the production of melanin. However, factors such as blood flow under the skin, exposure to ultraviolet light, age of the person, and sex of the person will ultimately determine the actual skin color.

The importance of genetic research

Research is being done to see how genetic diseases can be controlled or cured. There are also other diseases and conditions that might be affected by heredity. Some forms of cancer, for example, occur more often in certain families. Heart disease also occurs more often in some populations or families than in others. It is not yet known with either disease whether heredity is more important than environment. Research is being done to find out what part genetics plays in these disorders.

Immune response and organ transplant

One of the newest benefits of the science of genetics is in the field of transplant surgery. Surgeons have learned how to take an organ from one person and put it into the body of another person. This requires a great deal of skill and much complicated equipment. Transplants have been done with many different organs, including the heart, kidneys, and liver. The benefits of this surgery are easily seen. It is similar to getting a new part for a machine when the old one has been damaged or worn out.

But even though doctors can put a new heart into a person who needs it, the operation is not always successful. Sometimes the body rejects the new organ. The rejection is caused by an immune response. Ordinarily, this response is helpful because it protects the body from bacteria and other invaders. In transplant surgery, the new organ is rejected just as the bacteria would be. In that case, instead of helping the body, the immune response has done harm.

By studying the patient's genes before the transplant, however, doctors can find an organ from a donor whose genetic makeup is like that of the person who needs the organ. Family members—brothers, sisters, and parents—are most often picked to be donors of such organs as kidneys. Identical twins are the best donors for each other because they have the same genetic makeup. The closer the genetic makeup, the lower the risk of rejection. Maybe you have read that a heart patient was waiting for just the right donor in order to have transplant surgery. Choosing the right donor depends upon genetic knowledge.

Of all the biological sciences, genetics has grown most quickly. It has given insight into basic life processes and has added to the control of disease.

Key Words

amino acids	genes	recessive gene
amniocentesis	genetic code	recessive
carrier	genetics	inheritance
chromosomes	inherited	recombinant DNA
cystic fibrosis	lethal genes	sex-linked
DNA	medical geneticist	inheritance
dominant gene	melanin	sickle-cell anemia
dominant	multifactorial	sickle-cell trait
inheritance	inheritance	Tay-Sachs disease
Down's syndrome	mutation	trait
family pedigree		

Main Ideas

- Genes and DNA are necessary parts of the chromosome.
- DNA controls cell makeup and function.
- The medical geneticist is a specialist in the area of genetic counseling.
- Many birth defects are passed on genetically from one generation to the next.
- Some traits are determined by more than one set of genes. These fall under the heading of "multifactorial inheritances."

Understand the Reading

1. Which cells in the body have no chromosomes?
2. What is the relationship between genes and chromosomes?
3. Explain the job of a medical geneticist.
4. Will all genetic defects be seen at the time of birth? Explain.
5. Explain what a carrier is.
6. Why are carrier tests important?
7. What is the difference between sickle-cell trait and sickle-cell anemia?
8. What is the difference between a normal hemoglobin and a sickle-cell hemoglobin?
9. List four symptoms of sickle-cell anemia.
10. Explain recessive inheritance. Use Tay-Sachs disease as an example.
11. Explain dominant inheritance.
12. Explain sex-linked inheritance. Use color blindness as an example.
13. What do researchers think causes the extra chromosome in children with Down's syndrome?
14. What causes the body's rejection of a transplanted organ?
15. List six traits that have multifactorial origins.

Apply Your Knowledge

1. Using the illustrations on page 136 as a model, construct a family pedigree chart for yourself to see how certain traits have been passed on to you. Bring your pedigree chart to class for discussion.
2. With the help of a librarian in your school or public library, locate an encyclopedia of science or a science reference text. In the book, look up James D. Watson and Francis H. C. Crick. Read about their remarkable discovery in the world of genetic science. Pass along this information to your classmates in a report.
3. Investigate one of the genetic disorders mentioned in the chart on page 133. Look up the disease in an encyclopedia or medical reference text. Report what you learn to the class.

Chapter 11
Environmental Hazards

After reading this chapter, you will be able to:

☐ Identify the major causes of air pollution.

☐ Identify the major causes of water pollution.

☐ Explain what steps can be taken to reduce the danger of noise pollution.

☐ Name the sources and dangers of radiation in the environment.

"Look at that!" Rob shouted over the blaring music of his radio. "That truck should be ticketed for all the fumes coming out of its exhaust pipe."

"I know what you mean," replied Rob's father as he lit his pipe, his eyes fixed on the smoke curling out of the chimney of the Morgan house next door.

"That Rob," grumbled Mrs. Morgan, glancing out her window while her husband added another log to their fireplace. "He's going to deafen everyone in the neighborhood with that sound box of his blasting away!"

Everyone thinks pollution is someone else's fault!

The pollution problem

Science and technology have contributed greatly to the quality of life as we know it in the 1980s. Infectious diseases have been conquered, food production is high, and our life span has increased. Unfortunately, our improved standard of living has also produced a tremendous increase in environmental pollution. Smog, acid rain, noise, and radiation are several types of pollution that can affect your lifestyle and interfere with your wellness goals. Most people contribute directly and indirectly to some form of pollution.

Keeping the environment healthy is the responsibility of government, society, and each individual. Today, many new problems must be solved in order to save our natural resources and to protect people from environmental dangers. The government has passed new laws to make our environment a safe and healthy one to live in. But there are still many dangers that may affect our health in the future. The success of laws to control these dangers depends on the cooperation of each individual.

Air pollution

The air that you breathe contains such gases as oxygen, nitrogen, and carbon dioxide in certain amounts. But many people live in areas where the air contains pollutants that may be harmful to their health. Air pollution is a very common problem in cities of more than 100,000 people. Automobile exhaust and industrial wastes are often the cause of air pollution in cities. The five basic pollutants of air are carbon monoxide, sulfur oxide, nitrogen oxide, hydrocarbons (organic compounds made of hydrogen and carbon), and particulates (small particles that float in the air).

Sources of air pollution

Carbon monoxide is a colorless and odorless gas that is poisonous in large amounts. Most of the carbon monoxide in the air comes from automobile exhaust. Nitrogen oxide and hydrocarbons are also produced as by-products of engine combustion. The more vehicles there are on the road, the greater the possibility of pollution. Unleaded gasoline and some antipollution automobile parts decrease the number of pollutants in the air. But transportation vehicles still cause the greatest amount of air pollution.

Industry

Industries are responsible for the second greatest amount of air pollution. Fuels that are used in some industries may give off large amounts of sulfur dioxide, nitrogen oxide, and harmful particles of dust and ash. Sulfur dioxide is made when fuels containing sulfur, such as coal, are burned. Certain industrial processes may give off more of one pollutant than another. This depends on the kind of fuel used and the product that is being made.

Individuals

Still another source of air pollution is the individual. Each time a person smokes a cigarette, the air is polluted by cigarette smoke. When a person burns trash or drives a car with a poor exhaust system, air pollution is increased. More pollution is created when people burn wood in fireplaces or use soft coal in furnaces.

Air pollution in the home

Is your home energy-efficient? Do you have weather stripping, insulation, and double-glazed storm windows and doors to make your home airtight? Researchers have found that your home should have some air exchange with the outdoors. They have found many toxic fumes and other pollutants slowly being released from construction materials, fireplaces, and furniture. If your home is sealed tightly, be sure to open the windows occasionally so pollutants don't build up to a harmful level.

We must all be on the lookout for sources of pollution around us.

Some Typical Pollutants Released into the Home
Carbon monoxide from gas heaters and stoves
Benzopyrene from cigarettes
Radioactive materials from some types of brick, concrete, and soil
Asbestos from insulation in older homes
Formaldehyde from furniture made of particle board
Pollen from indoor plants
Particulates brought in by humans and pets

How many of these pollutants might you and your family be breathing in?

Since we are indoors the majority of the time, people with allergies and respiratory illnesses should also ventilate their homes. They should check their stoves and gas heaters for leaks. Wood-burning stoves and kerosene heaters are energy savers. But without proper ventilation, they can increase the level of carbon monoxide.

Effects of air pollution

Air pollution affects people directly and indirectly. It harms them directly by making them physically sick. And it harms them indirectly by spoiling the beauty of their surroundings and by being expensive to prevent.

Respiratory disorders

Breathing polluted air might make the eyes water, the nose run, or a cough develop. Many serious illnesses are more likely to happen to people who have been exposed to polluted air for long periods of time. Chronic bronchitis, emphysema, and lung cancer are more common in air-polluted areas. In Chapter 12, you will learn that cigarette smoking is closely related to the development of lung cancer. Heart diseases, especially heart attacks, occur more frequently in places where there is a high level of carbon monoxide in the air.

Accidents

Automobile accidents are another source of concern because they occur more often in places where the air is polluted. These accidents may be caused by poor visibility in the polluted air or by increased exposure to carbon monoxide. People with watery eyes, headaches, and breathing problems often find it difficult to drive in air-polluted areas.

High economic cost

The federal government spends billions of dollars each year to control air pollution. The expense for medical treatment of diseases caused by air pollution is also enormous. Air pollution can add to the rusting and corrosion of automobiles and machinery. This makes it necessary to

Care must be taken to keep the air we breathe free of harmful pollutants.

repair or replace these items more often. Even farm crops may be harmed or stunted in growth by air pollution.

Although no place is completely free of air pollution, the amount of air pollution in an area depends on various factors. Some factors are weather conditions, geographic location, and type of industry found in the area. Certain heavily populated cities, such as Los Angeles and London, have an air-pollution problem referred to as **smog**. Smog originally meant the combination of smoke and fog. Now it refers to any area of polluted air in which visibility is poor. In Los Angeles, the

Many people live in areas where the air is not healthy to breathe. More heart attacks and cases of lung disease occur in such places.

Smog is a serious problem, especially in big cities. Automobiles create the greatest amount of smog. Industries create the second greatest amount.

smog contains a large amount of gasoline vapors. At times it also contains **ozone**. Ozone is a very active form of oxygen that is produced by the action of sunlight on atmospheric impurities. Ozone may cause watering of the eyes and irritation of the nasal membranes. It also increases breathing problems associated with emphysema.

Normally, the polluted air near the earth's surface is warmer than the air above it. This lighter, warmer air rises and carries the pollution away with it. But sometimes the polluted air close to the ground is cooler and heavier than the air above it. Then the cool, polluted air becomes trapped beneath the warmer, lighter air above. This is known as a **temperature inversion**.

Sometimes there is not much wind flow, so the polluted air cannot rise and remove pollutants. This may cause a serious air-pollution problem called a "killer smog." Smog disasters have occurred in several major cities because of the weather conditions. In such cases, some people with respiratory problems have died, and many others have had to go to the hospital.

Air pollution and acid rain

Acid rain has eaten away at the artistic carvings on Cleopatra's Needle, located in New York City's Central Park.

Because carbon dioxide in the atmosphere mixes with water vapor to form carbonic acid, rain is usually acidic in content. The normal pH (acid content) of rainwater is approximately 5.6 on a scale of 1 to 14, where 1 represents the highest acidity and 14 represents the lowest acidity.

When air pollution is severe, however, the acid level in rainwater jumps dramatically. During a rainstorm in Wheeling, West Virginia, acidity was measured at 1.5. During a fog in Los Angeles, the acidity of the rainwater was recorded at 1.7. New Hampshire has had rain with a pH of 2.1. All three readings are more acidic than lemon juice or vinegar. This condition is referred to as **acid rain**. In general, throughout the eastern United States, an average rainstorm is 25 to 60 times more acidic than pure rainwater.

The corrosive action of acid rain and acid snow damages steel, stone structures, forests, and outdoor works of art. Ponds and lakes become more acidic, too, as acid rainwater flows into them. Fish eggs, frogs, and other water life fail to hatch when a pH of 6 or lower is recorded. Microscopic organisms (planktons) in ponds and lakes disappear completely, and the food chain of the aquatic environment is destroyed.

Farmers with food crops are also affected by acid rain. Less produce is available for market; as a result, higher prices for food are passed along to the consumer. The cycle of waste and destruction caused by acid rain is a vicious one.

Preventing air pollution

Everyone can be more active in helping to prevent the problem of air pollution. Car exhausts and home-heating systems can be checked regularly and kept in good working condition. Some home and trailer heaters, if not working properly, may give off harmful carbon monoxide. Automobiles should not be allowed to idle for more than a few minutes. Idling lets carbon monoxide escape into the air. Use of public transportation would lower the number of vehicles on the road. And strict laws about air pollution in industry must be enforced.

Water pollution

Water pollution was not a problem many years ago when the pioneers drank from clear streams. A farmer could easily dig a well and find water that was clean and free of harmful substances. Today, huge increases in population with many people living close together have added to the water-pollution problem. Human and industrial wastes are the largest water pollutants.

Human waste may contain organisms that cause serious illnesses. Industrial wastes, such as chemicals, oils, and detergents, may also cause illnesses and poison wildlife. In some cases, small amounts of certain pollutants may even cause tumors if taken into the body for long periods of time.

Sources of water pollution

Sewage is one source of water pollution. Sewage is made up of human waste, food-processing waste, and garbage. Many communities are unable to treat all the different kinds of sewage. This means that the wastes may increase the amount of water pollution in those communities. Some cities still dump large amounts of waste into nearby rivers and seas. Bacteria harmful to fish in the water breed in the decaying sewage. The breakdown of the sewage often takes oxygen from the water, and fish cannot get enough oxygen to survive.

Chemicals are another source of water pollution. Fertilizers used by farmers contain nitrates. When bacteria in the soil react with the nitrates, a toxic nitrate compound is formed. The compound seeps into the community drinking water. People drinking the contaminated water can suffocate because the chemicals interfere with the oxygen-carrying function of the red blood cells. Other chemicals, such as detergents and pesticides, may be spilled or washed into the water reservoirs. Ethylene dibromide (EDB) is an example of a pesticide that was used to fumigate grain, citrus fruit, and soil. Researchers found that EDB was **carcinogenic** (capable of causing cancer) and harmful to the reproductive system. When residues were found in drinking water and food products, the Environmental Protection Agency (EPA) banned all uses of EDB.

Sometimes water is removed from a river and used to cool industrial equipment. The heat is transferred from the equipment to the cold water. As the water heats up, it is piped back to the river. The warmed river water holds less oxygen than cold water. Fish and other organisms are killed by the change in temperature and decrease in oxygen. Contamination of water by heat is called **thermal pollution**.

Effects of water pollution

An **epidemic** is an outbreak of an infectious disease that affects a large number of people at the same time. Epidemics of hepatitis, typhoid fever, and different kinds of diarrhea have been traced to polluted water supplies. The long-term effects of chemical pollutants are not known for certain. But studies have shown larger numbers of tumors in fish that live in polluted waters.

Water shortages

To work properly, the human body needs to take in a little more than 2 quarts of water each day. Water is also needed to bathe, shave, prepare foods, and flush toilets. Appliances, such as washing machines, automatic dishwashers, and garbage disposals, use large amounts of water. Industries use a great deal of water to manufacture many products. Farmers need water for irrigation and for livestock. Cities use water for street cleaning, fire fighting, and sanitation purposes.

Many problems will develop if the supply of clean water is lowered because of water pollution. Pollution has become so bad in some countries that bottled drinking water must be bought.

If you doubt that water is pure, boil the water before drinking it. Do not bathe in polluted water. This could lead to skin diseases or other infections. Avoid eating fish that have been caught in badly polluted rivers. When camping, do not dump human waste into waterways. Also, remember that you can recycle many containers and other manufactured items. Everyone needs to be careful not to litter, especially in recreational areas.

Scientists are working to find better ways to get rid of sewage. Sewage treatment plants are being modernized. Laws are being made to stop the dumping of industrial wastes into waterways.

Scientists test water samples to control water pollution. They now think that some water pollutants cause cancer.

We must not only keep our water supply pure. We must also conserve this precious resource.

Toxic waste

What would you do with a substance that was corrosive, radioactive, infectious, caused mutation, caught fire easily, or was poisonous? Would you bury it? Burn it? Or would you take it out into the ocean and sink it? Approximately 130 billion pounds of **toxic waste** is produced by industry each year. According to the EPA, only about 10 percent of the toxic waste is disposed of safely and legally. What happens to the remainder? In many states, old unmarked trucks loaded with unmarked cans of toxic substances are abandoned in remote areas. Some are illegally dumped in landfills or flushed down rivers. Many of the 32,000 industrial dump sites are inadequate and are potential "time bombs."

Incineration and secured landfill are two expensive methods for disposing of toxic, or poisonous, waste. Incinerators must be built so that no pollution will escape into the air. Secured landfill must be made of a thick, solid clay base and sides to prevent seepage of toxins into the water supply. The problem of toxic waste is receiving international attention. The responsibility for toxic waste must be shared by consumers in each nation. The industries that create toxic waste are also making the products demanded by those consumers.

Noise pollution

The function of our ears is to hear sound. The ears were not made to absorb such sounds as airport noises, amplified music, and loud household appliances. The loudness of sound is measured in **decibels**. Exposure to noise above 85 decibels over a period of time can lead to hearing loss. The loss of hearing occurs gradually. Each time you are exposed to a loud noise, tiny hair cells in the inner ear are bent. These receptors cannot repair themselves and are not replaced by new ones.

Research has shown that noise pollution affects blood pressure, increases stress levels, disrupts sleep stages, and narrows the blood vessels

Sound	Noise Level in Decibels	Human Response
	0	Threshold of Hearing
	10	Just Audible
Broadcasting Studio Soft Whisper (15 feet)	20	
Library	30	Very Quiet
Bedroom Living Room	40	
Light Auto Traffic (100 feet)	50	Quiet
Air Conditioning Unit (20 feet)	60	Intrusive
Freeway Traffic (50 feet)	70	Telephone Use Difficult
Freight Train (50 feet) Alarm Clock Pneumatic Drill (50 feet)	80	Annoying
Heavy Truck (50 feet) N.Y. Subway Station	90	Hearing Damage (after 8 hours)
Garbage Truck Jet Takeoff (2,000 feet) Riveting Machine	100	Very Annoying
	110	
		Maximum Vocal Effort
Auto Horn (3 feet) Amplified Rock Music Jet Takeoff (200 feet)	120	
	130	
Jet Operation	140	
Carrier Deck		Painfully Loud
	150	

leading to the delicate hair cells in the ear, which deprives them of nutrients and oxygen. Even if you believe you are used to a noise, your body still reacts to it. To the body, noise means trouble is coming. Your heart beats faster, your blood pressure rises, and your muscles get tense. Over a period of time, these changes may lead to heart trouble, ulcers, and decreased resistance to infection.

Noise pollution interferes with rest and relaxation.

Unlike water, air, or radiation pollution, you can decide how much noise you are going to tolerate. There are some steps you can take to protect yourself against noise pollution. Be aware of noises that affect your body. Don't be embarrassed to wear ear protection when working around construction or to simply cover your ears when you anticipate a loud sound. Look for low-noise certification labels on appliances before you buy them. Don't turn the sound too high when you are wearing headphones.

Radiation pollution

Radiation pollution is a more recent kind of environmental danger. **Radiation** is an invisible form of energy that results from the splitting of atoms. Atoms are the tiny invisible particles of which all matter is made. **Gamma rays** are the most dangerous type of radiation that can get into body tissues. Materials that give off radiation are **radioactive substances**. Radioactive substances are naturally present in small amounts in the earth's surface. (Radium and uranium are two such substances.) In tiny amounts, radioactive substances are harmless. In concentrated amounts, they destroy bone marrow and damage chromosomes.

The largest amount of radiation is given off into the environment by nuclear weapons, such as the atomic bomb. Many countries now have nuclear weapons that are able to produce very serious radiation dangers.

People who come into contact with small amounts of radiation over a long period of time may develop health problems. X-ray machines, color televisions, and microwave ovens may give off small amounts of radiation. If these kinds of equipment work properly, there seems to be little danger from exposure. But overexposure to small amounts of radiation for long periods of time may cause serious medical problems.

Radiation can enter the body through the skin, lungs, or digestive system. The extent of the damage depends on how strong the radiation is, the length of exposure, the type of radiation used, and the type of

Nuclear power plants produce radioactive toxic waste.

cells that are exposed to the radiation. Cells that divide rapidly seem to be most affected by radiation. These cells can be found in the ovaries, testes, digestive tract, and bone marrow. One major concern about the effects of radiation is the possibility of mutation, or the change of genetic message within the cell. If ovaries and testes are exposed to enough radiation, chromosomes in the egg and sperm can be mutated, causing birth defects. If mutation occurs in other tissues, such as in the breast or bone marrow, cancer may occur. Some breast cancers and leukemias are related to radiation exposure.

Radiation prevention

The federal government has taken many steps to prevent the dangers resulting from radiation. Special safety precautions are taken in building radioactive substances and delivering them. Government agencies measure the amount of radiation from nuclear weapons testing and atomic power plants. Scientists from all over the world are working together to solve the problems of nuclear waste disposal.

X-ray machines are built to produce a large amount of radiation. Medical technicians who work near X-ray machines wear lead shields or operate the machine from behind a protective device. Such a device may be a wall made of lead. Pregnant women should avoid exposure to X-rays, particularly during the first 3 months of pregnancy.

Key Words

acid rain	ozone	smog
carcinogenic	radiation	temperature
decibels	radioactive	inversion
epidemic	substances	thermal pollution
gamma rays	sewage	toxic waste

- Progress and a growing population have changed the environment, creating many health hazards.
- Air pollution caused by motor vehicles, industry, and the individual causes serious health problems.
- Water pollution comes from sewage and industrial chemicals.
- Preventive measures can be taken to reduce the danger of noise pollution to the individual.
- Radiation pollution comes mainly from nuclear weapons, though small amounts come from certain appliances. This kind of pollution is especially dangerous and should be avoided.

1. What are the basic pollutants of air? Where do they come from?
2. What illnesses are connected with air pollution?
3. How does acid rain affect the economy?
4. List some causes of water pollution.
5. How can water pollution be prevented?
6. Why do fish often die from lack of oxygen in rivers used as sewage dumps?
7. What are the sources of noise pollution in our environment?
8. What are two acceptable methods of dealing with toxic waste?
9. What are some radiation hazards in the environment?
10. What is the federal government doing to prevent radiation dangers?

1. With a group of your classmates, find out as much as you can about nuclear energy use. Determine which countries use the most nuclear power as an energy source, and note accidents that have occurred. Then, stage a debate in class on the pros and cons of using nuclear energy.
2. Write to the Environmental Protection Agency for the latest information on pollution regulations. Review the information in class. Then invite a local health-agency official to your class. Discuss with the official how these regulations are enforced in your community.
3. Pittsburgh, Pennsylvania, is a city that once had a serious air pollution problem as a result of industry. Pittsburgh has since corrected the problem. Gather some information on the subject. Determine, in particular, when Pittsburgh had its problem, what caused the problem, and what steps city officials took to solve it. Organize your findings into a report to be delivered orally in class.

Chapter 12
Cancer Awareness

After reading this chapter, you will be able to:

☐ Identify the biological and environmental factors that cause cancer.

☐ Explain how the risk of cancer can be reduced.

☐ Name the three most common methods for treating cancer.

☐ Recognize the warning signals of cancer.

Each day, about 1,000 Americans die of cancer. Cancer, in fact, is second only to heart disease as a cause of death in the United States. But many of the factors that add to the increase in cancer can be controlled. Many Americans have been successfully treated and cured of cancer. Others have gained extra years of life through treatment. Knowing how to prevent cancer and how to detect it early are two of the most important parts of a wellness program.

There are more than 300 types of cancer. Some types grow and spread quickly and cause an early death. But other types may be completely cured. In all types of cancer, though, there is uncontrolled and irregular growth of abnormal cells. This growth can take place in any tissue or organ of the body.

What is cancer?

Normal cells divide in an orderly way. One cell becomes two cells, two cells become four, four cells become eight, and so on. Through normal cell division, body tissues and organs are formed. But cancer cells do not divide in an orderly and controlled way. When cancer cells divide, for example, one cell may become four or five. The four cells may become eleven cells, and these cells may continue to grow in a disorganized way. The cells are irregular in size and shape, and they no longer form useful tissues and organs. Cancer cells use nourishment needed by healthy cells. Also, the large mass of useless cancer cells crowds normal cells. This prevents healthy tissue from functioning.

A group of cells may grow together in a mass called a **tumor**. If the cells are normal and have an orderly pattern, the tumor is a **benign tumor**. Benign tumors grow inside a wall of tissue. They do not spread to other parts of the body or attack organs needed for life. A benign tumor usually does not cause serious medical problems. It may be removed by surgery.

What is a tumor?

If the cells in the tumor are not normal and grow in an irregular pattern, the tumor is a **malignant tumor**. Malignant tumors may break through the wall of tissue. They may spread to other parts of the body or attack body organs. Malignant tumors are cancers. The spreading of a disease from the place where it started to another part of the body is known as **metastasis**.

Cancer cells may be carried to other parts of the body by the blood or lymph system. Cancer may also grow into the tissue next to it. There is no set rate of growth for cancers. Some types grow more in a few weeks than others grow in many years. It is very important to discover cancer at an early stage. In this way, it is sometimes possible to stop it from spreading.

How does cancer spread?

Researchers are currently studying the role of chromosome breakage and fragile sites as an indicator of cancer.

What causes cancer?

There is no single cause of cancer. But a combination of environmental and biological factors is now known to affect the growth of different types of cancer.

Environmental factors

Carcinogens are substances that cause cancer. Different carcinogens cause different kinds of cancer. Exposure to asbestos for many years may cause a type of lung cancer. Smokers have a much higher rate of lung, larynx, and esophageal cancer than nonsmokers do. Too much exposure to the sun can lead to skin cancers. Even dietary habits are related to some types of cancer. Cancer of the bowel is very common in the United States, but vegetarians rarely develop it. Too much exposure to radiation may also cause some forms of cancer.

Biological factors

Some families have a "familial tendency" toward a certain type of cancer, such as breast or stomach cancer. This means that members of these families are more likely than other people to get a certain type of cancer. As you grow older, your chance of getting cancer will increase. For some unknown reason, cells that have been dividing normally for many years may suddenly begin to grow in a way that is not normal.

Reducing environmental risks

Steps can be taken to reduce environmental cancer risks by using some simple precautions in our daily lives. To begin with, avoid unnecessary X rays. Check with your dentist and doctor to see if the X rays are really necessary. Most medical X rays are adjusted to provide a very low dose of radiation. Exposure to larger doses or accumulation of doses over a period of time can increase the risk of leukemia, as well as cancers of the thyroid, skin, and bone.

Second, avoid prolonged exposure to ultraviolet light. A primary source of ultraviolet light is the rays of the sun. Like it or not, what this means is that *sunbathing is dangerous.* If you are still determined to "work on a tan" in spite of your awareness of the risks, then at least attempt to avoid sunbathing between 10 A.M. and 3 P.M. Ultraviolet rays are the strongest during these times. Equally important, use some type of sunscreen or lotion. If you have a light complexion, use the strongest sunscreen that contains PABA. Above all, avoid using sunlamps and tanning parlors. A tanned body and a healthy body are not necessarily the same thing. Malignant **melanoma**, a tumor containing dark pigment, occurs in 22,000 men and women each year.

Keep away from carcinogenic chemicals as much as possible. If you work around chemicals, use protective covering for your face and body.

Finally—don't smoke. If you are a smoker now, stop. Each year, smoking is related to over 300,000 deaths and costs taxpayers more than $27 billion in medical care. Smoking has been implicated in cancers of the mouth, pharynx, larynx, esophagus, pancreas, and bladder, as well as the lungs. If you work and there are people around you who

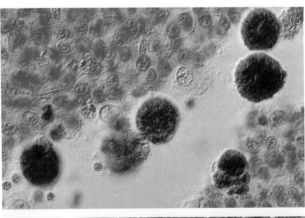

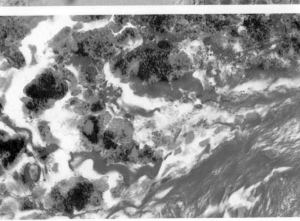

Normal cells (*top*) are regular in size and shape. Cancer cells (*bottom*) are not regular. They divide in an uncontrolled way.

smoke, request a work room free of tobacco smoke. Recent research has revealed that nonsmokers exposed to the fumes of other people's burning cigarettes run a higher risk of lung cancer than individuals not exposed to such smoke. You will read more about this in Chapter 20.

Reducing risks through sensible eating

Eating a smart diet can also reduce the risk of cancer. Although no single vitamin or food product has been proven to prevent cancer, there is evidence that there is a relationship between diet and cancer. Such an approach includes eating foods rich in vitamins A and C. Fruits and vegetables, especially the dark green and yellow vegetables, help lower the risk for cancers of the larynx, esophagus, and lungs. Be sure to include such vegetables as broccoli, cabbage, cauliflower, carrots, and brussels sprouts.

The American Cancer Society recommends including foods rich in vitamins A and C in your daily diet to reduce the risk of cancer.

Avoid eating too many salt-cured, nitrite-cured, and smoked foods. Excess nitrates may form nitrosamines, which can cause cancer in the stomach and esophagus. In general, reduce your intake of high-fat foods. Not only does this help control weight, but avoiding fatty foods can also reduce cancers of the breast, colon, and prostate.

Concentrate on foods with high fiber content. The theory is that the fibers in foods like wheat bran, oatmeal, fruits, and vegetables are not digested. Fecal material, along with carcinogenic chemicals that may adhere to the lining of the colon, is thus quickly eliminated.

Do not use alcohol excessively. Alcohol, combined with cigarette smoking or smokeless tobacco, increases the risk of cancers of the mouth, larynx, throat, esophagus, and liver.

Finally, avoid obesity. If you are overweight by 40 percent or more, the risk of cancer in the colon, breast, prostate, gallbladder, ovary, and endometrium of the uterus is high.

Early detection of cancer

Unfortunately, many types of cancer cannot yet be prevented. Therefore, finding these cancers early is very important. The chance of a cure is much greater when a cancer is found early. For example, colorectal (colon and rectal) cancer is second in incidence only to lung cancer. If it is found and treated in an early stage, the 5-year survival rate is 87 percent for colon cancer and 78 percent for rectal cancer. The survival rate drops if the cancer has spread. Adults with a family history of colorectal cancer, polyps (a type of growth) in the colon, or bowel inflammation should have regularly scheduled physical examinations.

Breast cancer is one of the most common types of cancer among women. About 1 out of 11 women will develop breast cancer sometime during their lives. As with most cancers, early detection increases the chance of cure. Today, the 5-year survival rate has increased to 96 percent. Most women discover lumps in their breasts themselves through monthly self-examination. Testicular cancer, the most common cancer in men aged 29 to 35, can also be detected through self-examination. The American Cancer Society has simple self-examination procedures. Cervical cancer can be effectively detected by a PAP test.

A yearly physical checkup for anyone over the age of 30 may help to prevent or detect cancer in the early stages. Sometimes a cancer that causes no symptoms may be found. If a tumor is found, a physician may suggest a **biopsy**. A biopsy is an operation to remove a small amount of tissue from the body so that a physician can look for abnormal cells.

Become familiar with the warning signals of cancer. The list on page 160 includes the seven of the American Cancer Society and two others. See a physician if you notice any of these signs. These conditions do not always mean that cancer is present, but you should be examined by a physician just to be safe.

Nine Warning Signals of Cancer	
1	a change in bowel or bladder habits
2	a sore that does not heal
3	any unusual bleeding or discharge
4	a thickening or lump in the breast or elsewhere
5	indigestion or difficulty in swallowing
6	an obvious change in a wart or mole
7	a nagging cough or hoarseness
8	weakness or fatigue
9	an unexpected weight loss

Treatment of cancer

The goal of cancer treatment is to destroy cancer cells or to remove them completely. Surgery, chemotherapy, and radiation therapy are the three standard ways of treating cancer. Any combination of these methods may be used. The method of treatment depends upon the location of the cancer, its size, and its type of growth. The effect of the treatment depends upon the type of cancer and how far it has spread.

Surgery

Sometimes a surgeon may remove a tumor completely by operating. This type of treatment can be very successful. But it is limited to types of cancer that produce tumors that can be safely reached and removed. Surgery is used to remove tumors in such organs as the colon, rectum, lung, prostate, and testicles. The use of laser beams as a tool for cutting and improved anesthesia have made surgery safer and more effective.

Chemotherapy

Chemotherapy is the treatment of cancer with powerful chemicals. Certain malignancies, such as **lymphoma** (cancer of the lymph glands) and **leukemia** (cancer of the blood cells), may be treated in this way. But sometimes patients suffer serious side effects. Even so, chemotherapy has become a useful method of treating and sometimes curing many cancers. Chemotherapy destroys the nucleus of a cell.

Radiation therapy

In radiation therapy, different kinds of radiation are aimed at cancer cells. The amount and direction of the radiation are controlled carefully. This is done to protect normal healthy cells. Cancer cells are usually more sensitive to radiation than normal cells are. So the cancer cells are destroyed first.

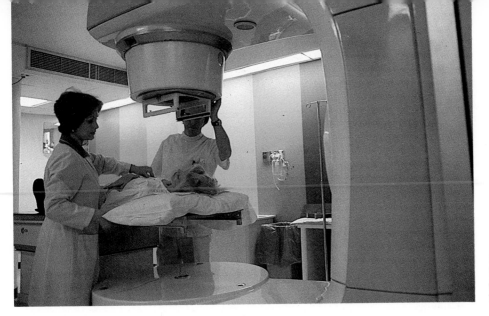

Radiation therapy is used to arrest cell growth and shrink tumors.

Radiation is used by itself or with chemotherapy or surgery. The purpose of the radiation is to stop cell growth and to decrease the size of the tumor before operating so that no cancer cells are hidden. Radiation is used to treat cancer of the cervix, head, neck, larynx, skin, and bone. One of the disadvantages of radiation treatment is that healthy cells are damaged. There are also the possibilities of radiation burn and the actual stimulation of cancer growth.

Cancer quacks

Some of the products sold by cancer quacks include laetrile, krebiozen, and nucleic-acid diets. Laetrile, also known as "vitamin B_{17}," is a substance containing cyanide extracted from apricot pits. There is no such vitamin as B_{17}. The National Institutes of Health studied laetrile extensively and found the product to be totally ineffective. Cancer quacks continue to sell their products to people who are desperate, afraid, and ignorant about cancer treatment.

The future

More and more people are beginning to realize that many cancers are curable. They are finding that techniques used by physicians to detect and treat cancer are frequently a combination of the common therapies discussed here, along with many new approaches. Some of these include:

- *Hyperthermia.* The use of heat to kill cancer cells. Using ultrasound and microwaves, heat waves measuring 109.4° to 120.2° Fahrenheit are sent to the tumor.
- *Monoclonal antibodies.* Vaccine that may stimulate the body to produce antibodies that seek out cancer cells and destroy them.
- *Cytokines.* Chemicals that have direct effect on the tumor; prevent metastasis of cancer cells.

Something to think about

Learn to identify the risks involved in various types of cancer.

Cancer Site	Risk Factors
Lungs	Cigarette smoking, exposure to such substances in work environment as asbestos
Breast	Family history, childlessness, first child after 30 (over two-thirds of time affects women over age 50)
Colon and Rectum	Personal history, family history, lack of fiber in diet, history of colorectal polyps or colitis
Prostate	Failure to seek regular detection through periodic health checkups (over four-fifths of time affects men over age 50, especially blacks)
Cervix	Frequency of sexual activity, multiple sex partners, first intercourse at early age, failure of women using oral contraceptives to undergo frequent screening
Bladder	Cigarette smoking, exposure to such substances in work environment as asbestos, failure to respond to evidence of blood in urine as early warning sign (over three-fifths of time affects men over age 65)
Mouth	Cigarette smoking, pipe and cigar smoking, use of smokeless tobacco, excessive use of alcohol
Skin	Excessive exposure to sun, light skin coloration, exposure to such substances in work environment as tar, pitch, and radium

- *BCG vaccine.* Used to stimulate immune response in patient's own body to fight off cancer.
- *Thermography.* Excessive heat given off by abnormal growths is used to detect them.
- *Magnetic Resonance Imaging.* Use of an electromagnet to form "pictures" of bodily organs that enable researchers to detect tumors.
- *Chemoprevention.* Use of folic acid and other vitamins and minerals to prevent recurrence of certain cancers.

Cancer will always be a problem if people do not help to prevent it or to discover it as early as possible. Many people continue to smoke despite the strong evidence that cigarette smoking can cause lung cancer. Many people also ignore the early warning signs of cancer. Many states have passed laws on smoking and the use of carcinogens. But the real responsibility for reducing cancer risks belongs to each person. Reducing cancer risks should be a high priority in your wellness goals.

Key Words

benign tumor	chemotherapy	melanoma
biopsy	leukemia	metastasis
carcinogens	lymphoma	tumor
	malignant tumor	

Main Ideas

- Cancer is caused by a combination of biological and environmental factors.
- Reducing cancer risks, early detection, and treatment are important factors in a wellness program.
- Cancer can be treated by surgery, radiation therapy, and chemotherapy.
- Scientists are constantly at work developing new ways to detect and treat cancer.

Understand the Reading

1. What is cancer?
2. What is the difference between a benign tumor and a malignant tumor?
3. How does cancer spread to other parts of the body?
4. Name some things in the environment that may cause cancer.
5. How can biological factors cause cancer?
6. List some of the things that can be done to reduce the risk of certain types of cancer.
7. What is a biopsy? When does a doctor suggest having one done?
8. List the nine warning signals of cancer.
9. What are the three standard ways of treating cancer? What are some newer techniques?
10. Why does radiation therapy kill cancer cells and not normal cells?

Apply Your Knowledge

1. Visit your local library's periodical division. Have the librarian help you locate newspaper and magazine articles on controversial treatments for cancer, such as laetrile and special diets. Prepare a report on these to present to your class.
2. Contact the local office of the American Cancer Society and obtain information on the prevention and early detection of cancer. Ask to receive current posters. Display your findings on a bulletin board in class.
3. Invite a physician from your community to speak to your class on current methods for detecting and treating cancer. Each member of the class should be prepared with questions for the doctor.

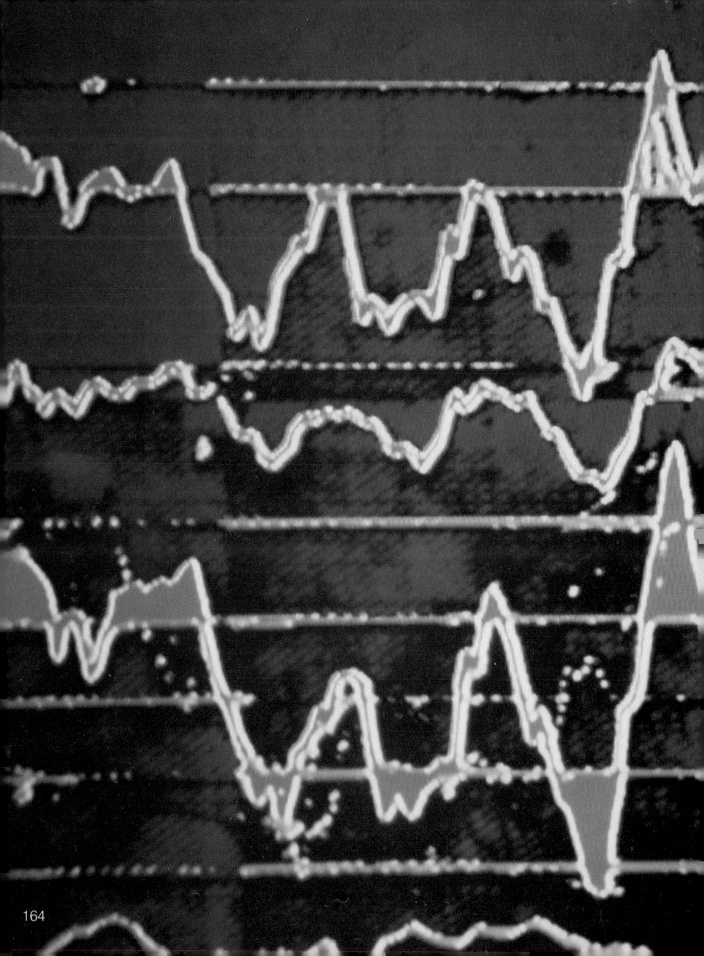

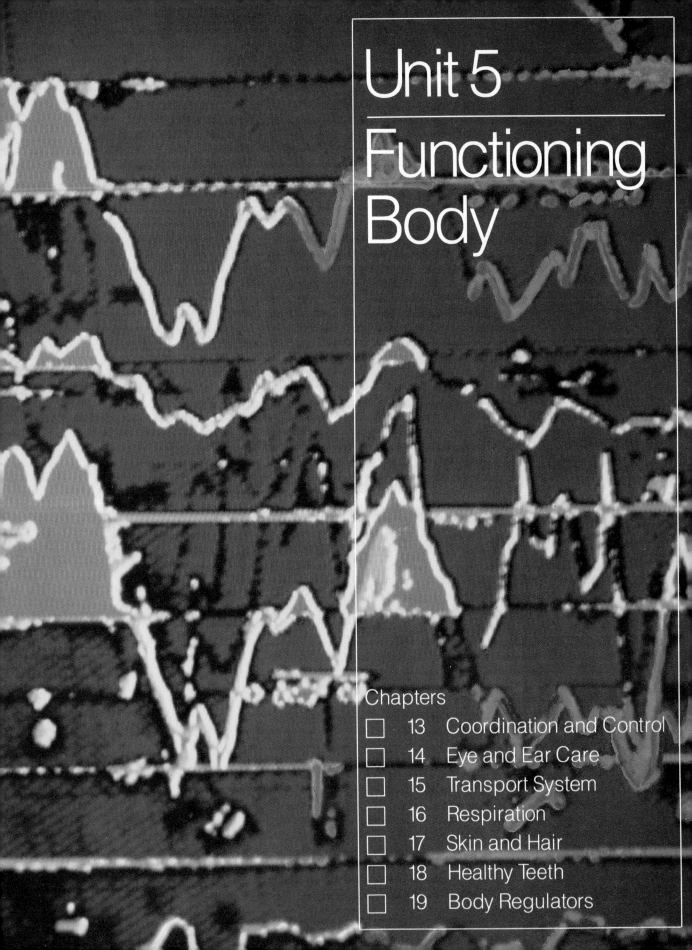

Unit 5
Functioning Body

Chapter 13

Coordination and Control

After reading this chapter, you will be able to:

☐ Identify the parts of the nervous system and explain the functions of each part.

☐ Name three kinds of neurons and describe their functions.

☐ Identify the major disorders of the nervous system and describe their symptoms.

☐ Learn how to care for the nervous system.

The brain is a remarkable organ. With it you are able to think, to reason, to understand, to remember, to make calculations, to imagine, and to feel. The brain enables you to sense your surroundings—to touch, to see, to hear, to smell, to taste. And the brain makes it possible for you to talk, to move—even to breathe.

The brain does not act alone. It is only one part, though the most important part, of the *nervous system*. Without the entire highly developed system, the brain could not do all the things it does.

The nervous system

The nervous system is made up of the **brain**, the **spinal cord**, and a network of nerves that runs to all parts of the body. The brain and spinal cord together make up the **central** (in the center) **nervous system**. This is the control part of the nervous system.

Neurons

In order to control something, you must be able to communicate with it. Twelve billion nerve cells, called **neurons**, are the nervous system's communicators. They carry messages, or impulses, back and forth throughout the body, enabling the brain and spinal cord to do their work.

A neuron is a single cell with a cell body, a nucleus, and one or more threadlike extensions called **nerve fibers**. The nerve fibers carry impulses between the cells. Those nerve fibers that pick up impulses are

Nerve cells are called neurons. Each neuron has tiny "arms" that carry messages to and from the neuron.

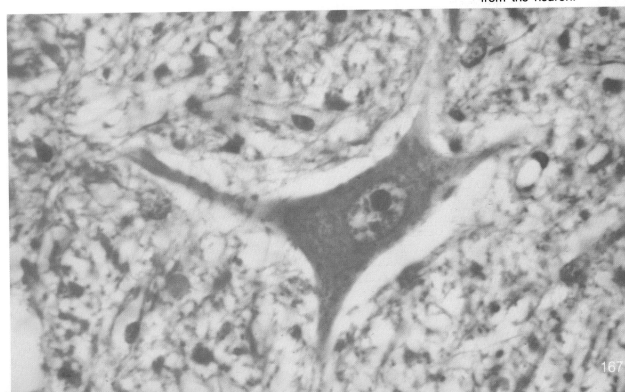

called **dendrites**. Those that carry impulses away are called **axons**. Some nerve fibers are very long. One set of nerve fibers goes from nerve cells in the fingertips all the way to nerve cells in the spinal cord.

The thinnest nerve fibers (1/25,000 inch in diameter) carry impulses at a rate of about 1 foot per second. Thicker nerve fibers can carry impulses as quickly as 450 feet per second. That is over 200 miles per hour!

Types of neurons

There are three types of neurons, each with a different function. **Sensory neurons** transfer impulses from the sense organs to the spinal cord or to the brain. The body's five sense organs are the eyes, the

Nerves are the body's communication system.

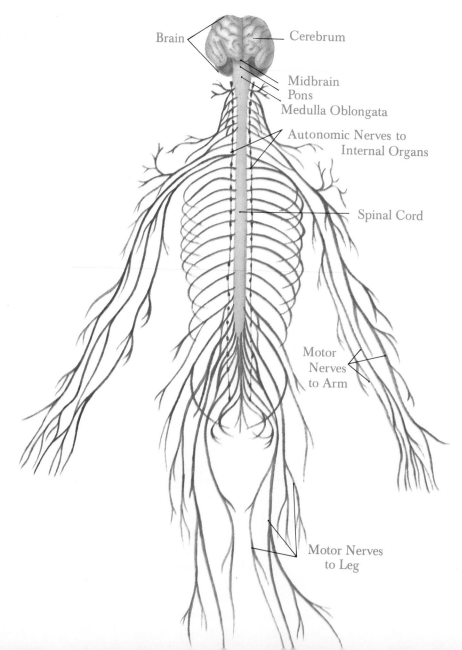

Brain — Cerebrum

Midbrain
Pons
Medulla Oblongata

Autonomic Nerves to Internal Organs

Spinal Cord

Motor Nerves to Arm

Motor Nerves to Leg

ears, the nose, the tongue, and the skin. These organs are all connected to the brain by sensory nerves. Suppose you bite into a bright red apple. Nerves in your tongue called taste buds send a message to your brain—"Delicious."

Motor neurons transfer impulses from the brain to muscles and glands. These impulses cause the muscles to contract or relax or cause the glands to function. To bite into an apple, your brain must send a message to your jaw muscles—"Open."

Association neurons connect sensory neurons to motor neurons. They function like the switches on a train track. They are located in the brain and in the spinal cord.

The nerves that carry messages between the two sides of the body and the brain and spinal cord make up the **peripheral** (on the side) **nervous system**. Those nerves that connect the brain and spinal cord to such organs and glands as the heart and sweat glands and regulate involuntary actions make up the **autonomic** (self-controlled) **nervous system**.

The brain and the spinal cord

The brain and the spinal cord are very delicate. They are protected against damage by a bony framework and protective membranes. The skull bone surrounds the brain. The backbone surrounds the spinal column. Membranes called meninges cover the spinal cord. The tissues of the brain and spinal cord are surrounded by a fluid called cerebrospinal fluid, which adds further protection.

The brain has always been a mysterious link between mind and body. How does it work? Scientists are still looking for more clues about the way it stores and sends messages. A human brain consists of about 3 pounds of spongy, pinkish-white tissue that is connected by a complex system of blood vessels. Its surface is wrinkled like a prune. The brain has several parts, and each part controls different activities of the body. All areas of the brain work together through a two-way communication system that involves the billions of neurons. This is why you can do several things at one time and can think and have feelings about what you are doing. Meanwhile, the actions of the glands and organs are being controlled automatically through the autonomic nervous system. The brain can also give directions to the autonomic nervous system.

Parts of the brain

The **cerebrum** is the large, upper part of the brain. It stores information and regulates memory, intelligence, and some emotions. Specialized areas control the senses of sight, hearing, smelling, touching, and tasting. In other words, you see and hear in the cerebrum. Other areas of the cerebrum control many other parts of the body. For example, if you think about moving your arm, the impulses travel from the arm center in your cerebrum to the arm muscles you wish to contract.

The brain—
a mysterious link
between mind and body

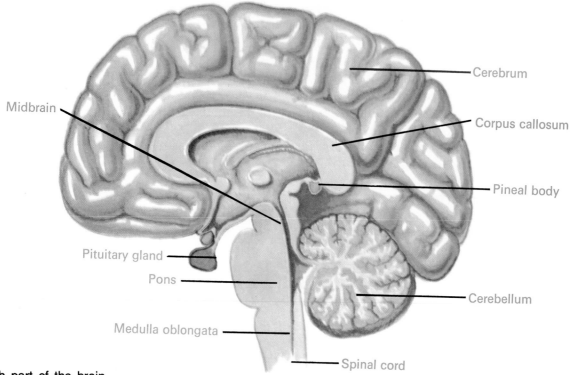

Midbrain

Cerebrum

Corpus callosum

Pineal body

Pituitary gland

Pons

Cerebellum

Medulla oblongata

Spinal cord

Each part of the brain controls a different activity.

Motor areas in the left half of the cerebrum control movements of the right side of the body. Motor areas in the right half of the cerebrum control movements of the left side of the body. This is because the motor fibers from the cerebrum cross over to the opposite side of the body as they enter the spinal cord. Ninety percent of all people are right-handed. The left side of the brain is dominant (or stronger) if you are right-handed. The right side is dominant if you are left-handed. By the time you were 10 years old, one side had become dominant over the other.

The Brain

Part	Job
Cerebrum	stores information and controls memory, intelligence, and some emotions
Cerebellum	coordinates muscle movements
Midbrain, Pons	link spinal cord with other areas of brain
Medulla Oblongata	regulates breathing, heart action, and blood circulation

Cerebellum. Beneath the back part of the cerebrum lies the so-called "little brain," or **cerebellum**. The activities of the cerebellum are carried on below the level of consciousness. That is, you cannot choose the responses that the cerebellum will make. It coordinates muscle movements so that posture and balance can be maintained.

Midbrain and pons. Two smaller parts of the brain connect the spinal cord with the other areas of the brain. These two parts are called the **midbrain** and the **pons**. These areas contain the centers of control for eye and facial movement and hearing.

Medulla oblongata. The **medulla oblongata** is the lowest portion of the brain. It tapers off into the spinal cord. The medulla oblongata regulates such important actions as breathing, heart action, and blood circulation. Nerve fibers from the upper brain pass through the medulla into the spinal cord.

Reflexes and habits

When you touch a hot object, your hand instantly jerks away. This happens before you feel any pain. Such an action is called a **reflex**. A reflex is an automatic reaction directed by the spinal cord. Because the message is so urgent, the nerves tell the muscles to react before they carry the message to the brain. Blinking the eye when an insect flies near it is another example of a reflex.

For the most part, reflexes protect you. You do not learn them. In fact, you do not even have to think about them. The nerve impulses travel over short pathways already set up in the nervous system. The pathway from the senses to the spinal cord and back to motor action is called a **reflex arc**.

Habits of action

Some of your actions are automatic because you have done them over and over. When nerve impulses have traveled over the same pathway a number of times, they tend to follow that pathway again. Such actions are **habits**. Learning to ride a bicycle is an example of forming a series of habits. When you begin, you must think of every move. You think of how to get on the bicycle; where to place your hands on the handlebars; when to push with each foot; and how to turn, balance, stop, and get off. After a while, you do not have to think about these things.

Habits are like reflexes because they do not demand constant thought. But they are different from reflexes because they must be learned. You can choose which habits you will develop, and you can change them if you wish.

Habits of feeling

In addition to habits of action, there are habits of feeling. For example, a dog jumps on a small boy and frightens him. The next time the boy sees a dog, his nerve impulses will probably travel the same pathway, causing him to be frightened. This is a **conditioned response**.

Like habits of action, habits of feeling can be changed. But this is not always easy. Fear of talking in front of the class or taking part in a play can be overcome by practicing until you are confident that you will perform well. When you practice, you are training your nerve impulses to travel over a different path.

Disorders of the nervous system

The organs of the nervous system are well protected against outside injury. But they are closely connected to all other organs by the bloodstream. This makes it possible for infection to spread to the nervous system. Other disorders may also affect the nervous system.

Epilepsy

Epilepsy is a condition in which epileptic attacks, or seizures, are caused by irritation of nerve cells in the brain. In mild cases, a person briefly loses consciousness or has a blank stare for a few seconds. In severe cases, convulsions occur.

An electroencephalogram, or EEG, is a painless test that enables doctors to diagnose brain disorders.

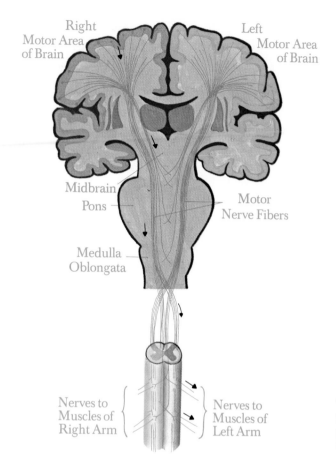

Right
Motor Area
of Brain

Left
Motor Area
of Brain

Midbrain
Pons

Motor
Nerve Fibers

Medulla
Oblongata

Nerves to
Muscles of
Right Arm

Nerves to
Muscles of
Left Arm

The nervous system
makes one unbroken
pathway to pick up and
send information.

Anyone who suffers from epilepsy should be under a doctor's care. With good medical treatment, a patient may remain free from seizures. People with epilepsy look and feel normal between attacks. Since attacks can now be controlled with medication, a person with epilepsy can lead a normal life.

Stroke

Strokes, or cerebral vascular accidents, are the third most frequent cause of death in the United States. Only heart disease and cancer cause more deaths. Strokes are rare in the young, but they often disable older people. Many people who have strokes have had high blood pressure. A study has shown that strokes occur twice as often in women between the ages of 45 and 54 who are cigarette smokers. A stroke occurs when the blood flow to an area of the brain is suddenly blocked. This blockage is usually caused by formation of a clot in a small blood vessel. As a result, the part of the body controlled by that area of the brain is partly or completely paralyzed. Frequently, speech is also affected. If the stroke is severe, it may cause unconsciousness or even death.

Prompt medical treatment and physical therapy can greatly improve the condition of the stroke patient. Understanding and assistance from members of the family are also essential.

Meningitis

Meningitis is the inflammation of the membranes that surround the brain and spinal cord. Usually, the inflammation is caused by a viral or bacterial infection. Meningitis is often a serious illness, and certain types are extremely contagious.

Multiple sclerosis

In **multiple sclerosis**, the covering that surrounds the nerves is destroyed. The symptoms depend on which nerves are damaged by the disease. Some cases may show loss of control of arm or leg movement. Other cases may show loss of vision or an unusual pattern of numbness. Multiple sclerosis may be caused by a slow-growing virus in the central nervous system.

Poliomyelitis

Poliomyelitis is caused by a virus that attacks nerve cells that control various groups of muscles. The result is paralysis of those muscles. Vaccinations to protect against polio have been developed in the past 30 years. It has been estimated that over 15 million children are not protected from polio because they have not been vaccinated. Some school systems do not allow children to enter school until they have had all the vaccinations they need.

Taking care of the nervous system

Anything that happens anywhere in the body is likely to influence the nervous system in one way or another. Likewise, anything that influences the nervous system affects the rest of the body.

Protection

Nerve tissue is soft and can be damaged. Most nerve tissue is protected behind bones or within muscles. Extra care must be taken to prevent serious injuries to the central nervous system. Helmets should be worn when riding motorcycles, bicycles, or horses to protect against head injury. Many head injuries in automobile accidents can be prevented if seat belts are worn and headrests are kept up. The use of seat belts is now a legal requirement in many states. Spinal-cord injuries may happen in driving accidents or careless football tackling. Improper use of skateboards and trampolines and diving into shallow water head first may also cause permanent nerve injuries.

The X ray revealed the inner person for the first time. But X rays produce shadowy pictures with few details beyond that of the skeleton. Having too many X rays is also known to be dangerous.

The CT scanner was developed next. It gives off much less radiation than regular X rays and allows doctors to see many details beneath the shadows.

Finally, the MRI, or Magnetic Resonance Imaging scanner, was developed. A patient undergoing an MRI scan lies on a board and is pushed head first onto a large plastic block. As the patient stays perfectly still in the darkness, radio waves move across a magnetic field and record the action of hydrogen atoms in the body.

The result? Scientists obtain a much clearer picture of the difference between healthy and diseased tissue. The MRI makes it possible to diagnose potentially serious health conditions when they are still in early and more curable stages. And there is no apparent risk of radiation.

Something to think about

Introducing the see-through human

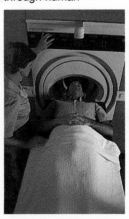

Food

A well-balanced diet should provide enough thiamine (vitamin B_1) for the nervous system to function properly. Some good sources of vitamin B are liver, peas, green beans, whole grains, and milk.

Oxygen

In order for you to think and act normally, the brain depends on the blood to provide a certain level of oxygen. The brain uses 25 percent of the oxygen you breathe in. Every minute, a pint of blood flows through your brain to carry in oxygen and food and to carry out wastes.

If the level of oxygen in the brain drops, a person may become confused and dizzy. If oxygen is not available for just a half minute (30 seconds), the person may lose consciousness. Eventually, the person may go into a **coma**, or deep sleep. If the oxygen supply carried by the blood is cut off for 5 minutes, permanent brain damage results. For this reason, artificial respiration should be given immediately if someone stops breathing.

Drugs and poisons

Nerve cells are more sensitive to certain drugs and poisons than other body cells are. Alcohol and morphine, for example, act on the cells of the central nervous system. Other drugs relieve pain by blocking the path of the pain impulse to the brain.

Lead and arsenic may be poisonous to the central nervous system if large amounts are taken into the body. Young children who chew on objects that are covered with paint containing lead may develop permanent brain damage.

Rest and sleep

Since the nervous system works nonstop, periods of rest make it work better. If you are worried or under emotional strain, the extra nerve impulses may cause a feeling of tiredness. Boredom, excitement, extra weight, poor diet, and some illnesses may cause you to feel more tired than normal, too. People need a good night's sleep for their bodies to work properly. Sleep is such an important bodily activity that you will spend 30 percent of your life sleeping.

Your own body will help determine how much sleep you need. The amount of sleep needed and the patterns of sleep vary from person to person. Generally, 8 hours each night are recommended. Many people do fine with less, but some people need more.

Did you ever notice that on the morning of a "special day" you got up earlier than usual and didn't feel that your sleep was cut off? Do you find yourself sleeping longer on the weekends? These are ways that your nervous system helps your body adapt. Did you ever have trouble waking up and then roll out of bed promising yourself that you would get to bed early that night? That is a danger signal that you are shortchanging your body on the sleep it needs.

During the day, two opposite physical processes can relieve a feeling of tiredness: rest or exercise. Rest is more relaxing after physical activity. After a tense or confining situation—an examination, for example— jogging, a bicycle ride, a long walk, or other physical exercise would probably relax you.

Key Words

association neurons	conditioned response	nervous system neurons
autonomic nervous system	dendrites	peripheral nervous system
axons	epilepsy	poliomyelitis
brain	habits	pons
central nervous system	medulla oblongata	reflex
cerebellum	meningitis	reflex arc
cerebrum	midbrain	sensory neurons
coma	motor neurons	spinal cord
	multiple sclerosis	stroke
	nerve fibers	

- The nervous system is the communication network for the body. Through this network, the body acts on the mind and the mind acts on the body.
- The nervous system is composed of the brain, the spinal cord, and billions of nerve cells.
- The brain is a complex organ. With the spinal cord, it controls the nervous system.
- Care should be taken to protect the nervous system and to keep it in good working order.

1. Describe the structure of a neuron.
2. Explain how motor neurons are different from sensory neurons.
3. Which system regulates involuntary actions?
4. Explain how our reflexes protect us.
5. List four diseases that affect the nervous system.
6. If you are right-handed, which side of the brain is dominant? Explain why.
7. How are the brain and the spinal cord protected?
8. Describe the functions of each area of the brain.
9. Explain three precautions that you can take to avoid brain injury.
10. Explain why rest is important in the care of the central nervous system.

1. Bring a variety of unsweetened fruit juices and paper cups to class. Select nine volunteers to take part in a "taste test." Volunteers are to take a sip of each juice and report what they taste. Three of the volunteers should wear blindfolds, three should seal off their nostrils so that they can't smell, and three should wear blindfolds *and* seal off their nostrils. Each student in the class should write his or her predictions before the volunteers take a sip of each of the juices. Record the results, and compare them with the predictions. What does this tell you about the sense of taste and its relationship to other senses?
2. Try to arrange for a doctor specializing in sports medicine to speak to the class. Ask the doctor to describe common reflexes used by athletes during sporting activities.
3. Investigate the subject of aphasia in a library reference book or encyclopedia. Read about the various effects of this disease, and write a report on your findings.

Chapter 14

Eye and Ear Care

After reading this chapter, you will be able to:

☐ Explain the functions of the eyes and the ears.

☐ Describe the structure of the eyes and the ears and explain how they work.

☐ Identify and describe the major disorders of the eyes and the ears.

☐ Explain how to protect the eyes and the ears.

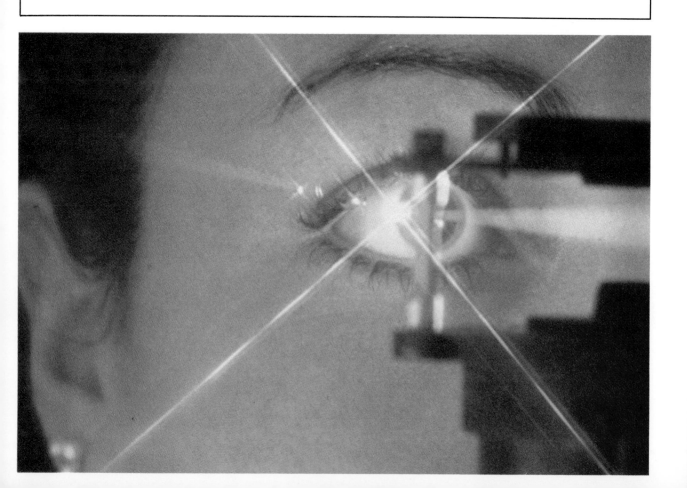

Think for a moment about your five senses. Which are most important to you? Which give you the most important information about your environment?

Most people would answer that sight is the most important sense. Hearing would be a close second.

Through our eyes and our ears, we pick up vast amounts of information about our surroundings. This information is relayed to the brain, which interprets the information and directs our actions. Just consider how many things you have seen and heard since you got up this morning. Without your eyes and your ears, how could you have obtained this information? Obviously, your eyes and ears are important sense organs, which should be cared for properly.

Structure of the eye

The eye is a highly complex sensory organ. The main parts of the eye are the eyeball itself and the **optic nerve**, which connects the eye to the brain. All the eye's vision-sensing components are in the eyeball. The optic nerve transmits visual information to the brain.

The eyeball is filled with a jellylike liquid called **vitreous humor**, which maintains the rounded shape of the eyeball. On the outside of the eyeball is a strong white covering called the **sclera**. Many blood vessels beneath the sclera nourish the tissue of the eye. The **retina** is underneath the sclera at the back of the eyeball. The retina is a thin, filmlike tissue made up of thousands of nerve cells.

At the front of the eyeball is the **cornea**, a colorless and transparent dome. The cornea keeps bits of dust and dirt from entering the eyeball. Behind the cornea is the colored **iris**, and at the center of the iris is a

The Eye

Part	Job
Vitreous humor	maintains eye's rounded shape
Sclera	prevents eye from being easily punctured
Retina	sends impulse along optic nerve to brain
Cornea	keeps eye free of dust and dirt
Iris	controls size of pupil
Pupil	regulates amount of light entering eye
Lens	controls change in shape of image
Optic nerve	connects eye to brain

small opening called the **pupil**. The iris is really a ring of muscles that controls the size of the pupil. Images enter the eye through the pupil.

The eye's **lens** is behind the pupil. The lens is attached to the eyeball by a pair of **ciliary muscles**, which can change the shape of the lens from thick to thin in order to focus.

Each eyeball is set in an eye socket in the skull. The sockets are composed of protective bones and are lined with a cushion of fat. The eyeballs are attached to the eye sockets by muscles that move the eyeballs from side to side and up and down.

Also protecting the eyes are the eyelids, which keep particles out of the eyes, and the eyebrows, which shade the eyes and keep out perspiration. A **tear gland** about the size of an almond is found just above and toward the outer edge of each eye. These glands bathe the eyes with a fluid that lubricates the eye. The fluid contains bactericide, a substance that kills bacteria and protects the eye against infection.

How the eyes work

You know how difficult it is to see in the dark. This is because vision depends on the reflection of light. Light rays shine on an object. The light does not go through the object, but bounces off it. Some of this reflected light enters the eyes. The source of light can be the sun, the stars, a lamp, or even a flashlight.

The eyes work much as a camera does. To see how the eyes work, let's follow the path of some rays of light as they go through the eyes.

Light rays reflected off an object carry an image of that object to the eyes. The rays of light pass through the cornea of each eye and enter the eyeball through the pupil. In dim light, the pupil expands to let more light enter; in bright light, it contracts to keep out excess light. The light hits the eye's lens. By changing shape, the lens focuses the image of the object on the retina. To bring faraway objects into focus,

The pupil becomes larger (*left*) or smaller (*right*) depending on the amount of reflected light.

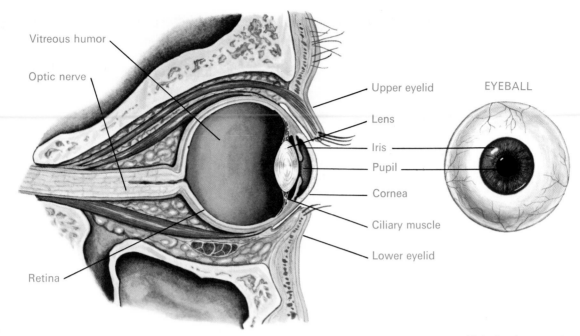

Vitreous humor

Optic nerve

Upper eyelid

EYEBALL

Lens

Iris

Pupil

Cornea

Ciliary muscle

Lower eyelid

Retina

This is the structure of the eye. The eyelids and surrounding bones protect the eye from injury.

the lens becomes thinner. To bring nearby objects into focus, the lens becomes thicker.

Remember that the retina is composed of thousands of nerve cells. It receives a picture of the object and transmits impulses about the picture to the brain through the optic nerve. The picture is upside down. In the vision centers of the brain, two pictures are received— one from each eye. The brain combines the two pictures into one three-dimensional image and turns it upright.

Visual problems may be caused by inherited defects in the shape of the eye. They may also be caused by disease, injury, aging, or weakness of the eye muscles.

Visual problems

How can the shape of the eye cause normal or poor sight?

Most defective vision is caused by an eyeball that is not regular in shape. If the eyeball is too long from front to back, the retina is too far from the lens. So distant objects are blurred because the light rays from them focus in front of the retina instead of on it. Changes in the muscles of the eyes do not correct the blurred vision. But objects very close to the eyes can be seen clearly. This condition is called nearsightedness, or **myopia**. If the eyeball is too short from front to back, the retina is too close to the lens. Then nearby objects are blurred because light rays from them focus behind the retina. But distant objects can be seen clearly. This condition is called farsightedness, or **hyperopia**.

In nearsightedness, distant objects appear blurred.

In some people, the curved surfaces of the cornea and the lens are not regularly shaped. Light rays are not bent uniformly, so they do not form a clear image on the retina. This condition is called **astigmatism**.

Strabismus

Three pairs of muscles make each eyeball move. Usually, the muscles of both eyes work together. Sometimes, however, an imbalance of the muscles causes one eye to pull more strongly than another. When this happens, one eye is pulled in one direction more than the other eye so that both eyes do not focus properly. This condition, **strabismus**, results in one or both eyes turning inward or outward. It can cause double vision. In some cases, the brain begins to ignore the picture from one eye. If the picture from that eye is always ignored, the eye weakens. It then begins to lose its ability to see. This condition is called **amblyopia**, or dim vision.

Amblyopia can also be the result of having one eye that sees more clearly than the other. Eventually, the weaker eye can almost completely lose its ability to see.

Cataracts

In older people, the lens of the eye sometimes becomes cloudy, causing blurred vision. This cloudiness is called a **cataract**. Cataracts can be caused by disease or radiation, but usually they are due to aging. If the cataract interferes too much with seeing, the lens can be surgically removed. Afterward, contact lenses or glasses can be worn, or a plastic lens can be inserted to replace the damaged lens. Cataract surgery is not considered very dangerous, and it usually works well in restoring vision.

Five Tips for Preventing Eye Strain	
1	Make sure you have plenty of light when you do close work.
2	If you read in bed, hold the book 14 to 16 inches from your eyes.
3	Don't read too much on a moving car or bus.
4	When you read or study for a long time, give your eyes a rest periodically by looking at a faraway object.
5	If you have eyeglasses, wear them.

Glaucoma

If it is not found in its early stages, **glaucoma** can lead to total blindness. It is thought that about 2 million people in the United States have glaucoma. More than 67,000 people are legally blind because of it. Glaucoma has been commonly thought to be a disease of older people. This is because its symptoms are often not seen until a person ages. However, the disease may begin early in life and then become worse as one ages.

Aqueous humor is a fluid that feeds the lens and cornea. In glaucoma, tiny openings that let the aqueous humor flow out of the eyes are closed. This makes fluid pressure build up. The pressure causes damage to the optic nerve. Finally, the nerve is destroyed and vision is lost.

If found in its early stages, glaucoma can be treated by lowering the pressure in the eye. People over the age of 35 should be tested for glaucoma every 2 years.

Eye infections

Swelling of the eyelid, or **blepharitis**, is a condition caused by bacteria. The edges of the eyelids become swollen and scaly. The infected parts also may cause itching and burning. A doctor's attention is always necessary.

The conjunctiva is the mucous membrane that covers the front part of the eyeball and the inside surface of the eyelid. **Conjunctivitis** is an infection that causes the membrane to become red and to itch and burn. The eye also waters a great deal. The upper and lower eyelids are often stuck together in the morning. Different bacteria and sometimes viruses or allergies cause conjunctivitis. The infection may be contagious when caused by bacteria or viruses. Immediate attention by a doctor is needed.

Tiny glands along the edge of the eyelids sometimes become infected. This causes a **sty**. Sties can be very painful. Redness, swelling, and pus

Five Tips for Preventing Eye Infections
1 Use only your own washcloths and towels.
2 Do not touch the area around your eyes with dirty hands.
3 Insert, remove, and clean contact lenses as directed.
4 Wet contacts with the proper solution, not saliva.
5 Stop using eye cosmetics that cause irritation or redness. Make sure applicators for eye cosmetics are clean. Buy new mascara at least every six months.

in the form of a small yellow or white spot are common symptoms. They usually disappear after about a week.

Correcting vision problems

Many vision problems can be adjusted with corrective lenses worn as glasses or contacts. Corrective lenses bend light rays as they enter the eye so that a clear picture is formed on the retina.

If you wear glasses, it is important to keep them clean. Every bit of dirt on the lenses keeps out needed light. The frames also need care. Crooked frames may put the lenses out of alignment. It is very important for people with astigmatism to keep their glasses in top condition.

Some people choose to wear contact lenses to improve their appearance. Many people also use soft or hard contact lenses for better eyesight. They also make it easier to see out of the sides of the eye and do not fog up with changes in temperature and humidity. When contact lenses first became available, people complained that they were uncomfortable and could not be worn for long periods. Today, however, new types of contact lenses are being developed. Now some lenses are made to be worn for many days or even months without removal. New lenses made of silicone or special plastic are also being tested. These lenses allow the greatest possible amount of oxygen exchange with the cornea.

Injuries to the eyes

Any part of the eye may be injured. But the danger is greatest for the cornea. If you rub your eyes when you have particles in them, you may scratch the cornea. This could leave scars, which would impair vision. It is now possible to replace a scarred or cloudy cornea with a healthy cornea from another person's eye. This medical operation is called a corneal transplant.

In order to help others, people sometimes make wills donating their corneas to medical science. Sometimes, too, when people die suddenly in accidents, their families donate their corneas as a living memorial to them. Corneas that are donated are kept in eyebanks in some large cities. They are then ready for use when they are needed.

Damage to the retina is usually caused by changes inside the body. For example, people with high blood pressure or diabetes may have small blood vessels in the retina that bleed and blur their sight. Looking directly at the sun can also burn the retina and injure vision for life.

The use of sharp sticks, stones, and pointed toys can lead to serious eye injuries or even blindness. Firecrackers sometimes cause loss of sight, as well as painful body burns. Careless use of rifles, shotguns, and air rifles causes many cases of blindness in one or both eyes.

Little pieces of metal that are being filed, sawed, or ground may fly into the cornea, injuring it and causing scars. They may also damage the retina. Injuries can be prevented by wearing goggles or using protective screens while doing this kind of work. Blows to the eye can also damage the eye. Sports goggles are sometimes suggested for people active in contact sports.

Guard against chemical injuries to the eye.

Many household products, such as ammonia, liquid bleach, and cleaning agents, can cause serious damage to the eyes. Strong acid or alkali may cause lifelong harm. Before you use an aerosol spray, make sure the nozzle is pointed away from your eyes. If you should get any chemical in your eyes, wash your eyes again and again with water. As for any eye injury, get medical help as quickly as possible.

When taken into the body, some substances may cause blindness. Methyl alcohol, commonly called wood alcohol, is one example. It should never be swallowed. Remember that half of all blindness that occurs is preventable.

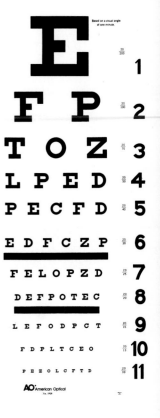

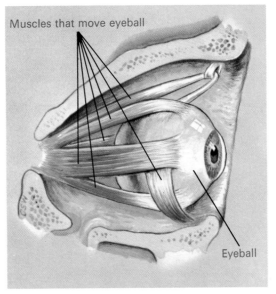

The action of three pairs of muscles moves the eye.

Muscles that move eyeball

Eyeball

Eye examinations

Checkups can help prevent eye problems.

An eye examination includes both examination of the eyes and a vision test. Most often, the vision test involves having the person stand 20 feet from an eye chart. On the chart are lines of letters in different sizes. If the person can read the letters that most people can read at 20 feet, the person is said to have 20/20 vision. At 20 feet, if the person can read only the letters that people with normal vision can read at 40 feet, the person has 20/40 vision. One use of a vision test is to find out if a person needs a complete eye examination. Some people may need eye examinations every few months. But others need them only every few years. People over age 35 should have an eye examination every year. Children should have eye examinations by the time they are 4 years old. Such conditions as amblyopia cannot be corrected if not caught at an early age.

A doctor who specializes in the care and diseases of the eye is called an **ophthalmologist**. Ophthalmologists can give their patients medical treatment and prescribe glasses or contact lenses. The prescriptions for glasses or contact lenses are filled by an **optician**. The optician grinds the lenses and makes the glasses.

Other specialists who give eye examinations are called **optometrists**. They are not medical doctors, but they have been trained to make measurements and to fit glasses and contact lenses. When eye disease or injury is suspected, patients should be referred to an ophthalmologist.

The visually handicapped

The braille alphabet makes it possible for blind persons to read with their fingers.

In the United States, there are about 500,000 legally blind people. There are also more than 11 million others who are visually handicapped. Students who have a severe vision problem may join a class directed by a teacher who is specially trained. They may also take part in regular classes for some subjects. Or they may enroll in a regular class and get extra help from a special teacher.

Students with such vision problems often use textbooks printed in large type. Books that are not printed in large type may be listened to

on records or tapes. People who have serious vision problems are often taught touch typing. Their listening skills are trained so that they depend more upon their ears and less upon their eyes for learning.

Blind people are often taught to read and write in braille. Braille is a language that is read by touch. Paper is punched with sharp instruments into patterns of raised dots. The dots stand for the letters of the alphabet. Blind people read by moving their fingers over these patterns. Many textbooks are translated into braille so they can be used by blind students.

With the learning resources available today, blind students can do most of the things their sighted friends can do. Often their other senses are much sharper. They may also have a strong will to achieve and to become fully independent. These assets can lead them to overcome obstacles and to succeed in a wide range of careers.

Structure of the ear

Can you imagine what your life would be like if you could not hear any sound? Your hearing plays an important role in helping you to adjust to your surroundings. Sounds let you judge the distances of objects and warn you of any danger. Of all the senses of the body, hearing is the last to disappear when you fall asleep. It is also the first sense to be aroused when you wake up.

The ear is organized into three parts: the **external ear** (outer ear), the **middle ear**, and the **inner ear**.

The external ear

Sound goes into the middle ear via the **external auditory canal**, an S-shaped channel that goes about 1 inch into the temporal bone. Within the auditory canal are many wax-producing glands. The wax and the many hairs that line the canal stop foreign objects from getting into the deeper part of the auditory canal.

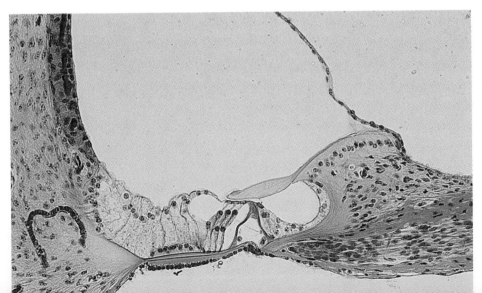

The bones of the ear are very small. The cochlea, shown here, has been magnified 480 times.

The middle ear

The middle ear is a small, drumlike cavity in the skull. It is found just inside the external auditory canal. A membrane called the **eardrum** separates the middle ear from the outer ear. Three tiny, movable bones go across the middle-ear cavity. They are named according to their shape: the hammer (**malleus**), anvil (**incus**), and stirrup (**stapes**). These bones amplify vibrations, or sound waves, that travel from the eardrum to the oval window of the inner ear.

A tube called the **eustachian tube** connects the middle ear with the back of the nose and throat. The tube opens into the middle ear and lets air into it. This balances the air pressure on both sides of the eardrum. When you swallow, the eustachian tubes open and adjust the air pressure in the middle ears. Riding in a fast elevator or an airplane may cause an unpleasant feeling in the ears. This feeling is caused by the sudden change in pressure on the outside of the eardrums. Swallowing or yawning opens the eustachian tubes and lets the pressure inside the ears become the same as the pressure outside.

Most hearing defects in young people are caused by infections that reach the middle ear through the eustachian tubes. Swelling in the middle ear interferes with hearing by keeping the bones from moving. Many infections of the middle ear may thicken the membranes and lower their ability to carry sound waves.

If an abscess (a buildup of pus) forms in the ear and breaks the eardrum, hearing may be harmed seriously. But if the break is small and on one side, the eardrum may still be able to move when sound waves strike it.

This is the structure of the ear. The ear not only allows you to hear—it helps you to keep your balance as well.

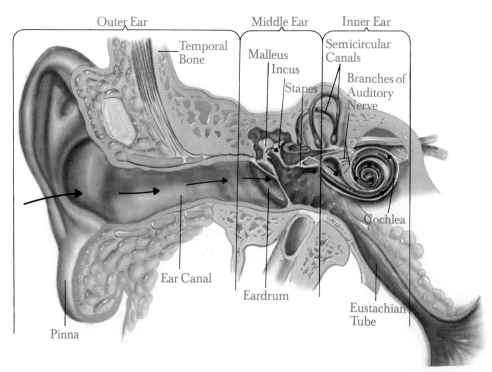

Outer Ear

Temporal Bone

Middle Ear

Malleus

Incus

Stapes

Inner Ear

Semicircular Canals

Branches of Auditory Nerve

Cochlea

Ear Canal

Eardrum

Eustachian Tube

Pinna

Inner-ear problems would make a balancing act like this one impossible.

The inner ear

The inner ear lies in the solid bone of the skull. It is located behind the top of the nose. The **cochlea**, which looks like a snail shell, is filled with liquid. It contains nerve endings from the auditory nerve. When sound waves strike the eardrum, the three bones of the middle ear move. The stapes rocks back and forth against the membrane of the oval window of the inner ear. This starts waves of motion in the cochlea. These waves then start impulses that are transmitted by the auditory nerve to the brain. In the brain, the nerve impulses are understood as sounds.

Sound waves may also reach the inner ear through the bones of the skull. If you were to put the handle of a vibrating tuning fork against the back of the ear, the sound would be carried through the bones of the skull.

The **vestibule** is found between the cochlea and the semicircular canals. When the head is held to one side, gravity causes tiny solid particles inside the vestibule to touch nerve cells. These nerve cells carry impulses to the brain. The impulses help you figure out the position of your head in relation to gravity.

The **semicircular canals** control balance. These three small canals lie at right angles to each other. Each canal is filled with fluid and has nerve endings that connect to a part of the auditory nerve. Changing the position of the head changes the pressure of the fluid in the canals. This sets up the nerve impulses that tell you how to keep your balance.

Unusual disturbance of the fluids in the semicircular canals causes dizziness. Seasickness, carsickness, and airsickness may be caused by the effect of motion upon the semicircular canals.

Hearing disorders

Most people can hear a wide variety of sounds, from high to low and from soft to loud. The sounds used in everyday speech are neither very high nor very low. The loudness of any sound is measured in decibels. Having normal hearing means being able to hear speech sounds as low as 15 decibels, which is whispering. Unfortunately, more than 18 million people in the United States have hearing disorders. There are over 3 million children who cannot hear even a loud conversation.

An instrument called an **audiometer** is used to measure a person's ability to hear. With an audiometer, a trained person can find out how loud a sound must be before the person being tested can hear it. People who have hearing problems should see an ear specialist to find the cause. An **audiologist** can test the ears for hearing problems. An **otologist** is a doctor who specializes in the care of the ears.

Hearing disorders are grouped into three major types: conductive loss, nerve loss, and central loss.

Conductive loss. **Conductive loss** is caused by any block to the passage of sound waves through the outer or middle ear. Some causes are: (1) too much wax or an infection in the external auditory canal; (2) an eardrum that is torn or inflamed; (3) broken or joined malleus, incus, or stapes, which stops movement; and (4) thick fluid in the middle ear.

One of the most common causes of conductive loss in young adults is **otosclerosis** (*oto* = ear / *sclerosis* = hardening). In this disease, the stapes becomes joined to the oval window by a spongy growth of bone. Then the stapes cannot rock back and forth against the membrane of the oval window. When this happens, sound cannot be transmitted well.

Most deaf people are not totally deaf. They can hear loud sounds and can understand what people say when people speak slowly and clearly. In such cases, hearing aids that make sounds louder can be useful.

Medical operations for correcting and repairing torn eardrums, joined bones, and other causes of conductive loss have improved. More people now are able to recover their hearing through operations.

Nerve loss. **Nerve loss** is caused by damage to the special sensory cells in the cochlea. The cells can be damaged in many ways. These include: (1) allergic reaction to drugs, such as antibiotics; (2) loud environmental noises; (3) **rubella** virus, or German measles, caught from the mother by the unborn child; and (4) infection spreading from the middle ear to the area near the cochlea.

Once a sensory cell is damaged in the cochlea, no medical operation can correct it. Hearing aids help many people with nerve loss. An otologist can discover the person's problem, and a hearing health professional can fit the right kind of hearing aid.

Central loss. **Central loss** is caused by damage to the auditory nerve that leads to the brain from the cochlea. It is also caused by damage to the brain center for hearing. If the brain center is injured, it does not matter how well the sound is carried by the eardrum, bones, and sensory cells. The brain cannot understand it. Luckily, central loss is rare.

Will aging affect hearing?

As people grow older, changes take place in their inner ears. These changes make it impossible for older people to hear as well as they did when they were younger. The ability to hear high tones is the type of hearing most affected by age. Many people who have poor hearing do not know that they cannot hear well. Others may not admit that they have a difficult time hearing. In either case, serious problems can develop when people feel left out of what is happening around them. Older people who cannot hear well may also have a harder time taking

"Hearing ear" dogs can alert their owners to noises that the person is unable to hear.

191

Wearing headphones can make you dangerously inattentive to your surroundings. Worse yet, they can cause hearing loss.

care of their basic needs. Hearing aids can often help them to communicate better.

Care of the ears

The major cause of defective hearing in young people is infection that travels up the eustachian tubes into the middle ears. Therefore, it is important to protect yourself against diseases that enter through the nose and throat. Learn to blow your nose gently so that bacteria will not be forced up into your ears. When you swim, keep water from getting into your nose. If you have a cold, do not go swimming. If you have a damaged eardrum or other ear problems, ask your doctor's advice about swimming or traveling in an airplane.

Another way that infection enters the middle ear is through the ear canal. The thin skin that lines the ear canal also lines the eardrum. Therefore, an infection in the auditory canal can spread easily to the eardrum. Do not use hard instruments to clean wax out of the ears. The wax can be removed from the ears with a damp cloth. Have your doctor remove any excess buildup of wax in the ears.

If an infection should develop, get medical help immediately. A doctor can prescribe medication or make an opening in the eardrum to drain the infectious fluids. Immediate treatment can prevent infection from leading to hearing loss.

Noisy surroundings may damage your ears. Even loud music can cause permanent ear damage. The risk can be lowered by taking a "quiet break" from a noisy environment every 30 minutes. Try wearing ear plugs when such breaks are not possible.

Most people learn to speak by imitating other people's speech. Deaf people cannot hear other people talk. They also cannot hear the sound of their own voices. Despite this fact, people with little or no hearing can learn to speak well enough to be understood. Deaf people can also communicate by using a hand alphabet called sign language. They can understand and speak to others in a language that spells out words or phrases with the fingers and hands. Certain positions of the fingers and hands stand for letters, words, or ideas. Deaf people can also learn to understand the speech of others by watching lip movements. The study of speech reading should be started early. Mothers and fathers of deaf children can learn to teach speech reading to them while they are very young.

Education of the deaf

Key Words

amblyopia	external auditory	optometrist
aqueous humor	canal	otologist
astigmatism	external ear	otosclerosis
audiologist	glaucoma	pupil
audiometer	hyperopia	retina
blepharitis	incus	rubella
cataract	inner ear	sclera
central loss	iris	semicircular
ciliary muscles	lens	canals
cochlea	malleus	stapes
conductive loss	middle ear	strabismus
conjunctivitis	myopia	sty
cornea	nerve loss	tear gland
eardrum	ophthalmologist	vestibule
eustachian tube	optic nerve	vitreous humor
	optician	

Main Ideas

- The eyes and ears are complex and important sensory organs.
- In order to see well, the eyes must be in perfect working order. If they are not, corrective lenses should be used.
- Visual problems may be caused by disease, defects, or injuries.
- Most eye injuries are caused by carelessness and neglect.
- The semicircular canal of the ear is important for balance.
- Hearing problems can be caused by disease, defects, injury, or loud noises.
- Most middle-ear infections occur when bacteria travel through the eustachian tube.
- Prompt treatment of infections and regular hearing tests may help in preventing serious hearing loss.

Understand the Reading

1. What is the job of the ciliary muscles?
2. What is the job of the vitreous humor?
3. List five structures that help to protect the eyes.
4. Explain why tears are important.
5. Describe the path of a light ray as it enters the eye and becomes an image on the retina. How is this image transmitted to the brain?
6. How does the lens change for near and far vision?
7. What does 20/40 on a vision test mean?
8. What is the shape of the eyeball in farsightedness? What is its shape in nearsightedness? How do lenses help to correct these defects?
9. How is myopia different from astigmatism?
10. What causes strabismus?
11. Explain what happens in glaucoma.
12. What are the differences between a sty and conjunctivitis?
13. Explain the work of an ophthalmologist, an optometrist, and an optician.
14. What is the job of the hammer, anvil, and stirrup?
15. Describe the path of sound waves from the time they enter the ear until they become nerve impulses that reach the brain.
16. How is the eustachian tube related to defective hearing in young people?
17. What is the job of the semicircular canals?
18. What is the major difference between conductive loss and nerve loss?
19. Explain how deaf people can communicate.
20. Discuss how you can prevent hearing problems.

Apply Your Knowledge

1. Obtain a decibel meter from your local health department. Check the decibel levels of several areas of your school, including the cafeteria and gym. Compare your findings with the figures in the chart on page 150. Discuss the results of your experiment with your class.
2. Do some research on Louis Braille, the inventor of the braille alphabet. Prepare a report for the class on the life of this pioneer.
3. Research the subject of American sign language at your library. Determine the ways in which "signing" is similar to and different from spoken language. In a report, tell your classmates what you have learned.
4. Do some research on the method by which seeing-eye dogs are trained. In a class presentation, describe the step-by-step procedure.

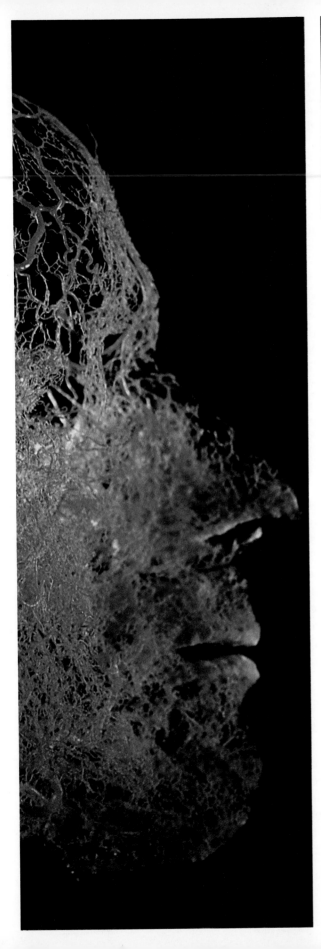

Chapter 15
Transport System

After reading this chapter, you will be able to:

☐ Identify the main parts of the body's transport system.

☐ Explain the importance of blood and describe its makeup.

☐ Identify and describe some of the diseases of the blood.

☐ Describe the structure of the heart and explain how it functions.

☐ Identify and describe some of the diseases of the heart.

☐ Explain how to take care of the body's transport system.

It collects and transports food.
It collects and transports oxygen.
It collects and transports wastes.
It even transports heat.
What is it?

The answer is blood. Blood carries all the supplies your body needs. The average adult has about 6 quarts of blood pulsing through 100,000 miles of blood vessels. The pumping action of the heart keeps the blood moving throughout the entire body. Blood, blood vessels, and the heart make up your body's circulatory system, or *transport system*.

The blood

Blood is a fluid tissue made up of plasma, red blood cells, white blood cells, and cells called platelets. **Plasma** is the liquid part of blood. It is 91 percent water mixed with salts and proteins. The red blood cells, white blood cells, and platelets all float inside the plasma.

Red blood cells

The blood in a human body has about 30 trillion **red blood cells**. Placed side by side, these cells could cover an area about as large as a football field. Red blood cells are the oxygen carriers in blood. They contain a substance called **hemoglobin**, which picks up oxygen in the lungs and carries it to all parts of the body. Hemoglobin gives blood its red color. When hemoglobin is carrying oxygen inside the red blood cells, the blood becomes bright red. When blood reaches the tissues of the body, hemoglobin releases the oxygen and gives it to the cells to use. Then the hemoglobin changes to a bluish-red color. Blood that has a lot of oxygen is red. Blood with less oxygen is bluish.

Red blood cells are continually being formed in the **bone marrow**— the soft, inner part of bone. Red blood cells live only about 30 days. Worn-out cells are destroyed in the spleen and the liver. In the time that it takes you to read this sentence, about 15 million red blood cells in your body will die. And about 15 million new ones will be formed.

White blood cells

White blood cells, called **leukocytes**, are also made in the bone marrow. They are larger than red cells, but there are fewer of them. White blood cells work to fight infection. These white cells squeeze between the cells in the walls of the tiniest blood vessels, or **capillaries**, and enter the body's tissues. When bacteria or viruses enter the body, white cells collect in large numbers around them. White cells surround the disease organisms and eat them. They also can eat polluted particles that stick to the lungs and can even slowly break up splinters. But if a white cell eats more disease organisms than it can handle, it dies. The

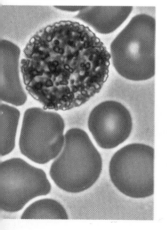

White blood cells help keep the body free of disease.

yellow pus found in some infections is really a mixture of dead white cells, active white cells, and disease organisms.

A doctor can often tell whether or not someone has an infection by counting the number of white blood cells in a drop of the patient's blood. When there is an infection in the body, the bone marrow makes more white blood cells to fight against the infection.

Some infections, especially virus infections, lower the number of white blood cells instead of increasing it. Certain drugs may also lower the number of white blood cells in a person who is sensitive to these drugs.

Platelets

Platelets are smaller than red blood cells, and there are fewer of them in the blood. When you bleed, platelets help to form a clot that stops the bleeding. The clot then hardens into a scab that covers the wound. This covering helps prevent infection.

Like any other body tissue or body organ, blood is subject to certain diseases.

Diseases of the blood

Anemia

Anemia is a disease that occurs when the blood lacks hemoglobin, red blood cells, or both. This means the body cells of an anemic person do not get enough oxygen. Decreased oxygen causes tiredness. It also causes a person to run out of breath easily.

One cause of anemia is a diet without enough iron, the mineral needed to make hemoglobin. Infections may cause anemia and may stop the body from making hemoglobin. Loss of blood from a wound can cause a drop in plasma and red blood cells for a time. This can also result in anemia. When this happens, a person becomes thirsty and drinks a lot of liquid to make up for the fluid that was lost. The bone marrow also makes new blood cells to replace those that were lost. Loss of blood from internal bleeding may be another cause of anemia. One sign of bleeding inside the digestive system could be dark or black bowel movements. Occasionally, some women develop anemia because of heavy blood loss during menstruation.

Leukemia

When there is a great increase in the number of white blood cells in the blood, the disease called **leukemia** may be present. The cause of leukemia is not known. But scientists think the disease is a cancer of the white blood cells. This disease is found mainly in young people and causes many deaths each year.

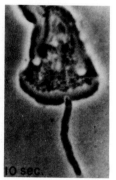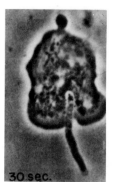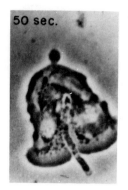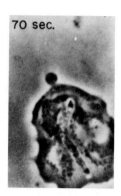

A white blood cell can surround and devour a bacterium in less than a minute.

Researchers are trying to develop a cure for leukemia. The use of certain drugs, X-ray treatments, or both can slow down the growth of the disease. With the right treatment, more than 75 percent of the people who have leukemia live through the first year of the sickness. And some people with leukemia now live for 5 years or longer.

Some kinds of leukemia are less serious than others. Some people live for a long time with chronic leukemia.

Hemophilia

Some diseases cause the blood to clot too slowly or not to clot at all. One such disease is **hemophilia**. A person with hemophilia can bleed to death very easily. The slightest bump or scrape can cause a dangerous problem for anyone who has this disease.

People with hemophilia sometimes bleed inside the body, especially into the joints. And even a small operation may be serious for a person who has a clotting problem. This is why every patient's blood is tested for clotting before operations are performed.

Hemophilia is an inherited disease, one that is passed on to children by their parents. The disease is found mostly in males. Fortunately, however, hemophilia is not a common disease. If a hemophiliac is hurt, a clotting factor (a medicine that causes blood to clot) is given to help stop the bleeding.

Blood types

Human blood falls into four major classes, or blood types: A, B, AB, and O. About 4 percent of Americans have type AB, about 10 percent have type B, about 41 percent have type A, and about 45 percent have type O. The same types of blood are found in both sexes and in all races. Blood of one type will mix safely with blood of the same type. And some blood types may mix with two or three other types. For example, type O is known as the "universal donor" blood. Type O can be given to people with almost any of the other blood types. It was once thought that AB could mix with blood of any other type, but problems were discovered.

Today, a doctor must determine what type of blood the patient and the donor have to see if they will mix safely. If the wrong blood type is given, the blood cells in the donated blood clump together. When this happens, the person receiving the new blood becomes very ill and sometimes dies.

Rh factor

About 85 percent of the population has a substance called **Rh factor** in their red blood cells. Blood that has the Rh factor is called Rh-positive. Blood that does not have the Rh factor is called Rh-negative. The presence or absence of the Rh factor does not affect a person's health in any way. However, Rh-positive blood should never be given in a transfusion to a person who has Rh-negative blood. The Rh-negative blood will react against the new blood.

The Rh factor can be very important during pregnancy. If an Rh-negative mother is pregnant with an Rh-positive baby, the mother's body will react by developing antibodies to fight what it thinks is a foreign substance. This does not hurt the first Rh-positive baby, but can pose a danger for the second Rh-positive child. Because the woman's body is now sensitized to Rh-positive blood cells, the antibodies in her blood will begin to destroy the blood of the developing second child.

To prevent this, Rh-negative women are injected with a serum called Rhogam after the first pregnancy. It is important, therefore, for both parents to be tested for the Rh factor when a first child is expected.

Blood banks

There are blood banks in most cities. Blood of all types is collected from healthy donors and stored under refrigeration. Blood banks store whole blood, that is, the plasma and the blood cells. Whole blood can be kept for only a few weeks under ordinary refrigeration. But it may be kept for much longer if it is frozen.

Whole blood may be divided into parts that can be given separately in transfusions. Plasma, packed red blood cells, platelets, and gamma globulin (a protein in blood plasma) are the main parts of blood that are used in transfusions.

A blood transfusion is the transfer of blood from one person to another. Someone who gives blood is called a **donor**. The blood received by the patient in a transfusion takes the place of blood that has been lost. It gives the person red blood cells to carry oxygen. The donor's red blood cells stay in the body of the person who receives them for only a few days before they are eliminated from the body. By then, the person is usually able to make new blood.

Blood banks provide communities with ready supplies of blood for emergencies.

The role of lymph

Lymph is a clear fluid that washes all the cells of the body. It comes mostly from blood plasma that has passed through the capillary walls into adjacent lymph vessels. Lymph moves along the lymph vessels as it is squeezed and pushed by contractions of muscles and blood vessels around it.

Everything that the cells need for their work is carried by the lymph from the bloodstream. Wastes from the body cells are returned by the lymph to the veins. Then the blood in the veins carries the wastes to organs in the body whose job it is to excrete, or get rid of, them. The lymph system, then, passes substances between the blood vessels and the body's cells.

This is the lymphatic system. Lymph flows through capillaries and lymph vessels that eventually join to form the thoracic duct.

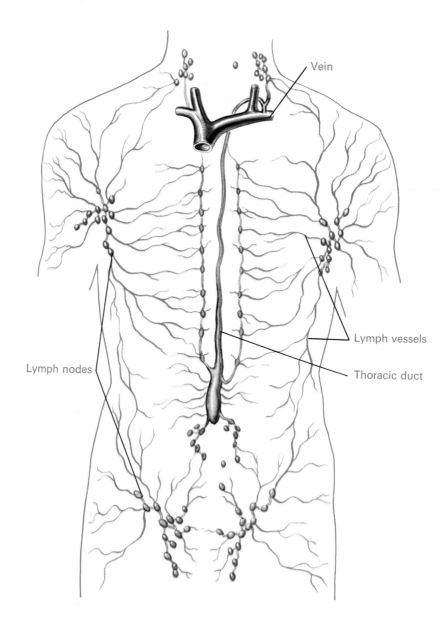

Vein

Lymph vessels

Thoracic duct

Lymph nodes

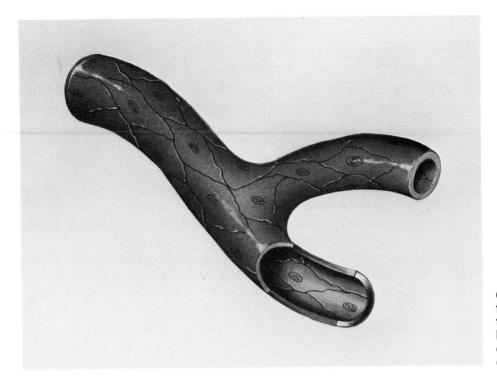

Oxygen and digested food leave the capillary through spaces between the cells in order to nourish nearby cells.

Lymph nodes

Along the lymph vessels are small structures called **lymph nodes**. The lymph nodes are a collection of the white blood cells. The lymph nodes also destroy disease organisms that enter the lymph vessels. When an infection starts in the body, the white blood cells in the nearest lymph nodes divide in order to surround and destroy the disease organism. If the number of white cells becomes large enough, the lymph nodes will enlarge to make room for them. This enlarging of the lymph nodes sometimes makes them feel sore.

The heart and blood vessels

The heart is a pear-shaped organ made of muscle. It pumps blood to all parts of the body. If you are somewhat active, about 5 to 9 quarts of blood are pumped through the heart each minute.

Contraction of the heart squeezes blood out of the heart into the **arteries**. These are blood vessels that carry blood away from the heart. Arteries branch again and again to form smaller and smaller arteries. Finally, the smallest arteries branch to form tiny capillaries. Most of the material that leaves the blood does so through the thin walls of the capillaries. Materials that enter the blood from the cells also pass through the capillary walls. The capillaries join to form small **veins** that then form larger veins. It is the veins that carry blood back to the heart.

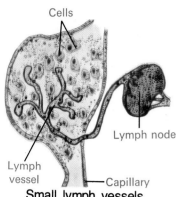

Cells

Lymph node

Lymph vessel

Capillary

Small lymph vessels pick up waste from the cells and carry it to lymph nodes.

Circulation of the blood

A wall of muscle divides the heart into two sides. The heart works like two pumps that act together. Each side of the heart—each pump—is divided into an upper part and a lower part. The upper part of each side is called the **atrium**, or auricle. And the lower part is called the **ventricle**. The heart, therefore, has four chambers.

The blood in the veins from all over the body (venous blood) enters the right atrium. This blood has given much of its oxygen to the tissues. It also has taken carbon dioxide and other waste materials from the tissues. The blood then flows from the right ventricle to the **pulmonary artery**. This artery carries the blood out of the heart to the lungs. The blood loses carbon dioxide in the lungs and picks up a fresh supply of oxygen.

The blood is carried back to the heart by the **pulmonary vein** and enters the left atrium. It is pumped from the left ventricle into the **aorta**, the largest artery in the body. The aorta and its branches carry blood to the kidneys and other vital organs. Two other branches, the coronary arteries, carry blood to the heart muscle itself.

The blood circulates very quickly. It flows all the way around the body in about 1 minute. Blood passes through the heart in only 1 or 2 seconds. It goes from the heart to the lungs and back to the heart in 10 to 15 seconds. It also goes from the heart to the brain and back to the heart in 10 to 15 seconds. Blood travels to the toes and back to the heart in about 20 to 25 seconds.

The heart rests between beats. During the period when the blood is flowing between the two atria (plural of atrium) and the two ventricles, the heart is relaxed. This resting time is called **diastole**. The contraction of the heart is called **systole**. Diastole lasts a little longer than systole. Out of 24 hours each day, the heart rests for about 15 hours.

When the heart beats, a wave of blood starts out at the heart and moves through the arteries. When you count your pulse, you are counting a series of these waves. The pulse rate is the number of times the heart beats each minute. The heart of a human infant beats about 130

Transport System

Part	Job
Left ventricle	pumps oxygen-rich blood into aorta
Aorta	distributes blood to arteries
Arteries	carry blood (and oxygen) to all organs of body
Veins	return oxygen-poor blood to heart
Right ventricle	pumps blood to lungs for new oxygen supply

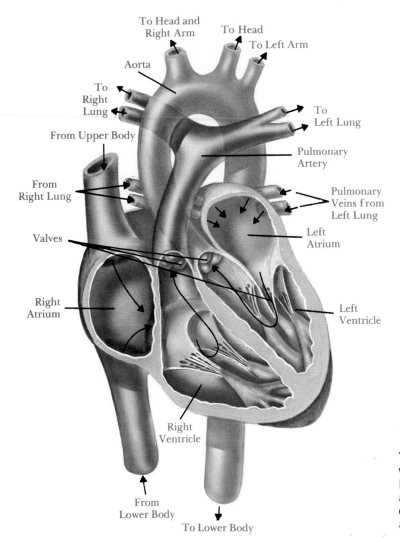

To Head and Right Arm

To Head

To Left Arm

Aorta

To Right Lung

To Left Lung

From Upper Body

Pulmonary Artery

From Right Lung

Pulmonary Veins from Left Lung

Left Atrium

Valves

Right Atrium

Left Ventricle

Right Ventricle

From Lower Body

To Lower Body

The heart is a pump with four chambers. Each chamber plays a part in delivering oxygen-rich blood to all parts of the body.

times per minute. This rate becomes slower with age until the adult rate is reached. This usually happens in the late teens. The pulse rate then averages about 80 beats per minute in women and 72 beats per minute in men.

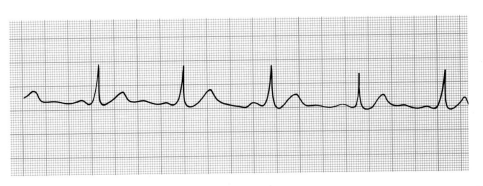

An electrocardiogram is a visual record of the heart's action. It enables doctors to diagnose heart disease.

Valves of the heart

There is a set of **valves** between the atrium and ventricle of each side of the heart. The pressure of the blood as it collects in each atrium causes the valves to open. Much of the blood enters the ventricles before the atria contract. When the ventricles contract, the pressure of the blood forces these valves to close. In this way, blood cannot flow backward into each atrium. There is another set of valves at the opening to each of the arteries that receives blood from the ventricles. When the ventricles contract, these valves open in order to let blood pump into the arteries. When the ventricles relax, the pressure of the blood in the arteries closes the valves. The blood now cannot flow backward into the ventricles.

Infections sometimes damage heart valves so that they cannot close tightly. Blood leaks back through the damaged valves with each heartbeat. When leakage occurs, the heart must work harder. If the damage is very great, the heart may not be able to keep enough blood moving through the body.

As the heart valves close, they make sounds. The closure of the two sets of valves creates vibrations in the chambers. The sound of these vibrations is heard as "lub dub" (the heart beat). If a valve does not close completely or if it is smaller than normal, a blowing or swishing noise is made by the blood passing through the defective valve. This noise may be heard with an instrument called a stethoscope. The sound is known as a **heart murmur**. Many young people have heart murmurs that are considered to be normal. A doctor should listen to the murmur and decide whether or not it is abnormal.

Return of blood to the heart

The blood from the legs must travel a long distance against gravity to get back to the heart. The walls of the veins are thinner than those of the arteries. They put little pressure on the blood. Blood from the lower part of the body moves upward mostly because the muscles used in walking and running squeeze the blood along as they contract. Valves in the veins keep the blood from dropping down again.

Sometimes the walls of the veins stretch, and blood collects in the veins above the valves. This condition is known as **varicose veins**. Varicose veins can cause discomfort. They may also be dangerous if enough blood collects to break the walls of the veins. Resting with the feet raised or wearing elastic stockings may help varicose veins in the legs. Sometimes an operation is necessary.

Changes in circulation

Your blood circulates night and day throughout your life. Sometimes your heart beats very fast. Sometimes it beats slowly. Athletic training and good physical condition seem to lower the pulse rate. It is increased by excitement, tobacco, fever, and some diseases.

When you eat, more blood is sent to your digestive tract. When you exercise, more blood goes to the muscles. In a healthy person, the heart usually sends the different parts of the body the blood they need.

There are nerves in the heart and the blood vessels. But you cannot control the impulses that travel over these nerves. Nerve impulses are started by the need for food or oxygen somewhere in the body or the gathering of waste materials. These impulses speed up or slow down the rate of the heart. Other nerve impulses cause some of the small arteries to contract and push the blood to other arteries. Yet other impulses will cause arteries to enlarge so that more blood goes through.

Fainting may occur when the brain does not get enough blood. A person may faint when emotionally upset, ill, or very tired. Bending or lying down with the head lowered lets blood run down into the brain. This eases the feeling of faintness.

Changes in circulation may be caused by emotions. When you become excited, your heart beats faster. When you are embarrassed, the blood vessels in your face and neck enlarge and let more blood flow to these areas. This makes you blush. Being sad may make your heart beat more slowly. When you are frightened, the blood vessels in your skin may become smaller. This removes blood from the surface of your skin and makes your face paler.

Blood pressure

Blood pressure is the pressure of blood against the walls of the arteries. The walls of the arteries are elastic, or stretchable, and contain involuntary muscles. There is usually enough blood in the arteries to keep them more or less always stretched. The pressure of the walls keeps the blood flowing into the smaller arteries and capillaries. When the heart beats, more blood is forced into the arteries, making the pressure greater.

High blood pressure is serious and should be treated by a doctor.

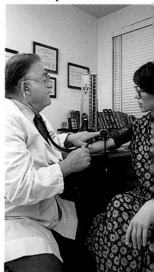

A healthy person's blood pressure goes up when the person stands, runs, or becomes excited. But when the blood pressure stays high all or most of the time, it is said to be abnormal. This condition is called **hypertension**, or high blood pressure.

High blood pressure may be dangerous. The pressure in the arteries may become so high that the heart wears itself out trying to pump blood into the aorta. Some of the small arteries may break and let the blood escape into the tissue and clot there. When clotting occurs in the brain, the parts of the brain affected by the clot cannot work properly. This can cause a stroke.

The causes of high blood pressure are not all known. Heredity, overweight, and emotional tension are related to high blood pressure. Too much salt in the diet may cause hypertension in some people.

Hypertension may begin at an early age. For that reason, blood pressure should be checked regularly in children and teenagers. With drugs and the right kind of diet, hypertension may be cured if discovered at an early age. It is only in later stages that it cannot be cured but can only be controlled.

Heart disease

The leading cause of death in the United States is heart disease. This may be because the average life span today is longer in this country than it was years ago. There are more older people today and, therefore, many cases of heart disease. The time to begin to guard against diseases of the heart is in adolescence or young adulthood. Although heart disease occurs in some young people, it usually afflicts people during middle and old age.

Heart disease includes almost any condition that weakens the heart or interferes with its proper work. Any infection that gets into the bloodstream may affect the heart by causing heart disease. Diphtheria, scarlet fever, syphilis, and many other diseases may harm the heart.

Congenital heart disease

A child may be born with abnormal heart valves or other defects in heart structure. Heart disease that has been present since birth is known as **congenital heart disease**. Some types of congenital heart disease are very serious. Other types may cause only minor problems. Many congenital heart defects can be corrected with heart surgery. A special machine called the **heart-lung machine** causes the flow of blood to bypass the heart. With the use of this machine, surgeons are able to operate on the heart.

Rheumatic heart disease

Children and young adults may get a type of heart condition called **rheumatic heart disease**. Rheumatic heart disease is the lifelong damage that is a result of **rheumatic fever**. Rheumatic fever may develop 2 to 6 weeks after a throat infection caused by a type of bacteria called streptococcus. A person usually has fever and swelling in the bone joints. Swelling could begin in the heart muscle and heart valves. This could cause scars to form. Scarring in these places is the permanent damage called rheumatic heart disease.

Not all sore throats are caused by streptococcal bacteria. But those that are should be treated with antibiotics to prevent rheumatic fever. When a child or young adult has a sore throat, a doctor may take a **throat culture**. A throat culture is made by rubbing a sterile cotton swab on the throat and then onto a culture plate. Since doctors have been using throat cultures and such antibiotics as penicillin, there have been fewer cases of rheumatic heart disease.

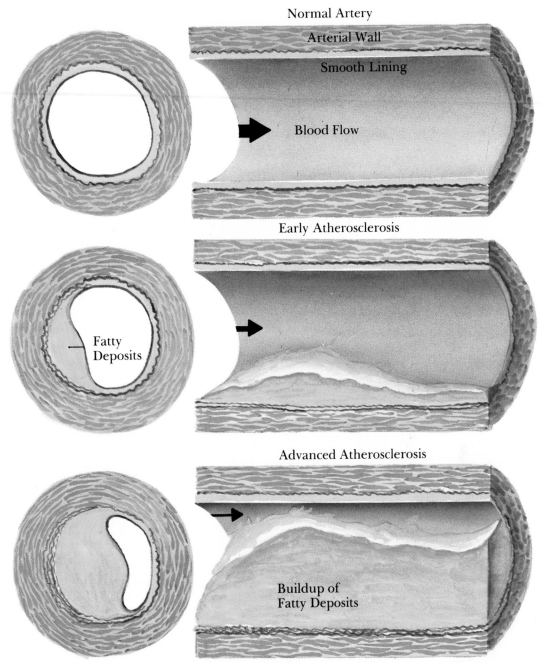

Normal Artery

Arterial Wall

Smooth Lining

Blood Flow

Early Atherosclerosis

Fatty
Deposits

Advanced Atherosclerosis

Buildup of
Fatty Deposits

Coronary artery disease

The vessels that carry blood to the heart muscle are called **coronary arteries**. Two common forms of heart disease involve the coronary arteries. As people become older, deposits of a fatty material called **cholesterol** collect on the walls of these arteries and narrow them. This produces **atherosclerosis**. Another condition, **arteriosclerosis**, involves the hardening of the walls of the arteries. Arteriosclerosis is a slow

Normal arteries (*top*) have no fatty deposits on the walls. In early atherosclerosis, fatty deposits collect on the walls of the artery (*middle*). In advanced atherosclerosis, the artery is almost completely obstructed (*bottom*).

process that takes many years to develop. A human heart must work harder to pump blood through vessels with either atherosclerosis or arteriosclerosis.

If a vessel carrying blood to the heart muscle becomes blocked, the heart muscle may be damaged. If the heart cannot get enough blood, a **heart attack** may develop. Usually, a person feels severe chest pain with nausea and sweating during a heart attack.

Many people have symptoms, such as mild chest pain, before a severe heart attack. A doctor should be called when chest pain is first noticed. Many people survive heart attacks if help is gotten quickly.

Many people who have narrow arteries from coronary artery disease do not have heart attacks. Some, however, develop chest pain whenever they try to exercise or when they are under stress. This chest pain is called **angina pectoris**. It occurs when the heart muscle does not get as much blood as it needs. This pain is usually relieved by rest or by medicine.

This team of surgeons is performing an operation on a human heart. Such operations have saved thousands of lives.

Angina pectoris is often a warning that surgery is needed. Patients with angina pectoris may have a dye injected into the coronary arteries. Using X rays, doctors can trace the dye as it goes through the circulatory

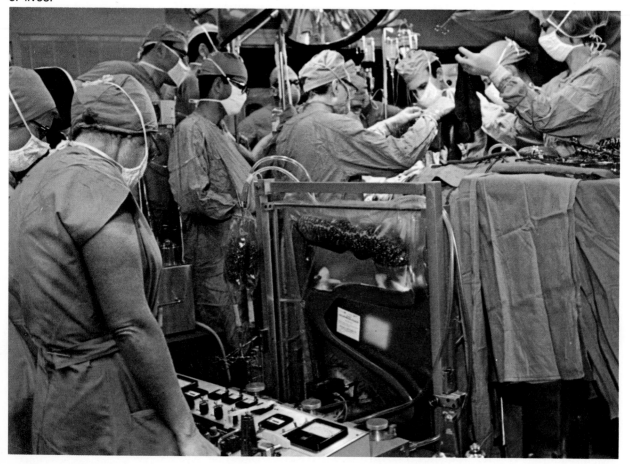

The idea is simple enough: A patient's heart is severely damaged by heart disease, so the heart is replaced with a healthy one. Unfortunately, the problems surrounding transplant operations for hearts and other organs are anything but simple. There is a shortage of transplant organs for those who need them, and donor organs cannot be kept alive for long outside the human body.

An even bigger transplant-related problem involves the human body's own disease-fighting mechanism—the immune system. This system, whose job is to fight and destroy invading organisms, mistakes the heart for such an organism and rejects it.

The solution to this problem is a group of powerful drugs that temporarily prevent the immune system from working. These drugs have brought about an increase in transplant operations and a better survival rate for patients.

system to see if anything is blocking the coronary arteries. If a blockage is seen in one of the three main coronary arteries, the patient may be advised to have cardiac surgery. In coronary bypass surgery, a blood vessel taken from the leg is attached to the blocked artery above and below the blockage. In this way, the blood flowing through the coronary artery is able to "bypass" the blockage.

There are many reasons for the increase in coronary heart disease in the United States. The conditions that make the chance of a heart attack greater are called **risk factors**. People who smoke cigarettes or have untreated hypertension have a greater than average chance of having a heart attack. Lack of exercise and overweight also may increase the chances of heart disease. High blood levels of cholesterol and sugar are two more risk factors.

Care of the circulatory system

Circulatory disorders, such as heart disease and strokes, often cause disability and death. These illnesses occur mostly in adults, especially in older people. But studies show that prevention must begin at a much earlier age. The process of atherosclerosis takes many years to develop into a complete blood-vessel blockage. There are many things you can do to decrease your chances of someday having a serious circulatory problem.

Exercise regularly.

There was a time when people walked long distances to get where they were going. Modern transportation has made walking unnecessary. Moreover, many jobs do not require physical activity. The circulatory system

Your circulatory system
needs some exercise
each day to keep it fit.

needs some exercise each day to keep it fit. Such exercises as walking, swimming, and jogging can be helpful to the circulatory system.

Choose a proper diet.

High blood levels of cholesterol are thought to lead to a higher rate of heart attacks. The average American diet has much more cholesterol and other fats than the body needs. Amounts of these substances should be limited. (See Unit 8.) Too much weight can also overwork the circulatory system. A diet that keeps body weight at normal limits should be followed.

Maintain normal blood pressure.

The circulatory system works best under normal conditions. High blood pressure is a serious disorder that should be treated with medications. Blood pressure can be checked easily with a blood-pressure cuff. If there is a history of strokes, heart attacks, or high blood pressure in someone's family, the person's blood pressure should be checked at least once a year.

Don't smoke.

Many more heart attacks occur in heavy smokers than in people who don't smoke. Just one cigarette speeds up the heartbeat and increases the blood pressure. Smoking interferes with the blood's ability to give oxygen to the tissues. In addition, smoking may be harmful to any one of the blood vessels in the circulatory system.

The more cigarettes a person smokes, the more likely that person is to have a heart or blood-vessel disease. But a person who stops smoking immediately begins to lower the risk of having a serious health problem. Even so, it takes years for a heavy smoker to lower the risk factor to that of a person who never smoked at all.

Key Words

anemia	donor	pulmonary artery
angina pectoris	heart attack	pulmonary vein
aorta	heart-lung	red blood cells
arteries	machine	Rh factor
arteriosclerosis	heart murmur	rheumatic fever
atherosclerosis	hemoglobin	rheumatic heart
atrium	hemophilia	disease
blood pressure	hypertension	risk factors
bone marrow	leukemia	systole
capillaries	leukocyte	throat culture
cholesterol	lymph	transport system
congenital heart	lymph nodes	valves
disease	plasma	varicose veins
coronary arteries	platelets	veins
diastole		ventricle

Main Ideas

- The heart is a pump. It keeps blood circulating through arteries, capillaries, and veins.
- The blood carries everything the body tissues need—oxygen, digested food, water, hormones, and other substances. These substances pass from the bloodstream through the lymph to the cells.
- Waste products from the cells are carried back through the lymph and the blood vessels to some of the body's organs, where they are excreted.

Continued

211

- Plasma is the liquid in the blood that carries the red and white blood cells. Red blood cells carry oxygen. White blood cells fight infection. Platelets help to clot blood.
- The heart and the blood vessels automatically increase or decrease the rate of flow of the blood. In this way, they adjust to the changing needs of the body.
- Heart disease is the leading cause of death in the United States. Certain things can be done to help reduce the chances of having a heart attack.

Understand the Reading

1. What are the main jobs of plasma, red blood cells, white blood cells, and platelets?
2. What are blood types? Why is it important to know what your blood type is?
3. Without looking at the diagram of the heart, make a sketch showing the four chambers and the valves. Use arrows to show the direction of the blood flow through the heart. From which side is the blood pumped to the lungs? From which side is it pumped to the rest of the body?
4. How do capillaries, veins, and arteries work together? In what direction does the blood flow through these vessels?
5. What are the dangers of high blood pressure?
6. Why is it important to discover high blood pressure in young adults?
7. What are some of the causes of heart disease? How can they be avoided?
8. What is rheumatic fever?
9. What happens to the arteries of a person who has arteriosclerosis?
10. Name four things you can do to decrease your chances of developing a serious circulatory problem.

Apply Your Knowledge

1. Contact the American Red Cross chapter in your community and ask about the blood-donor service. Find out who can give blood, how it is collected, how it is stored, and what use is made of it. Report your findings to the class.
2. Interview a cardiologist (a doctor who specializes in heart problems). Ask what sorts of exercises are recommended to patients who have had heart attacks. Find out what sorts of diets are prescribed. Pass your information along to the class.
3. Read about the subject of organ transplants and artificial hearts. Determine when the first work was done in these pioneering areas. Make a report of your findings to the class.

Chapter 16
Respiration

After reading this chapter, you will be able to:

☐ Describe the respiratory system and explain how it functions.

☐ Explain the difference between breathing and respiration.

☐ Explain the importance of respiration.

☐ Identify the diseases of the respiratory system and describe their symptoms.

☐ Explain how to care for the body's respiratory system.

If you had to, you could live for several days without water and for weeks without food. But you could live only a few minutes without air.

Air is a mixture of gases: about 78 percent nitrogen, 21 percent oxygen, 0.4 percent carbon dioxide, and traces of water vapor and other gases. It is the oxygen in air that is most important for humans. Without oxygen, the body cannot turn food into energy.

Oxygen is taken into the body each time you breathe. It enters your body through your nose or mouth and is carried to your cells via your *respiratory system. Respiration* is the process by which the cells of your body take in and use oxygen and give off a waste gas, carbon dioxide.

Structure of the respiratory tract

The respiratory tract consists of the air passages that move air into and out of the body and the lungs. From the lungs, oxygen is carried to the cells of the body through the bloodstream.

Upper respiratory tract

The nose is the main passage through which air enters the body. Some air also enters the body through the mouth. From these passages, air goes through the throat and enters the **trachea**, or windpipe, a long tube that extends down the neck. The walls of the trachea are made mostly of involuntary muscle and cartilage. A thin piece of cartilage, the **epiglottis**, covers the entrance to the trachea and prevents food from entering it.

In the upper part of the trachea is the **larynx**, or voice box. It is often called the Adam's apple. The vocal cords are inside the larynx. At the lungs, the trachea divides into two large branches called **bronchi**, or bronchial tubes. One tube goes to each of the two lungs.

All the body's air passages, including the nose, are lined with membranes that produce mucus, a lubricant coating secreted by the glands. These membranes are covered with small, hairlike parts called **cilia**. Mucus and cilia together screen out most of the bacteria, dust, and other harmful particles in air before the air gets to the lungs.

As air passes through the upper respiratory tract, it picks up moisture and warmth. Moist, warm, and filtered, the air is in better condition for use by the lungs.

Lungs

Inside each lung, the bronchial tube divides again and again into smaller tubes that end in tiny air sacs called **alveoli**. There are many thousands of these tiny air sacs in the spongelike lung tissue. Surrounding each

The Respiratory System

Body Part	Structure	Job
Nose	Structure on face with two holes lined with cilia	Pathway that cleans air before it reaches trachea
Epiglottis	Flap of cartilage at top of trachea	Prevents food from entering trachea
Trachea	Tube in upper chest cavity	Carries moist, clean air from nose to bronchi
Bronchi	Large tubes connecting trachea and lungs	Deliver air from trachea through smaller bronchial tubes to alveoli
Alveoli	Tiny sacs in lungs	Deliver oxygen to blood; receive carbon dioxide

air sac is a network of blood vessels. It is through these blood vessels that oxygen is picked up by the bloodstream and carbon dioxide is expelled.

The lungs hang in the **chest cavity**. This cavity is completely enclosed and airtight. The walls of the chest cavity are made of the ribs, the muscles between the ribs, and the breastbone. The floor of the chest cavity is formed by the **diaphragm**, a large sheet of muscle that separates the abdominal cavity from the chest. The inside of the chest cavity and the outside of the lungs are covered with smooth, moist membranes called the **pleura**.

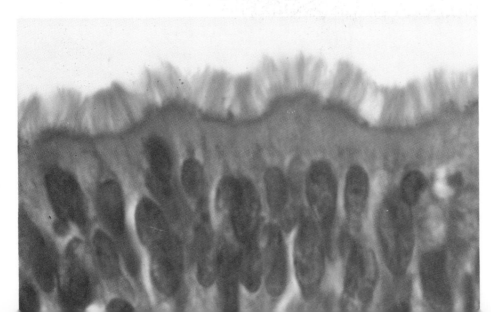

Tiny, hairlike projections called cilia prevent harmful substances from entering the lungs.

215

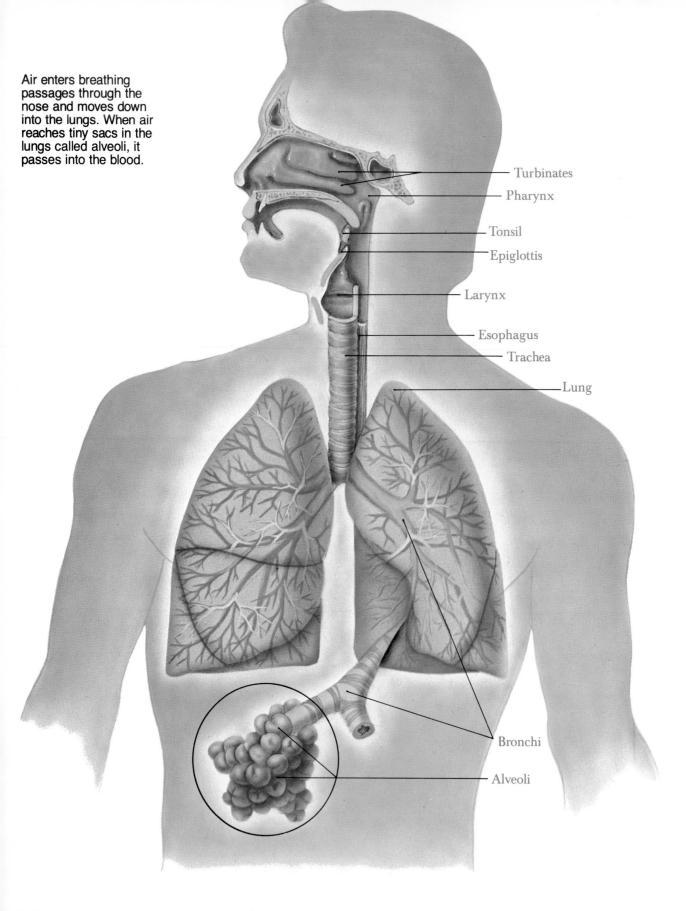

Air enters breathing passages through the nose and moves down into the lungs. When air reaches tiny sacs in the lungs called alveoli, it passes into the blood.

Turbinates

Pharynx

Tonsil

Epiglottis

Larynx

Esophagus

Trachea

Lung

Bronchi

Alveoli

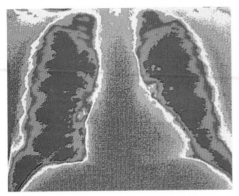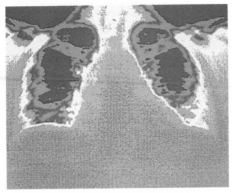

These two photographs show the same pair of lungs—fully expanded (*left*) and at rest (*right*).

Breathing

Breathing is the way you move air into and out of the lungs. Inhaling—also called **inspiration**—is the process of taking air into the lungs. Exhaling—also called **expiration**—is the process of forcing air out of the lungs. Both the chest walls and the diaphragm move in rhythmic fashion during breathing. To take air into the lungs, the muscles between the ribs lift the ribs upward and outward—away from the lungs. The diaphragm moves down. To force air out of the lungs, the ribs move downward and inward—toward the lungs. The diaphragm moves up.

During quiet, normal breathing, an adult takes in about 1 pint of air with each breath. This amount of air is only about one-eighth of what the lungs can hold. A person who runs or does hard work takes in deep breaths of air and fills more of the lungs.

Respiration

Have you ever blown on a fire to get it started? For fuel (wood, for example) to be converted to energy (heat), there must be sufficient oxygen. Likewise, for your cells to convert food into energy, there also must be oxygen. The process of producing energy from food with the help of oxygen is called **oxidation**. Oxidation takes place during cell respiration. The blood carries oxygen and food in the form of dissolved sugars to the cells. The oxygen enables the cells to oxidize the food and turn it into energy. During cell respiration, carbon dioxide is released back into the bloodstream. It is then carried to the lungs, where it is expelled through the upper respiratory tract. Respiration is complete.

Respiration is controlled mainly by a nerve center in the brain called the **respiratory center**. The respiratory center monitors how much carbon dioxide there is in the blood and regulates breathing accordingly. Suppose, for instance, you were to hold your breath. Carbon dioxide accumulates in the blood. The respiratory center senses this buildup of carbon dioxide. It sends out nerve impulses to the muscles used for breathing. These nerve impulses make you take a deep breath, whether you want to or not. Breathing then speeds up for a time until the carbon dioxide in the blood is lowered to the normal amount.

If you inhale oxygen deeply and quickly for a minute or two, you decrease the amount of carbon dioxide in the blood. Quickly exhaling too much carbon dioxide causes dizziness and even fainting. This is called **hyperventilation**. When this happens, the respiratory center sends out fewer impulses to the muscles used for breathing. This causes breathing to slow down until the level of carbon dioxide in the blood returns to normal.

Changes in breathing

An adult at rest breathes 15 to 20 times per minute. Children breathe faster. Exercise and some illnesses make a person breathe more quickly than usual, although other illnesses slow down breathing. People breathe in many different ways at different times. Talking, for example, requires many changes in breathing. And when you laugh or cry, you inhale deeply and exhale with many short breaths.

Yawning is inhaling deeply with the mouth wide open. Did you know that you may yawn even when you are not tired? Yawning is sometimes the lungs' way of taking in more needed air. For example, when you are in a hot, stuffy room with little air, you may not inhale enough oxygen by breathing normally. This causes the carbon dioxide in your blood to build up. To get rid of this waste, the respiratory center may signal the body to inhale deeply by yawning.

Breathing dust or bits of food into the trachea makes you cough and sneeze to blow them out. Since sneezes usually get rid of unwanted matter, they should never be blocked. Stopping a sneeze could cause

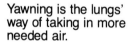
Yawning is the lungs' way of taking in more needed air.

nosebleed, ringing in the ears, and even sinus trouble. Instead, cover your mouth and nose loosely with a handkerchief when you feel a sneeze coming on.

Hiccupping is caused by jerky movements of the diaphragm that end with a click caused by the sudden closing of the vocal cords. You can usually control hiccups by holding your breath, by sipping water, or by trying hard to breathe slowly and regularly.

All of these kinds of breathing changes are very small. They are reactions to many different causes: to smoke, dust, and gas in the air you breathe; to the amount of oxygen and carbon dioxide in your blood and muscles; and to the way you feel. You have very little control over these changes in breathing. But your body's ability to breathe to fit your needs and feelings is an example of how your body works as a unit—a total organism.

Air pressure and oxygen

At sea level, air pushes down with a pressure of about 15 pounds per square inch. The higher you go above sea level, the thinner the air, the lower the air pressure, and the less oxygen in the air. Lowered amounts of oxygen in the air affect people. At 10,000 feet above sea level, many people feel light-headed and dizzy from the lack of oxygen. However, the human body can get used to small changes in the oxygen supply. Breathing speeds up for a time to increase the intake of oxygen, and the heart beats faster than normal. The number of red blood cells also increases so that more oxygen can be carried. This adjustment occurs over a period of several weeks. People who live at high altitudes become permanently used to having less oxygen in the air.

Athletes who are used to sea-level air pressure cannot compete at high altitudes without giving their bodies the time to adjust to the change. A team that is not used to high altitudes sometimes arrives at its destination a week early to give the players' bodies time to make extra red blood cells.

Many airplanes fly at heights where there is not enough oxygen for human needs. For this reason, most airplanes are pressurized. This means that their cabins are airtight and that air is pumped in to keep the level of air pressure higher than it really is outside the plane. Extra tanks of oxygen are carried on airplanes in case there is a sudden loss of cabin air pressure.

Underwater divers may get air through hoses kept on the water's surface, or they may carry air tanks on their backs. Carrying tanks with them lets them swim freely over a wider area. The tanks may hold compressed air. In special cases, they may carry oxygen mixed with other gases. Such a tank, together with its needed parts, is called a *scuba* (the word stands for *s*elf-*c*ontained *u*nderwater *b*reathing *a*pparatus). Air is usually exhaled directly into the water. This is why you see bubbles rising in pictures of scuba divers.

Divers must return to the surface slowly to prevent the nitrogen gas in their tanks from forming bubbles in their blood.

Air-pressure changes

The human body adjusts easily to small changes in air pressure. However, some precautions must be taken when a person goes to an area where the air pressure is very different from normal air pressure. People building tunnels deep underwater often work in caissons. Caissons are large, watertight chambers in which the air pressure is kept very high. The air pressure inside the caisson equals the pressure of the water outside. It is important to keep the air pressure high to prevent water from rushing into the caisson. Before going into the caisson, workers must spend some time in another chamber called an air lock. In this chamber, the air pressure first equals that at sea level. Then it gets higher at small intervals until it is equal to the pressure of the caisson in which the people will be working. After this slow adjustment, the workers may safely enter the caisson. When they leave the caisson, the workers must pass through the air lock again, where the process is reversed. The air pressure is slowly lowered from the high pressure of the caisson to sea-level pressure.

A large and quick change in air pressure affects the body. When a person goes into a high-pressure area, the higher pressure forces more air into the person's lungs. Nitrogen, a gas in air that is usually not absorbed by the lungs, is forced into the blood by the added pressure. This causes no problem as long as the person stays in the high-pressure area. But if the person returns to a lower-pressure area without letting the body adjust to the change, she or he may have problems. The nitrogen forms bubbles in the blood, which can block some of the small blood vessels and cause painful muscle cramps, dizziness, and nausea. These are symptoms of the **bends**, or caisson disease. In very serious cases, paralysis and death may result. Slow **decompression** can keep people from getting the bends. Decompression involves returning to the low-pressure area slowly to give the nitrogen time to pass out of the blood without forming bubbles. The nitrogen then goes back into the lungs and out of the body.

220

As they take in air, the lungs and air passages are constantly bombarded with bacteria, viruses, and irritating particles. Cilia and mucus protect the lining of the upper air passages against intrusions. Coughing also helps rid the respiratory system of irritating substances. But illnesses of the upper respiratory tract occur easily, especially during the winter months.

Bronchitis

Acute **bronchitis** is swelling of the bronchi. It often comes with a viral infection and may last as long as 2 weeks. Chronic bronchitis may be the result of an infection that lasts a long time. It may also result from long-term exposure to irritants, including cigarette smoking. Coughing is the main symptom of bronchitis.

Emphysema

Coughing, breathing difficulties, and a fast heartbeat are symptoms of **emphysema**. The alveoli lose their elasticity. They first become enlarged and later are permanently destroyed. Waste air full of carbon dioxide cannot be expelled from the lungs to let in fresh air. Less oxygen is then available for the blood. The heart and lungs work double time trying to keep a normal supply of oxygen in the blood.

As a crippling disability, emphysema ranks second only to heart disease. In recent years, deaths from emphysema have increased even more rapidly than those from lung cancer. Tobacco smoking seems to be the chief factor contributing to emphysema. Air pollution, asthma, and infections and irritations of the lungs are also thought to be likely causes. Infections sometimes move into the lungs when bronchitis, asthma, and sinus infections are left untreated.

To treat emphysema, ways must be found to let air pass into and out of the lungs. Some people learn to use their extra lung capacity. Oxygen or oxygen mixed with compressed air may be given to some patients. Reducing or removing the mucus that forms in the bronchial tubes may give relief.

Pleurisy

Sometimes infection or injury makes the pleura rough and sticky. This condition is called **pleurisy,** and it makes breathing difficult and painful.

Asthma

Asthma is a disease of the lungs that makes breathing difficult. In asthma, inflammation from white blood cells and a buildup of fluid cause the mucous membranes of the bronchi to swell. This swelling narrows the openings of the tubes. The muscles of the walls of the bronchi contract, making the air passages even narrower. Thus, air that has been breathed into the lungs is trapped. Untreated, asthma may develop into emphysema.

Asthma has many causes. About 15 percent of asthma cases are due to allergies to something in the environment. Dust, molds, pollen, feathers, and certain foods are the most common substances that may cause an allergy. A doctor may use skin or blood tests to find out which substances are the cause. Other causes of asthma are infections, exposure to cold air, and irritants in the air. Asthma can be a very serious illness. Treatment should be under a doctor's care. Using too many home cures or over-the-counter medicines may be harmful.

Pneumonia

Pneumonia is an infection of the lung tissue. The infection may cause fluid to build up in the lungs so that breathing becomes difficult. Cough and fever are the main symptoms of pneumonia. By listening to a person's chest or by taking a chest X ray, a doctor can tell if a person has pneumonia. The treatment given depends on the kind of infection the person has. Antibiotics are often needed, along with rest and plenty of liquids.

Scientists are always looking for ways to cure pneumonia. In 1977, a vaccine for one type of pneumonia was developed. It is currently being used with elderly people, who suffer the greatest number of deaths from this disease.

Care of the respiratory system

It is important to keep the respiratory tract warm and moist. During the winter months, the air may be very cold. It is not healthy to expose the air passages to very cold air for too long a time. Sometimes the air you breathe may be too dry. Adding moisture to the air of a room with a humidifier may be helpful, although there is disagreement among experts as to whether humidifiers actually provide any benefit.

Industrial gases, smoke, and certain fumes may be very irritating to the upper respiratory tract. Such irritants can cause harm to the mucous membranes and cilia. Asbestos and coal dust may cause lung disease if exposure continues for many years. Try to keep away from polluted air whenever possible.

Cigarette smoking does more harm to the respiratory systems of more people than all the other irritating substances put together. Cancer of the lungs and larynx, chronic bronchitis, and emphysema are all linked to cigarette smoking. The harmful substances in cigarette smoke may destroy the cilia, the mucous lining, and the bronchi. Then there is little to safeguard the person against respiratory infection.

Although not everyone who smokes gets lung cancer, many victims

would never have gotten the disease if they had not smoked. In spite of the many warnings that cigarette smoking is harmful to health, some people continue to damage their respiratory systems through this habit.

Key Words

alveoli	diaphragm	oxidation
asthma	emphysema	pleura
bends	epiglottis	pleurisy
bronchi	expiration	pneumonia
bronchitis	hyperventilation	respiration
chest cavity	inspiration	respiratory center
cilia	larynx	respiratory system
decompression		trachea

Main Ideas

- The intake of oxygen and the release of carbon dioxide by the body are processes needed for life.
- The respiratory tract consists of the air passages and the lungs.
- Breathing is the process of taking air into the lungs and expelling carbon dioxide out of them.
- Respiration is more than breathing. It is what your cells do when they take in oxygen from the blood and expel carbon dioxide back into the blood.
- Breathing adjusts automatically, depending upon the need for oxygen.
- There are many diseases of the respiratory tract. Cigarette smoking is a key factor in many of these diseases.

Understand the Reading

1. How does the body use oxygen?
2. Trace the passage of air from the nose to the alveoli. How is the air cleaned?
3. Enumerate some of the differences between breathing and respiration.
4. What muscles do we use in breathing?
5. How is breathing controlled? Why can you hold your breath for only a few moments?
6. What causes hiccupping, yawning, and coughing?
7. What happens to air pressure the higher you go above sea level? How does a person's body adjust to living at a high altitude?
8. What is bronchitis?
9. What is emphysema?
10. What are common causes of asthma? Why does a person who has asthma find it hard to breathe?

Apply Your Knowledge

1. Ask a librarian to help you obtain journal, newspaper, or magazine articles on the special systems that have been used to provide oxygen for space travelers and for people who live underwater for days or for weeks. Write a report for class based on your research.
2. Ask a teacher or physician to come to your class and demonstrate the use of a spirometer. Have several students volunteer to test their breathing before and after they have undergone physical exertion. The remaining students should write their predictions in advance of the experiment. Compare the predictions of the students with the actual results of the experiment. In a class discussion, try to arrive at an understanding of why the predictions might have differed from the test results.
3. Obtain the lungs of a sheep or pig from a local meat market. Have your teacher assist you in obtaining permission from the school to carry out an experiment in one of the biology labs. Wearing rubber gloves and a rubber lab apron, find the animal's trachea and bronchi. Insert a glass tube into the trachea and attempt to inflate the lungs. Describe how the lungs feel. Based on your reading of the chapter, attempt to explain why they feel as they do.
4. Obtain a copy of one of several books that have recently been published outlining new approaches to chronic breathing diseases. (One such book, which appeared in 1985, was actor Paul Sorvino's book on breathing exercises for asthmatics.) Write a report on the book.

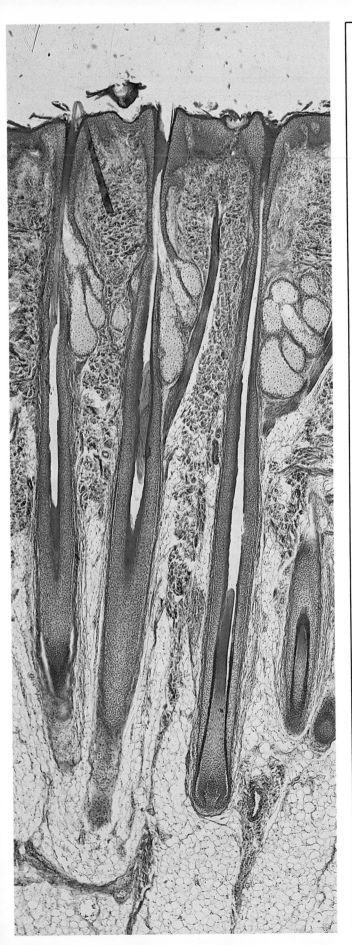

Chapter 17
Skin and Hair

After reading this chapter, you will be able to:

☐ Describe the structure of the skin.
☐ Explain the skin's function.
☐ Describe the makeup of hair and nails and explain how they grow.
☐ Identify the major skin problems.
☐ Explain how to treat the major skin problems.
☐ Explain how to care for the skin and the hair.

You know that the heart and the lungs are organs of the body. You may not know that the skin, too, is a body organ, the body's largest. Skin covers about 17 square feet of body surface in adults. It has a complex structure and many important functions.

Skin structure

The skin has two main layers. The **epidermis** is the outer layer of the skin, and the **dermis** is the under layer of skin. The dermis gives the skin its strength and elasticity, or ability to stretch.

Epidermis

The epidermis is a thin layer of cells. Along the inner surface of the epidermis, new cells grow and push the older cells to the outer surface of the skin. The skin cells that reach the surface are no longer alive. Millions of these cells are rubbed off onto clothing and towels each day. New cells replace the dead cells and constantly make a new outer covering. The thickest epidermis is on the soles of the feet. The thinnest epidermis is on the eyelids.

The inner portion of the epidermis contains cells that produce a skin coloring called **pigment**. Tanning of the skin is caused by the increased production of pigment that is triggered by the sun. **Pores** are tiny openings in the epidermis that lead to sweat and oil glands in the dermis.

Dermis

The dermis is a network of connective tissue and fatty tissue. It is thicker than the epidermis. The dermis contains blood vessels, nerves, and glands. The sweat glands, oil glands, and hair roots are in the dermis.

Functions of the skin

Your skin performs many functions for you throughout the day. It protects you, keeps you warm, tells you about your environment through touch, and helps you express your feelings to others.

Protection

The skin's most important function is to serve as a watertight container. Everything inside the body is wet—or at least moist. The skin prevents the air around you from drying up the body's tissues and fluids. The skin is the body's main defense against the entry of disease organisms. An infection usually cannot get started unless there is a break in the skin. As long as the skin is clean, it quickly gets rid of infectious

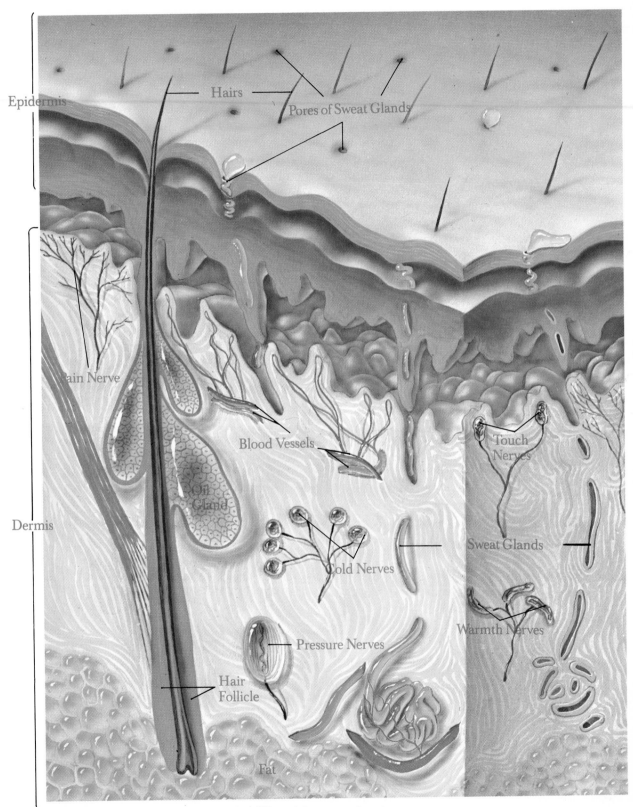

Epidermis

Dermis

Hairs

Pores of Sweat Glands

Pain Nerve

Blood Vessels

Touch Nerves

Oil Gland

Cold Nerves

Sweat Glands

Pressure Nerves

Warmth Nerves

Hair Follicle

Fat

This cross section of skin shows the different layers and parts.

organisms that may touch its surface. The skin also acts as a cushion for bumps and a covering for delicate inner tissue.

A suntan is the skin's way of protecting the body, too. The skin releases pigment to protect against injury from too much sunlight. The pigment that is made in the inner layers of the epidermis is called **melanin**. Melanin acts as a protection against the ultraviolet rays of the sun. It gives color to the hair, skin, and eyes. Some people have **freckles**. Freckles are small areas of the skin with many cells that produce melanin when exposed to the sun. Dark-skinned people have more melanin in their skin than light-skinned people do. People who have no melanin in their skin at all are called **albinos**. Albinos are very rare. It is not safe for them to be in the sunlight for long periods of time.

A **mole** is a growth in the pigmented layer of the skin. Moles may be found anywhere on the body's surface. Usually they appear during the early years of life. Most moles are harmless. But some types of moles may develop into cancer. If a mole grows, changes color, or is constantly irritated, see a doctor. If the cells that produce melanin begin to grow rapidly and in an abnormal pattern, a tumor called a **malignant melanoma** may develop. This is a rare type of cancer that usually can be treated if discovered early.

Regulating body temperature

The skin plays a role in regulating the body's temperature. The dermis contains a large amount of fat (adipose) tissue, which acts as insulation to help contain body heat. In addition, the dermis contains many tiny blood vessels. These serve to hold heat in or let it out of the body. For instance, when the body begins to heat up from exercise or outside temperatures, the flow of blood increases in the blood vessels. Heat that has been carried by the blood to the surface of the body can escape through the skin. Redness of the skin, especially on the face, is a sign that heat has been carried by the blood to the skin.

When outside temperatures are cold, the blood vessels in the skin contract. Less blood can flow through the blood vessels, and less body heat can escape.

The pores in the skin also help to control body heat. As the body heats up, the pores release perspiration. Perspiration comes from the 2 to 3 million sweat glands in the human body. On a hot summer day, about 2 to 3 quarts of perspiration must be released through the pores to keep the body from overheating. Perspiration is made up of water, salt, and body wastes. The water evaporates from the skin's surface. This evaporation helps the body cool down.

Sensation

You receive information about the environment from a network of nerve endings in the dermis. The sense of touch helps you to know the

Perspiration is released through pores in the skin.

Learning what causes skin problems will help to avoid them.

texture, shape, and weight of objects. Pain, cold, and warmth are sensations that warn against possible dangers that might occur.

Expression

Your skin offers clues about how you are feeling. The look on your face will often tell others if you are angry or happy. Excess sweating on the forehead and palms may show that you are worried or nervous. Blushing of the skin may show that you are embarrassed. Well-cared-for skin, hair, and nails are often evidence of a healthy person who cares about personal appearance.

Skin problems

Skin problems, even small ones, may cause unneeded discomfort and worry. It is often easy to prevent these problems if you understand what causes them.

Contact dermatitis

Certain substances may irritate the skin and cause **dermatitis**, or inflammation of the skin. The redness and blisters on the skin that develop after contact with one of these substances are symptoms of contact dermatitis. Several plants, such as poison ivy, poison oak, and poison sumac, cause contact dermatitis in many people. The oils on such plants irritate the skin of people who are sensitive to them. This may happen either through direct contact with the plant or by touching something that has touched the plant, such as a ball or a dog. People sensitive to these plants should learn to recognize and avoid them.

Allergic dermatitis

Hives are small lumps on the skin that look like insect bites. In serious cases of hives, the lips, eyelids, hands, and other parts of the body may

Is there a "perfect" tan? Whether you get your tan under the sun or under a sunlamp, there is no perfect (safe) tan. It is tempting to believe that once you have a tan, your skin is safe from the burning rays of the sun. Though the skin does try to protect itself by producing melanin, the resulting change in skin color can block out only 50 percent of the sun's ultraviolet rays.

If you try to tan too quickly, your skin may be injured and become red or blistered. Overexposure to the sun may cause a serious burn that needs medical treatment. Frequent overexposure can age the skin and lead to cancer. This is true of exposure to the so-called "safe" sunlamps used by tanning parlors, as well as exposure to the sun.

In short, spending time under the "rays" is unwise. If you do decide to get a suntan, it is important to limit your exposure at first. Then, slowly increase the time spent in the sunlight. Try a brief exposure of 20 minutes the first day. Add a few minutes each day, and let the suntan develop over 2 to 3 weeks. This gives the skin time to produce the melanin needed to protect the skin and develop a tan.

Some people, especially those with fair skin, may be more sensitive to sunlight than others. If you do not tan easily and your skin is sun-sensitive, you should stay out of the sun as much as possible and use a strong sunscreen when you are exposed to the sun. The harmful ultraviolet rays in sunlight are strongest at noon. So you should avoid that "peak-burning" time. Severe sunburn is less likely before 10 A.M. and after 2 P.M. (standard time).

Sunscreens are substances that are put on the skin to protect it from the sun's rays. Sunscreens are applied about 15 minutes before going into the sun. They have no effect when used after sunbathing. The best commercial sunscreen preparations contain PABA (para-aminobenzoic acid) or forms of this substance.

Suntan lotions can be helpful in getting a tan and in keeping the skin moist during tanning. But suntan lotions do not protect the skin from the sun. Certainly they will have little or no bearing on the damage the sun will do to the skin over the long run.

swell. Itching is usually severe. Hives may be caused by a reaction to some substance the body is allergic to. Some people are sensitive to certain pollens, chemicals, drugs, or foods. To prevent hives, a person should find out what causes this allergic reaction and should avoid the substance. Treatment with medication prescribed by a doctor usually gives relief.

Fungal infections

Ringworm and **athlete's foot** are common skin infections. Both are caused by a **fungus.** A fungus is a form of plant life that lives best in dark, warm, moist areas. Ringworm (*Tinea capitis*) causes itching and sores of the scalp. These sores tend to heal in the center and to spread outward. The ringlike appearance gives this infection its name. It is not really caused by a worm at all. Ringworm is very hard to treat at home. If you suspect you have ringworm, you should see a doctor.

Athlete's foot (*Tinea pedis*) usually begins with a slight itching, redness, and cracking of the skin between the toes. People often pick up the infection in shower rooms or on swimming-pool decks. The term "athlete's foot" is not really correct. Many people who are not athletes get this disease.

To prevent athlete's foot, wash the feet carefully with soap. It is very important to wash between the toes and to dry the feet thoroughly. Always use your own towel. Avoid footwear that causes your feet to perspire. If you think you have athlete's foot, you should see a doctor for proper diagnosis and treatment.

Boils

Boils are skin infections that often begin in a hair root. An area of swelling and redness with a center of pus may be seen on the skin's surface. The bacteria that cause this infection may spread to other people. For this reason, people with boils should not prepare or serve food. Boils should not be squeezed or pinched. This may cause the infection to spread to other parts of the body. A boil may become a serious infection and should be treated by a doctor. (A carbuncle is a number of boils that are close together. A sty is a small boil on the eyelid.)

Impetigo

Impetigo is a skin infection caused by bacteria. Symptoms include thickly crusted sores. The disease is extremely contagious among infants and small children. To treat the disease, doctors usually suggest cleansing the skin with soap and water and then applying a medicated ointment. Sometimes antibiotics are also necessary.

Acne

Acne is most often a skin infection caused by an oily secretion called **sebum.** Sebum provides an ideal growing place for bacteria.

When a pore becomes clogged, it appears as a blackhead. If bacteria enter the clogged pore, a yellow-white core, or pimple, develops. Do not squeeze blackheads and pimples. The infection may be forced inward. Squeezing may also cause permanent damage to the skin surface.

Poison ivy (*top*), poison oak (*middle*), and poison sumac (*bottom*) are three plants that cause contact dermatitis.

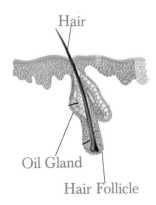

Hair

Oil Gland

Hair Follicle

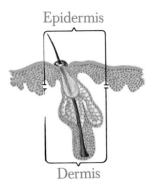

Epidermis

Dermis

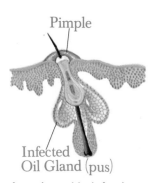

Pimple

Infected
Oil Gland (pus)

Acne is a skin infection caused by bacteria that enter the blocked pores. To prevent acne, wash often with soap and water and eat a well-balanced diet.

Acne is not considered a dietary disease. But some doctors tell their patients not to eat fats, fried foods, chocolate, and candy. Reactions to foods vary with different people. If you find that certain foods cause skin blemishes to appear, don't eat those foods for a while. Substitute another food from that basic food group. Eating from the four basic food groups is necessary for good health. And good health is needed for clear skin.

To prevent acne and preserve a healthy complexion, follow the skin-care rules below. If your skin does not clear up after you follow these suggestions for a few weeks, see your doctor. The doctor may decide to treat your acne with antibiotics.

1. Wash the affected area of the skin with soap and warm water every morning and night. Also wash in the afternoon after school. Dry the skin with a towel. This helps to remove the dead cells and some of the excess oils from the pores.
2. Avoid greasy creams and oily preparations. There is already too much oil on the skin.
3. Eat a well-balanced diet. Avoid any foods that seem to make acne worse.
4. Get enough rest and exercise.
5. Keep your hands away from your face.

Acne often improves during the summer months. This is due to the drying action of sunlight that prevents the buildup of oily material in the pores. For this reason, limited exposure to sunlight may be very helpful for some people.

Scabies and pediculosis

Scabies is an infection of the skin caused by tiny mites that burrow into the skin. Scabies occurs most often in the spaces between the fingers; in the elbows, wrists, and armpits; along the belt line; around the breasts; in the genital region; and on the buttocks. The mites release waste products that cause the skin to blister and to itch considerably.

Scabies can be acquired through contact with an infected person. It can also be picked up from bedding, clothing, or towels that have been used by an infected person.

Pediculosis is a skin disorder caused by various species of lice. Pediculosis usually causes itching.

Head lice infest the hairs of the head. Body lice infest the hairs of the body. Crab lice, or pubic lice, usually infest the pubic hairs, but can also be found in the hairs under the arms or even in a mustache.

232

Like mites, lice are acquired through contact with an infected person. To keep from getting lice, avoid borrowing or sharing clothes and such personal items as hairbrushes. During the course of its life, a female may lay hundreds of oval eggs, called nits, which are deposited on human hair.

To treat pediculosis, both lice and nits must be killed. Your doctor can recommend shampoos or ointments that will do the job. Nits can be removed from the hair with special combs. To prevent reinfestation of mites or lice, it is important that all clothing, towels, and bedding be washed in hot water and detergent.

Good hygiene helps prevent head lice (here greatly magnified).

The hair and nails

Hair and nails are outgrowths of the epidermis layer of the skin. Each hair grows from a hair root in the dermis. It grows through a hair **follicle** (the tissue around the hair) to become a hair on the skin. Living cells in the follicle push upward as they grow together and harden to form a surface hair. The hair above the skin's surface is made up of layers of dead cells that contain protein. The amount of pigment in these cells determines the color of the hair. As a person becomes older, the amount of pigment decreases. The hair may turn gray and then white.

The nails grow out of the skin beneath them and out of the **cuticle**. The cuticle is the nonliving epidermis that surrounds the edges of fingernails and toenails. When your hair and nails are cut, you do not feel any pain. That is because the hair and nails do not contain nerve endings. But pulling the hair and nails does cause pain. This is because the force of the pull reaches into the dermis, where the nerve endings are located.

Care of the hair

Healthy hair improves your personal appearance. Anyone can have healthy hair by taking care of it regularly.

Brushing

Brushing the hair increases the circulation in the scalp and decreases the buildup of dirt. It also spreads the hair's natural oil evenly through the hairs. The oil makes the hair soft and glossy. Brushing the hair once or twice daily is usually enough. Brushing too often may cause hair loss because hair is slowly pulled and lifted from its roots.

Shampooing

You should wash your hair at least once each week with shampoo to keep the scalp and hair clean. If your hair is oily or you have dandruff, you might want to wash it every day.

Regular shampooing helps control dandruff.

Dandruff

Ordinary dandruff is made up of dead cells. These come off the scalp in the same way that cells come off the epidermis all over your body. Sometimes the scalp is too oily. The oil causes the dead cells to clump together and become noticeable. Regular shampooing and brushing usually prevent dandruff. But sometimes a special shampoo may be needed. If most of the dandruff does not disappear with good hair care, see your doctor for treatment. Dandruff can be one cause of hair loss.

Hairdressings and sprays

Hairdressings and sprays may help keep hair in place. But if you use them, wash your hair frequently. These substances tend to build up in the hair. Dirt may also cling to them. If you use these preparations often, you should wash your hair periodically with a shampoo that helps clean the hair of such commercial additives.

Some people are allergic to hair sprays. They wheeze and cough when using them. If this happens to you, do not use hair spray.

Hair coloring

There are different ways to change the color of hair. One way is to add color with dyes, which darken the natural color of the hair. Another way is to "strip," or bleach, the hair's natural color. Depending on how much color-removing chemical is used, the hair may be lightly or completely bleached. After bleaching, a new color is sometimes added. A natural brunet, for example, may become a blond after stripping hair color and then adding blonding chemicals.

Hair bleaches and dyes are harmful to some people. Some scientists think that frequent use of dyes may cause cancer. Care should be taken before any such process is used. Always test for an allergic reaction first.

Key Words

acne	follicle	melanin
albinos	freckles	mole
athlete's foot	fungus	pediculosis
boils	hives	pigment
cuticle	impetigo	pores
dermatitis	malignant	ringworm
dermis	melanoma	scabies
epidermis		sebum

- The epidermis and the dermis are the two main layers of the skin.
- The skin keeps the body moist, protects the body, helps to control body temperature, and serves as an organ of sensation and expression.
- To function properly, the skin needs to be kept clean. Proper care can prevent many skin problems.
- Hair and nails grow from the upper layer of the skin. Proper care keeps hair healthy.
- There are two types of dermatitis, contact dermatitis and allergic dermatitis. Both cause the skin to break out in a rash and to become inflamed.
- Overexposure to the sun can age the skin and lead to cancer.
- Care of hair and nails improves your appearance.

1. How is the dermis different from the epidermis?
2. What are the four general functions of the skin?
3. When are moles harmful?
4. How does the process of perspiration help regulate body temperature?
5. Give some examples of contact dermatitis.
6. Why is it important to limit exposure to the sun?
7. How can athlete's foot be prevented?
8. How do pimples and blackheads form? Describe what can be done to help prevent the development of acne.
9. What determines the color of the hair? Why do some older people have gray hair?
10. Why don't you feel pain when your hair and nails are cut?

1. With the help of a librarian, locate reports in health magazines on the hair-transplant controversy. Determine the reasons men have given for choosing transplants to replace lost hair and the benefits and dangers of different transplant procedures. If you are able, locate some photographs showing some of the damage these procedures have done. Report your findings to the class.
2. Invite a dermatologist to speak to your class. Each student should prepare at least three questions to ask the specialist. Possible subjects include the following: foods to avoid, foods to eat, use of prescription acne-clearing preparations versus over-the-counter preparations, and why teenagers are more likely than preadolescents or adults to develop acne.

Chapter 18

Healthy Teeth

After reading this chapter, you will be able to:

- ☐ Identify the main parts of the tooth.
- ☐ Identify the kinds of teeth and explain their functions.
- ☐ Describe the sequence of tooth development.
- ☐ Identify the causes of tooth decay and other dental problems.
- ☐ Explain how to maintain healthy teeth and gums.

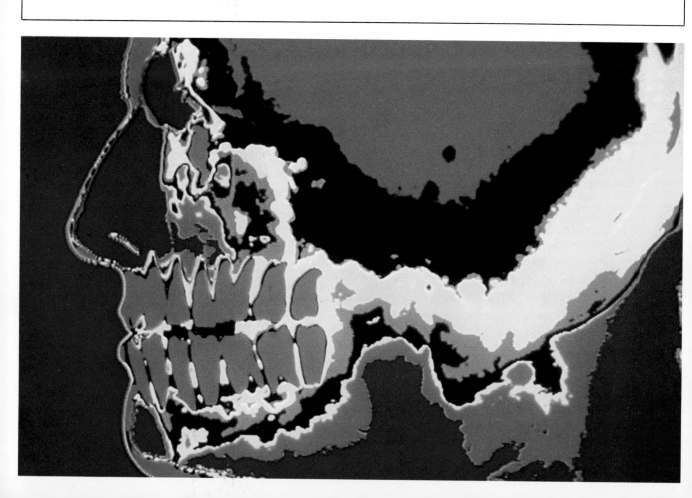

How many times have you heard comments like these? "He has a nice smile." "Her smile is her best feature."

Such comments usually mean a person has a fine set of teeth. Healthy, gleaming teeth do a lot to brighten a person's face and make that person attractive.

Teeth are, of course, an important part of our looks. They are also important to the overall health of our bodies. It is important, therefore, that you begin and continue to practice good dental hygiene.

The teeth

The teeth are powerful tools for cutting, tearing, crushing, and grinding food. Teeth help to prepare food for digestion. They break up solid food so that digestive juices can mix with it easily. The first of these digestive juices is the saliva in the mouth. Saliva adds fluid to food and begins the digestion of starches. When you chew food thoroughly, saliva can act upon it more effectively. So thorough chewing is important for good digestion.

Structure

Each tooth is made up of three parts. The **crown** is the part that can be seen outside the gums. The **neck** is the thinner part of the tooth that is surrounded by the gums. The **roots** are firmly planted in the jawbone.

The inside of each tooth is made up mainly of a type of bone tissue called **dentin**. The dentin in the crown of a tooth is covered by a layer

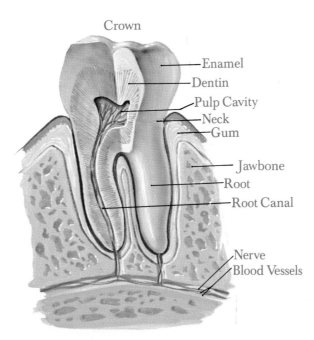

Crown

— Enamel
— Dentin
— Pulp Cavity
— Neck
— Gum
— Jawbone
— Root
— Root Canal
— Nerve
— Blood Vessels

These are the parts and position of a tooth. Teeth are alive. Cell activity in the teeth, gums, and jawbone goes on all the time.

of hard **enamel**. Enamel is the hardest substance that the body makes. Within the dentin of the tooth is the **pulp cavity**. This cavity holds nerves, blood vessels, and lymph vessels. These nerves and vessels enter the tooth through the root canal that goes from the tip of the root to the pulp cavity.

Except for the enamel, the teeth are alive. Chewing causes blood to circulate in the gums and teeth. **Cell metabolism**—the chemical change that occurs in cells to support life—is going on all the time in the teeth, gums, and jawbone.

Different functions

Most people have 32 teeth, 16 in the upper jaw and 16 in the lower jaw. The names of the different teeth describe what the teeth do. The 8 sharp teeth in front are called **incisors**. They cut, or incise, food. Next to the incisors are the 4 **cuspids**, or canines. These fanglike teeth are used for tearing food. Behind the cuspids are the 8 **premolars** and the 12 **molars** (from the Latin word for "millstone"). These teeth crush and grind food.

While most people have the 32 teeth described above, some have fewer than the usual number. And some have more.

Development

During a lifetime, people have two sets of teeth. The first set is called **primary teeth**, or "baby teeth." The second set is called **permanent teeth**. When a baby is born, all the primary teeth and some of the permanent teeth are already formed in the jawbones. There are 20 primary teeth, 10 in the lower jaw and 10 in the upper jaw.

When a child is about 6 years old, the permanent teeth begin to push through the gums. The first permanent teeth to appear are the first four molars. When the child is about 12, the second four molars push up behind the first molars.

The third and final set of four molars is called the wisdom teeth. They usually come in after the age of 16. Sometimes the wisdom teeth come in at the wrong angle and press against the second molars. They are then called "impacted" wisdom teeth. If this happens, the impacted wisdom teeth may have to be removed. A dentist may extract, or pull out, the problem teeth after giving the patient a local **anesthetic**, such as novocaine. A local anesthetic temporarily deadens the nerves in the tooth and surrounding gum so that the patient will not feel pain. Sometimes, though, it is necessary for a dental surgeon to cut through gum tissue to remove impacted wisdom teeth. In such a case, a patient may be given a general anesthetic to put her or him to sleep during the extraction.

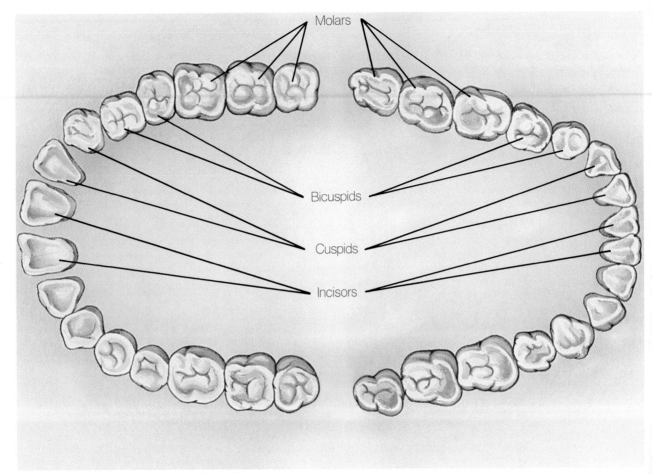

The various types of teeth are shown here.

As the primary teeth come in, a child should be taught to brush them. Visits to the dentist should start early, at the age of 3 or 4. Not taking care of the primary teeth may cause dental problems for the child later on. An infection at the roots of the primary teeth may affect the permanent teeth below them. If a primary tooth decays so badly that it has to be removed, the space may close up before the permanent tooth comes in. This often causes crowded, irregular, or crooked permanent teeth.

Care of the teeth

Diet

To build good teeth and to keep them strong and healthy, the body needs foods with vitamin D and the minerals calcium and phosphorus. Foods with a great deal of sugar—candy, cake, cookies, pies, and sweet drinks—add to tooth decay. People who eat many sugar-rich foods often have more tooth decay than those who eat fewer of these foods. Bacteria

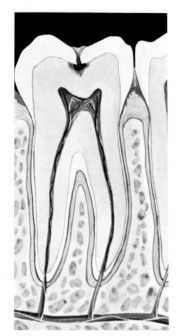
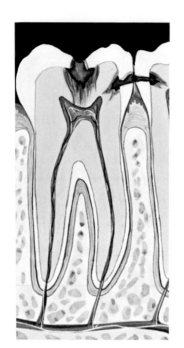
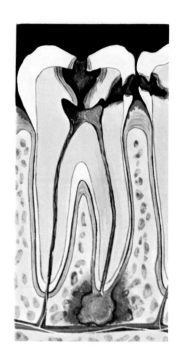

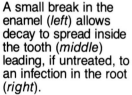
A small break in the enamel (*left*) allows decay to spread inside the tooth (*middle*) leading, if untreated, to an infection in the root (*right*).

in the mouth mix with the sugar. This forms an acid that may dissolve the hard enamel covering the tooth and start internal tooth decay. Most damage is done within 20 minutes after having sweet foods or drinks. So for snacks between meals, it is better to have such foods as raw fruits, celery, carrot sticks, and unsweetened drinks or milk.

Fluorides

Some years ago, researchers found that there was less tooth decay in communities where **fluorides** were found naturally in the drinking-water supply. Since then, adding the chemical sodium fluoride to drinking water has lowered the average amount of tooth decay by about 60 percent. Fluorides seem to make tooth enamel harder and better able to resist decay.

If your water supply is fluoridated, you probably have enough fluoride for strong, healthy teeth. If you are not sure about fluoridation in your community, ask your dentist. If your water is not fluoridated, your dentist may use a fluoride solution on your teeth or may suggest that you take fluoride tablets or drops at home. Fluorides in toothpaste may also be helpful. Toothpastes containing fluorides that have been proven effective carry the seal of the American Dental Association.

Cleaning the teeth

Plaque is a sticky, colorless layer of bacteria that forms constantly in the mouth. When plaque interacts with sugar, it produces acid. Acid dissolves the enamel, producing tooth decay. It is important to remove plaque in order to prevent dental disease. Teeth should be brushed after each meal and at bedtime. Use a brush that has a flat brushing surface and soft bristles with rounded ends. Hold the brush at an angle against the gum line, where the plaque forms. Move it back and forth, using a gentle, scrubbing motion. Remember to brush all the surfaces of the teeth—inner and outer. Replace your toothbrush when it begins to show signs of wear.

Dental floss, a special waxed or unwaxed thread, is also very helpful in fighting tooth decay. Dental floss can reach particles a toothbrush cannot get to. It can remove the plaque that is located in the spaces between the teeth and at the gum lines. The correct way to use dental floss can be learned with a little practice. For the floss to be effective, it must be used in the right way.

If you cannot brush your teeth after a meal, rinse your mouth thoroughly with water. This may help to remove food particles.

Visits to the dentist

In addition to cleaning your teeth at home, it is wise to visit your dentist about once every 6 months. If you do this, dental problems can be treated before they become serious.

The dentist carefully cleans and examines the teeth and gums. The teeth and gums should be x-rayed to find small cavities, root abscesses, or other hidden problems. If cavities are found, the dentist first removes any decay by drilling it out. This prevents the decay from spreading down into the pulp of the tooth. Then the dentist inserts a filling into

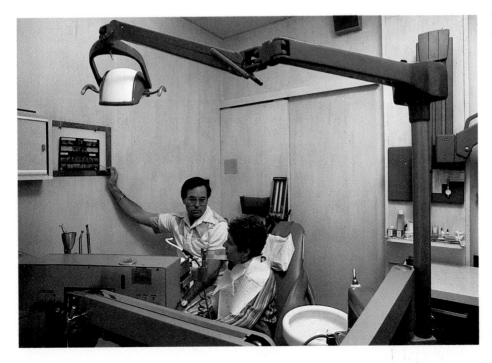

You should see your dentist every 6 months.

It used to be that braces to straighten crooked or protruding teeth were a treatment endured mostly by teenagers. However, with recent improvements in metal braces and the development of plastic and so-called invisible braces, more and more adults are using them. It is no longer necessary to encircle teeth with an array of metal wires—metal braces are bonded right on the teeth. Clear plastic braces are popular with adults and are less noticeable, although they tend to discolor and loosen faster than the old-fashioned metal fasteners. Invisible braces, which are mounted along the back of the teeth, are a major innovation. Because they can't be seen, they are attractive to adults. However, they involve a controversial technique. Some dentists claim invisible braces are more difficult both to put on and to keep on. It is also claimed that they interfere with speech and lengthen the time of treatment. Whether or not people use metal, plastic, or invisible braces, researchers are looking to the future. To shorten the treatment time, people may have "electric" braces several years from now. A battery current will surge through the braces during sleep to speed up the straightening process. Miniature magnets attached to the teeth may also be used to close a gap more quickly.

the tooth. The filling must be fitted carefully so that it will not become loose. A careful fit also cuts down the chances for decay to start around the filling's edges.

Dental problems

Regular and careful care of the teeth can help to prevent dental problems from occurring. When such problems do arise, though, they should always be treated without delay. They can affect not only your mouth, but also your appearance and the health of many other parts of your body.

Dental caries

The most common dental problem, of course, is tooth decay. The scientific name for tooth decay is **dental caries**. About 95 out of every 100 Americans have some tooth decay. "Bottle propping," or giving a bottle to a baby at nap or bedtime, is the most common cause of tooth decay in the infant or young child. This can result in destruction of the upper incisors and lower posterior teeth. It is also important to see

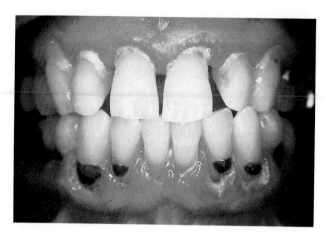

This painful swelling of the gums is known as periodontal disease.

to it that infants receive formulas that do not contain large amounts of sugar, since this also leads to decay.

A high rate of tooth decay is also a problem for many people in their late teens. A proper diet, fluorides, regular cleaning with toothbrush and dental floss, and professional dental care can aid in preventing most tooth decay.

Root abscesses

If decay has spread to the root of the tooth, bacteria may cause an infection, or **abscess.** A root abscess is usually painful. Toxins (poisons produced by the bacteria)—and even the bacteria themselves—may spread from the abscess to other parts of the body. An abscess in the upper jaw may go directly to one of the sinuses and cause a serious sinus infection.

Malocclusion

Irregular or crooked teeth make it impossible for the teeth of the upper jaw to close in a normal bite on those of the lower jaw. The result is **malocclusion,** or improper bite. Malocclusion sometimes causes people to breathe through their mouths. It may also interfere with speech and make a person look less attractive. Care of the primary teeth and of the 6-year molars is helpful in stopping malocclusion. Proper care includes filling cavities and either replacing lost primary teeth or using retainers that keep the spaces open until the permanent teeth grow in.

The treatment of malocclusion is known as **orthodontics.** A dentist who gives this treatment is called an **orthodontist**. Orthodontics usually includes the use of braces that gently move the teeth into place. This process of moving, or straightening, teeth may take months or even years to complete.

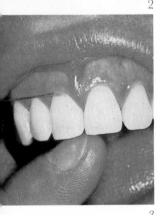

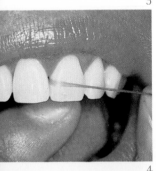

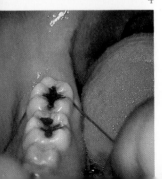

Gum problems

Teeth cannot be fully healthy without healthy gums. Healthy gums are firm. They are either pink or light red in color. Biting and chewing are natural ways of helping to keep gums healthy since these actions improve the circulation of blood.

Unhealthy gums become bright red or purplish, soft, and swollen. They also bleed easily. This condition of the gums is called **gingivitis**. Gingivitis is usually caused by poor care of the mouth and teeth. If a toothbrush or dental floss is not used properly, the gums may be injured and may swell. Pockets form in the swollen areas, which leads to infection. But regular brushing done in the right way and proper use of dental floss often stop swelling of the gums. A well-balanced diet with enough vitamin C may also help to stop gingivitis.

When plaque is not removed, it hardens to form a limelike layer on the teeth, especially near the necks of the teeth. This limelike layer is called **calculus**, or tartar. The only way to remove it is with a professional cleaning called a **prophylaxis**. Prophylaxis is done by a dentist or dental hygienist, who scrapes away the calculus. This helps to prevent gingivitis, since a buildup of calculus irritates the gum tissue.

Gingivitis may not be easily spotted at an early stage because there is no pain or discomfort. But if your gums begin to bleed when you brush your teeth, contact your dentist. A **periodontal membrane** surrounds the tooth and holds it in place. If the gingivitis is severe and involves the periodontal membrane, it may result in the loosening and eventual loss of teeth. The advanced stage of gingivitis is known as periodontal disease. A **periodontist** is a dentist who specializes in the treatment of periodontal disorders. Periodontal disease usually affects those over 25 years of age. It is the chief cause for loss of teeth. For this reason, prevention should begin early in life with proper brushing and use of dental floss.

Bad breath

Halitosis is another name for bad breath. Most people who take good care of their teeth do not have this problem, since most mouth odors are caused by tooth decay and periodontal disease. Infections of the nose, tonsils, or sinuses can sometimes cause bad breath. Substances in the air breathed out by the lungs can also be the cause. Getting rid of the causes of bad breath is better than simply freshening the breath with a mouthwash. A mouthwash has only a short-lived effect.

1. To floss your teeth, break off a piece of floss 18 inches long.   **2.** Wrap all but 3 inches around the middle fingers of each hand.   **3.** Guide the floss between two teeth with the thumb and forefingers. Bend it against the side of one tooth.   **4.** Holding the floss tightly, scrape the floss up and down against the side of the tooth.   **5.** Repeat these steps on the rest of your teeth.

Smile Power...

American Dental Association

"What Lovely Teeth You Have, My Pretties!"

American Dental Association

Good oral hygiene is your own job. You should choose foods that do not add to dental decay. Avoid snacks that have too much sugar. Brush your teeth after eating and before going to bed. Clean your teeth with dental floss when necessary. Visit your dentist twice a year for checkups. If your water supply is not fluoridated, ask your dentist for another way to get fluoride. If you take proper care of your mouth and teeth, most dental problems can be stopped or controlled.

Responsibility for dental health

Key Words

abscess	gingivitis	periodontal membrane
anesthetic	halitosis	periodontist
calculus	incisors	permanent teeth
cell metabolism	malocclusion	plaque
crown	molars	premolars
cuspids	neck	primary teeth
dental caries	orthodontics	prophylaxis
dentin	orthodontist	pulp cavity
enamel		roots
fluorides		

Main Ideas

- Teeth help to prepare food for digestion.
- During a lifetime, a person has two sets of teeth.
- Daily mouth care is important to dental health.
- Dental care is important in keeping a healthy and attractive appearance.
- Proper diet, cleanliness, fluoridation, and regular visits to the dentist are the best ways to protect your teeth.
- Most dental caries can be prevented.
- Teeth that have begun to decay should be found early and filled. This keeps the decay from spreading.
- Malocclusion can be treated by an orthodontist.
- Diseases of the teeth and gums should be treated by a dentist.

Understand the Reading

1. Draw a picture of a tooth. Label the crown, neck, roots, dentin, enamel, pulp cavity, and root canal.
2. What is the function of teeth?
3. Diet is important in the formation of teeth and in stopping tooth decay. What kinds of foods should be included in the diet? Which foods should be eaten in small amounts? Which foods make good snacks?
4. How is sodium fluoride important in dental care?
5. What is plaque, and how can it be removed?
6. Imagine that you just sat down in the dentist's chair. List some of the things you expect the dentist to do to your teeth.
7. Why is it important to have cavities filled while they are small?
8. Discuss ways to prevent malocclusion.
9. Why is care of the gums important? In what ways can you keep your gums healthy?
10. Describe the way the mouth looks if a person has gingivitis.

Apply Your Knowledge

1. Arrange a class trip to a dentist's office or a dental clinic. Ask the dentist to explain the use of some of the instruments and the X-ray machine. Ask to see X-ray photos of primary teeth about to be pushed out by permanent teeth, dead teeth, root abscesses, and dental caries.
2. Contact an official in your community health department and determine whether sodium fluoride is added to the water in your area. Ask: (1) when the practice was started, (2) how much fluoride is being used, (3) what the rate of dental caries was before fluoridation, and (4) what results, if any, have been found so far. Make a report to the class.

Chapter 19
Body Regulators

After reading this chapter, you will be able to:

☐ Explain the importance of hormones and describe how they are carried throughout the body.

☐ Identify the endocrine glands and describe what body activities each regulates.

☐ Identify the major diseases associated with hormonal imbalance and describe their symptoms and treatment.

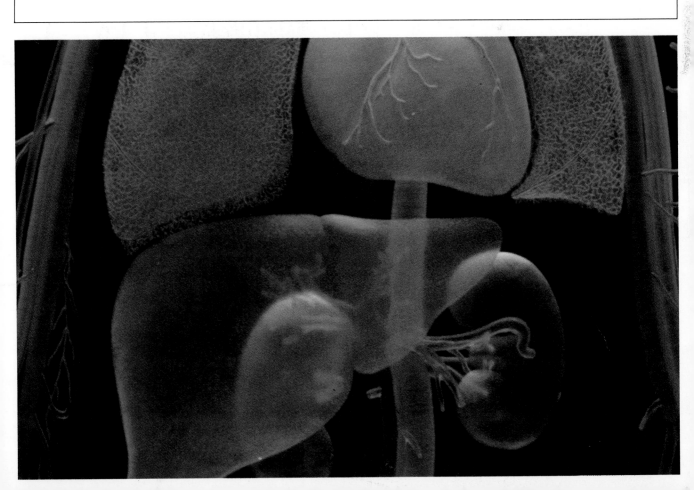

The nervous system controls many bodily functions. Other bodily functions are controlled by special chemical regulators called *hormones*. Hormones regulate such life activities as growth, behavior, and body development. They are carried to the body's cells through the bloodstream.

Hormones are produced by special glands called the *endocrine glands*. The endocrine glands are located in the head, neck, and trunk. Each gland produces different hormones with different functions.

The endocrine glands are different from other glands. The endocrine glands do not have ducts, or tubes, that lead out to other parts of the body. The hormones produced in the endocrine glands pass directly from the cells of the glands into blood vessels surrounding the glands. For this reason, the endocrine glands are sometimes called glands of internal secretion, or *ductless glands*.

Pituitary gland

Deep inside the brain is the **pituitary gland**. Of all the endocrine glands, it is thought to have the most influence on the others. In fact, it is sometimes called the "master" gland. The pituitary gland produces several hormones. One, the **thyroid-stimulating hormone**, causes the thyroid to produce its hormone. Another hormone produced by the pituitary is called **ACTH**, or the adrenocorticotrophic hormone. This hormone causes the adrenal glands to produce their hormones. Other pituitary hormones may affect the functioning of the ovaries and testes.

The pituitary gland also produces the hormones that control body growth. An excess of these hormones may cause bones to grow unusually large and long, which causes **giantism**. A deficiency of growth hormones may lead to **dwarfism.**

The pituitary gland, in a sense, helps control the temperature of the human body. The **hypothalamus**, a part of the brain located above the pituitary gland, sends hormones to this gland. These hormones from the hypothalamus regulate body temperature.

Thyroid gland

Perhaps the best known endocrine gland is the **thyroid gland**, which is located in the neck. The thyroid produces the hormone **thyroxin**. Thyroxin controls the rate of metabolism in all the cells of the body. If too much thyroxin is produced, cell metabolism is speeded up. People with too much thyroxin in their blood tend to suffer weight loss, anxiety, rapid heartbeat, diarrhea, and sometimes changes in the eyes.

On the other hand, too little thyroxin in the blood slows down cell metabolism. People with too little thyroxin in their blood tend to suffer weight gain, depression, slow heart rate, hoarseness, constipation, and feelings of coldness.

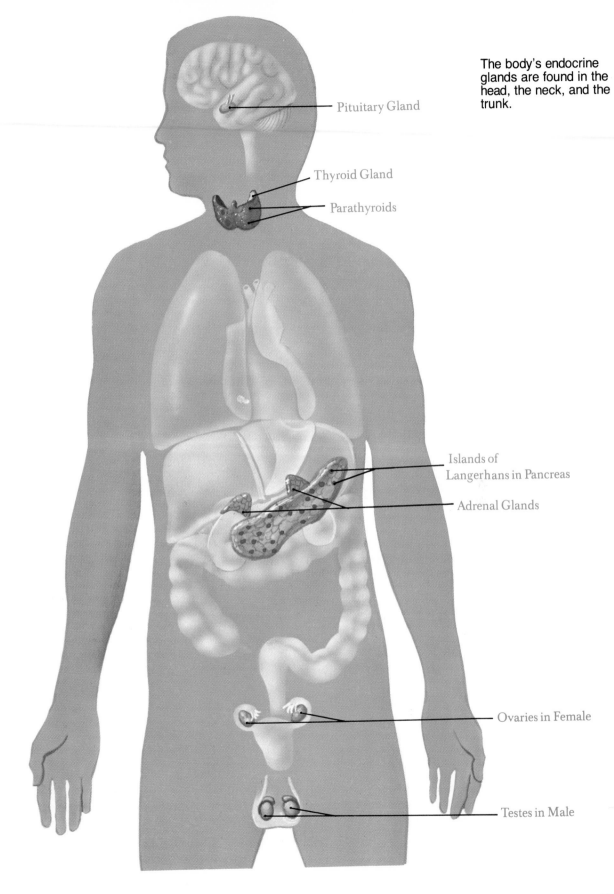

Pituitary Gland

The body's endocrine glands are found in the head, the neck, and the trunk.

Thyroid Gland

Parathyroids

Islands of Langerhans in Pancreas

Adrenal Glands

Ovaries in Female

Testes in Male

Iodine and the thyroid gland

The thyroid gland needs iodine in order to work properly. If the body does not get enough iodine, the cells of the thyroid must work harder to produce thyroxin. The thyroid enlarges in order to perform the extra work. This swelling in the neck is called a **goiter**.

Iodine is usually obtained from our food and water. Because seawater contains iodine salts, people who eat seafood usually get the iodine they need. In places where the soil has iodine in it, the food and water will naturally supply enough iodine. But some soils, especially in places once covered by glaciers, have no iodine. In these areas, people need to supplement their diets with iodine. A good source of iodine is iodized salt, which is ordinary table salt to which iodine has been added.

Thyroxin and cretinism

An infant who produces too little thyroxin grows slowly. The skin becomes thick, and the hair is dry and dull. The infant is usually overweight, has trouble keeping warm, and is slow in acting and thinking. These are symptoms of **cretinism**. Cretinism can lead to physical and mental retardation. Today, cretinism is rare because it is routinely tested for in newborns. Early symptoms of cretinism can be helped with thyroxin treatment.

Parathyroid glands

There are four **parathyroid glands**. These important glands are located within the thyroid gland in the neck. Secretions from the parathyroids are needed for the metabolism of calcium and phosphorus. Calcium and phosphorus are needed to build all body tissues, especially the bones and teeth. Calcium is also needed for the clotting of blood and the healthy working of muscles and nerves.

Islets of Langerhans

The **islets of Langerhans** are tiny clusters of gland tissue found in the pancreas, which is located near the stomach. The islets of Langerhans produce several hormones, one of which is **insulin**, a very important substance needed to enable sugar to enter body cells to be used for energy. If the insulin-producing cells of the islets of Langerhans do not function properly, diabetes develops.

Diabetes

Leslie's first symptom of disease was increased urination and excessive thirst. She waited anxiously for each class period to end so she could get a drink of water. After school, she drank several cans of soda. Her terrible thirst was then joined by a tremendous appetite. She began to eat often throughout the day. Despite the huge amount of food she ate, she did not gain weight. In fact, she lost weight. Before long, Leslie began to feel very tired. She sometimes lacked the energy even to talk with her friends.

Leslie's symptoms were signs of **diabetes mellitus**, a common disease caused by failure of the islets of Langerhans to secrete insulin. She was eating plenty of food, which meant that there was more than enough sugar in her bloodstream. But without insulin, her body could not get the sugar into the cells for energy. So Leslie's cells were starving.

Leslie's kidneys needed large amounts of water to remove the extra sugar in her blood. So Leslie had to urinate frequently and she was always thirsty. She finally went to a doctor, who gave her a blood test and urinalysis. The above-normal amounts of sugar in her urine and in her blood showed that Leslie had diabetes.

Only about 10 percent of all diabetics show symptoms before the age of 15. But when diabetes occurs in a young person, as in Leslie's case, it is called insulin-dependent. This means that insulin must be taken by a shot to sustain life. Most cases of diabetes mellitus appear in people over the age of 40. This diabetes is usually controlled through weight loss, diet, and exercise. It is called noninsulin dependent. Occasionally, oral medication may be required for the noninsulin-dependent diabetic to help the body lower blood sugar. People who are obese have a greater than normal chance of developing diabetes later in life.

Today, most people who have diabetes are able to lead almost normal lives. They must eat regular meals that are low in fat and exercise regularly. A person who has insulin-dependent diabetes must take insulin to make up for the amount not produced by the glands. Taking insulin does not cure diabetes, but it can control the disease. The person with insulin-dependent diabetes must also monitor his or her own blood-sugar level daily to maintain control. Keeping a normal blood sugar is important because unregulated diabetes leads to long-term problems with the eyes and kidneys.

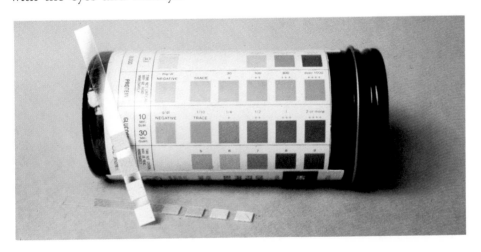

The materials shown here make it easier for the diabetic to test the amount of sugar in the urine.

If too much insulin is injected, too much exercise is taken, or too little food is consumed, the diabetic's blood-sugar level may become too low. This is called **hypoglycemia**, or **insulin reaction**. The symptoms of insulin reaction include pale, cold, and clammy skin; shallow breathing; nervousness; blurred vision; stupor; and possible loss of consciousness if not treated by eating sugar. Most people with diabetes learn to tell when they are having an insulin reaction. They can quickly restore the proper blood-sugar level by eating a food that contains sugar.

Adrenal glands

The two **adrenal glands** are located in the trunk of the body, one above each kidney. They are 1 to 2 inches long. Each adrenal gland has an inner part and an outer part. Each part secretes a different hormone.

Adrenalin is one of the hormones secreted by the inner part of the adrenal glands, or medulla. Adrenalin speeds up and strengthens the heartbeat. It increases muscle tone in the skeletal muscles and slows down activity in the digestive tract. These changes prepare the body for action—fighting, running away, or doing something that the person would not have the strength to do under normal conditions. When a person is frightened or angry, for example, more adrenalin is produced.

Adrenalin can be made in laboratories. It is used to treat many disorders. Sometimes it is given to people who are having severe attacks of asthma. It can be used to speed up blood circulation in a person suffering from shock or suffocation. In some cases, an injection of

The two adrenal glands are found one above each kidney. The medulla, or inner part of each gland, produces the hormone adrenalin.

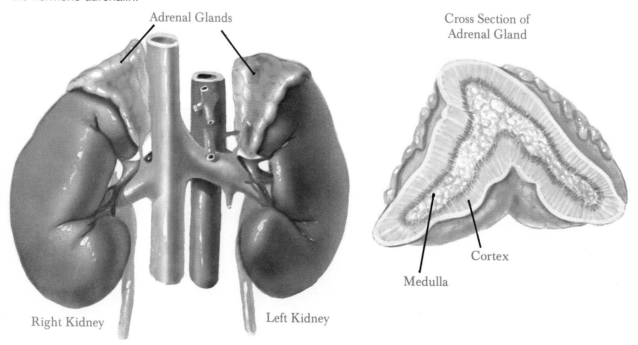

Adrenal Glands

Cross Section of Adrenal Gland

Cortex

Medulla

Right Kidney

Left Kidney

Gland	Job
Pituitary	Produces thyroid-stimulating hormone, ACTH, and other hormones; influences activities of other endocrine glands; regulates body growth; regulates body temperature
Thyroid	Produces thyroxin; controls the rate of metabolism in the body's cells
Parathyroids	Produce parathyroid hormones; regulate the body's use of calcium and phosphorous
Islets of Langerhans	Produce insulin; regulate the body's use of sugar
Adrenals	Produce adrenalin and cortisone; speed up and strengthen the heartbeat; increase muscle tone; slow down digestive activities; prepare the body for action; control the body's use of salts, fats, and glucose; help the body react to stress
Gonads	Produce estrogen (female hormone) and testosterone (male hormone); control development of the reproductive organs; control development of secondary sexual characteristics
Pineal	Produces pineal hormone; thought to regulate daily rhythms
Thymus	Produces thymus hormone; thought to help in fighting infections

Adrenalin is the body's "emergency" hormone. It gives us the boost of energy sometimes needed at critical moments.

adrenalin into a heart that has stopped beating will cause the heart to start beating again.

The outer part of the adrenal glands is the cortex. It produces a hormone called **cortisone**. Cortisone decreases swelling and helps the body react to stress. A synthetic (man-made) form of cortisone can be used to treat kidney disease, arthritis, and other disorders. Cortisone should be used only under the watchful eye of a doctor because it can have harmful side effects. Other hormones from the cortex also control the body's use of salts, fats, and glucose (one form of sugar).

Gonads

The **gonads**, or sex glands, are organs that produce reproductive cells. In females, the gonads are the ovaries, which lie in the lower part of the abdomen. They release mature egg cells and produce several sex-

253

related hormones, including **estrogen**. In males, the gonads are the testes, which are in a small outer pouch below the abdomen. The testes produce sperm and the hormone **testosterone**.

Both the ovaries and the testes develop before birth. They produce sex hormones in small amounts during childhood. They begin to produce greater amounts of the sex hormones in most girls between the ages of 11 and 14 and in most boys a year or two later. The sex hormones cause the secondary sexual characteristics to develop in young men and young women.

Pineal and thymus glands

Two other endocrine glands, the **pineal gland** and the **thymus gland**, are now being studied by researchers. Much less is known about these glands than is known about the other endocrine glands.

The pineal gland, located in the center of the brain, plays a role in regulating daily rhythms. It seems sensitive to light and darkness. It also works with other endocrine glands.

The thymus gland is located in the upper chest. It is somewhat large at birth, but seems to decrease in size thereafter. By the time one becomes an adult, it is very small. The thymus is believed to produce substances that help to fight infections.

Care of the endocrine system

The endocrine system usually takes care of its own chemical balance. If the system is not working well, a person can have such symptoms as unusual thirst, unexplained weight change, extreme tiredness or nervousness, or signs of abnormal growth and development. Such symptoms signal the need for a doctor's care. Blood tests can be used to check the functioning of the glands. For example, blood tests can quickly show if you have a thyroid disorder or diabetes.

Key Words

ACTH	giantism	parathyroid glands
adrenal glands	goiter	pineal gland
adrenalin	gonads	pituitary gland
cortisone	hormones	testosterone
cretinism	hypoglycemia	thymus gland
diabetes mellitus	hypothalamus	thyroid gland
ductless glands	insulin	thyroid
dwarfism	insulin reaction	stimulating
endocrine glands	islets of	hormone
estrogen	Langerhans	thyroxin

■ The endocrine glands secrete hormones that are carried by the blood and that control various activities of the body.

■ Too much or too little secretion of a hormone from one or more of the endocrine glands may cause a disturbance in the working of the body.

■ In many cases, modern scientific knowledge has made it possible to control disorders caused by hormonal imbalance.

Understand the Reading

1. Name the glands that make up the endocrine system.
2. Which gland is sometimes called the master gland? Why?
3. List the functions of the pituitary gland.
4. What is another name for an enlarged thyroid gland? What causes an enlarged thyroid to develop?
5. What is cretinism? How is this disorder controlled?
6. Which glands in the body secrete hormones that are needed to metabolize calcium and phosphorus?
7. Explain how producing too much or too little insulin can cause disorders.
8. Which hormone helps to prepare the body for action or stress? How?
9. Which gland secretes cortisone? What does cortisone do in the body?
10. What hormone is produced in the ovaries? Which one is produced in the testes?

Apply Your Knowledge

1. Do some research on the discovery of insulin. Report your findings to the class.
2. Collect articles in newspapers and magazines about research on hormones and on the endocrine glands. Attach your clippings to a class bulletin board. Appoint members of the class to report every few weeks on new developments in this area.
3. Ask a pharmacist to explain what kinds of problems synthetic cortisone is used to treat and the slightly unusual way in which the drug is administered. Then, read magazine and newspaper articles to investigate the use of this substance by athletes. Based on your interview with the pharmacist, determine why improper use of synthetic cortisone can lead to devastating results and even death. Report your findings to the class.
4. Interview an endocrinologist about the use of radioisotopes to treat problems of the endocrine system. Ask for information on the kinds of specific problems that are treated in this fashion. Present your findings to the class in a report.

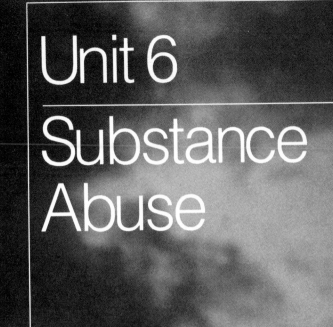

Unit 6
Substance Abuse

Chapter 20
Tobacco

After reading this chapter, you will be able to:

- ☐ Identify the substances in tobacco that are harmful to the human body.
- ☐ Name the major diseases caused by tobacco use.
- ☐ Explain how passive smoking can harm nonsmokers.
- ☐ List mistaken reasons given by smokers for not quitting the habit.
- ☐ Identify the types and dangers of smokeless tobacco products.

David and Cathy were standing in the school yard after lunch. As Cathy lit up a cigarette, she noticed David giving her a funny look. "You're not going to start lecturing me about this, are you?" she said. "I know how bad cigarettes are for you, but I'm going to stop before anything bad happens to me."

"I sure hope you're right," David said. "But it sounds to me like you're gambling with your health."

Don't gamble with *your* health. If you use tobacco now, stop. If you haven't started, don't. Remember, a wellness program isn't defined only by what you *do*, but equally by what you *don't* do.

Tobacco use

Medical and scientific knowledge leaves no doubt about the harmful effects of tobacco smoking. In fact, the Surgeon General of the United States Public Health Service has stated, "... cigarette smoking is the chief, single, avoidable cause of death in our society and the most important public health issue of our time."

Smokers and nonsmokers alike share the high cost of smoking. Each year in the United States, accidents and diseases related to smoking cost billions of dollars in added health-care expenses and lost work output. Especially tragic are the many home fires caused by smoking.

Substances in tobacco smoke

Tobacco smoke consists of more than 3,000 components. It is a mixture of gases, vapors, and tiny suspended particles. Each cubic centimeter of tobacco smoke that enters the mouth contains millions of these particles. One of the harmful gases in this smoke is carbon monoxide. Carbon monoxide reduces the oxygen-carrying capacity of the blood. It is believed to be responsible for the reduced wind (shortness of breath) of smokers. There is often several hundred times as much carbon monoxide in tobacco smoke as is thought to be safe. The particles in smoke also contain **nicotine** and **tobacco tars**.

Nicotine

The nicotine in tobacco smoke is a powerful, colorless poison. When absorbed into the bloodstream, nicotine affects the nervous system. A drop of pure nicotine injected into the body would cause death in a few minutes. Every smoker absorbs some of the nicotine in tobacco smoke. The reason a person does not die after smoking is that the amount of nicotine absorbed at any one time is less than a fatal dose.

The beginning smoker often has symptoms of mild nicotine poisoning. Even regular smokers sometimes show the same effects. These symptoms include dizziness, faintness, rapid pulse, clammy skin, and sometimes nausea, vomiting, and diarrhea. Nicotine is responsible for tobacco addiction and for many diseases of the heart and blood vessels.

Tobacco tars

The tars in tobacco smoke contain a large number of chemicals. Some of these, called carcinogens, produce cancer if applied to the skin of animals. Others, called cocarcinogens, act with other chemicals to cause cancer. Tars are also responsible for bronchitis, emphysema, and other diseases of the respiratory tract associated with smoking. Switching to low-tar, low-nicotine cigarettes may not reduce the amount of tar since smokers of these cigarettes often smoke more, inhale more deeply, or puff more often. The reason appears to be an addiction to nicotine. Also, additives have been included in the newer brands, and the nature and amounts of the additives are not known. For these and other reasons, the U.S. Surgeon General has stressed that there is no "safe" cigarette.

Effects of smoking on the body

In most people, smoking dulls the senses of taste and smell. Tobacco tars cause unattractive brown stains on the teeth and fingers of cigarette smokers, and both nicotine and tobacco tars are irritating to the respiratory tract. Smoking is also responsible for bad breath and the likelihood of developing facial wrinkles as one grows older.

The heart rate increases after smoking. In one group of young people studied, the average increase after a single cigarette was 21 beats per minute. Occasionally, the heartbeat becomes irregular, and there is pain in the chest. Smoking also causes the small arteries to contract, or become smaller. This cuts down the flow of blood through them. Decreased blood flow lowers the temperature of the skin. This is often accompanied by an increase in blood pressure.

Smoking and disease

Experts estimate that each year over 300,000 Americans die prematurely from the effects of smoking. The more serious diseases related to smoking include coronary heart disease, cancer, chronic bronchitis, and emphysema. Smoking is also one of the causes of long-lasting and uncomfortable minor ailments.

Coronary heart disease

Smoking puts a strain on the heart and blood vessels. It also reduces blood flow through the lungs and causes the lungs to absorb less oxygen. These effects cause shortness of breath. They also keep the heart from getting enough oxygen. There are many more deaths from coronary heart disease among cigarette smokers than among nonsmokers.

Cancer

According to the American Cancer Society, cigarette smoking is responsible for 30 percent of all cancer deaths. Smoking has been linked to cancer of the lungs, larynx, pharynx, oral cavity, esophagus, pancreas, and bladder. In a recent year, more than 120,000 persons in the United States died of lung cancer. Of these deaths, it is thought that more than 80 percent were due to cigarette smoking. There are 15 different known cancer-causing substances in each cigarette.

The chances of developing lung cancer depend upon many factors: the age at which smoking begins, the number of cigarettes smoked each day, how deeply the smoke is inhaled, the total number of years of smoking, and the total number of cigarettes smoked over those years. Among men, lung cancer continues to be the leading cause of cancer deaths. Lung cancer recently became the leading cause of cancer deaths among women. Although the proportion of adults who smoke has declined, present smokers, especially women, are smoking more heavily.

Researchers have also reported the damaging effects that cigarette smoking has on certain kinds of workers. Asbestos workers who smoke have 60 times as great a chance of developing lung cancer as do nonsmoking asbestos workers. Those industrial workers who smoke are

There is no longer any doubt among scientists about the health dangers linked with cigarette smoking.

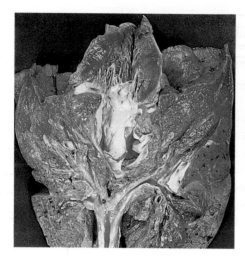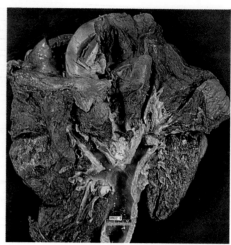

Much of the damage done to lungs through smoking (*right*) can be reversed (*left*).

especially susceptible to lung diseases due to the combined effects of smoking and exposure to toxic industrial substances.

Pipe and cigar smokers usually do not inhale as much as cigarette smokers do. Therefore, their risk of developing lung cancer is not as great as that for cigarette smokers. Nevertheless, the risk of lung cancer does exist, and it is still a greater risk than that for nonsmokers. Exposure to smoke in the upper respiratory tract is approximately the same for all smokers. Therefore, the chances of developing cancer of the pharynx, larynx, mouth, and esophagus are as great for pipe and cigar smokers as for cigarette smokers. Pipe smokers have the added risk of developing lip cancer.

Chronic bronchitis and emphysema

Heavy smokers often develop a chronic cough caused by irritation of the linings of the nose, throat, and lungs. In time, this irritation may be followed by chronic bronchitis and emphysema (see Chapter 16). Emphysema may begin with a slight difficulty in breathing at times. Later, an activity such as a short walk may result in breathlessness. After a time, emphysema reaches a point where the individual cannot perform normal activities. About 80 percent of all cases are related to smoking.

Passive smoking

Ann Casey is a 24-year-old artist. She likes movies, concerts, sports events, and eating out in restaurants. But only recently has she been able to enjoy these activities. Ann is one of the large number of individuals who are allergic to tobacco smoke. This past year, her community established no-smoking areas in all public facilities. So Ann now enjoys activities that she once thought she would never be able to attend.

People who have asthma, emphysema, or heart ailments cannot be in a smoky environment. Many of them are not as fortunate as Ann. They live in cities or towns that have not yet established smoking regulations. Such regulations guarantee smoke-free areas at restaurants, public meetings, and entertainment facilities.

Passive (involuntary) **smoking** occurs when a nonsmoker unwillingly inhales smoke from a burning cigarette, cigar, or pipe. In a smoky environment, the nonsmoker breathes many of the same particles in tobacco smoke that a smoker inhales. The chemical components in smoke-filled surroundings come from two sources—mainstream and sidestream smoke. **Mainstream smoke** is the smoke inhaled and then exhaled by the smoker. **Sidestream smoke** is the smoke that goes directly into the air from the burning end of a cigarette, cigar, or pipe. Sidestream smoke can be seen, for example, when a cigarette is burning in an ashtray. The sidestream smoke is not filtered in any way. Many substances, including those known to cause cancer, are therefore found in much higher concentrations in sidestream smoke than in mainstream smoke. In smoke-filled environments, there may be more carbon monoxide and other pollutants in the air than there are during air-pollution emergencies! Many people—especially those suffering from chronic heart or lung diseases—are seriously affected by severe air pollution. Many others experience discomforts, such as stinging eyes, headache, nausea, or nose and throat irritation. Some people have serious allergic reactions to the chemicals in tobacco smoke. Recent research has shown that the more smokers one lives with, the higher one's risk of cancer.

Effects on babies and children

Studies have shown that a pregnant woman harms her unborn baby when she smokes cigarettes. Infants born to smoking mothers weigh less and are more likely to have impaired growth and development.

Children have more respiratory infections than most adults have. Children are also more likely to be sensitive to the effects of sidestream smoke. Studies have shown that children whose parents smoke at home have twice as many respiratory illnesses as do children with nonsmoking parents. Children who have asthma suffer a great deal if they live in a household where people smoke. Asthma attacks can even be brought on by cigarette smoking.

"I knew smoking could become a habit. But I never planned on smoking that long."

"I never thought I'd have trouble stopping when I wanted to. I guess everybody feels that way."

A person may start smoking for any one of many reasons. The person then keeps smoking because a habit has been formed. Smoking leads to a strong dependence on tobacco, and this addiction to the nicotine in tobacco is very hard to overcome.

The smoking habit

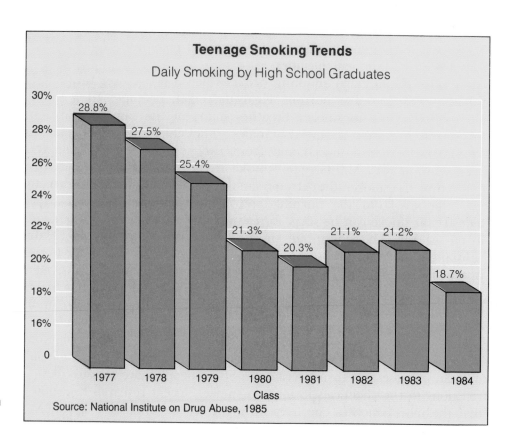

Teenage Smoking Trends
Daily Smoking by High School Graduates

28.8% (1977)
27.5% (1978)
25.4% (1979)
21.3% (1980)
20.3% (1981)
21.1% (1982)
21.2% (1983)
18.7% (1984)

Class

Source: National Institute on Drug Abuse, 1985

These are teenage smoking trends over an 8-year period.

Mistaken reasons for smoking

Some people smoke because they think that tobacco relieves tiredness. This may be because the nicotine in the smoke causes a temporary increase of sugar·in the blood. More sugar means more fuel for the muscles. After a brief time, though, the fuel is gone and the tiredness is greater than before. Some say that smoking relaxes them and eases nervous tension. This may be true for regular smokers who crave tobacco. A cigarette gives them temporary relief. But the feeling of relief from tension may simply result from the fact that smoking gives smokers something to do with their hands. There is no evidence that cigarette smoking has any other soothing or calming effects.

Many young people begin smoking because their friends smoke. They feel that smoking will lead to being accepted by their peers. Before you begin smoking for this reason, turn the logic around. Ask yourself: Would *you* refuse to accept someone as a friend because that person refused to pick up one of *your* bad habits?

Quitting the habit

Convincing evidence of the harmful effects of smoking has caused over 30 million people to stop smoking. Others go on smoking out of habit

"Our society teaches youngsters to poison themselves, and we convince them they are having a good time." These are the words of Dave Wagnon, a drug-education specialist in the Richardson school district in Richardson, Texas. Concerned about drug abuse among students, members of the Richardson district decided to take action. They set up a comprehensive drug-education program for both elementary and high-school students. The program includes seminars for students, brochures for parents, videotapes about drugs, and intervention teams to recognize problems and concerns and offer help. A unique part of the program is called STARS, Students Teaching About the Risks of Smoking. STARS is based on two major ideas: Young people will listen more readily to other young people, and the critical time to reach students is around the fifth grade. To help the fifth graders learn to make choices and to say no for good reasons, high-school volunteers are recruited and instructed about smoking and decision making. Armed with information, they go into the fifth-grade classrooms to talk with the pupils. Nearly half of the elementary schools in Richardson have been reached by the STARS program.

Something to think about

Students teach the risks of smoking

If your friends tell you that smoking makes you mature, don't listen.

because they do not make a strong effort to stop. Willpower, time, and discomfort are involved in breaking a well-established habit such as smoking.

Many cigarette smokers who would like to stop smoking are concerned about gaining weight when they quit. According to a report from the U.S. Department of Health and Human Services, the facts are these: Only a third of all people who quit smoking gain weight by substituting food when they first quit. A great majority—two-thirds—either stay at the same weight when they quit or *lose* weight by starting a physical-fitness program.

The benefits of breaking the smoking habit are worth the effort. People who quit smoking have a better chance of living long and healthy lives. If there is no disease present, the body begins to repair the damage that smoking caused as soon as someone stops smoking. The person will cough less, breathe more easily, and enjoy a general feeling of well-being. Many programs are now available to help people stop smoking. Also, free or inexpensive kits and manuals on how to quit smoking are available from the American Lung Association, the American Heart Association, and the American Cancer Society.

Smokeless tobacco

Believing that it is smoke alone that is harmful in cigarettes, a number of individuals have taken up the habit of using **smokeless tobacco**. This is tobacco that is made to be chewed, sniffed, or "dipped" rather than smoked.

Generally, there are three forms of smokeless tobacco: snuff, chewing tobacco, and plug tobacco. **Snuff** is a finely ground mixture of tobacco leaves and stems. The word *snuff* has its origin in the fact that people inhale, or snuff, this ground tobacco. **Chewing tobacco** is made from different kinds of loose-leafed, low-grade tobacco. Users take a small portion and place it between the cheek and gum, or "dip" it. **Plug tobacco** is compressed tobacco that is sold in brick form. Pieces are cut or bitten off the plug. Plug tobacco is used in the same way as chewing tobacco.

Smokeless tobacco products have been sold in the United States since colonial days. However, in recent years, there has been an increase in their popularity, especially among young people who view smokeless tobacco as a healthier choice than smoking. Some athletes point out, "It can't hurt you like cigarettes can." The news for the users, however, is not good.

Within 20 minutes, nicotine from oral tobacco is absorbed into the bloodstream and causes the heart to beat faster and the blood pressure to rise. This is because nicotine is a stimulant. The gums may recede, the teeth may become discolored and loosen, and the biting surfaces may wear away. This damage is due to the repeated, direct, and prolonged contact of the tobacco with the gums and teeth. The user of smokeless tobacco has bad breath and a decreased ability to taste. Since

There is no such thing as "safe" tobacco. These smokeless products carry their own share of risks.

most chewing tobacco contains sugar, the incidence of dental caries increases among chewers. More important, chewing tobacco or rubbing snuff against the soft mouth tissues can cause **leukoplakia**, a condition that often leads to cancer. Leukoplakia appears as a white patch on the soft tissues of the mouth. It is often the result of irritation of the tissues from a tobacco product. There is an increased risk of cancer of the mouth, throat, larynx, and esophagus from the use of these products. Also, as with smokers, users of smokeless tobacco develop a strong dependence on it.

Many people have "bought" the message that smokeless tobacco products are safe alternatives to smoking. To counter this myth with facts, some states have insisted on health warnings on smokeless tobacco packages, as well as restrictions on advertising of these products. Massachusetts is one such state. Many other states are thinking about passing similar laws.

Key Words

chewing tobacco	nicotine	smokeless tobacco
leukoplakia	passive smoking	snuff
mainstream smoke	plug tobacco	tobacco tars
	sidestream smoke	

Main Ideas

- Tobacco smoke consists of nicotine, tars, and other harmful substances.
- Cigarette smoking is a major cause of heart disease, various types of cancer, chronic bronchitis, emphysema, and several other diseases.
- Tobacco smoke is not only harmful to smokers, but to nonsmokers as well.
- The use of smokeless tobacco products can be addictive and cause mouth cancer and other mouth disorders.

Understand the Reading

1. What are some of the symptoms of nicotine poisoning?
2. Why is switching to low-tar, low-nicotine cigarettes not an effective way of reducing tar for many smokers?
3. Of the 120,000 deaths from lung cancer in the United States in a recent year, what percentage was due to cigarette smoking? What percentage of emphysema cases are related to smoking?
4. Explain the difference between mainstream and sidestream smoke.
5. List three discomforts that nonsmokers might experience in a smoke-filled room.
6. What are some harmful effects of cigarette smoke in infants born to smoking mothers?
7. Does tobacco relieve tiredness? Explain.
8. What percentage of smokers gain weight after quitting?
9. How is snuff generally used? How are plug tobacco and chewing tobacco used?
10. What happens to the body soon after oral tobacco is absorbed into the bloodstream?

Apply Your Knowledge

1. Collect as many magazine and newspaper advertisements for cigarettes as you can. Post them on a bulletin board in class. When you have gathered a large number of ads, discuss with your classmates the kind of individual the cigarette manufacturers seem to be appealing to. Also discuss what you think is the manufacturer's message to the public. Consider the claim made by a representative of a tobacco company that the advertisements are directed toward people who already smoke, not toward nonsmokers.
2. Investigate the regulations regarding smoking in public places that have been passed in some cities and states. Summarize your findings in a written report.
3. Obtain a copy of your state's law on the sale and delivery of tobacco. Write a summary of the law and its penalties.

Chapter 21
Alcohol

After reading this chapter, you will be able to:

☐ Describe the effects of alcohol on the human body.

☐ Explain the effects of alcohol abuse on mental health.

☐ Identify some of the organizations formed to help alcoholics and their families.

☐ Explain what it means to have an alcohol problem.

Why do people drink alcoholic beverages? Some people drink because they like the taste. Others drink because they think it is sophisticated. Still others drink because alcohol seems to relax them and ease their worries for a time. Whatever reason people give for using alcohol, it is important for them to understand that they are using a potentially dangerous drug. Like other drugs, alcohol can have serious consequences when it is abused.

Alcoholic beverages

Wine and beer have been used since earliest times. Both are made by the process of **fermentation**, which is caused by the action of certain yeasts on the sugars found in fruit and grain. In ancient times, fermented drinks were less likely to have disease-causing germs than was most drinking water. So in those days, people tended to drink more alcoholic beverages than water.

Wines contain from 8 to 16 percent alcohol. There is less alcohol per ounce in beer than in wine. But beer is usually drunk in larger amounts than wine is. Stronger alcoholic beverages, such as brandy, whiskey, gin, and rum, are made by **distillation**. This is a process of purifying liquids by heating them until they become gases. Then they are cooled back to liquid form again. Stronger alcoholic beverages contain from 40 to 50 percent alcohol.

Alcohol is high in calories. But alcohol does not have important nutrients, such as proteins, vitamins, and minerals. People who drink a lot of alcohol and eat little food often suffer from malnutrition. Because alcohol is high in calories, it is also fattening. One serving of beer (12 fluid ounces) has about 150 calories.

Effects on the body

Alcohol is absorbed by the blood from the stomach and small intestine. The blood absorbs alcohol most quickly when it is drunk on an empty stomach. The blood absorbs it more slowly when it is drunk with food. Alcohol in the blood reaches all the organs in the body. It has some effect on most of them. But its greatest effect is on the brain.

Alcohol is a powerful drug. Specifically, it is a depressant. It dulls the nerve centers of the brain that control judgment, attention, memory, and self-control. A person who has been drinking acts more on feeling than on thought and judgment. The drinker may feel overconfident and act on impulse. This is very true when the person is active and in the company of other people. A person who drinks while alone is likely to be made depressed and sleepy by the alcohol. Typically, these effects begin to appear after a person has drunk about $1/3$ ounce of alcohol. This is the amount of alcohol contained in $2/3$ ounce of whiskey. A bottle of beer, a highball, and a cocktail each has more than this amount.

Fact: The amount of alcohol in 12 ounces of beer, 5 ounces of wine, and 1½ ounces of 80-proof liquor is the same.

12 oz.   5 oz.   1½ oz.

Alcohol is used up, or metabolized, by the liver at the rate of one-half ounce per hour. Therefore, a given amount of alcohol drunk over several hours will have less effect on a person than the same amount taken over a short period of time.

Drinking a large amount of alcohol—1 ounce or more—may make a person loud, talkative, affectionate, or quarrelsome. The drinker may not consider what other people think of this conduct. The alcohol is also likely to make the person dizzy and lightheaded. Movements become slow, and muscular coordination is upset. This causes an unsteady walk and slurred, mixed-up speech. A person in such a condition is said to be **intoxicated**. After many drinks, a person may pass out. Upon waking, the person usually feels uncomfortable and irritable. He or she is usually very thirsty, has a headache, is dizzy, and may suffer from nausea and vomiting.

The blood vessels of the skin become larger after the use of alcohol. This causes the face to flush and gives a false feeling of warmth. The rise in blood flow through the skin really causes the body to lose heat, not save it. So the idea of drinking an alcoholic beverage to keep warm is incorrect.

The regular intake of large amounts of alcohol may lead to indigestion and loss of appetite. The heart, liver, and kidneys may be badly damaged. Heavy drinking over a long period of time can lead to early death from heart or liver disease. And drinking large amounts of alcohol at one time may lead to paralysis of one nerve center in the brain after another. Finally, the nerve centers that control the actions of the heart and lungs may become paralyzed. The result is death from alcohol poisoning. For this reason, "drinking contests" sometimes end in tragedy for the winner.

People who drink too much often defend their habit by asking, "What difference can one little drink make?" This is a good question. If "one little drink" contains half an ounce of pure alcohol, then one little drink consumed within two hours is enough to affect the average person's judgment. Two drinks consumed in the same period of time is enough to cause clumsy speech and walk. Three drinks in two hours can make a person loud, emotionally volatile, irrational, and 100 times more likely to have a traffic accident. With six drinks, a person can become totally incapable of voluntary action. For some people, this is the equivalent of a surgical anesthetic. And seven drinks? Seven drinks in two hours can cause coma or difficulty in breathing or even death.

Misuse of alcohol

Every so often, many people enjoy alcoholic beverages in small or moderate amounts. But alcohol can be habit-forming, or addictive. Alcohol addiction is a serious illness known as **alcoholism**.

As with many of the "abuse" problems of our times—whether the object of the abuse is food or alcohol or other drugs—the experts find the cause of the problem to be a combination of biological, social, and psychological factors. For example, some studies indicate an inherited tendency toward alcohol abuse. Other studies have shown that the way alcohol is handled socially in a particular country can make a difference. Still other people become heavy drinkers to escape from conflicts or emotional problems they have not learned to handle.

It is impossible to tell which drinkers will become alcoholics. Most alcoholics began with an occasional drink. This is why it is important to recognize that alcohol is a drug that may cause addiction. There are more than 13 million alcoholics in the United States. About one-third of them are in their teens. And almost as many women as men are alcoholics.

Effects on mental health

The effects of alcohol on mental health are even more striking than its effects on physical health. The personality of the alcoholic goes through many changes. Alcoholics lower their standards of conduct. They lose self-respect and the respect of others. Sometimes they are not reliable as workers and lose their jobs. They may begin to care only about themselves and their problems. Their biggest worry may be where to get the next drink.

Teenagers who use alcohol to help solve problems slow down their progress in learning how to manage their lives. Adolescence is thought of as the time when a person changes in mind and body from a child to an adult. But when a teenager chooses to use a drug to help solve problems, mental growth (maturity) is slowed down. Using a drug to escape problems, instead of using the mind to solve them, can keep a teenager from developing into a true adult.

Parents who are alcoholics may affect the physical and mental health of their children. An alcoholic parent cannot be relied on. So the children of such a parent may feel insecure. They may also often be embarrassed by the parent's behavior. In more serious cases, a parent may spend money on alcohol instead of providing the family with the proper food, clothing, housing, and medical care. In extreme cases, an alcoholic parent may become violent. Broken homes, lost jobs, serious accidents, child neglect, poverty, and sometimes crime may be caused by the use of too much alcohol.

Fetal alcohol syndrome

FAS, or **fetal alcohol syndrome**, is the name for a group of birth defects caused when a pregnant woman drinks. FAS has a wide range of severity. Infants may be born with abnormally small heads; mental retardation; and deformities of the heart, limbs, or face. Typically, FAS children with facial deformities have slitlike eyes; protruding foreheads; short, turned-up noses; cleft palates or short upper lips; receding chins; and deformed ears. They may have extra or missing fingers and toes.

One study indicates that a mother who drinks six or more drinks of any alcoholic beverage per day increases the risk of FAS for her child to nearly 75 percent. Among women who drank only one or two drinks per day, another study showed a 14 percent rate of birth defects. And even drinking heavily once at one of the many crucial periods in fetal development can cause deformities or brain damage. Alcohol or some product of alcohol metabolism is probably the cause of these defects, but the exact way in which these malformations occur is not clearly understood.

Researchers at the University of North Carolina studied the effects of alcohol on the fetuses of mice that were 7 days pregnant. This is about the same as 3 weeks of pregnancy in humans—a time when most women do not even realize that they are pregnant. The researchers found that ethanol, which is in all alcoholic beverages, caused the brains of fetal mice to be abnormally small and narrow. This led to facial distortion and other FAS symptoms.

The National Council on Alcoholism advises that the only safe decision for an expectant mother is to totally avoid alcohol during pregnancy.

Automobile accidents

A safe driver must be in full control and have alert reflexes. He or she must make correct decisions and act quickly. A person who has been

Sobering Statistics	
If your blood alcohol concentration is . . .	Your risk of being involved in a traffic accident is increased by . . .
0.10%	7%
0.15%	25%
0.18%	60%
0.20%	100%

drinking is a menace on the highway because alcohol weakens the person's judgment and self-control. The drinker also often feels a false confidence about being able to drive.

The amount of alcohol in a person's blood is called the BAC, or **blood alcohol concentration**. It is usually expressed in terms of percent. A blood alcohol concentration of 0.06 percent usually results from drinking 2 to 3 ounces of whiskey or other distilled liquor or two to three 12-ounce bottles of beer. A driver with a BAC of 0.06 percent is twice as likely to have an accident as a driver who has not been drinking. If the alcohol concentration in the person's blood is 0.1 percent, the person's risk of having an automobile accident is seven times as great as that of a nondrinking driver. What is the legal blood alcohol concentration for drivers in your state?

People who have been drinking are involved in automobile accidents that cause thousands of deaths each year. A study of 1,134 fatally injured drivers in one state showed that 65 percent of the drivers who were responsible for the accidents had been drinking. And of 353 fatally injured pedestrians, 59 percent of those under 65 years of age had been drinking. In a single year in another state, it was reported that 6 out of 10 drivers and pedestrians killed in traffic accidents had been drinking. More than half of those who were killed had drunk enough to be intoxicated.

Help for the problem drinker

On a typical Friday or Saturday night, Brian would drink five or six beers with friends. One Friday evening, Brian drank until he lost consciousness. His friends were worried about him. They wondered what to do.

Any person who is unconscious needs medical help. In this case, Brian could have died from alcohol poisoning if he had drunk too much alcohol in too short a time. His life might also have been in danger if he had taken another drug before or while he drank the beer. Some drugs can cause death when mixed with even a little alcohol. If simply left to "sleep it off," Brian could have choked to death on his own vomit. His life might have depended on how much his friends knew about the dangers of drinking too much alcohol and on how quickly they acted to get help for him.

If someone you are with loses consciousness from drinking too much alcohol, call a doctor or an ambulance immediately. While waiting for help, place the person on his or her side, keep the air passages open, and remove any food or gum from the mouth. If the person's breathing stops, give mouth-to-mouth resuscitation if you know how. When the doctor or ambulance arrives, tell the doctor or trained ambulance driver what the person drank and how much.

If someone you are with has drunk far too much and might lose consciousness, stay with the person and send for medical help.

Life can be very unhappy for alcoholics and their families.

Early identification

If you drink only beer, can you still be an alcoholic? If you drink only on weekends, can you still have a serious alcohol problem? The answer to both of these questions is yes. Alcohol problems are not defined by what kind of alcohol you drink, when you drink, or even how long you've been drinking. Having an alcohol problem depends on how important alcohol has become to you and how seriously drinking is affecting your life. According to the Department of Health and Human Services, a person with an alcohol problem is anyone who:

■ Drinks in order to get to school or work.
■ Drives a motor vehicle while intoxicated.
■ Does something under the influence of alcohol that he or she would not have done without alcohol.

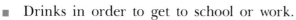

A person with an alcohol problem needs to be helped to deal with emotional troubles that contribute to the problem.

- Becomes injured seriously enough as a result of alcohol to need medical attention.
- Comes into conflict with the law as a result of being intoxicated.
- Has been intoxicated four times in a single year.

Helping a person with an alcohol problem is hard to do. It is, in fact, impossible unless that person sees that there is a problem and wants to do something about it. Just as important, the person must want help in solving the problem. A person may have to go into a hospital or other facility for **detoxification**, or withdrawal from the drug. But if the person receives early treatment for the alcohol problem, entering a hospital is not usually needed. Once a person decides to get help, there are many different community organizations, such as churches, health centers, and family service agencies, to help with the treatment program.

The aim of treatment is to make the individual a happier, more self-aware person who does not need alcohol in order to function. The person learns how to deal with the fears, tensions, feelings of inadequacy, and other conflicts that contribute to a drinking problem. There are also many facilities to help people cope with an alcoholic in the home.

Alcoholics Anonymous

Many alcoholics get help from an organization called **Alcoholics Anonymous** (AA). All AA members are former drinkers. They try to help each other during times of crisis. They give each other extra strength to overcome the physical and psychological need for alcohol. This is done on a day-to-day basis. The AA member makes no promise to reform. But every day, the person pledges not to take a drink that day. Over a period of time, the alcoholic may be able to break the habit and to regain a feeling of self-respect and usefulness.

Al-Anon, an associate organization of AA, is for spouses of alcoholics. Whether or not the alcoholic is receiving help from Alcoholics Anonymous, the husband or wife can get help from Al-Anon to cope with the alcoholic spouse.

Alateen

A high school boy in Pasadena, California, whose father was an alcoholic, talked with some friends who had the same problem. Their discussion later included a counselor. It led to the development of **Alateen**, an organization for the children of alcoholics. There are now about 2,000 chapters all over the United States. Local Alateen chapters are listed in the telephone book.

The purpose of Alateen is to help its members cope with problems that come up in homes where one or both parents drink too much.

Meetings are informal with frank, sincere, and honest discussions. Members do not criticize alcoholics or look for sympathy. Instead, they try to understand their own problems. This helps them to overcome feelings of inferiority and hopelessness. It also helps them to face and adjust to their situations objectively and realistically. They report that they find it helpful to talk with other young people who have similar problems.

M.A.D.D.

On May 3, 1980, 13-year-old Cari Lightner of Fair Oaks, California, was walking with a friend inside the bicycle lane on a highway when she was struck from behind and killed by a hit-and-run drunk driver. Cari's mother, Candy, was stunned to learn that the driver, a middle-aged man with two previous drunk-driving convictions, was unlikely to go to jail for killing Cari. Candy Lightner quit her real-estate job and launched **M.A.D.D.** (Mothers Against Drunk Drivers). What began as a one-woman crusade for personal justice has resulted in over 100 chapters spread throughout almost every state. The goals of the organization include:

- Reducing the number of deaths and injuries caused by drunk drivers by fighting plea bargaining, probation, and light fines and sentences.
- Providing assistance for the victims of drunk-driver crimes through individual and family counseling, support groups, and information and referral services.
- Sponsoring community awareness and education programs and keeping the issues of drunk-driver crimes in the public eye.

Candy Lightner, founder of M.A.D.D., is shown here speaking in Washington.

Candy Lightner's experience with Mother's Against Drunk Drivers is an example of what one citizen can do to bring about change.

Students Against Driving Drunk (**S.A.D.D.**) began as a project in a high school in Massachusetts following the alcohol-related traffic deaths of several students at the school. Students signed S.A.D.D. contracts with their parents, promising to call home at any hour when a "sober" ride home was not available. In return, the parents pledged "to come and get you at any hour, any place, no questions asked, and no argument at that time. . . ." S.A.D.D. now has over 100 chapters throughout the nation. Each chapter organizes its own campaign against drunk driving.

An important decision

Whether or not to use alcohol is an important decision. A person's health and safety often depend on if, how much, and under what circumstances alcohol is consumed. For these and other reasons, more and more people—young and older people alike—are exercising their right not to drink. When offered alcohol as a way to have a good time, many teenagers have a ready "no" answer. Some plan in advance how they will respond to different situations. Others respond spontaneously. Here are some of their responses:

- "It's not for *me*."
- "Thanks, but I want to *remember* this party."
- "I don't need alcohol to have a good time."
- "Not tonight."
- "No, thanks. I'm driving."
- "I'm not interested."
- "I have a better time without it."
- "I'd just as soon drink a soda."
- "No thanks."

Can you think of other responses that might be appropriate, depending on the circumstances?

Key Words

Alateen	blood alcohol	fetal alcohol
Alcoholics	concentration	syndrome
Anonymous	detoxification	intoxicated
alcoholism	distillation	M.A.D.D.
	fermentation	S.A.D.D.

- Alcohol is a dangerous, habit-forming drug.
- Drinking too many alcoholic beverages can lead to serious mental and physical health problems.
- Many automobile accidents and other tragedies are caused by the use of alcohol.
- There are definite signs that a person has an alcohol problem.
- There are many community organizations available to help the problem drinker and the drinker's family.

1. Is alcohol a drug? Explain some of the effects it has on the brain.
2. Does alcohol warm you up? Explain.
3. Describe a serious mental health risk for teenagers using alcoholic beverages.
4. What is the danger in not seeking help for a person who loses consciousness from drinking?
5. What is FAS? What is the risk of FAS to the unborn child of a woman who drinks a great deal of any alcoholic beverage on any given day?
6. Why is it dangerous to drive while under the influence of alcohol? What does BAC mean?
7. Give four indications that a person has an alcohol problem.
8. What is detoxification? What is the aim of detoxification?
9. Describe an Alateen meeting. Who specifically is Alateen intended to help?
10. Describe how M.A.D.D. started. What are some of M.A.D.D.'s goals?

1. Do some research on Prohibition in an encylopedia or history text. When did it take place? What factors led to it? How was it enforced? Finally, what led to the repeal of Prohibition? Report to the class on what you have learned.
2. Investigate what regulations exist in your state concerning the purchase, sale, possession, and consumption of alcoholic beverages. Find out which laws apply to adults and which to minors. Write a summary of the laws and their penalties.
3. Find out what resources are in your community to help the problem drinker and the drinker's family. Determine how well facilities that offer these resources are publicized and whether the resources that exist are sufficient to handle the problem. If possible, interview community officials and representatives of the facilities. Present your findings to the class.

Chapter 22
Drugs

After reading this chapter, you will be able to:

☐ Identify the main types of drugs used to maintain health.

☐ Explain what leads people to abuse psychoactive drugs.

☐ Name and describe the four kinds of commonly abused drugs.

☐ Identify a healthful alternative to drug use.

Of the 180,000 commercials the average television viewer sees before the age of 18, the majority sell "harmless" drugs. Advertisers spend billions of dollars to make you believe that wine, beer, cola, aspirin, coffee, diet pills, sleeping pills, and cold remedies are useful in making you "feel good fast." The media have convinced people that drugs are glamorous, easy to take, and totally risk free with almost instantaneous effects. People who cannot cope with daily stresses or those who are simply bored learn this drug message well. But how safe are these "harmless" drugs? And what is the likelihood, once a person has developed the "drug habit," of moving on to substances that are clearly unsafe?

Drugs for health

Most drugs are used to restore or maintain health. Certain drugs prevent disease. For example, in 1967, 20 million people had smallpox. The World Health Organization organized a campaign against the disease. As a result of this, smallpox was almost completely eliminated. **Vaccines**, such as the one used against smallpox, help the body to fight bacteria and viruses that can cause disease. **Antibiotics** and other drugs fight infections that have already developed in the body. Penicillin has been used successfully to treat many diseases, including some sexually transmitted diseases. Still other drugs are useful in controlling those diseases that cannot be cured. Epilepsy and diabetes mellitus are two examples of diseases that can be controlled with medication.

Many different kinds of drugs are used to relieve pain. **Analgesics**, such as aspirin, allow people to be comfortable while they recover from illness or injury. Aspirin is probably the most widely used drug. Besides relieving pain, aspirin can reduce fever and inflammation. **Anesthetics**, such as novocaine or sodium pentothal, cause numbness or insensitivity to pain. With these drugs, physicians can perform surgery or other procedures that would otherwise be too painful.

Space-age drugs

Each year, pharmaceutical companies (drug manufacturers) develop new drugs to treat ulcers, high blood pressure, depression, migraine headaches, insomnia, fatigue (extreme tiredness), and constipation. It may not have been obvious to you as you read this list of ailments, but they all have something in common. All can be caused by stress, and stress is part of our fast-paced society. A first step in a wellness approach to health is to slow down and learn to take things in stride.

Psychoactive drugs and drug abuse

Sometimes stress gets out of hand. Medications have been created to help people deal with stressful situations. These medications are called **psychoactive drugs**. Psychoactive drugs seem to change a person's mood or behavior.

Countless new drugs are manufactured each year.

In many cultures, psychoactive drugs have been used for pleasure, escape, and relaxation, as well as for treatment of disease. In certain Native American cultures, such drugs have been used for religious and mystical experiences. But psychoactive drugs can also be used destructively. In the United States, it is thought that hundreds of thousands of people are physically or psychologically dependent on drugs.

Why people abuse psychoactive drugs

Many people believe that the social environment is a very important cause of drug use and abuse. Because many drugs are easy to get and people now are more aware of them than before, drug use has increased. Popular attitudes toward drugs are important, too. Some people claim that drug advertising is too widespread. They feel that advertising has made Americans believe that drugs can change anything—even their lives. Dissatisfaction and frustration may also lead people to use psychoactive drugs.

People in troubled emotional states are more likely to use drugs than well-adjusted people. People who are anxious, depressed, or bored may also use drugs. They may return to the use of drugs again and again in order to feel comfortable. Peer-group pressure also influences many young people's experimentation with drugs. Using drugs may seem to be a way to keep one's membership in certain social groups.

Some drugs are more likely to be abused than others because of the way they act in the body. A drug's capacity to produce tolerance and dependence may cause a person to use it again and again. **Tolerance** means that a person's body becomes used to the effects of a drug that is taken regularly. Larger and larger doses are needed to produce the effect. For example, a half glass of wine or liquor might make an inexperienced drinker "high." Later on, that same drinker might need a half bottle to produce the same effect. An expensive drug that produces tolerance may become extremely costly to a user.

Physical dependence takes time to develop. It may take weeks or even months for a person's body to become dependent on a drug. After that, the person must have regular doses of it. If a person who is physically dependent on a drug does not get the amount of the drug that the body has come to need, that person will suffer **withdrawal symptoms**. Trembling, hallucinations, nausea, and vomiting are some of the symptoms of withdrawal. Sudden withdrawal from a drug can be fatal.

It is important to realize that not all psychoactive drugs cause physical dependence, or **addiction**. However, regular users develop another kind of dependence on these drugs called **psychological dependence**. This kind of dependence results from a mental or emotional need, not a physical one. The problems produced by psychological dependence are similar to those caused by physical dependence.

What effects do psychoactive drugs have on a person's body? Which drugs produce tolerance? Which drugs are likely to cause physical

Most people experience some degree of depression or anxiety at some time. Finding someone to talk with is a good way to cope with this. Drugs should never be used except under a doctor's direction.

Your Life-Style and Drug Dependency

Researchers have found that there are many patterns of social development that are closely related to drug use. Your life-style is an important indicator. Complete the following questionnaire to see if your life-style could lead to drug dependency.

Directions: Count the number of times you respond *yes* to the questions.

1. I am more of a leader than a follower.
2. I prefer to be with people who do not use drugs.
3. I am a member of a school club or a religious youth group.
4. I exercise to stay physically fit and also to relax.
5. I have responsibilities at home.
6. I have several close friends.
7. I am confident in my school work.
8. I make friends easily.
9. I read the labels and warnings on products I consume.
10. I have developed both short- and long-term goals.
11. I am looking forward to a rewarding future.
12. I have a healthy life-style.
13. I have decided on several wellness goals.
14. I have a good relationship with my family.
15. I have good relationships with my teachers.
16. I have hobbies or take part in recreational activities or competitive sports.
17. I eat nutritiously.
18. Stresses that I have are manageable.
19. I have good role models.
20. I feel good about my race.
21. I feel that I am an asset to my family.
22. I like the community in which I live.
23. I am aware of the potential danger of all drugs.
24. I feel very little peer pressure.
25. So far, growing up has not presented too many problems.

If you answered *yes* to 20 or more questions, the chances are good that your life-style will keep you from using drugs. If you answered *yes* to fewer than 15 questions, you may decide to change a specific part of your life-style to avoid drug dependence.

dependence? Don't depend on friends and classmates for answers to these questions. The facts provided in this chapter are only part of the information that is available to you. Study as much of the current literature on drugs as you can. Your life or the life of someone you know may depend on how much you know about the effects of drugs.

Most of the commonly abused psychoactive drugs can be divided into four major categories: depressants, narcotics, stimulants, and hallucinogens.

Commonly abused drugs

Depressants

Depressants slow down the activity of certain areas of the brain and spinal cord. These drugs cause muscles to relax and the rates of breathing and heartbeat to slow down. Alcohol is the most widely used drug in this group. It is discussed separately in Chapter 21. The effects of alcohol are very similar to the effects of other depressants. Keep this in mind as you read about them.

Barbiturates. Next to alcohol, **barbiturates** are the most widely used kind of depressant. Barbiturates slow down a person's reaction time, just as alcohol does. They also produce drowsiness and possibly slurred speech. They may reduce anxiety, but they also decrease mental functioning and memory. And high doses of barbiturates may result in coma and death.

Barbiturates are extremely dangerous when they are taken with alcohol. Taken together in doses that would not be fatal by themselves, barbiturates and alcohol depress brain and nervous system functioning so much that they can actually stop a person's breathing. Many accidental deaths have occurred because people who had been drinking alcoholic beverages took what would have been an otherwise safe amount of barbiturates in the form of sleeping pills.

Tolerance to barbiturates develops quickly. These drugs tend to produce both strong psychological and physical dependence. Sudden withdrawal from them can be dangerous or even fatal. Medically supervised, gradual withdrawal from barbiturates is safer and less painful for someone dependent on them.

Tranquilizers. **Tranquilizers** are depressants that help to calm a person's emotions without interfering with alertness or the ability to think clearly. Tranquilizers are less likely to cause dependence than barbiturates. But using tranquilizers in large doses over a long period of time can create tolerance and dependence.

Narcotics

Some abused **narcotics** are opium, heroin, morphine, and codeine. All of these drugs are derived from the opium poppy flower. **Morphine** is one of the best pain relievers known to medicine. **Codeine** is a weaker pain reliever than morphine and is used especially in prescription cough medicines. **Heroin** is made by heating morphine in the presence of acetic acid. Heroin has the same effects as morphine, but is about 20 times more powerful than morphine. In the United States, heroin is illegal, even for doctors to prescribe, because it is so addictive. Heroin users in America often become involved in crime and illegal trade to pay for their habit. Users take the risk of dying from an overdose. Overdoses usually occur because users cannot be sure of the strength of the black-market heroin they are buying. Overdoses also occur because of changes in individual tolerance levels.

Opium-based drugs are highly addictive, and physical dependence develops quickly. Withdrawal symptoms include runny nose and eyes, weakness, depression, nausea, vomiting, diarrhea, and muscle cramps. These symptoms reach their peak within 24 hours and are usually over in about 48 hours. Complete withdrawal, however, may take as long as 6 months. But the problems caused by withdrawal from heroin or morphine are actually less severe than those caused by withdrawal from alcohol or barbiturates.

Methadone. **Methadone** is a synthetic drug made in chemical laboratories. Since the 1950s, it has been offered to heroin addicts as a legal substitute for heroin in drug programs in the United States. Methadone has also been used as a painkiller in both Europe and the United States since World War II. It relieves addicts of their cravings and helps them to function in everyday society. But, like heroin, methadone is addictive. By itself, methadone has little mood-altering effect. However, it is especially dangerous to combine this drug with other depressants. Deaths from overdoses have occurred when methadone was used in combination with alcohol, barbiturates, or heroin.

Methadone can be an effective part of a withdrawal program for heroin addicts. Such a program usually includes psychological counseling and general health care. Heroin addicts must be helped to confront their own psychological dependence on drugs. Most drug abusers build their lives around obtaining and using a drug. This is especially true of people using illegal substances. Changing an entire life-style is difficult, but it must be done if addicts want to break their drug habits successfully.

There are other medical problems associated with narcotics abuse. Serious infections may result from injections with needles that are not sterile. Malnutrition is also common. Drug abusers often neglect the other needs of their bodies.

Each year, many babies are born with an addiction to heroin. These infants are born to women who were users of heroin during pregnancy. The infants need medical care to help them withdraw gradually from narcotics. Drugs, such as heroin, tranquilizers, barbiturates, alcohol, and even aspirin, pass from a mother's bloodstream through the placenta to the unborn child. Thus, pregnant women must be especially thoughtful and careful about drug use. It has been found that many drugs affect the normal development of unborn babies. This is true even when the drugs are used in commonly prescribed doses.

Stimulants

Stimulants speed up processes in the body. They cause the heart to beat faster, circulation and respiration to increase, and blood pressure to rise. Some of the stronger drugs in this group cause **euphoria**, or strong feelings of well-being. Nicotine is a harmful stimulant; it is discussed in Chapter 20 on tobacco and smoking.

Caffeine. **Caffeine** is a widely used stimulant in America. It is used by people of all ages. Caffeine can be found in beverages, such as coffee, tea, cocoa, and cola drinks. It is also present in chocolate and in nonprescription drugs used for overcoming tiredness. The use of caffeine is socially accepted and even supported in the United States. Products containing this drug are easy to buy and relatively inexpensive. A normal dose of caffeine, such as the amount in a cup of coffee or tea, can relieve drowsiness and muscle fatigue for a while by increasing the pulse rate. Caffeine also increases urination.

Caffeine, a psychoactive drug, is found in such beverages as coffee.

Caffeine can be abused if too much of the substances that contain caffeine are consumed. Drinking five or more cups of coffee a day may cause physical dependence. The physical effects of caffeine abuse include nervousness and insomnia. Excessive stimulation of the heart can produce palpitations (rapid heartbeat) and other problems. Caffeine can also complicate the health problems of people with high blood pressure and peptic ulcers.

Amphetamines. **Amphetamines** are synthetic stimulants. Methamphetamine, or "speed," is a commonly abused drug in this group. Medically, amphetamines have been used to treat depression, overweight, uncontrolled and excessive sleeping, and overactive children. The immediate effects of amphetamines include a quick elevation of mood and a sudden feeling of power or energy. Users report that they are able to concentrate intensely and that tiredness is reduced. Abusers of these drugs often become thin, nervous, and aggressive. They suffer from lack of appetite, poor nutrition, and lack of sleep. They may also experience delusions (false ideas about themselves) and other emotional disorders.

Psychological dependence and tolerance develop quickly with these drugs. People who use amphetamines depend on these substances in order to feel happy. Physical dependence and withdrawal symptoms do not appear to be problems with amphetamines.

Cocaine. **Cocaine** is a substance that comes from the leaves of the coca plant. Pure cocaine has been used as a local anesthetic for surgery of the eyes, ears, nose, and throat. Cocaine sold on the streets usually contains large amounts of such fillers as powdered sugar, amphetamines, and quinine. The fillers mimic some of the effects of cocaine and increase profits for the dealer.

These harmless-looking plants are lethal substances in the wrong hands.

Cocaine causes blood vessels to narrow so that heart rate, blood pressure, and body temperature increase. The muscles controlling the iris constrict and cause the pupils of the eyes to dilate. If cocaine is used over a period of time, the user will experience loss of appetite and weight, malnutrition, inability to sleep, hallucinations, and paranoia. Users become psychologically dependent and are often deeply depressed when they withdraw. Cocaine was once thought to be a "safe" and "nonaddictive" drug. Today, researchers and physicians consider cocaine to be extremely dangerous and addictive. *Crack* is cocaine in small chips or pellets, smoked in a pipe. Because it is smoked, it is more potent and much faster-acting than powdered cocaine. Crack is very, very dangerous. A roller coaster effect is caused by the feeling of depression after use and an immediate craving for more; people become addicted to it in as short a time as days or weeks.

Hallucinogens

Hallucinogens include drugs like **LSD** (lysergic acid diethylamide), mescaline, and psilocybin. These drugs are usually swallowed. As the name of these substances suggests, they cause hallucinations, or sense distortions, in the user. Mescaline, peyote, and psilocybin are obtained from plants. Mescaline and peyote come from the peyote cactus. Psilocybin is obtained from certain mushrooms. Other hallucinogens, such as LSD, are produced in chemical laboratories.

The effects of these drugs depend on the mental state of the individual user and on the surrounding environment. Some users may experience intense mood swings from complete joy to utter depression or terror.

Though tolerance can develop with frequent use, hallucinogens cause little psychological dependence and no physical dependence.

PCP (phencyclohexylpiperidine) has qualities of both depressant and hallucinogenic drugs. It is an extremely dangerous drug. Used in combination with other drugs, it intensifies their effects. The effects of this drug vary widely from one individual to another. "Angel dust," as PCP is sometimes called, produces either depression or stimulation of the central nervous system, depending upon the dosage and the way it is taken into the body. Low doses produce effects like those of alcohol intoxication. Higher doses may produce acute psychosis, convulsions, coma, and even death. At certain times, PCP may produce extreme agitation, hallucinations, and psychotic behavior. This can include such violent acts as homicide, suicide, or self-mutilation.

Marijuana

Marijuana is a complex drug obtained from the hemp plant, which is known as *Cannabis sativa*. It contains over 150 known chemicals and the same cancer-causing lung irritants found in tobacco. The major mind-altering ingredient in marijuana is THC (delta-9-tetrahydrocannabinol). With improved growing methods, the amount of THC in marijuana today is ten times greater than the amount 5 years ago. With increased levels of THC, marijuana users risk the chance of affecting the normal functions of the reproductive and respiratory systems. **Hashish** is made from the flowering tops of the female hemp plant, which have higher concentrations of THC.

There is no doubt that marijuana, even when used in small amounts, is a dangerous drug. When smoked, it is potentially more damaging to the lungs than cigarette smoking. Marijuana is inhaled more deeply into the lungs and is held for a longer period of time. The irritating chemicals thus cause more damage to delicate lung tissue and increase the chance of THC absorption into the bloodstream. Since THC is absorbed by the body's fatty tissue, the reproductive organs, the lungs, and the brain store the chemical for several weeks and perhaps as long as a month. Marijuana users who smoke several times a week increase the amount of THC in their bodies.

Marijuana does not fit neatly into any of the four categories of abused drugs. It acts partly like a depressant and partly like a stimulant. Depending on the dose and the individual, marijuana can produce a wide variety of physiological effects. Studies made over the last 10 years indicate that some of the following effects will occur with moderate use:

—distortion of time perception
—increase in heart rate
—difficulty in understanding what is read
—impairment of short-term memory

—decreased judgment and coordination
—confusion and anxiety
—increase in appetite and thirst
—unpredictable behavior
—difficulty in forming concepts
—difficulty in tracking moving objects
—poor eye-hand coordination

Since some of the effects remain long after smoking, a person who drives under the influence of marijuana is taking a serious risk. Researchers are investigating the long-term effects of marijuana. Effects in males are found to include low sperm count and an increase in the number of sperm with abnormal appearance and movement. In females, there is evidence that THC blocks ovulation.

Experiments have shown that high doses of THC can also produce physical dependence in some people. A person smoking several marijuana cigarettes a day will experience irritation, stomach pains, sweating, insomnia, and other mild withdrawal symptoms when smoking is stopped. Psychological dependence is also very possible.

The younger the person using marijuana, the greater the impact on the systems of the body. Physicians and psychiatrists have expressed concern about its use by young people. Any drug that becomes central in young people's lives can prevent them from facing problems and developing strong and healthy personalities.

Ecstasy (XTC)

3,4-methylenedioxymethamphetamine, better known as MDMA or **ecstasy (XTC)**, is a new threat, although the drug is actually not new. In 1914, chemists accidentally created MDMA to reduce appetite. Ecstasy is usually classified as a hallucinogen, but it also has some characteristics of a stimulant. Many drug-treatment programs around the country are reporting serious health problems in MDMA users. The effects of the drug vary from uncontrollable contraction of the jaw muscles (clenching and biting of the inside of the cheek) to possible psychosis. Researchers at the UCLA Neuropsychiatric Institute have labeled MDMA unpredictable. Serious convulsions and death have resulted from large doses.

The Drug Enforcement Administration has classified ecstasy as a dangerous substance, and illegal possession is a serious offense.

Multiple-drug abuse

Polydrug abuse, or multiple-drug abuse, is a serious addiction to two or more drugs. Many polydrug users take additional drugs either to increase the effects or decrease the aftereffects of the other drugs. Marijuana, alcohol, cocaine, and diazepam (a tranquilizer) are the most common chemicals mixed by polydrug abusers.

Alcohol and marijuana are the drugs most often substituted when the drug of choice isn't available. When a person smokes marijuana and drinks alcohol, the mixture is very dangerous. Marijuana blocks the body's normal ability to eliminate some toxins in alcohol. The toxic alcohol then builds up in the bloodstream and organs.

Over 3,000 people die each year from mixing barbiturates and alcohol. Combining the two depressants has a serious effect on the central nervous system, which controls breathing and heartbeat.

Physicians have difficulty helping polydrug users who are brought into an emergency room. Symptoms that are normally used to diagnose drug abusers become confusing because the polydrug abuser may have taken a tranquilizer, a stimulant, and other drugs.

Drug abusers are not the only ones who need to be careful about multiple-drug use. For example, anyone who takes a drug to prevent blood from clotting should not take aspirin with the drug. Aspirin slows down the clotting time of blood so that severe bleeding may result. There are many other drug reactions that can take place in your body. You must investigate to learn about the chemicals in your food, medicines, and environment. A healthy body and mind will rely on drugs as little as necessary.

Runners sometimes talk about "runner's high." They describe the runner's high as a source of exhilaration that makes them feel as though they could run forever. Young people involved in other forms of exercise,

Alternative to drug use

Teach yourself to recognize—and practice—happy alternatives to drug abuse.

such as jogging and aerobic dancing, experience similar reactions. These exercise-related "highs" seem to be an acceptable, happy alternative to drugs.

Researchers have become interested in learning what is responsible for runner's high. The source of this power appears to be two kinds of chemicals released by the body. The first group of chemicals is called beta-endorphins. They block the nerve receptor sites to prevent the sensation of pain from reaching the brain. Have you noticed that you are less sensitive to pain when you are involved in vigorous physical activity? The second type of chemical is called adenosine triphosphate, or ATP. This chemical appears to cause blood vessels to widen so that the brain will receive large amounts of blood. Both ATP and beta-endorphins may be responsible for the "terrific feeling" that you experience after aerobics, swimming, or even an after-school run around the track. Terrific feelings can also be experienced when you excel in personal growth. When you continue to build feelings of self-worth and confidence, you are on your way to a drug-free life.

Key Words

addiction	euphoria	polydrug abuse
amphetamines	hallucinogens	psychoactive
analgesics	hashish	drugs
anesthetics	heroin	psychological
antibiotics	LSD	dependence
barbiturates	marijuana	stimulants
caffeine	methadone	tolerance
cocaine	morphine	tranquilizers
codeine	narcotics	vaccines
depressants	PCP	withdrawal
ecstasy (XTC)	physical	symptoms
	dependence	

Main Ideas

- Most drugs are used to restore or maintain health.
- The abuse of psychoactive drugs in our society is a serious and dangerous problem.
- The commonly used psychoactive drugs can be divided into four basic categories—depressants, narcotics, stimulants, and hallucinogens. Marijuana, however, has a variety of effects.
- Polydrug abuse and the use of XTC (ecstasy) are on the rise among drug users.
- The athlete's "high" is attracting more and more young people as a healthy alternative to drug abuse.

1. Describe the functions of vaccines and antibiotics.
2. What is tolerance? What effect does it have on a drug user?
3. What is the difference between psychological and physical dependence on drugs?
4. Compare the general effects of depressants and stimulants on the human body.
5. What can happen when barbiturates and alcohol are used together?
6. What are the medical uses for morphine, amphetamines, and cocaine?
7. What are some of the dangers of using marijuana?
8. What was the original medical use of MDMA? When was it first manufactured?
9. Why do physicians have difficulty helping polydrug users brought into hospital emergency rooms?
10. What two types of chemicals are believed by researchers to cause "runner's high"? Explain how each of them works in the body.

1. Collect articles on drugs and drug abuse from magazines and newspapers. These may be articles about or by individuals who have struggled with the problem of abuse. Try to find common characteristics of drug users, and develop a profile of the typical drug user. The following questions may help you in your development of such a profile: (1) Is there any relationship between the drug used and the background of the user? (2) How do individuals with drug problems finance their problem? (3) How do the individuals look back on their experiences as abusers of drugs? (4) What steps did these individuals take to overcome their abuse problems? When you have constructed your profile, make a report to the class.
2. Obtain a copy of your state's laws concerning the possession, use, delivery, and sale of controlled substances. Write a summary of the laws and the penalties for breaking them. Report your findings to the class.
3. Contact a drug treatment facility in your locality and arrange to interview a drug counselor. Determine: (1) the average length of time an individual spends at the facility during recovery, (2) what kinds of treatment are offered for various physical and psychological dependencies, and (3) whether there is any "follow-up" work to be done by the recovering addict after he or she is released. In a report to the class, summarize what you have learned.

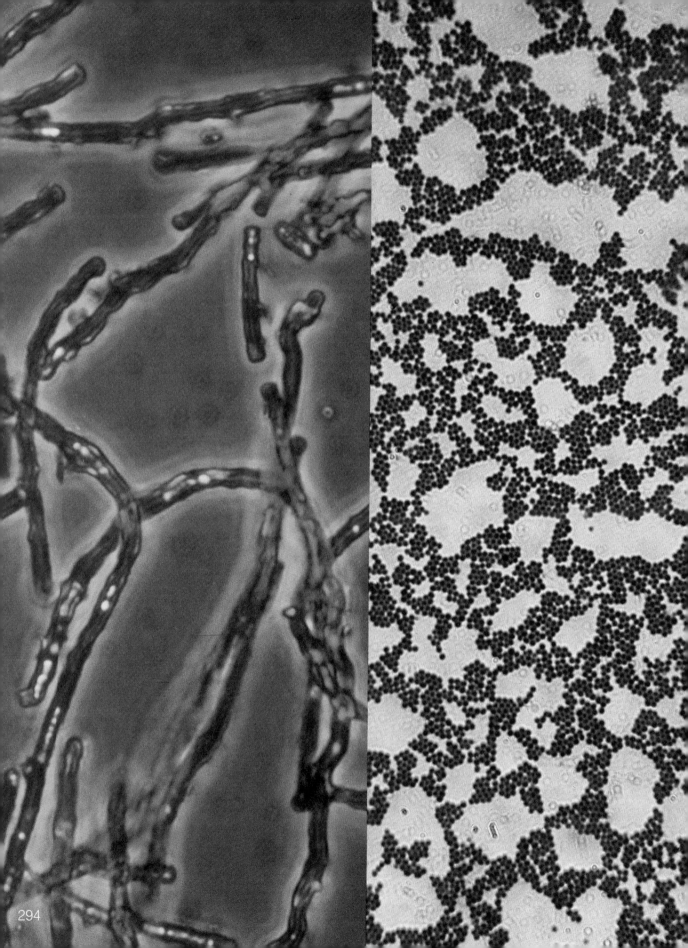

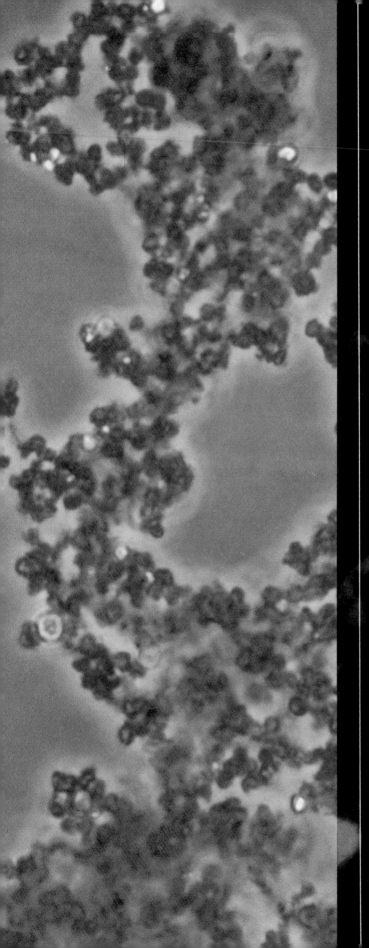

Unit 7
Communi-cable Diseases

Chapter 23

Infectious Diseases

After reading this chapter, you will be able to:

- ☐ Identify the causes of infectious diseases.
- ☐ Explain communicable disease.
- ☐ Explain how the body fights disease.
- ☐ Identify the most common infectious diseases and describe their symptoms.
- ☐ Explain how to prevent infectious diseases.

Smallpox. Plague. Typhoid fever. Diphtheria. These are some of the diseases that people have dreaded throughout history. At one period or another, each disease destroyed large segments of a population.

During the fourteenth century, one-fourth of the population of Europe, or 25 million people, died from the plague. No one knew what caused the plague. Some thought sickness was caused by "evil spirits."

Not until Anton van Leeuwenhoek invented the simple microscope in the seventeenth century did scientists have the tool to learn the causes of disease. Leeuwenhoek saw what he called "animalcules" with his microscope. His discovery led to an understanding that many diseases are caused by microorganisms too small to be seen with the naked eye. Not all microorganisms, of course, cause disease. Those that do are called *pathogens*, and sometimes, germs.

Pathogens and infection

The most common pathogens are **bacteria** and **viruses**. Bacteria are single-celled organisms with cell walls and without easily identifiable nucleuses. Viruses are not cells, but they do have genetic material and can reproduce in living tissue. Viruses are smaller than bacteria and cannot be seen under an ordinary microscope. However, many of them can be seen under the more powerful electron microscope. Some fungi (small, plantlike organisms) and some protozoa (small, animal-like organisms) also cause disease.

The diseases caused by pathogens or their products are called **infectious diseases**. Some, such as the common cold, cause minor illness. Others can cause serious illness or even death.

Many, but not all, infectious diseases are also **communicable diseases**, or **contagious diseases**. This means that they can be passed from one person or animal to another. These are the diseases that can lead to epidemics, such as the one that occurred in Europe in the fourteenth century. A chart presenting a partial list of infectious diseases and their occurrences appears on page 301.

Some infectious diseases can be passed from one person to another even though the infected person is not ill with the disease. People who can give a disease to others when they are not ill themselves are called **carriers**.

Sources of infection

Many of the pathogens that cause infectious diseases can live and reproduce only inside the human body or the body of an animal. These pathogens can spread from one person or animal to another in a number of ways. Some pathogens spread directly from person to person. For example, the mucus released in sneezing, speaking, or coughing

An outbreak of plague in the fourteenth century is thought to have killed more than half the population of Europe and Asia.

can spread pathogens. So can direct contact with saliva. Colds and influenza are often passed in these ways. Direct contact with open skin sores may also spread some bacteria and viruses.

Pathogens can also be spread indirectly, such as by handling the silverware or clothing of an infected person. Food may carry pathogens. Pathogens in the air may either land on food or be carried directly to the food by the person preparing it. Some intestinal infections, such as typhoid, are caused by pathogens in food that was contaminated by animal waste products.

Water polluted by sewage may also carry pathogens that cause intestinal diseases. Rats, houseflies, and mosquitoes frequently carry pathogens from such sources as garbage or sewage. Still other pathogens live on damp surfaces and can be carried on toothbrushes or towels.

Actions of pathogens in the body

Pathogens enter a human body in a number of ways: through the digestive or respiratory tracts, through breaks in the skin, or through the mucous membranes. After entering the body, the pathogens multiply. At first, they cause no symptoms of the disease. This period of time is called the **incubation period**. The incubation period of most infectious diseases may last from a few hours to several days. Once the pathogens have become sufficiently large in number, symptoms such as pain, fever, redness, and swelling occur, and you know you are sick.

Defenses against infection

You are always coming into contact with many pathogens. Yet, you are not always ill. This is because your body has an amazing system of defenses. This ability of the body to fight off infection is known as **resistance**. Resistance to infection depends on several factors. A healthy person is usually able to resist many infectious diseases. Poor nutrition, chronic illness, too much alcohol, and smoking lower resistance. So do emotional stress and age. The elderly and the newborn are more likely to get certain infections.

The body has some natural barriers to infection. Healthy, unbroken skin provides one barrier. Hairs in the nose and cilia in the throat help to screen out pathogens from the air we breathe. Stomach acid destroys some pathogens after they enter the body. But the body's best methods of defense are certain blood cells and substances made in the blood that help to kill some pathogens.

Leukocytes, or white blood cells, surround, kill, and digest invading organisms. Someone who has too few white blood cells is very open to infections. Some medications may lower the number of white blood cells in the body. **Antibodies** are protein substances made by certain specialized white blood cells. Antibodies circulate in the bloodstream and attack pathogens. Eating enough protein helps to make sure that your body will have the material it needs to make antibodies. **Antitoxins** are substances the body sometimes produces to neutralize (make inactive) harmful toxins (poisons) that pathogens sometimes produce.

Common infectious diseases

The common cold, influenza, hepatitis, and mononucleosis are some of the ordinary infectious diseases that affect people every year. Unfortunately, there are no cures for these diseases. But understanding something about their causes can help you from getting them.

The common cold

Every year, people miss many days of school and work because of the common cold. The average person may have three or four colds a year. A heavy smoker may have six or more. Many different viruses cause colds. Each cold you get may be caused by a different virus. The incubation period of a cold is very short—only about 18 to 48 hours. The cold itself usually lasts from 2 to 7 days. Runny nose, sneezing, sore throat, and slight headache are some of the symptoms.

There is no medication that will cure a cold. Your doctor may prescribe some that provide relief from its symptoms, however. A pain reliever, such as acetaminophen, is sometimes suggested to relieve the aches and fever caused by colds, but take no medication before consulting a physician.

It is very important to keep a cold from turning into a more serious disease. Rest and plenty of liquids will help. Breathing moistened or humidified air is often a very helpful way to clear the passages in the nose. If you have a very sore throat or a high fever or if your cold lasts longer than a week, you should see a physician.

Try to prevent colds. Enough rest, good nutrition, and proper clothing will help keep up your resistance. A cold is still contagious after symptoms have appeared. Stay away from someone who has a "new

Water fountains often carry bacteria and viruses that can cause communicable diseases.

cold," if you can. Try to stay away from crowds during the "cold" season. Do not pass your cold on to others. Practice good hygiene, such as covering your mouth and nose when you sneeze or cough.

Influenza

Influenza, commonly called the flu, is a very contagious disease caused by a virus. There are only two main types of influenza virus—type A and type B. But there are many kinds of A virus and many kinds of B virus. In one way, these viruses act in a strange manner—they undergo **mutations** (changes in structure) very rapidly. Every few years, a new kind of influenza virus appears. When this happens, there is usually an epidemic. Many people "catch the flu." For example, in the late 1960s, the Hong Kong flu spread all over the world. In 1972, the London flu appeared, and the Russian flu occurred in 1978. These flu epidemics often occur in the winter and spring.

Be sure to cover your nose and mouth when you sneeze.

Influenza usually has an incubation period of 1 to 3 days. The early symptoms are like the symptoms of the common cold. Then fever, cough, weakness, and muscle aches often develop. Sometimes a patient will also feel sad and depressed. Fluids, bed rest, and medications to ease pain are the best treatments. Again, young people should not take any medication for flu except under a doctor's order. Harmful side effects can develop in some young people.

Influenza is contagious from the time just before symptoms appear to about a week later. The virus is usually spread by coughing and sneezing. Some cases of influenza that occur during an epidemic can be rather severe. But the flu is usually not a serious disease. However, it can be dangerous for children with heart disease, elderly people, and people with chronic lung disease. Doctors often advise these people to be vaccinated each year. (See Chapter 25 for information about vaccinations.)

Disease	Number of Cases		
	1960	1970	1980
Amebiasis	3,424	2,888	5,271
Aseptic meningitis	1,593	6,480	8,028
Chicken pox	*	*	190,900
Diphtheria	918	435	3
Encephalitis	2,341	1,950	1,402
Hepatitis	41,700	65,100	60,000
Malaria	72	3,051	2,062
Measles	441,700	47,400	13,500
Meningococcal infections	2,259	2,505	2,840
Mumps	*	105,000	8,600
Pertussis (whooping cough)	14,800	4,200	1,700
Poliomyelitis	3,190	33	9
Rheumatic fever**	9,022	3,227	432
Rubella (German measles)	*	56,600	3,900
Shigellosis (bacillary dysentery)	12,500	13,800	19,000
STD	383,800	693,200	1,074,000 **
Streptococcal sore throat, scarlet fever	315,200	433,400	370,000
Tetanus	368	148	95
Tuberculosis	55,500	37,100	27,700
Typhoid fever	816	346	510
Typhus fever	272	407	1,244

Something to think about

Diseases across two decades

*Figures not available
**Partial report

Source: U.S. Centers for Disease Control, Atlanta, GA

Hepatitis

Many different viruses may cause swelling of the liver, a condition called **hepatitis**. People with hepatitis usually have headache, nausea, vomiting, fever, and pain in the abdomen. They may also have jaundice, a yellow discoloration of the skin, and darkened urine. Hepatitis is a serious illness and may cause other severe problems.

There are several types of hepatitis. Hepatitis A, which is also called infectious hepatitis, is the most common type. The A virus is usually found in water or in food that has been contaminated by feces. It may also be found in uncooked clams and other shellfish. The hepatitis virus can spread through saliva, feces, semen, and vaginal secretions. A doctor may inject someone who has been exposed to the type A virus with a medication called gamma globulin. This helps to protect against the disease.

Hepatitis B, which is also called serum hepatitis, is a more dangerous type. The type B virus spreads through the blood. A person who carries

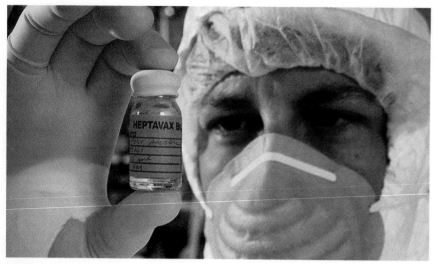
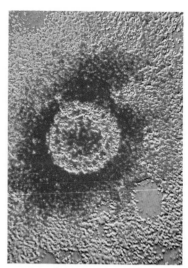

The means by which hepatitis B is spread are well known. The way in which mononucleosis is transmitted remains a mystery.

this virus cannot give blood, because it would infect the person who received it. Drug users who share the same needles to inject drugs into the bloodstream often get hepatitis. Vaccines have been developed to protect people against hepatitis B.

You should take extra safety measures whenever you are close to someone who has hepatitis. Do not share cups and utensils, and avoid close contact with the infected person. Good personal hygiene helps prevent hepatitis. Always wash your hands before eating and after using the toilet.

Mononucleosis

Mononucleosis, better known as "mono," is a fairly common viral infection among high school and college students. In fact, the greatest number of cases of mononucleosis is found among young people 15 to 19 years old. This disease often occurs in places where there are large groups of young people, such as in schools, in colleges, and in the military services. Mononucleosis is sometimes called the "kissing disease." This is because people thought it was spread by kissing. Actually, scientists are not sure how this disease spreads. It is caused by a virus that may be spread through the saliva. But the virus may be spread in other ways, too.

Patients with mono often complain of sore throat, nausea, chills, and fever. The lymph nodes and spleen may be enlarged. There are usually feelings of weakness and tiredness. These feelings can last for weeks, sometimes for months.

The symptoms of mononucleosis are like the symptoms of many other diseases. However, a physician can diagnose mononucleosis with a blood test. People with mono should be under the care of a doctor. They need plenty of rest and should avoid strenuous physical activity.

In the early 1980s, **AIDS** (acquired immune deficiency syndrome) was an infectious disease only a few Americans had heard about. Only a tiny percent of the population had the disease, and most of these victims were homosexual men. Now the disease is spreading. By 1985, occurrence of the disease had doubled. Some 6,000 people—approximately half of all reported cases—had died. Specialists feared that as many as 1 million Americans were symptomless carriers of AIDS. Women and heterosexual men were contracting the disease. Even children had fallen victim. AIDS had become a household word and a national concern.

AIDS is a disease that interferes with the body's ability to fight off infection, leaving the victim open to a host of infections that are often fatal. It is caused by a virus, human T-cell lymphotropic virus-III (HTLV-III), that destroys certain disease-fighting white blood cells.

The first symptoms of the disease are similar to those associated with influenza. These include swollen lymph glands, fatigue, fever, night sweats, diarrhea, and gradual loss of weight. The disease can also cause forgetfulness, impaired speech, tremors, and seizures.

Doctors do not know all the details about how AIDS is transmitted, but they believe the main way is sexually. The disease can also be transmitted directly into the bloodstream through disease-contaminated needles and from infected blood given in transfusions. Doctors do not think it is transmitted through tears or saliva, though research continues. The precise incubation period for the disease is not known, but researchers believe that people can harbor it for years without experiencing symptoms.

Dr. Joseph Gallo of the Centers for Disease Control was one of two researchers to isolate the virus responsible for AIDS.

Next to homosexual men, the group at greatest risk from AIDS is intravenous drug users. Babies of mothers with AIDS are also at risk. People requiring blood transfusions were formerly also endangered, but new methods of testing blood for possible AIDS contamination have been developed.

Any person who has symptoms of the disease or suspects he or she has been exposed to it should see a doctor immediately. Though the disease has no cure, doctors have had some success in treating it with various antiviral medications.

Preventing infectious diseases

Each individual must be responsible for disease prevention. Practice good personal hygiene, eat a nutritional diet with sufficient protein and fresh fruit and vegetables, and get enough rest and exercise to help keep up your resistance against common infections. If you think you have a communicable disease, get medical advice early. This stops other serious problems from developing and prevents the spread of the illness to others. For most bacterial infections, the doctor may prescribe an antibiotic. However, most viruses cannot be killed with antibiotics.

Each day, new discoveries are being made in the control of infectious diseases. More about the prevention and control of communicable diseases appears in the next two chapters.

Key Words

Main Ideas

- Communicable diseases are caused by pathogens passed from an infected person or animal to others.
- The human body has important natural defenses against disease: white blood cells, antibodies, and antitoxins.
- Common infectious diseases include the common cold, influenza, hepatitis, and mononucleosis. AIDS is a serious infectious disease that gained public attention in the early 1980s.
- Good hygiene, sensible nutrition, rest, and exercise help keep up your resistance to infectious diseases.

Understand the Reading

1. What is the difference between viruses and bacteria?
2. What is a carrier?
3. Describe several ways in which pathogens can spread directly from one person to another.
4. What do pathogens do once they have entered the body?
5. Name three factors that lower resistance to infection.
6. Describe how white blood cells kill invading organisms.
7. What is the incubation period of the common cold? Of influenza?
8. How can you avoid contact with the hepatitis virus?
9. Name some common infectious diseases that teenagers may get. How can these diseases be prevented?
10. Name the virus that causes AIDS. What do doctors believe is the main way AIDS is transmitted?

Apply Your Knowledge

1. In an encyclopedia or other reference book, research the bubonic plague. Note when and where it has occurred throughout history, as well as what steps have been taken to treat and prevent it. Write a report for class based on your research.
2. Invite a doctor or public health official to talk to your class about the prevention of infectious disease in your community. Each student should prepare at least three questions to ask. Try to determine what epidemics, if any, have occurred in your community in the last 50 years. Explain how they were dealt with.

Chapter 24
Immunizations

After reading this chapter, you will be able to:

- [ ] Describe how the body develops immunity to disease.
- [ ] Distinguish between natural and acquired immunity.
- [ ] Distinguish between active and passive immunity.
- [ ] Explain how vaccines are made and how they work.
- [ ] Identify and describe the diseases against which all people should be vaccinated.

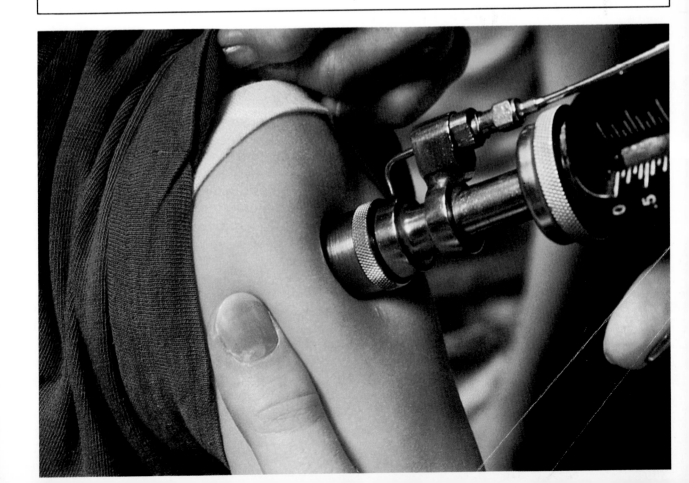

In 1960, close to 3,200 cases of poliomyelitis were reported. In 1980, only 9 cases of the disease were reported. Why the sudden drop? The answer can be summed up in a single word: vaccination.

Until the mid-1950s, polio epidemics were common in this country. In 1952 alone, almost 58,000 Americans were struck with this crippling disease. Then Dr. Jonas Salk developed a *vaccine*. Within 10 years, there were fewer than 100 cases of polio per year.

Vaccines for many other infectious diseases have also been developed. Smallpox has been completely eradicated, and diphtheria and scarlet fever have almost been wiped out.

To understand how vaccines work, you need to understand how the body's immune system works.

Active immunity

When pathogens cause infection in the body, certain specialized white blood cells make protein substances called **antibodies**. Antibodies and white blood cells attack the pathogens. Once the infection has been stopped, the number of antibodies decreases because they are no longer needed. If, however, the same pathogens enter the body a second time, some white blood cells with a kind of chemical "memory" rapidly produce more antibodies. Sometimes they are able to do this quickly enough to kill the pathogens before the infection begins. This ability of the body to form antibodies against pathogens before they can cause disease is called **active immunity**.

Sometimes very few pathogens enter a person's body, and no symptoms of the disease appear. However, the white blood cells still produce antibodies against the pathogens. Immunity may be built up when the same pathogens enter the body in small numbers many times. In these cases, a person may seem never to have the disease at all.

All people are born with some immunity, called **natural immunity**. Immunity the body builds up after having a disease or after being exposed to a disease is called **acquired immunity**. In acquired immunity, the body actively produces substances to fight a certain disease. A person who develops an immunity against such diseases as diphtheria, scarlet fever, measles, mumps, chicken pox, or polio usually is immune for life. The active immunity that follows after recovery from these diseases can last a lifetime.

Vaccines

Scientists and physicians have found that the body can be "fooled" into making antibodies and developing active immunity. Vaccines, or **immunizations**, made from weakened pathogens or from substances made by pathogens do this when they are introduced into the body. They are potent enough to cause the body to make antibodies, but not so potent

Dr. Jonas Salk developed a vaccine to combat polio.

as to cause the disease. Vaccines can be given to people by mouth or by injection. They are a safe way for the body to build up immunity against some diseases.

Different types of vaccine build up immunity for different lengths of time. Measles or mumps vaccines, for example, usually create lifelong immunity. Vaccines against tetanus, however, last only a few years. Follow-up doses of vaccines, called **boosters**, must be taken to keep up the body's level of antibodies.

Another type of vaccine, called a **toxoid**, is made from the poisonous waste products of disease-causing microorganisms. These poisons are treated chemically to make them harmless. But they still can cause the body to make antibodies. Tetanus toxoid is one example.

Side effects of vaccines

Like many medicines, vaccines can cause side effects. However, these effects are usually mild and last only a short time. They may include a slight fever, a sore arm, or a mild rash. A vaccine very rarely causes a serious side effect. For this reason, vaccines should be given only under the direction of trained health professionals. The positive effects of immunization are much greater than the risks of vaccination. People with unusual diseases or allergies, however, may not be able to take some vaccines.

Most, but not all, immunities involve the production of antibodies. With **passive immunity**, a person does not make antibodies, but acquires them in some other way. For example, infants are born with passive immunity to some infections because the antibodies were passed to them

Passive immunity

307

by their mothers before birth. This protective immunity lasts only for a few months. Soon after birth, babies begin to build up their own antibodies against infection.

Another form of passive immunity occurs when a serum made from the blood of another person or animal is given to someone who has been exposed to an infectious disease. The serum contains antibodies and helps to protect the person against the disease-causing microorganisms. The protection lasts only a short time because the person getting the serum is not actively making antibodies.

Responsibility and immunity

You are responsible for keeping up your own immunity against disease. In this country, state laws require the immunization of children as they enter school for the first time. Diseases that have crippled or killed children in the past have been brought almost completely under control by immunization. But the pathogens that cause these diseases are still in the environment. Surveys show that millions of children in the United States have not been properly immunized against many common, preventable diseases, and epidemics can still occur.

Your doctor, school nurse, or parents may be keeping a record of your immunizations. You should keep a record, too. In order to be effective, tetanus immunizations must be kept up to date with booster shots. These boosters should continue about every 10 years, even through adulthood. Other diseases against which people should be immunized include diphtheria, pertussis, poliomyelitis, measles, mumps, and rubella. Certain people who are at risk should also be immunized against

A program of wellness includes immunization against infectious diseases.

influenza. Your doctor can tell you which immunizations you should have.

Diphtheria, pertussis, and tetanus (DPT)

A combination DPT vaccine protects against three diseases—diphtheria, pertussis, and tetanus. This vaccine has been available since the early 1950s. But today, almost 10 million children under age 12 are not properly immunized.

Diphtheria is a serious infectious illness. In the late 1800s, 15 out of every 10,000 Americans died of diphtheria each year. The symptoms of this disease include sore throat and trouble with breathing and swallowing.

Pertussis is commonly called "whooping cough" because of the sounds many of these patients make as they fight to breathe in air. A major symptom of pertussis is very bad coughing spells. The disease often appears in children and is highly contagious. Pertussis can be fatal in infants. Prevention of the disease is very important.

Tetanus occurs in both children and adults. It is caused by pathogens that live in soil, dust, and manure. These germs often enter the body through small wounds or breaks in the skin. Once inside the body, tetanus bacteria make a poison that attacks the body's nervous system. This causes the muscles to lock in spasms, or abnormal contractions. Patients often have convulsions and may die from being overtired and having trouble with breathing. Because the muscles of the face are usually affected, many people call this disease "lockjaw." Even with the best medical treatment, about one-half of all tetanus cases are fatal. Immunizations are very important, especially for farmers and others who work near the soil.

A series of three DPT shots should be given to healthy infants during the first 6 months of life. At 18 months, a fourth dose is given. Then the fifth dose is given before a child enters school. From then on, boosters for diphtheria and tetanus given about every ten years can keep the level of protection high.

Antibiotic drugs produced from molds such as this are used to treat many diseases caused by bacteria.

Poliomyelitis

Poliomyelitis is a contagious disease that used to be called infantile paralysis because it mostly affects young children. All healthy infants and young people between the ages of 8 weeks and 18 years should have the polio vaccine.

The disease can cause lifelong **paralysis**, a condition of not being able to move some or all parts of the body. Polio is fatal in about 1 out of every 10 cases. Sometimes the breathing muscles are paralyzed, and patients must be helped to breathe with machines.

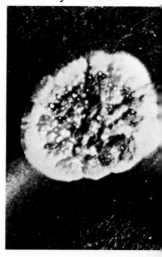

Around 1980, an event occurred that caused deep concern among immunologists. One-time sufferers of polio began to have relapses (experiencing symptoms of the disease again). This was the first time that a disease for which a vaccine had been discovered reappeared as a public health problem.

Called **postpolio syndrome** (more technically, *postpolio sequelae*) by researchers, the epidemic is estimated to have affected about 25 percent of the nation's 300,000 polio survivors. Many who thought they had seen the worst of this crippling disease have found themselves once again relying on crutches and wheelchairs.

Public health specialists have cautioned the general public not to interpret the outbreak of postpolio syndrome as evidence that the virus is active again. While researchers look for an explanation for this odd epidemic, individuals are urged to undergo standard vaccination treatments against polio and other diseases for which vaccines exist.

Measles, mumps, and rubella

Measles is a serious childhood disease. It begins with a cough, a fever, and a red rash behind the ears and on the back of the neck. Added problems, such as pneumonia, blindness, or brain damage, may follow.

Mumps often occurs in children, although it may also appear in teenagers and adults. The first symptoms of this contagious disease are fever and painful, swollen glands under the jawbone. In severe cases, mumps can cause brain damage or sterility.

In the eighteenth century, smallpox was a dangerous disease. Today, thanks to medical science, the disease is no longer a threat.

Rubella is most dangerous to pregnant women. A woman infected by rubella virus early in pregnancy has almost 1 chance in 4 of giving birth to a deformed baby. Rubella is often called German measles or three-day measles. Children should be immunized so that they do not catch this disease and spread it to pregnant women.

Knowledge of disease prevention

Scientists are developing new vaccines against many diseases. Knowing about the immunizations you and your family may need is important. By becoming immunized, you can protect yourself, your family, and your community from many serious diseases.

Key Words

acquired immunity	measles	poliomyelitis
active immunity	mumps	postpolio syndrome
antibodies	natural immunity	rubella
boosters	paralysis	tetanus
diphtheria	passive immunity	toxoid
immunizations	pertussis	vaccines

Main Ideas

- Immunization is the body's way of defending itself against a certain disease.
- Vaccines have been developed to build up immunity to standard infectious diseases.
- Children should receive proper immunization as a safeguard against epidemics.

Understand the Reading

1. What is the difference between active and passive immunity?
2. What is a vaccine?
3. Why should people be immunized even against diseases that are no longer common?
4. Name seven diseases that may be prevented by immunizations.
5. What is postpolio syndrome? What is unusual about it?

Apply Your Knowledge

1. Call your community health department. Find out what kinds of injections are required for U.S. citizens traveling to India, Western Europe, and Africa. Attempt to learn what health risks exist in those countries that require immunization treatments.
2. Plan an immunization schedule for a child from birth to the age of 16.

Chapter 25

Sexually Transmitted Diseases

After reading this chapter, you will be able to:

- ☐ Identify the common sexually transmitted diseases and describe their symptoms.
- ☐ Explain how sexually transmitted diseases are spread.
- ☐ Explain how sexually transmitted diseases can be prevented.
- ☐ Describe the treatment for the common sexually transmitted diseases.

Which of the following statements do you think are true?

- At least a half dozen common infectious diseases are transmitted sexually.
- After colds, the most common infectious diseases in the United States today are sexually transmitted.
- The cases of sexually transmitted diseases, *STD*, number about 20 million per year.
- You can have a sexually transmitted disease without knowing it.
- *Venereal disease, VD*, is another name for a sexually transmitted disease.

If you guessed that all the statements are true, you are right. Sexually transmitted diseases pose one of the greatest health hazards in the United States. Today, most communicable diseases occur less often than they once did. But STD continue to spread.

Types of STD

Sexually transmitted diseases are passed from an infected person to another person, usually through sexual intercourse or direct bodily contact involving the sex organs. Some STD can also be picked up from used towels and other surfaces. Because many victims do not know that they are infected, they spread the disease to others without knowing it.

Some STD are extremely dangerous and, if untreated, lead to serious illness and even death. Like other infectious diseases, STD are caused by pathogens. Most STD can be cured with such medications as antibiotics or sulfa drugs. A few virus-caused STD are not curable.

STD threaten the health of millions of people. Young adults are especially at risk. People who change sexual partners often are also at great risk. It is important to understand the dangers of STD and to learn their symptoms. Some of the most common STD are described here.

Chlamydia

Although the disease has been around for quite a long time, many people in the early part of this decade had never even heard the name **chlamydia**. That is mainly because, unlike most STD, chlamydia often causes no symptoms.

Experts estimate that chlamydia affects between 3 and 5 million people each year. This makes it the most common STD. Chlamydia is caused by a tiny bacterium, *Chlamydia trachomatis*, that looks like a virus. Both men and women can have the disease, but women and their babies suffer most. The Chlamydia bacterium affects the womb and may result in an infection that spreads through the entire reproductive system.

This can not only destroy a woman's chance of having children but can threaten her life. Babies born to women infected with chlamydia develop conjunctivitis (an eye infection), followed by ear and lung infections, which can cause death.

While chlamydia sufferers often have no symptoms, occasionally symptoms *do* occur. In women, these include vaginal itching, abdominal pain, and bleeding between periods. In men, chlamydia infection is a possibility when there is a burning sensation during urination, discharge from the penis, or burning and itching around the urethra. Whenever these symptoms occur, medical attention should be sought at once.

Gonorrhea

Next to chlamydia, **gonorrhea** is the most commonly occurring STD. Gonorrhea is about twenty times more common than syphilis and more than five times as common as chicken pox. More than 2 million cases of gonorrhea were reported in the United States in a recent year, and not all cases were reported.

Gonorrhea is caused by bacteria called gonococci that show up in pairs. The symptoms of gonorrhea begin 2 to 10 days after sexual contact with an infected person. The male usually has pain and burning when he urinates. There may also be a puslike discharge from the penis. The female may have a vaginal discharge, but often she has no symptoms at all. After a while, both male and female symptoms may disappear, and the person may think the disease is cured. But the bacteria continue to live in the inner mucuous membranes. In this way, a person may become a carrier of the infection without knowing it. Medical advice should be sought whenever exposure to the disease is suspected. A physician can take samples of fluids from the cervix, the vagina, and the urethra to find out if there is a gonococcal infection. Gonorrhea organisms in the fluids may be seen in the laboratory under a microscope or may be grown in a culture bottle.

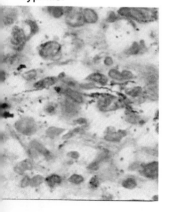

Shown here are spirochetes, the bacteria that cause syphilis.

Gonorrhea infections can usually be treated successfully with antibiotics, such as penicillin. However, having the symptoms disappear does not mean the disease is cured. So a follow-up visit to the doctor is often needed to make sure that the infection is gone. If the infection is not treated, many other serious problems, such as crippling arthritis or sterility, may develop. Also, a pregnant woman may pass the infection to her infant, who may be born blind.

Syphilis

Syphilis is caused by spiral-shaped bacteria called spirochetes. The bacteria enter the body through a small break in the skin or through mucous membranes. They travel throughout the bloodstream. The bacteria can be picked up through open sores. But they cannot be picked up from toilet seats or towels because they cannot live outside the body.

The first stage, or **primary stage**, of the disease includes a painless open sore called a **chancre**. The chancre usually appears 2 to 6 weeks after contact. It is very infectious. The male may see an open sore on his penis. The female may not have any external sores. Since the sore may disappear without treatment, the person may mistakenly think there is no longer a problem. If the patient is not treated, a skin rash and mouth sores may appear about 6 weeks later. The rash is often on the palms of the hands and soles of the feet. Mild, flulike symptoms may occur. This is the **secondary stage** of the disease. The rash and other symptoms may disappear, but spirochetes will stay in the bloodstream unless proper treatment is obtained.

For many years, there may be no symptoms while the spirochetes attack other parts of the body, such as the heart and the brain. This is known as the **latent stage**. After many years, **late syphilis**, the final stage, may cause heart failure, mental illness, or blindness. For this reason, it is very important to treat syphilis at an early stage. A doctor may take a blood test or may examine a piece of the sore under a microscope to make the diagnosis. Syphilis can be treated and cured with penicillin.

A pregnant woman may pass the syphilis infection to her unborn baby. Therefore, a blood test is often done early in pregnancy to diagnose and treat syphilis before it can cause deformities in the newborn.

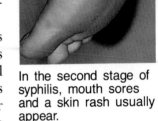

In the second stage of syphilis, mouth sores and a skin rash usually appear.

Genital herpes

Genital herpes is caused by the herpes simplex II virus. Herpes simplex I virus usually causes cold sores and fever blisters in the mouth. Herpes simplex II infections usually appear in the genital area. Herpes II virus is introduced into the body mainly by sexual contact. Cases of genital herpes are rapidly increasing in number. Each year, about 500,000 people are infected with this virus for the first time.

The first symptoms of genital herpes are usually noticed several days to 3 weeks after sexual contact. The first symptom is often pain in the genital area. A small skin lesion called a **vesicle** may then appear in the genital area. A vesicle is a blisterlike elevation on the skin. It can be as small as a pinhead or as large as a pea. It contains clear fluid. When a vesicle breaks, the area underneath it swells and becomes sore. Muscle aches, fever, and headache, symptoms usually associated with colds or the flu, may be associated with the herpes infection.

It is important to let the doctor decide if the vesicles are herpes or another disease. If genital herpes is diagnosed, one should avoid sexual contact during the time of active infection to keep from spreading the infection. There is no known cure for herpes, although certain medications are available that provide relief from the discomfort of the disease. Even after treatment, herpes infections may appear again and again. In some people, this reappearance can be triggered by changes in the temperature of the environment or by emotional stress. The

It's a fact of life...
VD gets around

Each individual bears responsibility for his or her own actions.

disease is easily spread any time the blisters are present, so contact should be avoided at that time.

In women, there are two serious problems that may develop that would require further treatment. Pregnant women with genital herpes may transmit the infection to their infants during childbirth if proper safety measures are not taken. Women who have repeated herpes infections also appear to have more abnormal Pap smears and a higher risk of cancer than other women do. The American Cancer Society recommends that all women have Pap smears every 3 years following two consecutive yearly tests in which the results were negative. This is particularly important for women who have had genital herpes infections.

Scabies, pediculosis, genital warts, and trichomoniasis

The STD mentioned so far can lead to very serious complications if untreated. There are other STD that are just as widespread and contagious, though they are usually not as dangerous if contracted. Nevertheless, precautions should be taken to avoid these diseases. You have already read about two of these STD, scabies and pediculosis, on page 232 in the chapter on skin.

Often called venereal warts, **genital warts** affect as many as 1 million people per year. They are found in the genital or rectal area. Genital warts are caused by a virus and sometimes grow large enough to block the vagina, anus, or urethra. They can be removed by medical, surgical, or laser therapy.

Trichomoniasis, or "trich," as it is usually called, is a common infection of the vagina. It is usually transmitted through direct sexual contact, but it can also be passed through the use of wet washcloths and towels. Men carry the organism responsible for trichomoniasis but usually have no symptoms. There is evidence that women who are infected have an increased risk of developing cervical cancer.

Preventing and treating STD

An individual must be responsible for her or his own social actions. All of the STD discussed in this chapter, as well as AIDS (which was discussed in Chapter 23), are prevented by not having sexual contact with infected people. The surest prevention is to refrain from sexual intercourse.

These diseases do not go away on their own. There is no self-medication to treat them. Anyone who notices symptoms of an STD should go to a doctor or health clinic for expert diagnosis and treatment. A toll-free referral service (1-800-227-8922) gives information on medical facilities in your area that treat STD. Any sore, ulcer, or discharge involving the sexual organs should be diagnosed and treated by a doctor.

In addition, there are diseases with similar symptoms that may *not* be transmitted sexually. A physician should diagnose and treat these diseases as well.

People with an STD must tell their sexual partners so that the partners can also be examined. Those with a sexually transmitted disease must stop sexual activity until cured so as not to infect others. Finally, it is important to know that a person who has had an STD and has been cured can catch the same disease again.

Key Words

chancre	late syphilis	syphilis
chlamydia	latent stage	trichomoniasis
genital herpes	primary stage	venereal disease
genital warts	secondary stage	(VD)
gonorrhea	STD	vesicle

Main Ideas

- Sexually transmitted diseases are infectious diseases that are spread from person to person through sexual contact.
- Gonorrhea and syphilis are two common and serious STD.
- Gonorrhea and syphilis can be prevented and cured.
- Genital herpes is an STD that can be prevented but not cured.

Understand the Reading

1. How are sexually transmitted diseases spread?
2. How many cases of chlamydia are estimated to occur each year? Name some of the harmful effects.
3. What are the symptoms of gonorrhea?
4. How does a physician determine whether a person has gonorrhea?
5. Why can't a person get syphilis from towels or toilet seats?
6. What are the four stages of syphilis?
7. Why do doctors often give pregnant women a blood test for syphilis?
8. How can STD be prevented?
9. Does every person with an STD infection show symptoms? Explain.
10. Why should a person with an STD tell a sexual partner?

Apply Your Knowledge

1. Do some research on the methods used to treat gonorrhea and syphilis in earlier times. Report your findings to the class.
2. Paul Ehrlich was a German scientist who lived in the latter half of the nineteenth century. Find some information about him in a reference book or encyclopedia. In a class report, tell of his contribution to bacteriology.

Unit 8
Food, Digestion, and Nutrition

Chapter 26

Nutritional Needs

After reading this chapter, you will be able to:

☐ Recognize the differences among the four main food groups.

☐ Identify the basic nutrients needed by the human body.

☐ List the healthful and harmful properties of various vitamins and minerals.

☐ Explain the differences between "good" cholesterol carriers (HDL) and "bad" cholesterol carriers (LDL).

☐ Explain the significance of the body's basal metabolic rate.

Karen was worried. She had been having headaches and blurred vision lately, and her appetite had disappeared. Karen said nothing to her parents about these problems because she didn't want to worry them. But when her skin turned yellow and began to peel, she could not hide her "illness" any longer. Alarmed, her parents took her to the doctor. After a thorough examination and numerous questions, the doctor diagnosed Karen's ailment as hypervitaminosis A. It seems that Karen, without her parents' knowledge, had been taking huge doses of vitamin A. She had read in a popular teen magazine that vitamin A prevents acne.

Karen had "overdosed" on vitamins.

Using the Daily Food Guide

What you eat is really your own business. You have likes and dislikes. But if you let your likes or tastes alone tell you what to eat every day, you might find that your body's need for nutrients is not being met. You can eat a lot of food and still be poorly nourished.

Nutrients are the substances in food that provide energy, build and repair cells, and regulate body processes. They aid in growth and development. Eating a lot of just one kind of food may not give your body enough nutrients. But if you eat a variety of foods, there is a good chance that your nutritional needs will be met.

One way to be sure you are getting enough of the nutrients you need is to use a food guide when planning your meals and snacks. The U.S. Department of Agriculture recommends the **Daily Food Guide** shown on page 322. It classifies foods into four groups based on the nutrients they contain. The groups are: (1) meat, poultry, fish, and beans; (2) milk and cheese; (3) vegetables and fruit; and (4) breads and cereals. Notice that for each food group, the guide gives the number of servings needed each day and the serving size. It also provides examples of the foods you can choose from.

For many years, these were known as the "four basic food groups." Now the Department of Agriculture recognizes a fifth food group— fats, sweets, and alcohol. This group includes such foods and condiments as cooking oils, salad dressings, catsup, jams and jellies, and pastries— foods that are meant to complement, not replace, foods from the other four groups. No servings from this fifth group are recommended in the Daily Food Guide. Since these foods provide calories with few nutrients, they are called **empty-calorie foods**.

A balanced meal provides between one-fourth and one-third of the nutrients you need daily. The meal contains a serving from each of the first four food groups. If the serving sizes are adequate, a Swiss cheese omelet served with steamed broccoli and French bread is an example of a balanced meal.

Take a minute to check your favorite meal against the Daily Food Guide. Make a list of each food in the meal. Are all four food groups

Daily Food Guide				
	Meat, Poultry, Fish, and Beans Group	**Milk and Cheese Group**	**Vegetable and Fruit Group**	**Bread and Cereal Group**
A Serving Is	2–3 oz cooked lean meat, poultry, fish	1 cup milk	½ cup vegetable or fruit	1 slice of bread
Servings Daily	2	Children under 9: 2–3 Children 9 to 12: 3 Teenagers: 4 Adults: 2 Pregnant Women: 3 Nursing Mothers: 4	4 (Include 1 source of vitamin C and 1 source of vitamin A every other day.)	4 (Select only whole-grain, enriched, or fortified products.)
Equivalents	1 egg ½–¾ cup cooked dry beans, peas, soybeans, lentils 2 Tbsp peanut butter ¼–½ cup nuts, sesame seeds, sunflower seeds	1 cup plain yogurt ½ cup cottage cheese 1 oz cheddar or Swiss cheese (= ¾ of a serving) ½ cup ice cream (= ⅓ of a serving)	½ medium grapefruit or cantaloupe 1 medium orange, apple, banana 1 medium potato juice of 1 lemon	½–¾ cup cooked cereal, cornmeal, grits, noodles, rice 1 oz ready-to-eat cereal

included? If not, what other foods could you add to the meal to make it balanced nutritionally?

Get into the habit of mentally referring to the Daily Food Guide to check the nutritional value of the foods you are planning to eat. This will help you to make wise choices, whether you are preparing your meals at home or eating out in a restaurant.

Nutrients

Protein is needed for the never-ending building and replacement of body cells. Protein can also provide energy. When you eat chili con carne with beans, you are taking in proteins of animals and plants. Inside the small intestine, these large protein molecules are broken down. Smaller substances called **amino acids** are formed. Then, like tiny building blocks, the amino acids are joined together to form specific proteins that the body needs.

The proteins in the body are made up of about 23 amino acids. The body can make most of these amino acids. However, 9 of the amino acids cannot be manufactured by the body. These are called **essential amino acids**. They must be in the foods you eat.

Foods with high-quality protein contain the essential amino acids. The meat, poultry, fish, and beans group and the milk and cheese group are the best sources of such protein. Protein from the vegetable and fruit group or the bread and cereal group does not have as many essential amino acids. It is low-quality protein. Vegetarians who eat only plant foods have a difficult time getting all the essential amino acids. Some vegetarians get a well-balanced assortment of amino acids by including dried legumes, milk, cheese, and eggs in their diets.

Carbohydrate

Carbohydrate is the body's main source of energy. The energy provided by carbohydrate is needed by every body cell. Starches and sugars are carbohydrates. Starch is the carbohydrate in foods of the bread and cereal group and in vegetables. Fruit and milk contain the carbohydrate called sugar.

If you eat more carbohydrate than your body needs, the excess is stored in the liver and muscles in the form of glycogen (stored sugar).

Refer to the Daily Food Guide when planning your meals.

323

If you eat more than can be stored in this way, the excess is changed to fat and stored in fat cells. Many overweight people blame carbohydrate for their weight problems. But overeating, not carbohydrate, is what causes people to gain weight.

Fat

Fat is concentrated fuel for the body. It is found in many foods, such as nuts, meat, oils, eggs, chocolate, margarine, olives, avocados, and butter. Many people believe that fat is bad for them, so they avoid it as much as possible. It is true that eating large amounts of fat—more than 30 percent of your daily calories—can cause certain health problems for some people. But the body needs fat for several reasons. Ounce for ounce, fat supplies much more energy than carbohydrate or protein does. Fat also adds flavor to many foods and helps the body to absorb vitamins A, D, E, and K from the digestive tract. Fat stored in the body is a reserve source of energy. Finally, fat is important for insulating the body and acting as cushioning for vital organs.

Fats can be in a liquid or a solid form. Corn oil, sunflower oil, and cottonseed oil are called **unsaturated fats** or **polyunsaturated fats**. Unsaturated fats are usually in liquid form at room temperature.

Saturated fats are solids found in meat, butter, coconut oil, and palm oil. Margarine that is solid is also partially saturated. When you use saturated fat for cooking, it will become a liquid. But it will become solid again when placed in a cool environment.

A high intake of fat, especially saturated fat, is generally thought to be harmful because it may be related to cardiovascular disease. The dietary guidelines for fat recommended by the American Heart Association are to reduce fat to 30 percent of total calories, with 10 percent coming from each type of fat—saturated, partially saturated, and polyunsaturated.

Cholesterol

Cholesterol, most of which is produced by the body, aids in the production of hormones and cell membranes. Cholesterol can be found

Develop the habit of eating a variety of foods to obtain all your nutrients.

325

Red meat and other animal fats contain cholesterol.

in foods from animal sources, but it is not found in foods of plant origin. It is waxy and fatlike, but it is not a fat.

The National Institutes of Health and the American Heart Association have both concluded "beyond a reasonable doubt" that lowering elevated blood cholesterol levels will reduce the risk of heart attacks. They thus recommend that Americans restrict their intake of cholesterol to below 300 milligrams per day. Since cholesterol is found in animal products, it is advisable for people at risk for heart disease to adjust their diets and eat moderate amounts of egg yolk, whole milk and dairy products, and fatty red meats.

Cholesterol travels through the bloodstream by attaching itself to two types of protein. One of these types, low-density lipoproteins (**LDL**), deposits the cholesterol it carries along the artery walls, forming atheromas (fatty masses). LDL is thought of as the "bad" cholesterol carrier. High-density lipoproteins (**HDL**) help carry cholesterol through the arteries to the liver to be eliminated. On its path through the blood, HDL may even remove some fatty masses that have formed. HDL thus works a little like a vacuum cleaner. It is the "good" cholesterol carrier.

As a person ages, the ability to rid the body of cholesterol decreases. The possibility of developing cardiovascular disease increases. To find out if a patient has a high potential for developing cardiovascular disease, doctors measure the total cholesterol and divide it by the HDL cholesterol to find the numerical ratio. The lower the ratio, the less chance there is of a heart attack—and the higher the ratio, the greater the risk. Exercising seems to increase the body's manufacture of HDL, while daily stresses, smoking, and poor nutrition increase the body's manufacture of LDL.

Minerals

Many **minerals** are needed in small but steady supply to control the body's chemical processes. The following are the most important.

Iron. Iron is the mineral in hemoglobin that attracts oxygen. Without enough iron, your muscles do not get sufficient oxygen to contract properly. You may then feel tired or "washed out." This condition is known as **iron-deficiency anemia**. You can avoid iron-deficiency anemia by eating foods that are good sources of iron, such as meat (especially liver and kidney), dried beans, eggs, and enriched breads.

Calcium and phosphorus. These are minerals that are very important for strong bones and teeth. An adequate amount of calcium is essential for building stronger, denser bones. Growing teenagers need to establish the habit of consuming adequate calcium to lessen their chances of developing osteoporosis in adulthood.

Calcium also helps blood to clot, muscles to contract, and nerves to send messages. Good sources of calcium include milk, hard cheese, and yogurt. Dark-green leafy vegetables have some calcium, too. Meat, fish, poultry, eggs, and milk are high in phosphorus.

Fluorine. Fluorine prevents tooth decay. The best source of fluorine is drinking water that has fluoride salts in it.

Iodine. Iodine is needed for proper working of the thyroid gland. The body's need for iodine can be met by using iodized table salt.

Many other minerals are needed by the body. But if you include enough foods with iron, calcium, phosphorus, fluorine, and iodine in your diet, you will usually get all the other needed minerals along with them.

Simple iodized table salt provides iodine needed by the body.

Vitamins

Vitamins are important to your body. They are substances that help regulate body processes. Many people think that large amounts of vitamins will guarantee good health. Unfortunately, that is not really so. It is even possible to take too much of certain vitamins. **Fat-soluble vitamins**—vitamins A, D, E, and K—are stored in the body until they are needed. Unneeded amounts are not removed as waste in the urine, so taking large amounts can be harmful. An excess of the **water-soluble vitamins**—vitamins B and C—cannot be stored and is less likely to be a problem. You should know how much of each vitamin your body needs and eat to meet those needs.

Vitamin A. Vitamin A is very important for the health of the skin and the eyes. It also helps keep the linings of the mouth, nose, throat, and digestive tract free from infection. A diet extremely low in vitamin A may lead to the development of dry, rough skin. Such a diet may also cause difficulty in adjusting the eyes to dim light.

Vitamin A is found in egg yolks, liver, butter, milk, and cheese. Fortified margarine also contains vitamin A. The human body is capable of making vitamin A from carotene, a substance found in green and yellow vegetables and in fruits. Usually, vitamin A is not destroyed by cooking. Large amounts of vitamin A that are taken continuously can cause liver damage.

Vitamin D. Vitamin D is needed to grow strong bones and teeth. Because bones develop before birth, it is important for pregnant women to have plenty of calcium and vitamin D in their diets. A child with a serious lack of vitamin D may develop rickets, a condition in which the bones are poorly formed.

Vitamin D is found in fortified milk and in fish-liver oils. Vitamin D is also produced by the action of the ultraviolet rays in sunshine on certain oils in the skin. But in some environments, the hours of sunshine in a day are few, or heavy pollution lessens the full amount of sunlight. In these environments, fortified milk is important to the diet.

It is possible for human beings to get too much vitamin D by taking too many vitamin D capsules. This causes kidney and liver damage and deformed bones. Concentrated forms of vitamin D should be used only in the exact amounts suggested by a doctor. For the most part, it is safer to get vitamin D from foods than from capsules.

Vitamin E. Vitamin E is not a miracle nutrient. Don't believe everything you hear about vitamin E. It cannot cure ulcers, arthritis, cancer, heart disease, or warts. It cannot make you a better athlete. This vitamin prevents vitamin A from being destroyed too quickly. It also strengthens the cell membranes of red blood cells.

Vitamin E can be found in salad oils, margarine, whole-grain cereals, and most fresh, green leafy vegetables. The body will store excess vitamin E in tissues under the skin and in the ovaries or testes. Too much vitamin E intake, however, can interfere with the work of the glands and tissues.

Vitamin K. Vitamin K plays an important role in the clotting of blood. This vitamin helps the liver produce a protein that is needed for blood clotting. Foods that are good sources of vitamin K are dark green leafy vegetables and liver. The large intestine can also produce vitamin K. If

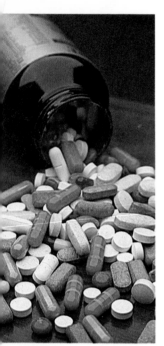

WARNING: Overdoses of some vitamins can be hazardous to your health.

you eat well-balanced meals, you will not have to worry about getting the right amount of this vitamin.

Vitamin B. Vitamin B is actually a group of vitamins that is sometimes called the vitamin B complex. It includes thiamine, riboflavin, niacin, pyridoxine, and vitamin B_{12}. The vitamin B complex is important for energy and growth.

Thiamine. Thiamine, or vitamin B_1, is needed by the nerves, muscles, and digestive system. With a serious lack of thiamine, nerve and muscle disorders can develop. A disease called beriberi, which affects the heart and the nervous system, can also develop. Pork, whole-grain and enriched cereals, lean meats, and dried legumes give the body thiamine.

Riboflavin and Niacin. Riboflavin, or vitamin B_2, and niacin are found in liver, cheese, leafy vegetables, beans, milk, eggs, and fish. Both of these vitamins are good for the skin, the nervous system, and digestion. A serious lack of niacin causes dry red patches to form on the skin. This is a disease called pellagra.

Pyridoxine. Pyridoxine, or vitamin B_6, is needed by the body for protein metabolism. Large amounts of vitamin B_6 may cause severe nervous disorders. People have misused this vitamin for bodybuilding, depression, premenstrual syndrome, and hyperactivity. Some of the symptoms of overdose include numbness of the feet and hands, loss of touch and temperature sensations, and, in extreme cases, inability to feel the location of the arms.

Vitamin B_{12}. Vitamin B_{12} helps increase the number of red blood cells and helps the body use protein, fat, and carbohydrate. It is found in liver, leafy vegetables, milk, eggs, and cheese.

Scurvy, caused by a vitamin C deficiency, plagued early sailors.

Vitamin C. Vitamin C, or ascorbic acid, is found in citrus fruits, such as oranges, lemons, limes, and grapefruits. Tomatoes, potatoes, and cabbage are also good sources. A person who tires easily, whose skin bruises easily, or whose gums bleed may need more vitamin C. Vitamin C cannot be stored in the body, so excess amounts are removed from the body as waste. But it is not a good idea to take extremely large doses of vitamin C, since this may cause diarrhea or kidney damage.

Recently, researchers have found that an excess of vitamin C interferes with the absorption of copper in the intestinal tract. Copper is important for releasing iron from storage in the body. Iron is used to form the oxygen-carrying hemoglobin of the red blood cells. Without copper, iron-deficiency anemia is possible.

There is also evidence that the body will begin to adjust to large amounts of vitamin C taken over a long period of time. If vitamin C intake is then decreased, minor symptoms of a disease called scurvy may appear.

Scurvy is caused by a severe lack of vitamin C. Long ago, sailors and others who were cut off from supplies of fresh food for long periods of time suffered weakness, pain in their legs and joints, and severe bleeding from their gums. Sometimes they lost their teeth. These are symptoms of scurvy. This disease sometimes caused death. Sailors on long voyages did not develop scurvy if they had a little lime or lemon juice each day. In fact, the name "limey" for sailor comes from the days when British sailors drank lime juice each day to prevent scurvy.

Water

Most people think that water is something to bathe in, swim in, and drink whenever they are thirsty. Actually, next to air, water is the most important substance needed for life. Water is found in every cell of the body.

Water has several important functions. It carries nutrients through the intestinal wall and into the bloodstream. It also helps to carry waste materials out of the body. The body's temperature-control system needs water in order to work properly.

On an average day, about 2 to 3 quarts of water can be lost through perspiration, urination, bowel movements, and breathing. If you exercise, you must replace the lost fluid. If you don't replace it, your body may become dehydrated and malfunction, somewhat like a car with an overheated engine. The symptoms of dehydration are headache, fatigue, and a feverish feeling. If dehydration persists, the likelihood of developing heatstroke increases (see page 382).

To make sure your body is getting the water it needs, you should drink 6 to 8 glasses of liquid daily. In addition to water, you can drink soup, milk, juice, tea, and other beverages. Many foods can also help you maintain the delicate liquid balance in your body. Most of the foods you eat are over 50 percent water. Some fruits and vegetables are as much as 95 percent water. Even dry foods, such as bread, flour, and crackers, contain from 5 to 30 percent water. You must increase water intake when you exercise, have a fever, or lose fluid through vomiting or diarrhea.

Without water, nutrients could not be carried from the intestine into the bloodstream, wastes could not be carried out of the body, and the body could not be kept at an even temperature.

Fiber

For many years, nutritionists have recommended that we include more **fiber**, or roughage, in our diets. Lettuce and other vegetables, fruits, and whole-grain breads and cereals all provide fiber. Fiber is the cellulose in the cell walls of the plant foods we eat. Cellulose, one kind of roughage, is a complex carbohydrate that our intestines cannot fully break down.

Fiber is fairly soft once it reaches the intestines. Yet this roughage helps to "scrub out" materials left after digestion and absorption have occurred. The bulk formed by fiber helps the muscles of the large intestine to contract and push the waste products toward the rectum. If the diet does not have enough fiber, the waste materials in the large intestine travel slowly and allow bacteria more time to multiply. Present studies suggest that the contact with bacteria over a long period of time increases the chance of intestinal cancer.

Fiber helps to clean out the materials left in the intestine after digestion has taken place. Whole-grain products have a high fiber content.

It is not hard to give your body the right nutrients. Three balanced meals a day should do it. A balanced meal follows the Daily Food Guide and has a serving from each of the four food groups.

Breakfast is an important meal. For most people, it has been 12 to 14 hours since the last meal. People need a good supply of nutrients for energy to begin the day's activities. A breakfast of juice, cereal, eggs, and milk contains foods from the four food groups. It may provide about one-third to one-fourth of the day's nutrients. Some instant breakfasts are easy to prepare and may be useful at times, though they may not contain foods from all the food groups. However,

Breakfast, lunch, and dinner

When advised to add fiber to their diets, many people have a response similar to this one: "Fine, I'll add fiber. But where do I find it?" The answer to this question is simple: Fiber is all around us—in foods that we eat frequently. Experts advise including about 15–30 grams of dietary fiber each day.

Consider the following common foods and their fiber contents.

Food	Fiber Content (in grams)
apple, 1 small	3.1
banana, 1 medium	1.8
cabbage, ¾ cup	2.2
cauliflower, ½ cup	1.2
pear, 1 medium	2.8
peas, ½ cup	3.8
potatoes, ¾ cup	3.1
tangerine, 1 medium	2.1

The list goes on. Let your imagination guide you in working fiber into your diet. A fruit salad made of the fruits in the table above, for instance, would be as delicious as it would be healthful.

many of them lack the roughage that fruits and whole-grain cereals provide. Other important nutrients may be missing, too.

You should eat about one-third of the day's required nutrients at lunch. You can find foods from the four food groups in the school cafeteria or in a restaurant. You can also carefully pack a lunch at home that includes something from each food group.

For many people, dinner is the biggest meal of the day. A dinner of meat, poultry, or fish, along with vegetables, salad, a roll or a slice of bread, and milk, represents all four food groups. Such a dinner provides about one-third of all the nutrients needed for the day.

Snacks, too, can make an important contribution to the diet. Nutritious snack foods can be found in all four food groups.

You can plan healthful meals, even on a small budget. Learn as much as you can about the nutritional value of foods. Your own knowledge will help you to shop wisely and eat well. Remember that less-processed foods may be more nutritious than highly processed foods, such as pre-prepared foods. You can get high-quality protein from inexpensive foods, like eggs and cottage cheese. Certain foods, such as rice and beans, combine to provide more high-quality protein than either food alone would. Combining foods to get the most protein value from them is called **protein complementarity**. Another hint for better eating on a small budget is that whole-grain breads and cereals contain more nutrients than foods made of refined white flour.

Nutrients such as carbohydrates, fats, and proteins provide energy. Energy is released in the cells. The body uses and releases energy for breathing, circulation of the blood, and all physical activities that take even the slightest effort.

The **basal metabolic rate** (BMR) is the minimum level of energy you need to use to keep your body's vital functions—for example, respiration, circulation, and maintenance of body temperature—operating while at rest. The BMR tells something about how your body uses the energy in the food you eat. Usually, the younger you are and the larger your body is, the higher your BMR will be. Males, on the average, have a higher metabolic rate than females.

You can find your BMR by following these steps:

1. First, use chart A (page 334) to determine what the surface area of your body is. Using a ruler or straightedge, line up the points representing your height and your weight. Your surface area is the point on the middle line where the ruler crosses. Record your approximate body surface area on a sheet of paper.
2. Use chart B to determine the amount of heat loss per square meter of body surface for 1 hour. Find the number that corresponds to your sex and age. Record your approximate heat loss on the paper.
3. Then, multiply your body surface area times your heat loss.
4. Finally, multiply your answer by 24 to determine your BMR for 1 day.

Calories

Energy is measured in **calories**. A calorie is neither a nutrient nor a substance found in foods. A calorie is a measure of energy. Technically, a calorie is the amount of heat necessary to raise the temperature of 1 gram of water by 1°C. The number of calories in a food tells how much energy that food provides.

All of the foods that supply fat, carbohydrate, and protein are sources of calories. When you take in more calories (energy) than you use, your body stores the extra calories as body fat. Each day, a moderately active

333

Chart A

Height in.	cm	Surface area m²	Weight lb	kg
6'0" 2"	190	2.5	280	130
	180	2.4	260	120
10"		2.3	240	110
8"	170	2.2 2.1	220	105 100
5'6"	165	2.0	200	95 90
4"	160	1.9	190 180	85 80
2" 5'0"	155 150	1.8 1.7	170 160	75
10"	145	1.6	150 140	70 65
8"	140	1.5	130	60
4'6"	135	1.4	120	55
4"	130	1.3	110	50
2"	125	1.2	100	45
4'0"	120	1.1	90	40
10"	115	1.0	80	35
8"			70	

Chart B

Age	Males	Females
12	45.3	42.0
13	44.5	40.5
14	43.8	39.2
15	42.9	38.3
16	42.0	37.2
17	41.5	36.4
18	40.8	35.8
19	40.5	35.4

young person uses about 20 to 25 calories per pound of body weight. A very active person may need more calories per pound. Those who exercise very little may need as few as 17 calories per pound. Boys and men generally need more calories than girls and women do. Height, weight, and age—as well as the season of the year and the climate of the geographic area in which one lives—also affect the number of calories needed.

Key Words

amino acids
basal metabolic rate
calories
carbohydrate
cholesterol
Daily Food Guide
empty-calorie foods
essential amino acids

fat
fat-soluble vitamins
fiber
HDL
iron-deficiency anemia
LDL
minerals
nutrients

polyunsaturated fats
protein
protein complementarity
saturated fats
unsaturated fats
vitamins
water-soluble vitamins

- The recommended daily servings of food from the Daily Food Guide provide a good diet for most people.
- Nutrients in food supply the body with energy, regulate body processes, and provide materials for building and repairing cells.
- Carbohydrate and fat are the major energy sources for the body, while protein helps to build and repair body cells.
- Cholesterol is a fatlike substance that may be deposited on the walls of the arteries. A low level of cholesterol in the blood reduces the risk of heart attack.
- Vitamins and minerals help to regulate body processes. They are needed regularly in small amounts rather than in large amounts.
- Water is also an important nutrient.
- Fiber is important for good health, even though it is not fully digested.
- The minimum level of energy needed to maintain the body's vital functions is the basal metabolic rate (BMR).

1. What is the difference between foods and nutrients?
2. Why is it important to have variety in your diet?
3. Which food groups will give you the high-quality protein that your body needs?
4. List two reasons why fat is important in your diet.
5. What is protein needed for?
6. What is the difference between saturated and polyunsaturated fats?
7. Why is it important to know how much cholesterol is taken into the body?
8. What is the function of iron in your body?
9. How can iron-deficiency anemia be avoided?
10. If you were not getting enough vitamin C, what symptoms might you have?

1. Using the Daily Food Guide on page 322, make up a meal plan for a day that includes three balanced meals. Be imaginative in your selections, and choose dishes that you like. Compare your menu with those of other students.
2. Invite the school dietitian or a dietitian from another food facility in your community to speak to the class. Ask the dietitian to explain how vegetarians are able to plan meals that provide high-quality proteins.

Chapter 27

Snacks and Special Diets

After reading this chapter, you will be able to:

- [ ] Explain why breakfast is an important meal.
- [ ] Describe the features of a safe diet.
- [ ] Explain why fad diets are not sensible approaches to weight loss.
- [ ] List the dos and don'ts of special diets for athletes.

In a spacious and comfortably furnished apartment, a teenager fixes himself a predinner snack. He dumps the contents of a 1-pound bag of frozen french fries onto a baking sheet and pops it into the oven. While he is waiting for them to bake, he eats the remainder of the blueberry pie his mother had served for dessert the previous night. Then he swallows a few generous spoonfuls of ice cream.

Both the teenager and his parents would be surprised to learn that he suffers from a health problem: he is malnourished.

Snacking

One of our favorite activities is snacking. Snacking has become a social custom in this country. For many people, it has become part of their regular eating habits. Some schools stress nutritional snacking. And many schools provide milk, fruits, and vegetables at breaks during the school day. Other schools are using automatic vending machines that stock many different kinds of foods. However, soft drinks and candy, though not the best snacking foods, are the most popular items sold in vending machines.

There is nothing wrong with snacking. You can eat as often as four or five times a day. However, you should eat a balanced daily diet without excess calories. Some nutritionists even suggest eating smaller amounts of food more often. In that way, you can use nutrients better. Snacks can help you get the nutrients that may be missing from your meals.

Not all snack foods are nutritious, however. Some foods do not fit into the traditional food groups. They are empty-calorie foods—the main thing they offer is calories. Carbohydrate and fat are the major nutrients in such snack foods as chips, candy, jam, and carbonated drinks. Compare the nutritional values of the snacks listed in the table below. Which snacks are healthiest?

Some Snacks and Their Nutritional Values						
	Carbonated beverage	Fresh orange juice	Raw carrot	Malted milk	Pizza	Chocolate bar
Amount =	1 cup	1 cup	6–8 strips	1 cup	1 medium slice	1.5 oz
Calories =	96	110	20	245	185	160
Protein =	0	2 g	1 g	11 g	7 g	2 g
Calcium =	0	27 g	18 g	317 g	107 g	33 g
Iron =	0	.5 mL	.4 mL	.7 mL	.7 mL	.4 mL
Vitamin A =	0	500 IU	5,500 IU	590 IU	290 IU	0
Thiamine =	0	.22 mL	.03 mL	.14 mL	.04 mL	.10 mL
Riboflavin =	0	.07 mL	.3 mL	.49 mL	.12 mL	.05 mL
Vitamin C =	0	12.4 mL	4 mL	2 mL	4 mL	0

The importance of breakfast

Many people eat a light breakfast—or none at all. But breakfast is an important meal. By morning, your body has digested dinner from the night before. It has stored some extra carbohydrate in the liver in the form of glycogen. The amount is equal to about 600 calories.

However, about 350 to 400 calories are used up even when you are asleep. With more than half of the stored carbohydrate used between dinner and breakfast, the need to renew your energy supply becomes important. If you eat a good breakfast, you are restoring calories you will need during the morning hours. But if you do not eat a good breakfast, your energy level may drop as the morning wears on. Then around 10 A.M., you may eat a high-carbohydrate snack, such as a candy bar or doughnut, to supply the missing energy. But you may not be getting all the nutrients your body needs, only calories.

It is very easy to talk about the importance of breakfast. Actually, eating a proper breakfast takes more planning when you have very little time. But remember, good breakfast habits can be learned. Try making a breakfast sandwich or mixing orange juice the night before to save you some time in the morning. The good eating habits you learn today will be a great help for the rest of your life.

If you eat a good breakfast, your energy level is more likely to stay high all morning.

Weight control

During childhood and adolescence, a healthy person usually gains regularly in height and weight. During the adolescent spurt of growth, however, you will gain at a fast rate for a few years. Then less rapid gains will be made until you reach adult size.

Height-weight-age tables show weight ranges at different ages and heights. These tables are useful only in a general way. That is, they show average ranges. They do not show what any one person should weigh. A person with a large frame would probably weigh more than a person of the same age and height who has a smaller frame. The graphs on page 341 show ranges in weight and height at different ages.

Diet for the underweight

People who are underweight may be unhappy about the way they look. Some may worry not only about their looks, but also about a lack of energy and more frequent sickness.

Unusual thinness may be caused by a long-term illness. Infection, stress, or other illness can interfere with appetite. If a person has a digestive disorder, the nutrients in food may not be absorbed in the right way. If there are physical problems, it is best to have a doctor prescribe the proper weight-gain diet.

Most often, underweight reflects a person's lifestyle or ideas about food in general. Some thin people pick at their food. They hesitate to

338

Instead of snacking on potato chips or candy, have a cold, delicious piece of fruit.

try new or different foods. Overactive people may forget to eat. Too strict a weight-reduction diet may also result in underweight. Sometimes the dining table may become the family battleground when one person is not willing to eat what is being served. Eating then becomes a chore, not a pleasure.

If you are underweight, examine your ideas and feelings about food. Think about why you might be underweight. When you are satisfied with the reasons you have found, you might want to set some goals for yourself. Merely eating more food may not improve your health and appearance. Any new diet must have nutrients as well as calories.

If you really want to gain weight, you should get up early enough to have breakfast. Eat more of your favorite foods. Eat even if you aren't hungry. If your appetite is small, eat several smaller meals. Select nutritious but higher-calorie foods. Eat snacks about 2 hours before a meal. Snacking too close to mealtime raises the blood-sugar level (the amount of sugar in the blood). This may lessen your appetite.

Exercising also helps to stimulate the appetite. After school, eat a snack that is both nutritious and high in calories. Then, exercise for at least a half hour.

No single food can help you to gain weight. So it is better to try a variety of foods to keep up your interest in eating. And remember, gaining weight takes time. Don't try to fatten yourself up in a week. Work slowly and carefully at changing your eating habits.

What is "overweight"?

No one gains 25 pounds all of the sudden. There is a gradual weight gain during your growth period. But some people gain more rapidly than they should. Weigh yourself regularly, and look for bulges and flabbiness. Also compare your weight with your height and body type.

If you find a difference of 2 or 3 pounds in weight from one morning to the next, don't panic. There is no need to go on a diet. On some days, your body tissue may hold more fluid than on others. On days when you exercise, you may lose these 2 or 3 unwanted pounds of fluid. Staying at your best weight and looking attractive does not mean staying extremely thin. Some people think they are overweight when they are not. As a result, they may not eat enough of the proper foods and get enough nutrients to stay healthy.

It is easier to take off a little extra weight than to go on a yearlong diet to lose 10 to 15 pounds. Once you develop an eating habit that makes you gain weight, it becomes hard to break. If you are gaining too much weight or gaining too quickly, try to figure out why. Sometimes problems at home, at school, or with friends may make you eat or snack too much. You may not even be aware of the total number of calories you are taking in.

Diet for the overweight

Hundreds of how-to-diet books are written by different people. But what may work for them may be harmful for you. You may not need professional advice to lose 2 or 3 pounds. But before you try to lose 10 pounds or more, check with your doctor. Your doctor can recommend a reducing diet that will suit you. Remember, no matter what you weigh, your body needs the nutrients from a balanced diet.

Overeating is one of the major causes of being overweight. The number of calories consumed is greater than the number of calories burned. The following eating rules will help you eat fewer calories than you burn.

- Try to eat only at mealtimes when you are at the table.
- If you do snack, eat fruits or vegetables, not high-calorie foods.
- Let everyone know that you will not have second helpings during a meal. Eat smaller helpings.
- Instead of gulping down food, take small bites and rest between them. During the course of a meal, pause for a few minutes. Slowly increase the time it takes you to eat your meals.
- Substitute exercise for snacking.

A pound of body fat equals 3,500 calories. To lose 1 pound per week, you can eat 500 fewer calories per day than you burn. You can

Girls' Weight Range

Boys' Weight Range

lb

172
164
156
148
140
132
124
116
108
100
92
84
76
68
60
52
44
36
28
20

1 2 3 4 5 6 7 8 9 10 11 12 13 14 15 16 17 18
Age in Years

1 2 3 4 5 6 7 8 9 10 11 12 13 14 15 16 17 18
Age in Years

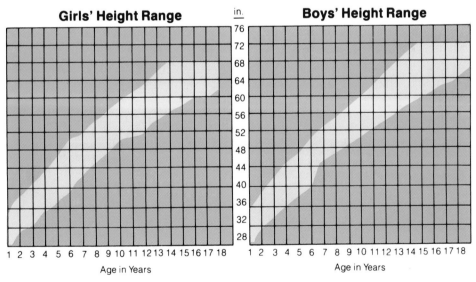

Girls' Height Range

Boys' Height Range

in.

76
72
68
64
60
56
52
48
44
40
36
32
28

1 2 3 4 5 6 7 8 9 10 11 12 13 14 15 16 17 18
Age in Years

1 2 3 4 5 6 7 8 9 10 11 12 13 14 15 16 17 18
Age in Years

The color areas in these charts show the average ranges of height and weight for girls and boys.

either reduce the calories in meals and snacks that you eat, or you can burn more calories through exercise. Examine the illustration on page 342, and compare the number of calories used for various exercises.

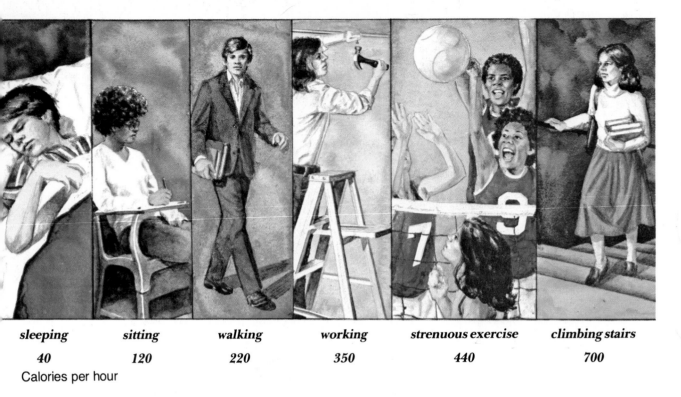

sleeping	sitting	walking	working	strenuous exercise	climbing stairs
40	120	220	350	440	700

Calories per hour

Fad diets

Fasting diets, high-carbohydrate diets, liquid-protein diets, high-fat diets, grapefruit diets, low-carbohydrate diets, and many more untested fad diets come and go. Many of the fad diets can harm the body's metabolism. One of the famous low-carbohydrate diets is known to cause feelings of tiredness—and it is high in fat and cholesterol. It also causes water loss, dizziness, and kidney trouble. Medical experts and nutritionists have all called the low-carbohydrate diets dangerous ones.

Before going on any diet, check with your doctor.

342

Amount of Exercise Needed to Burn Calories in Selected Foods	
Food	**Exercise Time**
1 medium-sized piece of apple pie	55 minutes active exercise
1 medium-sized doughnut	24 minutes active exercise
1 medium-sized slice of cake	32 minutes active exercise
1 18-ounce carbonated beverage	20 minutes active exercise

It takes time to gain extra weight, so it makes sense that it will take time to lose it. Fad diets that promise quick weight loss are useless and can be harmful. With them, you may lose weight in fluids. But real tissue weight will not be lost. Many are not nutritionally balanced. In the long run, fad diets won't help you take off pounds permanently.

Diet aids are risky.

Diet pills are another popular but risky way to lose weight. Some pills do help, but they do it by interfering with healthy body functions. Laxatives may speed food through the digestive tract so quickly that it cannot be absorbed. Diuretics may increase urination, causing a loss of water and needed salts. Other pills cause nervousness or drowsiness. Diet pills should never be taken except under a doctor's supervision.

A good weight-reducing group may help.

Several worthwhile organizations have been set up to help people lose weight. Members receive a medical examination when they join. A doctor or dietitian helps them to decide how much weight they should try to lose. A doctor also helps decide how quickly they should lose weight. Members go to regular meetings. At the start of each meeting, they are weighed. Awards are given to the members who reach their weight-loss goals. Members also help one another to keep from losing faith in their own goals.

Anorexia nervosa and bulimia

Often, instead of getting their ideas about weight from doctors and nutritionists, people get them from advertising. Today, it is fashionable to be extremely slim. Being very thin might be necessary for people who earn their living as models or movie stars. But for most people, extreme thinness is not always healthy or even physically attractive.

Anorexia nervosa. In an effort to conform to society's weight standards, some young people who think they are overweight begin to diet. They are then unable to stop dieting, and their weight may drop well below

Singer Karen Carpenter was a victim of anorexia nervosa.

100 pounds. These people may suffer from a psychological illness called **anorexia nervosa**. The word *anorexia* means "lack or loss of appetite for food." Appetite is psychological and is dependent on the memory of past experiences. Hunger is physiological and is caused by the body's need for food.

With anorexia, there is a loss of appetite resulting from fear, depression, anger, or other emotional states of mind. If people are suffering from anorexia, nothing can convince them that they are thin enough. By strictly controlling their intake of food, anorexics have a false sense that they are controlling their lives. If parents or friends encourage and even force them to eat more food, they may do so to avoid arguments. But often they will afterwards go to the bathroom and induce vomiting.

Approximately 90 percent of anorexia patients are girls and women. Their condition may be connected with an unwillingness to progress from childhood to adulthood. The unnatural thinness caused by anorexia can be a means of clinging to a child's body. The malnutrition associated with it can lead to serious physical illness and even death.

Bulimia. **Bulimia** is an uncontrollable craving for food that leads to eating huge quantities of food (binging), followed by forced vomiting (purging) or abuse of laxatives. Similar to an anorexic, a bulimic is terrified of obesity. Some anorexic patients exhibit bulimic behavior by eating more than 5,000 calories per day and then vomiting.

Since the salivary glands are involved each time the patient vomits, the glands become swollen and cause the cheeks to look puffy. When important minerals, such as potassium, are lost during vomiting, the heart muscle may be affected. This can lead to cardiac arrest. Damage to the esophagus (food tube that connects the mouth and stomach) and to the enamel of the teeth is the result of the action of strong acid from the stomach.

Like anorexia, bulimia is a self-destructive emotional disturbance and is a symptom of other life problems. For this reason, psychiatric counseling is an important part of the patient's therapy. Since each patient responds differently, there is no universal cure. Various types of therapy are used, ranging from behavior modification to hospitalization.

Special diets

Because of activities they are involved in or because of their food preferences, some people follow special diets. But no matter what diet a person follows, it should be made up of foods that meet the body's need for balanced nutrition.

The athlete's diet

Do athletes need salt pills, special amounts of vitamins, or extra helpings of steak? Some athletes think so. Have you ever heard an athlete say that if you eat steak on the day of a game, you will be stronger because of added muscle growth? The athlete is partly right, but mainly wrong. Steak is high in protein and does build new tissue, but not extra muscle cells. Only exercise can do that. And if the steak contains more protein than the body needs, it will be stored in the body as fat.

All the vitamins an athlete's body needs can be found in the different foods eaten each day. Too much of vitamins A and D can harm the body. As mentioned in Chapter 26, vitamin E taken in large amounts will not improve an athlete's ability. If you are an athlete, make sure you are getting enough rest and eating a nutritionally balanced diet. If you are active, you may need more calories. But as you eat more food to satisfy your hunger, you will probably get enough calories.

Excess weight loss

Have you ever tried to lose 5 to 15 pounds of weight quickly to impress the coach or to make the gymnastics team? The advice from coaches, nutrition experts, physical education authorities, and doctors is "don't." Your performance will be poor if you are dehydrated and low in energy. You may make the team. But endurance and power depend on a good diet, so you may not be able to compete week after week. Maintain competition weight instead of constantly gaining and losing.

Remember, the nutritional needs of athletes are really no different from those of nonathletes, except for calories. There is no "superfood" that can make you more active or give you speed. You are better off eating a balanced diet made up of foods from the four food groups in the Daily Food Guide.

Eating and exercise

For top performance during a game, it is best to eat at least 3 hours before you play. Nutritious meals that are easy to digest will help you to keep up strength and endurance without upsetting your stomach. Many coaches even suggest eating five small meals instead of three large ones during the sports season. It takes a full meal about 2 to 4 hours to leave the stomach and enter the small intestine. If food is still in the stomach by game time, you may have cramping, nausea, and even vomiting. Fatty foods should not be eaten before a sports event. They take much longer to digest. Try to include 2 to 3 cups of water during the meal. If you eat 3 to 4 hours before the game, drink another cup of liquid 1½ hours before the event. Don't take salt tablets. A normal diet will supply enough salt.

"Energy" foods and fluids

Will candy bars before a game give extra energy? These, like other foods, must be digested. After digestion, which may take several hours, glucose is ready for use by the cells. Most of the reserve energy that you need for an event is formed several days ahead. Eating large amounts of glucose, cubes of sugar, hard candy, and dextrose pills may cause the intestinal tract to draw extra fluids from the body tissues. This will add to any dehydration problem during physical activity. Nutrition experts say that an athlete should drink water in small amounts at frequent intervals during an event. For prolonged activity, noncarbonated soft drinks and fruit juices provide an additional energy source and replace fluids.

Vegetarian diets

Vegetarian is a term that includes all people who do not eat meat. Most vegetarians will include eggs and milk in their diets. They are called **lacto-ovo-vegetarians** (*lacto* = milk/*ovo* = egg). Others use only dairy products, such as milk, cheese, and butter. They are known as **lacto-vegetarians**. The few who eat only nuts, fruits, grains, and vegetables are pure vegetarians.

Nutritionists do not recommend a pure vegetarian diet for most people. Without the meat, poultry, fish, and beans group or the milk and cheese group, the body may find it hard to obtain needed amino acids, iron, and vitamin B_{12}. Pure vegetarians, especially, must be very careful to combine plant foods in order to obtain all the important amino acids in adequate amounts.

When soybeans are added to such foods as cereals, a high-quality protein is made. Throughout the world, many people who eat large amounts of plant food and little meat rely on soybeans and cereals for their protein.

Key Words

| anorexia nervosa bulimia | lacto-ovo-vegetarians | lacto-vegetarians vegetarian |

Main Ideas

- Nutritious snacks should be chosen.
- Eating a nutritious breakfast will lower the chance of midmorning tiredness.
- Your input of calories must equal your output of energy if you are going to maintain your desired weight.
- Many fad diets are nutritionally unbalanced, ineffective, and potentially dangerous to health.
- Vegetarian diets need careful planning to provide high-quality protein and iron.
- The exaggerated emphasis on being thin has led to two serious eating disorders, anorexia nervosa and bulimia.

1. Why are jam, candy, and carbonated beverages called empty-calorie foods?

2. Examine the table on page 337 and find out which snack is the best source of each of these nutrients:
   (a) vitamin C   (d) riboflavin
   (b) calcium   (e) thiamine
   (c) vitamin A   (f) iron

3. Why is breakfast an important meal?

4. What is the best way to gain weight if you are underweight?

5. Discuss several safe ways to lose weight.

6. Using the chart on page 342, estimate how many calories you will use if you do the following:
   (a) walk for 20 minutes
   (b) clean your room for 15 minutes
   (c) sit and watch television for 1 hour
   (d) play volleyball for 1 hour
   (e) take a nap

7. Why are diet pills dangerous?

8. What serious health problems accompany anorexia nervosa and bulimia?

9. Should athletes eat high-energy foods just before a game? Should they drink any fluids during a game? Why or why not?

10. What is the difference between the diets of pure vegetarians and lacto-ovo-vegetarians?

1. Determine who among your classmates enjoys cooking. Then, based on what you have learned in this chapter about nutritional snacks, develop recipes for several snacks that are both good to eat and nutritious. (These should be foods that can be prepared for the most part without a stove.) Ask volunteers to supply ingredients, and have your class "chefs" create some of these tasty snacks in class.

2. Use an encyclopedia to learn as much as you can about the typical diet of inhabitants of another country. Then use the Daily Food Guide on page 322 to attempt to determine if the diet is lacking any important nutrients.

3. In magazine and newspaper articles, research the claims made by Dr. Linus Pauling regarding the use of vitamin C as a cure for the common cold. When did Dr. Pauling first make these claims? What else is this noted scientist famous for? What evidence for or against Pauling's claims has been amassed since he first put forth his theory? Once you have found answers to these questions, report to the class on your findings.

Chapter 28

Nutrition:
Labeling and Consumers

After reading this chapter, you will be able to:

- ☐ Explain how to interpret the nutritional label on a food package.
- ☐ Identify the differences between healthful and harmful food additives.
- ☐ Explain why it is important to limit your intake of sugar and salt.
- ☐ Recognize some of the limitations of "health" foods.

Mrs. Karden was careful about the foods her family ate. She usually bought granola bars for them to snack on because she had heard somewhere that granola is a "healthy" food. That was Mrs. Karden's mistake: If she had read the label on the package, she would have found that what seemed like a healthful, nutritious treat was actually loaded with sugar!

Food labeling

You may know the nutritional values of certain foods and the kinds of nutrients that you need daily. But do you always know what to buy in the supermarket? Do you carefully read the labels on the products you buy, or do you simply look for color, brand, and design on the package? As you enter your favorite supermarket, there are over 12,000 items arranged to encourage you to buy on impulse. Your eyes first notice the brands of foods most often advertised in magazines and on television. Food manufacturers spend large amounts of money designing packages to attract your attention. They want you to think that the foods inside the packages are just as tasty and exciting as the pictures. Since you are not allowed to look inside the packages or to sample the foods by tasting them, you have to depend a great deal on your understanding of nutrition labeling to make the best purchase.

The nutritional information on a package should include the serving size and the number of servings per container. Calories, nutrients, and ingredients—what's in the food—are usually listed, too. Some products also list information about sodium, cholesterol, and unsaturated fat.

What is the U.S. Recommended Daily Allowance?

The dietary standards of the United States are established by the Food and Nutrition Board of the National Research Council of the National Academy of Sciences. The nutrition specialists on the Food and Nutrition Board are well qualified to set up the Recommended Daily Allowance, **RDA**, of all nutrients. The **U.S. RDA** gives the amount of each nutrient needed daily by most people in the United States. The term "U.S. RDA" was adopted to ensure proper nutrition labeling. Recommended allowances are more than most people need to avoid diseases associated with malnutrition that were once common in the United States.

Are the U.S. RDAs the same for everyone?

Our daily needs for various nutrients differ according to sex, age, body size, and activity. The RDAs are a guide for the general population. Both age and sex are considered in each recommendation. Revisions to the recommendations are made about every 5 years.

You should have a general idea of how many calories and nutrients you need each day. Then keep track of how many servings of different foods you eat. Based on the amounts you eat, you can easily figure out what percentage of each of your U.S. RDAs is satisfied.

Read labels carefully. They are a clue to the nutritional value of a product.

If you check many product labels, you will generally find an ingredients list. Any of the following terms, for example, may be used to indicate ingredients: "made from," "prepared from," "contains," and "content." These terms refer to the same thing: what makes up the food.

On a certain cereal box, you might see a long list of ingredients, beginning with milled corn, sugar, oat and wheat flour, and rice. These items are listed by weight. This means there is more milled corn by weight in the food than any other ingredient. The ingredient present in the second largest amount is sugar. Oat and wheat flour are third, and rice is fourth. **Additives** used in the food must also be listed. Additives are substances added to food in small amounts for the purpose of improving the food in some way or increasing its shelf life.

Food additives

Some food advertisers would have you believe that *additive* is a bad word. Advertising slogans frequently state that certain products are "free of additives." Some additives, however, are helpful. They replace nutrients that are lost during processing treatments, such as steaming, skinning, crushing, or deep frying. To replace these nutrients, vitamins and minerals are added to packaged foods. Products that contain them are said to be **enriched**, or fortified.

Preservatives. **Preservatives** are additives that keep bacteria, molds, and fungi from spoiling food. Our ancestors preserved their foods with sugar or salt or used drying or smoking methods. Salt and sugar are still being used as preservatives today, along with nitrites, sulfur dioxide, calcium propionate, and others.

Antioxidants. **Antioxidants**, which include vitamin C (ascorbic acid) and vitamin E (from tocopherols), attract oxygen. This oxygen attraction prevents stored foods, especially fats, from changing in color, taste, and smell. Synthetic antioxidants called BHA and BHT are also used. **Sulfites** are used in restaurants to keep vegetables and fruits looking fresh and crisp. Dried fruits, soft drinks, and alcoholic beverages also contain sulfites. This antioxidant is suspected of causing asthma attacks.

Acids and bases. These keep jams and jellies from hardening. They also put effervescence, or "fizz," into soft drinks.

Stabilizers and emulsifiers. These keep oil and water mixed and keep bottled salad dressings and mayonnaise from separating into layers.

Taste enhancers. Taste enhancers, such as monosodium glutamate (MSG) and salt, enhance, or "bring out," the flavors in certain foods. They are not necessary food ingredients. The National Research Council

Do you know how much fat there is in the packaged foods you buy? Before you answer, take a careful look at the nutrition label on a package of processed food. The label lists the *grams* of fat in a serving of the product, but it doesn't tell you the *ratio* of fat to other nutrients.

To find the percentage of fat in any processed food, do the following:

(1) Multiply the grams of fat in a single serving by 9.
(2) Divide the result by the number of calories per serving.
(3) Multiply the result by 100.

The answer you get will be the percentage of fat in a serving of that food.

Use this formula for some of your favorite "low-fat" foods. You might be in for a surprise.

---

has recommended that monosodium glutamate be eliminated from baby foods. The council thinks that babies should eat bland foods as long as possible so that they are not taught to crave certain tastes when they are older. Many manufacturers are decreasing the salt content of foods, too, since a high sodium content in the diet can be a factor in hypertension. Other food enhancers include cloves, ginger, and citrus oils, which add "spice" to foods.

Coloring agents. This group of additives makes foods look better. About 90 percent of these agents are artificial and have no nutritional value. One food coloring, red dye no. 2, is thought to cause cancer. It was ordered off the market by the Food and Drug Administration (FDA).

Flavoring agents. These are a mixture of 10 to 15 different ingredients. The effect of these additives most concerns researchers. Flavoring agents include over 1,200 natural and synthetic (artificial) flavors.

Improving agents. These include meat tenderizers and compounds that put a glaze, or shine, on baked goods.

In packaged foods, preservatives and antioxidants are needed. They prolong freshness and prevent bacteria from multiplying. In this way, foods can be stored for use when they are needed. They also prevent the formation of **toxins** (poisonous substances) produced by chemical changes in spoiled foods. And enrichment and restoration are important, since foods that are refined and processed lose some of their food value.

Using additives that prevent foods from spoiling also lets you have food that is grown far away from home. The foods don't spoil on the way to our communities. Such foods can also be sold at any time of the year, not just during a special season. Prices can thus be kept lower.

Harmful additives

Some additives may, of course, be harmful. Nutritionists believe that some additives in our food are unnecessary. Many additives are dangerous, except in small amounts. One such group of preservatives is called **nitrites**. Nitrites are added to hot dogs, bacon, and sausages to prevent the deadly bacterium called **botulinum** from growing. Botulinum causes **botulism**, a severe form of food poisoning that can kill. Unfortunately, nitrites can also produce cancer-causing agents. But botulism is a greater, more immediate threat to us than cancer. So nitrites are still being used in very small amounts in meats until researchers discover a safer preservative to replace them.

Commercially canned foods cooked at high temperatures are not likely to contain botulinum toxin. The high temperatures destroy the bacteria. However, if a can bulges or leaks or if a food has an unusual odor, it should not be used. The can and its contents should be returned to the store or discarded.

The cause of botulism can usually be traced to contaminated fish, soups, nonacid vegetables, and meat. Since the bacteria grow best where there is no oxygen, improper home canning of foods is the major cause of this deadly form of food poisoning. The bacteria produce a toxin that affects the nerves leading to the muscles of the eyes, throat, and chest. Although an antitoxin can save the patient, full recovery may take several years.

As a consumer, you should read food labels in order to make good choices. You might write to food manufacturers or to your legislator about the harmful additives in food.

The best way to lower your intake of bad food additives is to eat fresh foods and a varied diet. The greater variety in your diet, the less

Beware the use of terms like "all natural" in your food basket.

One of the best ways to lower your intake of additives is to eat fresh foods.

likelihood there is of consuming large amounts of any one additive. With so many packaged foods on the market, perhaps consumers have become lazy about taking the time to prepare and cook fresh vegetables, meat, fish, and fruit. By changing food-preparation habits, many people can improve the quality of what they eat.

Do we need extra sugar in our diets?

Sugar can be found in almost every food you eat. There are many different forms of sugar. Some of the more common simple sugars include sucrose, fructose, brown sugar, honey, and corn syrup. However, all sugars have approximately 4 calories per gram. Since there are very few nutrients in sugars, they are labeled as caloric sweeteners, or empty calories.

The body doesn't need the caloric sweeteners, but your "sweet tooth" may become addicted to them. The major concern about excess sugar, especially sucrose, in the diet is the likelihood of an increase in dental caries (tooth decay).

The U.S. Dietary Goals recommend that you limit sugar intake to not more than 10 percent of the total calories you eat in a day. Remember to look for other words that mean "sugar" on food labels. Even if the word "sugar" does not appear, you are buying a product with sugar if you see "dextrose," "corn syrup," "glucose," or "dextrins" on the label.

It would be hard to stop eating sugar altogether. Many foods, such as catsup, canned pinto beans, and even tomato soup, contain some sugar. The best way to cut down on sugar intake is by adding less sugar to such foods as breakfast cereal and by avoiding the "hidden sugar" in many canned and bottled foods.

How much salt is safe?

You use approximately 2 teaspoons of salt, or sodium chloride, every day. That is about 8½ pounds per year. Sodium is an important nutrient. It regulates body fluid, helps nerve impulses travel, and helps the heart

Hidden Sugar in Some Foods

Cakes and cookies		tsp.	Spreads and sauces		tsp.
Chocolate cake	1/12 cake (2-layer iced)	15	Jam	1 level Tbsp.	3
			Jelly	1 level Tbsp.	2½
Angel food cake	1/12 of large cake	6	Marmalade	1 level Tbsp.	3
Sponge cake	1/10 of average cake	6	Syrup, maple	1 level Tbsp.	2½
			Honey	1 level Tbsp.	3
Cream puff (iced)	1 average, custard-filled	5	Chocolate sauce (thick)	1 Tbsp.	4½
Doughnut, plain	3″ diameter	4			
Macaroons	1 large or 2 small	3			
Gingersnaps	1 medium	1			
Molasses cookies	3½″ diameter	2			
Brownies	2″ × 2″ × ¾″	3			

Pie		tsp.	Milk drinks		tsp.
Apple	1/6 medium pie	12	Chocolate	1 cup, 5 oz milk	6
Cherry	1/6 medium pie	14	Cocoa	1 cup, 5 oz milk	4
Raisin	1/6 medium pie	13	Eggnog	1 glass, 8 oz milk	4½
Pumpkin	1/6 medium pie	10			

Soft drinks		tsp.	Ice cream		tsp.
Sweet carbonated beverage	1 bottle, 6 oz	4⅓	Ice cream	⅛ quart (½ cup)	5–6
			Sherbet	⅛ quart (½ cup)	6–8
Ginger ale	6 oz glass	3⅓			

Fruits and fruit juices		tsp.	Candy		tsp.
Fruit cocktail	½ cup, scant	5	Chocolate bar	1 average size	7
Orange juice	½ cup, scant	2	Chocolate cream	1 average size	2
Pineapple juice, unsweetened	½ cup, scant	2⅗	Chocolate fudge	½″ square	4
			Chocolate mints	1 medium	3
Grapefruit juice, unsweetened	½ cup, scant	2⅕	Marshmallow	1 average	1½
			Chewing gum	1 stick	½
Grapefruit, commercial	½ cup, scant	3⅔			

Cooked fruits		tsp.	Dried fruits		tsp.
Peaches, canned in syrup	2 halves, 1 Tbsp. syrup	3½	Apricots, dried	4 to 6 halves	4
			Prunes, dried	3 to 4 medium	4
Rhubarb, stewed, sweetened	½ cup	8	Dates, dried	3 to 4 stoned	4½
			Figs, dried	1½ to 2 small	4
Apple sauce, unsweetened	½ cup, scant	2	Raisins	¼ cup	4
Prunes, stewed, sweetened	4 to 5 medium, 2 Tbsp. juice	8			

20 teaspoons of sugar is equivalent to 400 calories.

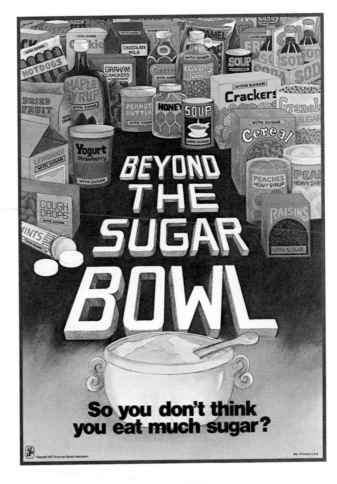

BEYOND THE SUGAR BOWL

So you don't think you eat much sugar?

In the United States, the average person eats 100 pounds of sugar per year.

to beat. The National Academy of Science has established a "safe and adequate" sodium intake of 1 to 3 grams per day. Americans currently consume 4 to 5 grams per day.

Doctors recommend that people who have high blood pressure or migraine headaches use less salt. They also advise people who tend to retain water in the body to lower their salt intake. People on salt-free diets should be careful not to use salt when they cook or flavor food. The label on food products will state one of the following:

- Sodium Free . . . . . . less than 5 milligrams (mg) per serving
- Very Low Sodium . . . . . . 35 mg or less
- Low Sodium . . . . . . 140 mg or less
- Reduced Sodium . . . . . . sodium reduced by 75 percent
- Unsalted . . . . . . no salt added to product that is usually salted

Are you confused by such words as "natural," "organic," and "health" when they are applied to foods? All three words are sometimes used to promote fad foods or fad diets. People who sell these products claim that their foods are safer and more nutritious than those that are

Are health foods more nourishing?

355

Salt Content of Snack Foods	
snack food	**salt content (mg/100g)**
Corn chips	741
Taco tortilla chips	868
Toasted corn	1,307
Salted peanuts	595
Granola snack bar	273
Corn-flavored snacks	1,014
Pretzel twists	2,370
Nacho chips	546
Sunflower seeds	721
Tortilla chips	468
Saltines	1,794
Nacho cheese chips	292
Salty rye crackers	819
Wheat crackers	566

conventionally grown and marketed. Other claims, bordering on quackery, suggest that certain foods will help prevent cancer or will cleanse the body of toxins. Remember, not all products sold in stores to promote wellness are safe.

Many people believe in eating health foods, such as granola cereals or organic honey. Honey does contain traces of vitamins and minerals, but it is still one of the simple sugars. Granola cereals are made with whole grains, but these cereals, too, are high in sugar. Many of the health foods are high in calories also, and many are expensive.

Open dating and unit pricing

Many preservatives are added to our foods. Even so, some foods will spoil or lose their flavor in a short period of time. **Open dating** helps consumers identify fresh food. Food manufacturers stamp packages with dates that tell when products should be removed from the shelves, when the food was packaged, or the latest date by which the food should be used. However, different dates may have different meanings. Consumers

Many people do much of their food shopping at health food stores.

356

Calories in Some "Health" Foods		
Food	**Amount**	**Calories**
Banana chips	½ cup	200
Bean sprouts	1 cup	40
Blackstrap molasses	2 tablespoons	80
Bran muffin	1 small	130
Brewer's yeast, dry	1 tablespoon	23
Brown rice, cooked	⅔ cup	150
Bulgur, cooked	1 cup	230
Carob powder	3 ounces	325
Carob bar	1.5 ounces	232
Coconut milk	1 cup	605
Coconut, raw, shredded, loosely packed	½ cup	225
Fruit, dried (apples, dates, apricots, raisins)	2 ounces	160
Granola	½ cup	260
Honey, all kinds	1 tablespoon	60
Nuts (most kinds)	1 ounce	160–170
Peanut butter, natural	2 tablespoons	200
Potato chips, natural	1 ounce	150
Pumpkin seeds, hulled	1 ounce	155
Soybeans, roasted	1 ounce	140
Sunflower seeds, hulled	1 ounce	160
Tofu	4 ounces	130
Wheat germ, toasted	¼ cup, dry	110
Yogurt, plain, low-fat	8 ounces	150
Yogurt, sweetened	8 ounces	200–260

need to learn what the dates mean. Some foods have a shelf life of 2 to 3 years. Others must be consumed within several days.

Different brands of food on supermarket shelves are often packaged in containers of different sizes and weights. **Unit pricing** is a method of showing the cost per unit of weight, regardless of the size of the container or the weight of the contents. Unit prices are posted on supermarket shelves. Using this information, you can quickly compare the costs of two different-sized packages of raisins, for example, by reading and comparing their costs per unit of weight.

Key Words

additives	**enriched**	**sulfites**
antioxidants	**nitrites**	**toxins**
botulinum	**open dating**	**unit pricing**
botulism	**preservatives**	**U.S. RDA**
	RDA	

Main Ideas

- Food labeling helps us to "see" what is inside a package.
- The Recommended Dietary Allowances tell us the kinds and amounts of nutrients we need. The U.S. RDA used on nutrient labels is based on the RDA.
- Additives that keep food from spoiling allow us to ship foods for thousands of miles and to enjoy them out of season. Other additives improve the nutritional value of food.
- Some additives are safe only if small amounts are consumed.
- Added sugar is not needed in the diet, and salt intake should be limited.
- Health foods may not satisfy consumer needs.
- Open dating and unit pricing help consumers make wise choices.

Understand the Reading

1. How often are recommendations for revising RDAs made?
2. Refer to the food label on page 349, and answer the following questions:
   (a) Is this food a good source of calcium? Why or why not?
   (b) How many servings are in this container?
   (c) How large is each serving?
3. Use the formula in "Something to think about" on page 351. Determine the percentage of fat in a packaged food that has 4 grams of fat and 180 calories per serving.
4. What is the job of antioxidants in food? Of stabilizers?
5. Why did the National Research Council recommend that monosodium glutamate be dropped from baby food?
6. How can nitrites be both helpful and harmful?
7. Does the body need sugar? Explain.
8. Why is some salt in the diet important? Why is too much salt harmful for some people?
9. What are the attractions of health foods for some people?
10. What is open dating? How does it help the consumer?

Apply Your Knowledge

1. Keep a record of every food you see advertised that makes claims of being "nutritionally beneficial." Visit a supermarket, and locate as many of those products as you can. Copy down the nutritional information listed on each product. Discuss your findings with the class.
2. Bring to class two samples of the same prepared food, one with additives, one without. Blindfold volunteers and feed each of them a little of each food. (The two foods should be labeled so that the rest of the class knows which is which.) After the volunteers have commented on the differences in taste, if any, conduct a class discussion.

Chapter 29
Digestion and Elimination

After reading this chapter, you will be able to:

☐ Name the organs involved in digestion and describe the function of each.

☐ Identify the organs that carry away waste.

☐ Identify the causes of major problems in the digestive tract.

☐ Explain how to prevent problems in the digestive tract.

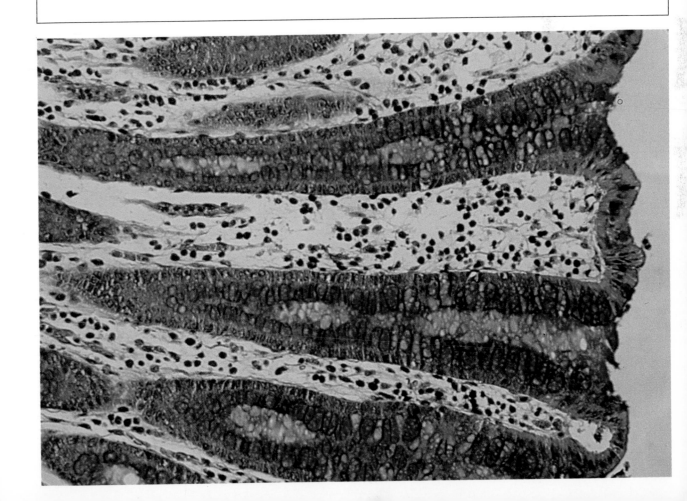

The digestive tract

The digestive tract is made up of a series of organs that move food through the body. The tract begins at the mouth and ends at the anus. The anus is the opening from the large intestine to the outside of the body.

The entire digestive tract is called the **alimentary canal**. The alimentary canal is about 30 feet long. Most of its length curls back and forth within the abdomen.

Throughout the digestive process, important work is done by **enzymes**. These enzymes are in digestive juices produced by many different glands throughout the body. Digestive enzymes are chemicals that break down food into simpler compounds. These simpler compounds are then absorbed into the bloodstream. The substances that are not absorbed into the bloodstream gather in the large intestine and are finally pushed out as waste, or feces.

The secretion of digestive juices and the movement of food through the digestive tract are involuntary. They are not under your control.

Digestion begins in the mouth.

The digestive tract begins at the mouth. The tongue, the teeth, and the fluids in the mouth prepare food for the later stages of digestion.

The tongue is an important tool. As food enters the mouth, the tongue guides it between the teeth. The food is then cut and ground by the teeth. This mechanical breakdown of food, or chewing, is called **mastication**.

The surface of the tongue is dotted with tiny, fingerlike projections called **papillae**. The papillae help the tongue "hold onto" food and move it. Without papillae, it would be hard, for example, to lick a yogurt cone. Cats and dogs have many papillae. They use their raspy tongues to lap up food and fluids. Tiny taste buds are located along the sides of the papillae. There are four different kinds of taste buds—sweet, salty, sour, and bitter. Each kind is located on a different part of the tongue's surface.

Three pairs of **salivary glands** secrete saliva, the liquid that pours into the mouth. Saliva moistens and softens food. It contains the enzyme called salivary **amylase**. This enzyme breaks down starch into a form of sugar called maltose.

A "ball" of food that has been chewed and is ready to be swallowed is called a **bolus**. The tongue pushes the bolus back toward the pharynx

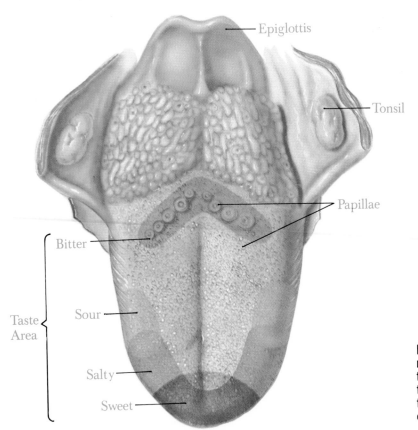

Epiglottis

Tonsil

Papillae

Bitter

Taste Area

Sour

Salty

Sweet

Digestion begins in the mouth. The tongue, the teeth, and the fluids in the mouth break up the food for the later stages of digestion.

(throat). The involuntary swallowing reflex then takes over. The soft palate and the **uvula** (a flap of gumlike tissue) close the nasal opening. The epiglottis covers the trachea (windpipe). These actions stop food from entering the air passages. The bolus is now on its way to the stomach and intestines.

The pathway to the stomach

After food is chewed and swallowed, it is moved along the **esophagus**, a tube that connects the mouth to the stomach. The esophagus is about 10 inches long. It passes down through the thorax (chest cavity) until it reaches the diaphragm. There it enters the abdominal cavity and connects to the stomach. The esophagus does not digest food, but it does secrete mucus that mixes with and moistens the food.

In the walls of the esophagus are rings of muscle that contract, one after the other. These waves of contractions are called **peristaltic waves**. These movements push the food along the digestive tract. Peristaltic waves are involuntary. You can't decide to stop or start them. Even if you were standing on your head, food would still be pushed or moved along the alimentary canal.

361

This is a diagram of the digestive system.

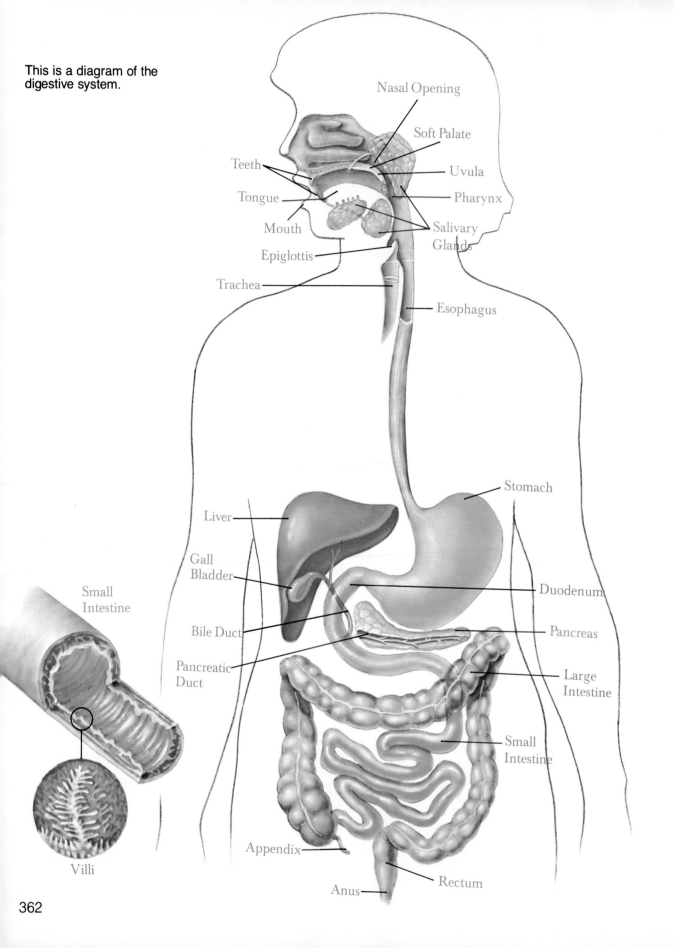

Nasal Opening

Soft Palate

Teeth

Uvula

Tongue

Pharynx

Mouth

Salivary Glands

Epiglottis

Trachea

Esophagus

Stomach

Liver

Gall Bladder

Duodenum

Bile Duct

Pancreas

Pancreatic Duct

Large Intestine

Small Intestine

Small Intestine

Appendix

Villi

Rectum

Anus

The stomach is a temporary storage place.

The stomach is a pouch that has digestive glands in it. The stomach works mainly as a temporary storage place for food during digestion. It gets larger as the body gets larger.

Glands in the walls of the stomach produce **gastric juice**. This juice contains the enzymes pepsin and rennin, which are needed for the digestion of proteins. Gastric juice also contains hydrochloric acid. This acid makes it possible for the pepsin to act. It also kills some of the microorganisms that enter the stomach in food. The stomach expands and contracts, mixing the food with the gastric juice. The food then becomes a thin, soupy liquid called **chyme**.

It takes 3 to 4 hours for the stomach to empty after an ordinary meal. Fatty foods stay in the stomach longer than other foods. Liquids may pass through the stomach in 10 minutes or less.

Many people think that the stomach is the most important organ of the digestive system. Actually, very little food is absorbed directly into the bloodstream from the stomach. A person could even live comfortably without a stomach, as long as meals were small and taken frequently.

The major part of digestion occurs in the small intestine.

The small intestine is a very important part of the digestive tract. It is a coiled tube about 20 to 25 feet long and about $1\frac{1}{2}$ inches wide when filled. The most important part of the digestive tract is the **duodenum**, the first section of the small intestine. Most of the digestive process is carried on in the duodenum. Secretions from the pancreas, from the liver, and from glands in the walls of the duodenum act upon the bolus as it passes through the duodenum.

The liver is part of the digestive system.

The liver is a large organ on the right side of the upper part of the abdomen. It is one of the most important organs in the body. The liver carries out many of the functions needed for digestion and other body processes.

Bile is a fluid secreted by the liver. It aids in the digestion of fat. Bile is stored in the gall bladder, a small sac under the liver. During digestion, the gall bladder contracts. This causes bile to flow through the bile duct to the duodenum.

Worn-out red blood cells are destroyed in the liver. Pigments from these cells give a dark yellowish-green color to the bile. These pigments also give feces their yellowish-brown color.

The pancreas aids in digestion and helps the cells use sugar.

The pancreas is a gland that lies along the lower side of the stomach. It is about 4 to 6 inches long. The pancreas is both an endocrine gland

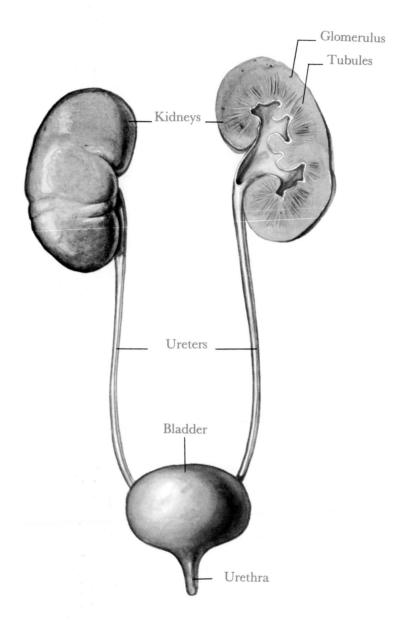

Glomerulus

Tubules

Kidneys

Ureters

Bladder

Urethra

The kidneys remove waste from the blood. The waste enters the bladder in the form of urine and is later excreted from the body.

and a gland of external secretion. It produces two kinds of secretions: pancreatic juice and the hormone insulin.

Insulin is an internal secretion. It passes from gland cells in the pancreas right into the bloodstream. Insulin helps the body cells use sugar.

Pancreatic juice is an external secretion. It flows from the pancreas to the duodenum through a duct called the pancreatic duct. The pancreatic duct joins the bile duct so that pancreatic juice and bile go into the duodenum through the same opening. Enzymes in the intestinal and pancreatic juices finish the digestion of fat, carbohydrate, and protein. They change fat to glycerol and fatty acids, carbohydrate to simple sugars, and protein to amino acids.

Digestion is completed in the small intestine. The food has been broken down and is ready to be absorbed by the bloodstream or removed as waste. Nutrients enter the bloodstream, and wastes are passed to the large intestine.

The villi of the small intestine absorb nutrients.

The inner lining of the small intestine has millions of tiny, fingerlike projections called **villi** (singular: villus). The villi add greatly to the surface area of the lining of the intestine. Nutrients are absorbed through this large surface area.

Each tiny villus has a network of small blood vessels and a lymph vessel. Lymph is a colorless fluid found in all body tissues. It carries substances between body cells and the bloodstream. The vessel walls separating the blood and lymph from the materials in the small intestine are very thin. Digested food substances can easily pass through these walls. Water, amino acids, simple sugars, mineral salts, and some vitamins enter the blood vessels. Digested fat and some vitamins enter the lymph vessel. From there, they enter the bloodstream. Nutrients absorbed into the blood go first to the liver, where some nutrients are stored for later use.

Elimination of wastes

Some of the body's wastes are carried by the lymph to the veins. Then the wastes are carried by blood in the veins to other organs that excrete, or remove, them from the body. Carbon dioxide and water are breathed out through the lungs. Water and salts pass out through the skin as perspiration. Among the most important organs that remove wastes are the large intestine and the kidneys.

The large intestine reabsorbs water and removes wastes.

Undigested food, bacteria, and dead cells from the lining of the small intestine are not absorbed by the villi. Instead, these substances pass into the large intestine. The substances are now in a highly fluid state. They are mixed with many digestive juices and contain much water. The walls of the large intestine absorb most of the water and return it to the bloodstream. This is one of the most important functions of the large intestine.

Many bacteria live in the large intestine. Most of them are harmless. Some serve a useful purpose by breaking down waste materials.

Movement of peristaltic waves along the large intestine is slow. It takes 12 to 20 hours for materials to pass through the large intestine. Feces (waste) are finally passed out of the body as a bowel movement.

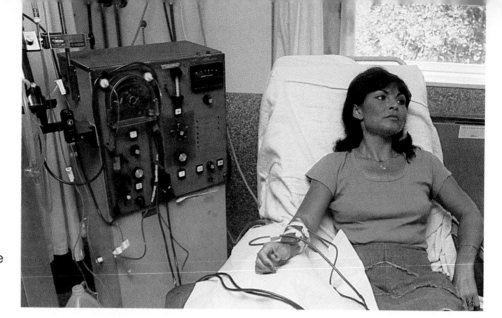

Machines such as these have saved many lives by artificially doing the work of the kidneys.

The urinary system purifies the blood.

The urinary system consists of two kidneys, two ureters (tubes from the kidneys to the bladder), a bladder, and the urethra (passage to the outside of the body).

All of the blood in the body circulates through the kidneys. Extra water, salts, and wastes containing nitrogen are filtered out of the blood into small tubes within the kidneys. The wastes then flow through the ureters to the bladder. These liquid wastes, called urine, are stored in the bladder until they are excreted.

Formation of urine takes place all the time. An average adult excretes from 1 to 2 quarts of urine every 24 hours. Usually urine is yellow. The color is lighter when there is a good deal of water in the urine and darker when there is less water.

Many kinds of wastes leave the body in the urine. Some of them change its color and odor. For example, a distinctive odor may be noted in the urine after eating asparagus. Even vitamins or certain drugs may change the color of urine.

Elimination of urine

When the bladder is full, pressure starts nerve impulses that cause release of urine. A person can stop the bladder from emptying by contracting the muscles in the wall of the urethra. Children usually learn to control urination when they are 18 to 30 months old. Control is easiest when the child is awake. Bedwetting, called **enuresis**, is common in preschool children. But sometimes it occurs in schoolchildren and adults, as well. This is generally caused by strain, extra excitement, or illness. Researchers have developed ways of breaking bedwetters of this habit by hooking them up to alarms that sound quietly when they wet the bed.

If bedwetting occurs often in an older child or adult, a physician should be consulted.

What will happen if the filtration system breaks down?

Any infection or poison carried in the blood may damage the kidneys. Salts from the urine may form hard masses, or stones, and lodge in the kidneys, ureters, or bladder. Small stones may pass out of the body with urine. Larger stones usually must be removed by surgery. The kidneys can also be damaged by such poisons as mercury or by large amounts of harmful substances, such as caffeine or alcohol.

A person can get along very well with only one kidney or even part of one kidney. If one kidney is removed, the remaining one can enlarge to twice its original size. It can do the work of two kidneys. However, if there is total damage to both kidneys, waste materials will collect in the blood. This can cause poisoning and even death.

Artificial kidney machines have saved many lives. Blood travels from the patient's artery through tubes into the kidney machine. Waste materials in the blood are filtered out by special artificial membranes in the machine. The clean blood then returns to the patient through a vein. Surgeons can also now perform operations that transplant a healthy kidney from a donor into another person whose kidneys are damaged or diseased.

More about the digestive system

A person has good digestion when movement of the peristaltic waves goes on smoothly and all of the digestive juices are secreted in the right amounts. The muscles and glands of the digestive tract have nerves that are part of the autonomic (involuntary) nervous system. Messages from the brain that travel over these nerves are not under your control.

Poor digestion is sometimes called indigestion. Indigestion may cause a loss of appetite, a bad taste in the mouth, a pain in the abdomen, vomiting, or diarrhea. Emotional strain can cause indigestion. Other causes include appendicitis, gallstones, or ulcers in the stomach or intestines. Any long-lasting digestive problem should be checked by a doctor.

How do emotions affect digestion?

Strong emotions, such as fear, anger, resentment, embarrassment, or excitement, can affect the digestive system. Messages sent by the nerves can cause problems with peristaltic waves and gland secretion. The mouth may become dry. A dry mouth means that the salivary glands are not producing saliva. At the same time, the stomach and intestines may be "dry" because other digestive glands are not working well. This is not a good time to eat a large meal.

On the other hand, pleasant thoughts about eating may aid digestion. The smell, taste, sight, and even the thought of food can make the mouth "water" (produce saliva). The other digestive glands also start to secrete. The muscles of the digestive system contract, sometimes making the stomach and intestines "growl" or "rumble."

Good eating habits help digestion.

Pleasant, clean surroundings and good company at mealtime aid digestion. It is best to eat slowly. Nagging, arguing, or worrying out loud at the table creates tension. This upsets digestion. A calm, relaxed atmosphere helps everyone to enjoy the food.

Many people wonder if they should drink water with meals. Small amounts of water between swallows of food help the work of the enzymes. However, it is not a good idea to use water to wash large bites of food down the throat. When people do this instead of chewing thoroughly, they make it harder for good digestion to take place. Drinking ice water with a meal may also interfere with the digestive process.

What causes vomiting?

Vomiting is caused by backward, or reverse, peristaltic waves in the stomach and esophagus. It comes with strong contractions of the abdominal and chest muscles. Nausea, a feeling of faintness and weakness, yawning, and extra secretion of saliva usually occur before vomiting.

Mealtimes should be times of happy sharing.

The center that controls vomiting is not in the stomach, but in the brain. Nerve impulses can travel to this center from many places in the body. Vomiting is always a sign of some kind of disturbance. Unpleasant sights, sounds, or even thoughts can stimulate the vomiting center. It is more easily stimulated in children than in adults.

Vomiting may be a symptom of a dangerous illness. Irritation in the stomach may start messages traveling over nerves that lead to the vomiting center. Irritations in the abdomen caused by appendicitis, gall bladder disease, injuries to the abdomen, or intestinal infection may also send messages of distress to the vomiting center. The same is true for some illnesses that do not seem related to the digestive tract, such as pneumonia, scarlet fever, and some kinds of heart disease.

Some people become nauseated when they travel by car, ship, or airplane. This is known as motion sickness. In such cases, nerve messages go to the vomiting center from the eyes and the semicircular canals of the ears. Lying down and closing the eyes can help someone with motion sickness to feel better. Medications have been used very successfully to treat motion sickness.

Diarrhea can lead to dehydration.

Diarrhea is a symptom of disturbance in the digestive tract or elsewhere in the body. In diarrhea, the feces are watery. Bowel movements also occur more frequently than usual. So large quantities of water are lost from body tissues. This may result in dehydration (water loss). If diarrhea is very bad and continues for some time, its cause should be discovered and treated. It is especially dangerous in infants and young children.

Common causes of diarrhea are nervous upsets, eating food to which one is allergic, and the presence of microorganisms in food or drink. A simple way to prevent many microorganisms from getting into food is by washing the hands before eating, cooking, or serving food.

Constipation and its problems

Constipation is a common condition in which the feces are hard and bowel movements are difficult. Most people have a bowel movement once a day. Some people have one only every 2 or 3 days. Others have two or three bowel movements in a day. The number and frequency of bowel movements is not as important as the regularity.

The usual reason for constipation is a diet that does not include enough roughage and bulk to cause peristaltic waves. Roughage, or fiber, is nondigestible material. It stimulates the muscles of the digestive tract. Sometimes the muscles in the wall of the intestines contract but do not relax. This stops the peristaltic waves. Another cause of constipation is lack of exercise. In this case, the muscles of the abdomen become too relaxed to be useful in bowel action.

Enemas are treatments sometimes used to relieve constipation. An enema usually is made of plain warm water. The enema is put into the anus with a tube. The liquid goes into the lower part of the large intestine. It stretches the walls of the intestine. Then the walls contract and force out both the water solution and the wastes. An enema does not act on the whole digestive tract. This is an important difference between enemas and laxatives.

Laxatives stimulate the muscles of the digestive tract. If laxatives are taken often and regularly, they can become habit forming. As time passes, larger doses or stronger laxatives will be needed to produce a bowel movement. As a result, muscles of the intestine may become overworked and suffer damage. It is best to take laxatives only on the advice of a physician.

Can everyone drink milk?

Milk and milk products pose a health hazard to the 30 million adult Americans who lack the lactase enzyme.

Approximately 30 million adult Americans are unable to drink milk because they do not have an enzyme that can digest the sugar in the milk. The milk sugar is called **lactose**, and the enzyme responsible for digesting it is **lactase**. The lactose passes from the small to the large intestine. Bacteria in the colon ferment the sugar to make it digestible. Some people can tolerate small amounts of milk or dairy products that have already been fermented. Commercially prepared enzymes are also available. Several drops of the enzyme are added to the milk to break down the lactose.

Ulcers can form in the stomach or duodenum.

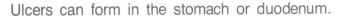

An **ulcer** is an eroded, or worn, spot in the digestive lining. Ulcers are usually in the stomach or in the duodenum. They may bleed or may "eat through" the wall of the digestive tract. In addition, they are usually very painful. Not all causes of ulcers are known. Cigarette smoking is an important factor in the formation of ulcers. Ulcers of the stomach are five times more frequent in cigarette smokers than in nonsmokers. Special diets, medications, and ways to decrease acid in the digestive tract are important in the treatment of ulcers. In some very serious cases, surgery may be needed to correct the problem.

Swelling of the appendix is called appendicitis.

The appendix is a small organ near the beginning of the large intestine. Its function is unknown. Infection or inflammation of the appendix is called **appendicitis**. The first symptom of appendicitis is usually pain. The pain may be sudden and very bad, or it may be mild. Later symptoms include nausea, vomiting, constipation, fever, and soreness in the lower abdomen. If these symptoms occur, call a doctor. In the meantime, remain quiet and eat nothing. Do not take a laxative. Do not use a hot-water bag or electric heating pad. Heat or a laxative can cause an infected appendix to rupture, or break. This spreads infection throughout the abdominal cavity. Keep in mind that most of the deaths resulting from appendicitis today could have been prevented with proper medical treatment.

What causes hemorrhoids?

Sometimes veins around the anus or in the rectum become swollen with blood. Such a swollen mass of veins is called a hemorrhoid. Hemorrhoids may bulge out near the anus. A blood clot may form in a hemorrhoid, producing a painful lump. Sometimes hemorrhoids rupture and bleed.

Constipation, straining during bowel movements, physical exertion, inherited tendencies, and pregnancy are all thought to be causes of hemorrhoids. Proper diet and controlled exercise can help a person who has hemorrhoids. In very serious cases, surgery may be needed to correct this condition.

Gas in the intestinal tract

Having gas (**flatus**) in the stomach or in the intestine is a normal condition. Sometimes it can be uncomfortable. The extra gas puts pressure on the wall of the intestine.

Gas is formed when you swallow air. Much of this gas will be belched from the stomach. A small amount can find its way into the large intestine. The bacteria in the large intestine can form other gases, such as hydrogen and methane.

371

To prevent too much flatus from forming, stay away from foods that you know are "gas-forming." People react in different ways to different kinds of food. Cabbage or beans, for example, may produce gas in some people, but may have no effect on others.

How common are intestinal infections?

Until recent years, worms of different kinds were found in the digestive tracts of many people. Such worms included ascaris, hookworm, tapeworm, and pinworm. For several reasons, infestations with worms are now much less common in the United States. People who handle, cook, and serve food are instructed to wash their hands often. They do this to protect themselves and others from the spread of worms and other organisms. Modern buildings and sewage disposal have lowered the number of breeding places for flies. Because few people go barefoot, hookworm is now rare. Meat inspection gives protection against some infections. And we now know that thorough cooking kills harmful organisms in food.

In many places throughout the world, intestinal infections and infestations are still common. Travelers should find out if the drinking water in places they visit is free of contamination. They should also find out if it is safe to eat raw fruits and vegetables and how carefully food is cooked and served.

Key Words

alimentary canal	duodenum	mastication
amylase	enuresis	papillae
appendicitis	enzymes	peristaltic waves
bile	esophagus	salivary glands
bolus	flatus	ulcer
chyme	gastric juice	uvula
	lactase	villi
	lactose	

Main Ideas

- The digestive tract breaks food down into simpler chemical substances. Some of these substances are absorbed as food, while others are eliminated as waste.
- The tongue helps in tasting, chewing, and swallowing. Taste buds are found along the sides of papillae on the tongue.
- The salivary glands secrete saliva. Saliva moistens food and has an enzyme called amylase that breaks down sugar into maltose.
- Food is pushed through the digestive tract by muscular contractions called peristaltic waves.

Continued

372

■ The major part of digestion takes place in the small intestine rather than in the stomach.

■ Sensible eating and exercise help keep the digestive system in good condition.

1. Put the following into the order in which they work in the digestive system: uvula, rectum, pharynx, duodenum, stomach, esophagus, tongue, large intestine.
2. List three functions of the tongue.
3. What is the function of the enzyme found in saliva?
4. What happens to food in the mouth? In the stomach? In the small intestine?
5. How does gastric juice help in the digestive process?
6. List two functions of hydrochloric acid in the digestive system.
7. How could a person function without a stomach?
8. What are the functions of the liver and bile?
9. Name the two types of secretion from the pancreas.
10. What does the large intestine do?
11. What is the function of the ureters?
12. Explain the work of the kidneys.
13. How do emotions affect digestion?
14. How can diarrhea be dangerous?
15. Name some causes of constipation. How can it be prevented?
16. Why is it unwise to make a habit of taking laxatives?
17. Describe the symptoms of appendicitis.
18. What should a person with appendicitis do until a doctor is reached? What kinds of treatments are dangerous?
19. How does flatus (gas) form in the digestive system?
20. How are intestinal infections and infestations spread?

1. Do some research on digestion in cows. If you can, obtain technical drawings that show the various parts of the cow's digestive system. In a report, tell your classmates about digestion in cows, and pass around the drawings.
2. Have a physician who specializes in internal medicine visit the class. Ask the doctor to discuss the relationship between taste and smell. In particular, attempt to learn what part of our sense of taste is actually determined by our sense of smell. At home, test what the doctor says by holding your nose and sampling some strong-flavored foods. Report what you find to your class the following day.

Unit 9
Safety and Emergency

Chapter 30
Personal Safety

After reading this chapter, you will be able to:

☐ Identify the major causes of accidents on the road.

☐ Identify the major causes of accidents at home, on the job, and out-of-doors.

☐ List the steps that can make your home a safer place from fire and other disasters.

☐ Describe what actions you can take to decrease the chance of being attacked.

The word *accident* implies forces over which we have no control. However, the facts show that many "accidents" can and should be prevented. Do you follow safety rules for the hobbies, sports, or jobs that you are involved in? Are you careful not to drive, work, or play athletic games when you are tired? When you are working with equipment or driving, do you give your full attention to what you are doing?

Automobile accidents

No one ever expects to be in a motor vehicle accident—and that is a major part of the problem. Sitting at the control panel of an object made of several tons of steel capable of traveling at high speeds leads to a feeling of power. Nothing, you think, can penetrate your "suit of armor." And probably nothing would—if yours were the only car on the road.

About 22 percent of all drivers are less than 25 years old. These young drivers usually see and hear better than older drivers. They also react more quickly. So you might think they would be good drivers. Yet drivers under 25 have more accidents per licensed driver than any other age group. They are in about one-third of the automobile accidents in the United States. At this rate, 1 out of every 3 people who are now 15 years old will be hurt in an automobile accident. About 1 out of every 100 will die.

Safety on the road

Accidents are the leading cause of injury and death among people of high school age.

What can be done to prevent serious injuries from car accidents and to lower the high death rate? One answer is seat belts. Having your seat belt fastened reduces your chance of being seriously injured by 50 percent and of being killed by 60 to 70 percent.

In spite of the fact that seat belts are now required by law in many states, only about 1 person in 8 buckles up regularly. Why? Surveys show most people aren't against the *idea* of seat belts. Some people say that seat belts are a "nuisance" and "inconvenient." Others say they don't want to be belted in case their car catches fire in an accident or plunges into a lake or river. Despite the regularity of such accidents on television, fiery crashes and sinking cars are extremely rare. Seat belts decrease your chances of being knocked unconscious or otherwise disabled on impact. You would thus be better able to help yourself and others escape from the car in any type of accident.

Another reason people give for not wearing belts is that they might be "thrown clear" in a crash if they aren't belted. Occasionally, a passenger is thrown clear in an accident. But actually, your chances of being killed are 25 times greater if you are thrown out of the vehicle than if you remain inside the car.

Motorcycle accidents

Many young people drive motorcycles and mopeds. Based on the number of miles driven, the chance of a cyclist being killed is about five times greater than that of an automobile driver. The chances of motorcycle passengers being killed are also higher than those of automobile passengers. Both drivers and passengers on motorcycles and mopeds are unprotected against the forces of a collision.

Major causes of motorcycle accidents include unsafe driving practices, not obeying traffic rules, weaving around and in between cars, and "stunting" (trick riding). Untrained or inexperienced cyclists also contribute to the death and injury tolls associated with motorcycle accidents.

Because of the danger of serious accidents from these practices, as well as from hazardous driving conditions, it is extremely important to use the proper equipment if you are going to drive or ride a motorcycle.

Number of Accidental Deaths by Age in a Recent Year

Age	Motor Vehicle	Falls	Drown-ing	Fires, Burns	Ingest. of Food, Object	Fire-arms	Poison (solid, liquid)	Poison by Gas
Under 5	1,426	155	803	846	407	45	73	32
5 to 14	2,747	89	856	478	58	271	33	19
15 to 24	19,040	515	2,278	564	127	702	522	320
25 to 44	16,133	1,066	1,858	1,017	340	604	1,372	417
45 to 64	8,022	2,116	902	1,245	726	233	650	275
65 to 74	2,991	1,840	307	749	594	61	218	83
75 & over	2,813	7,513	253	923	997	39	221	96

A motorcyclist's risk of death on the road is five times as great as that of an automobile driver.

A crash helmet, goggles, and heavy gloves should be worn at all times the cycle is in motion.

Bicycle accidents

Riding bicycles for pleasure or for heathful exercise is very popular. You know about some of the dangers of driving an automobile or a motorcycle. Riding a bicycle can be very dangerous, too. In fact, bicycles are involved in more injuries than any other vehicle.

Some of the causes of bicycle accidents are loss of control, riding too large a bike, and such mechanical problems as brake failure or chain slippage. Like motorcyclists, bikers sometimes perform foolish stunts with their bikes—such hotdogging maneuvers as riding on the rear wheel, the rear fenders, or the handlebars. Accidents resulting from such behavior seem especially pointless, particularly when someone other than the rider is injured.

To decrease the number of accidents, bicycle riders should obey the same traffic rules that automobile drivers and motorcyclists follow: Ride on the right side of the road, obey traffic signs and lights, and signal when you are about to stop or turn.

About 6,000 people drown every year in the United States. Most drownings occur when young people are swimming, fishing, boating, water-skiing, skin diving, and surfing—in other words, during leisure activities. If you enjoy these activities, the most sensible course of action you can take is to learn how to do them well and safely.

The most important rule to learn regarding water safety is this: Learn to swim well. This is an important precaution for all water sports and recreational activities in the water. Beyond this, you might want to remember the following safety tips suggested by the American Red Cross:

Safety in the water

■ Swim out-of-doors only when the water temperature will not chill your body.

- Choose a place to swim where you know the depth and current of the water. This place should be free from weeds that may trap you. Swim where a lifeguard is present. Never swim alone.
- Know how well you can swim, and do not take chances.
- Know how long you are able to swim. Stop before you get chilled or overtired.
- Do not swim long distances unless someone in a boat accompanies you.
- Do not swim out to help a drowning person unless you have had special training in lifesaving. Throw the person something that will float, such as an oar or a life belt.
- Learn how to handle a boat or a canoe correctly. Always wear a life jacket.
- Use boats that are in good condition. Do not overload them.
- Do not skate on ice that is less than 4 inches thick.
- Be careful when wading in streams. Slippery rocks and a fast current can cause anyone to slip and fall.
- Do not attempt to swim long distances underwater without coming up for air. Otherwise, you may lose consciousness and drown.

Safety out-of-doors

Camping and hiking are healthful and enjoyable activities. To get the most benefit from these ventures, you need to plan them well. It is important to anticipate and prepare for the unexpected.

The cardinal rule in hiking is: Don't do it alone. There are too many hazards when hiking by yourself in deserted areas. These dangers can usually be avoided by taking along at least one other person. The following are other tips for campers and hikers:

- Leave information about your travel route and time schedule with someone before you depart.
- Avoid fatigue by moving at a leisurely pace and making frequent rest stops.
- Drink plenty of fluids and eat regular meals to keep up your energy.

Outdoor recreation becomes a greater source of pleasure when safety precautions are followed.

380

- Keep a clean camp to prevent animals from becoming a problem. Do not keep food in your tent or sleeping bag.
- Carry a compass and some first-aid supplies with you at all times.
- Know the proper emergency signals and how to use them (three of anything: whistle blasts, flares, mirror flashes, etc.).
- Consider weather conditions: past, present, and future. Watch for signals of change.

Weather safety

Being caught outdoors in a thunderstorm can be a terrifying experience. Each year, about 200 people are killed and 550 injured from lightning. The danger of being struck by lightning is not great. If you follow these rules, you can lessen the danger:

- Seek immediate shelter. Your automobile provides safety because of its rubber tires.
- Get out of and away from water.
- Stay away from a tall tree or a single tree, regardless of its size.
- Try not to be the tallest object in an area. Don't stand on an open beach, hilltop, or exposed slope on a mountainside.
- Keep away from metal objects, such as bikes, fishing rods, wire fences, and railroad tracks.
- If you think lightning is about to strike, drop to your knees and bend forward. Make yourself as small a target as possible. Do *not* lie on the ground.

Preventing heat and cold injuries

Cold injuries. Cold temperatures can cause problems for the unprepared or unprotected. Continued exposure to cold and dampness for long periods may cause a serious problem called **hypothermia**. Other factors that may lead to this condition are wind, fatigue, and hunger.

The symptoms of this condition are not always clear. The person may shiver, have slow or slurred speech, sluggish movements, an uncooperative attitude, and drowsiness. If allowed to sleep, the person may be hard to awaken.

In very cold temperatures, such parts of the body as the face, ears, hands, and feet may develop **frostbite**. Frostbite can occur at any altitude, but there is a greater chance at higher elevations. The affected part of the body loses feeling. The skin may first appear flushed and then become pale and shiny.

The best way to prevent these injuries is to wear proper clothing. Several layers of clothing provide more protection than a single thick layer. Avoid wearing rain-soaked or perspiration-soaked clothing. The head, ears, hands, and feet should always be covered when exposed to cold. Applying an oil-based ointment to the lips, nose, and cheeks will help to protect these exposed areas.

Heat injuries. Prolonged exposure to an extremely hot and humid environment may lead to heat exhaustion or heatstroke (sunstroke). Heat exhaustion is usually caused by too much physical exertion and sweating over an extended period of time in a hot environment. A heatstroke is more serious. It is a profound disturbance of the heat-regulating mechanisms of the body. Sweating stops and heat builds up in the body. Body temperature must be lowered immediately, or death may occur.

Most heat problems can be prevented by limiting exposure to the sun, wearing light-colored and loose-fitting clothing, and avoiding strenuous outdoor activity on hot days. When exercising or working in hot temperatures, take frequent rests and replace fluid and salt loss. If you feel tired and nauseated or have a headache, dizziness, or muscle cramps, stop any activity. Rest and drink plenty of fluids. If you don't feel better, get medical help.

Insect bites

Many insects can pose a threat to outdoor fun. Bees are known to be attracted to bright colors, floral prints, strong perfumes, lotions, and scented soaps. Stings from bees, wasps, hornets, and yellowjackets do not usually pose a health threat. But a person who has an allergic reaction may stop breathing after being stung by one of these insects.

Ticks are present in almost all wilderness and wooded areas, especially during the late spring and summer. Being bitten by a tick is usually not serious. Certain species do carry serious diseases, however, such as Rocky Mountain Spotted Fever and Lyme disease. These ailments affect thousands of people every year. After a tick has been correctly removed (see Chapter 31), be alert to signs of redness or swelling where the bite was located. If fever, chills, headache, vomiting, or rash develops 1 to 10 days after the bite, the person should see a physician.

Safety on the job

Each year, more than 11,000 people in the United States die in accidents related to their jobs. Some **work-related accidents** are caused by the workers themselves. So it is important for workers to know safe work habits. Other work-related accidents are caused by unsafe buildings, tools, and equipment and by the lack of proper safety equipment. It is important for owners to provide a safe workplace for employees. The Occupational Safety and Health Administration (OSHA) is a government agency that sets standards for safety in the workplace. OSHA inspectors check to see if employers are meeting these standards.

Many accidents occur around machines. The most common unsafe practice is failure to turn off a machine before adjusting, repairing, or cleaning it. Lack of safety guards or poor use of safety guards causes a large number of accidents with saws. In the use of grinding wheels, eye protection and proper adjustment of the tool rest are important safety measures.

Accidents in the workplace are not spread evenly through the day. They reach a peak between 10 and 11 A.M. and again between 3 and 4 P.M. However, fewer accidents occur in the afternoon than in the morning. Workers must be allowed rest periods, which relieve tiredness and decrease the number of accidents.

In many places, nuclear energy is replacing present sources of energy. This means that more and more workers will have jobs in which radiation will be a danger.

Farming is becoming a more dangerous occupation. More than one-third of the accidental deaths on farms involve machinery. Powerful machinery should not be operated without training. Careless driving of tractors is the major cause of farm accidents.

Home safety

Each year, about 20,000 people in the United States die as a result of **home accidents**. More than 3 million people are injured. Many accidents happen at home because people tend to pay less attention to possible dangers in these more familiar surroundings. When is the last time you or another member of your family checked *your* home for possible safety hazards?

The majority of home accidents can be avoided by following these safety measures:

- Light stairways well. Provide handrails for stairways. Do not leave toys or other objects on stairs.
- Keep ice and snow off porches, steps, and sidewalks.
- Use a *steady* stepladder to reach high places.
- Be careful when walking on waxed floors or loose rugs.
- Keep electric cords in good condition. Do not use electrical appliances in places where they are near water.
- Keep knives, garden tools, plastic bags, boiling water, matches, household chemicals, and medicines out of the reach of children.
- Be alert for gas leaks around gas appliances.
- Do not use gasoline or flammable cleaning fluids indoors.
- Do not start an automobile in a closed garage.
- Be sure that all firearms (guns and rifles) are unloaded and out of reach of children.
- Arrange bedclothes so that babies cannot get blankets and pillows over their noses and mouths.
- Keep small objects (including toys) that might be swallowed away from babies.
- Place window guards on upper-story windows in homes where there are small children.
- Securely lock or remove any large container, such as an empty refrigerator, in which a child could suffocate.
- Use caution when working with power tools.

Fire prevention

Each year, large numbers of people die or are left homeless as the result of fires. There are many ways you can protect your life and home in case of fire.

One important step you can take is to buy and install a smoke alarm. This simple device sounds a warning buzzer when a room begins to fill with smoke. Call a family meeting to make sure everyone knows what to do, where to go, and who is responsible for smaller children and pets. Practice fire drills regularly. Prepare for fires that occur at night. Fire and smoke can kill you while you are sleeping. Make plans in advance to escape from your bedroom.

The Institute for Fire and Burn Education promotes burn research, fire education, and assistance to burn survivors. There is a state director in each of the 50 states. One of their services is to provide information to burn victims about a line of cosmetics formulated especially for them.

Most fires can be prevented. To this end, fireplaces, chimneys, and space heaters should be checked periodically since they are potential hazards. If a fire does occur, these simple steps could save your life:

Never run wildly if your clothing catches fire.

Instead...

Stop completely.

Drop to the ground.

Roll on the ground until the fire is extinguished.

- Don't act impulsively or panic. If you are trapped in a room that is filling with smoke, crawl under the smoke to available fresh air as quickly as possible.
- Don't attempt to stay in a burning house. Call the fire department from a neighbor's house.
- Never reenter a burning house.
- Sleep with bedroom doors closed to keep out smoke, heat, and gases in case of fire. If there is a fire, never open a door that feels hot. Escape by another exit or a window.

Preventing assault

Reports of **assault** appear frequently in today's newspapers. The following are simple, practical precautions you can take to reduce your chances of being assaulted.

At home. When you arrive home, always have your house keys in hand before you leave your car. Do not leave your keys in a secret hiding place—under the doormat, on a windowsill, or in the mailbox. Leave that extra set of keys with a trusted neighbor. Once inside the house, lock the door behind you. If it is nighttime, make sure the blinds or draperies are closed. Allow no stranger to enter your home to use the phone. (If the person claims there is an emergency, offer to make a phone call while the person waits outside.)

On the street. Don't walk alone at night. Walk at a distance from buildings, dark doorways, shrubbery, and other places where someone could be hiding. Keep someone at home informed about where you are going and when you expect to be home.

In a car.   First, and most important, never accept a ride from a stranger. When you leave a building to go to your car, have your keys ready. Check the back seat before getting into the car. Once you are safely inside, lock the doors. If you think you are being followed, drive to a nearby police or fire station, hospital emergency entrance, or well-lit all-night business establishment to call for help. If you know you are being followed, keep honking your horn and blinking your lights—attract attention.

Never hitchhike or pick up a hitchhiker. Also, don't stop to help a motorist in trouble. Instead, drive to the nearest phone and call for help for the person. Always park in a well-lighted area, and travel on main roads when possible. If you have car trouble, raise your hood and then lock yourself in the car. If someone stops to offer help, roll down the window slightly and ask the person to call the police or a repair truck for you. Don't leave the car until identified help arrives.

Rape and molestation are also hostile and violent crimes. They leave the victim feeling emotionally shattered and violated. Measures can be taken to prevent becoming the victim of a sex crime. The first line of defense is recognizing that *anyone* can be assaulted, regardless of age or gender. Boys as well as girls have been victimized by sex offenders.

Help for the victim

When someone is the victim of an assault, the person may need immediate medical attention. The police should be notified as well. Many communities have special emergency numbers or rape hotlines that permit victims of assault to speak directly with an expert. These people have special training, which enables them to reduce the victim's initial shock reaction to the attack.

Beyond the immediate need for safety and health care, victims of sexual assault have different needs. Victims have to cope with strong negative feelings, sometimes for a long time after the incident. The help of a professional counselor or therapist is almost always needed. The best thing you can do for someone who has suffered sexual assault is to be patient and understanding. Give the person as much "space" to deal with the problem as he or she needs.

Key Words

assault	home accidents	work-related
frostbite	hypothermia	accidents

Main Ideas

- Accidents are the leading cause of injury and death among people of high school age.
- Most accidents can be prevented.

Continued

- The use of seat belts reduces injuries and saves lives.
- Most accidents out-of-doors can be prevented by following appropriate guidelines.
- Many accidents at home occur because people don't pay enough attention to dangers in everyday situations.
- Every family member should know what to do in case of fire.
- To get the most benefit from camping and hiking, you need to plan these activities well and take certain precautions.
- There are many simple precautions you can take to reduce your chances of being assaulted.

Understand the Reading

1. What are some arguments that people give for not wearing seat belts? What is wrong with these arguments?
2. What are three causes of motorcycle accidents? Of bicycle accidents?
3. What is the most important rule regarding water safety? Give four other rules related to water safety.
4. How many people are killed each year by lightning? Name four precautions you could take to avoid injury by lightning.
5. What are some of the factors that cause hypothermia?
6. What sorts of things attract bees? What danger do insect bites pose to individuals with allergies?
7. What is the most common unsafe practice involving machines in industrial workplaces? Explain.
8. How many people are injured each year in home accidents? List five precautions that reduce home-accident risk.
9. What should you do during a fire if you are trapped in a smoke-filled room?
10. What should you do when driving alone at night if you spot a motorist in trouble?

Apply Your Knowledge

1. Interview the safety commissioner or some other local authority on traffic safety. Learn what are the most hazardous intersections and stretches of road in your community. Find out how many injuries and deaths have occurred at these spots. Discuss your findings with the class. Use photographs of the traffic hazards, if possible.
2. Suppose that a state official placed you in charge of a project to lower the number of injuries and deaths among the high-school-age population in your community or state. In a written report to the class, discuss what specific steps you would take to reach your goal.

Chapter 31
Basic First Aid

After reading this chapter, you will be able to:

- [ ] List the steps that must be taken in a medical emergency.
- [ ] Describe how to control serious bleeding.
- [ ] Explain what needs to be done for a poisoning victim.
- [ ] Explain how to treat shock, fractures, dislocations, and sprains.
- [ ] Identify the different degrees of burns.
- [ ] Tell how to treat victims of heat or cold exposure and snakebites.
- [ ] Tell how to treat victims of electric shock and convulsions.

Even when we are extremely cautious, accidents sometimes happen. A driver turns the wheel sharply to avoid hitting a dog and runs into another car. A sharp tool is accidentally knocked out of the hand of a careful, experienced factory worker. During an after-school basketball game, a student is knocked off balance and sprains his leg. When accidents happen, it is important to know how to care for people who have been injured. This on-the-spot care is called first aid. Learning first aid and when to use it should be part of your wellness program.

First aid

First aid is emergency treatment given to a person who is injured or ill. First aid takes place before medical or surgical care arrives. Fire and police departments in many communities have first-aid equipment and trained personnel to help in emergencies.

The term *first aid* may also be used to describe caring for small cuts, bruises, and other minor injuries. Proper care may keep a minor injury or sickness from becoming serious.

An **emergency** is a situation that requires very fast action. It is not always possible to tell which emergencies are serious and which are not. However, certain conditions, such as severe bleeding, failure to breathe, heart attack, and poisoning, must be spotted and cared for at once. General rules to follow are these:

- If there is more than one injured person, care for the most seriously injured first.
- Keep calm and act quickly and quietly. Speak in a normal tone of voice. Try not to worry the victim.
- Find out if the injured person is bleeding. Serious bleeding must be stopped as quickly as possible.
- Check for breathing. Make sure that the victim has an open air passage. If the victim is not breathing, start artificial respiration at once.
- Check for the victim's pulse. If there is no pulse, cardiopulmonary resuscitation (CPR) must be started. (See Chapter 32 for more information on CPR.)
- If there are signs of poisoning or drug use, begin the proper treatment at once.
- Do not move an injured person unless you must for the person's safety. Moving an injured person the wrong way may harm the person even more. Do not let the person sit up or stand until help arrives.
- Get trained medical help fast. However, do not leave the victim in order to get help unless you have no other choice.

Control of bleeding

Controlled bleeding can help a wound to clean itself. But uncontrolled bleeding can lead to death. If bleeding is not very serious, let it continue for a short while. Then wash the area very carefully with soap and water. Do not apply iodine or other antiseptics. Finally, cover the area with a clean dressing, such as sterile gauze.

It is possible for a person who is bleeding very heavily to bleed to death in just a few minutes. If there is very serious bleeding, or **hemorrhage**, the bleeding must be stopped at once. Place a clean cloth over the wound, and press down firmly. A sterile bandage is best. But any clean cloth, such as a clean handkerchief or part of a clean shirt or slip, will do. If no cloth is available, press your hand directly on the wound. Firm pressure will usually stop the bleeding. Keep pressing until medical help comes. Do not keep lifting your hand and looking at the wound to see if the bleeding has stopped. In addition to applying pressure to the wound, raise the injured part of the body if you are sure that no bones are broken. This will help to slow the loss of blood from the wound.

If bleeding continues, you can also apply pressure to the major artery leading to the wound. If the wound is in the arm, find the pulse between the elbow and the armpit on the inner side of the arm. Using your fingers, press the artery shut against the underlying bone. For a bleeding leg, press on the inner upper thigh. Use the heel of your hand to press hard. For severe bleeding, direct pressure over the wound, elevation, and pressure on the main artery should all be used together.

If pressure and raising the injured part of the body do not stop the bleeding, a **tourniquet** can be used, but *only as a last resort*. A tourniquet is a band of cloth or any other material that is pulled tightly around an arm or leg. The tourniquet is placed above the wound (between the wound and the heart). A tourniquet is dangerous because it cuts off the supply of blood to the tissues of the limb. The decision to apply a tourniquet is really a decision to risk a limb in order to save a life. A tourniquet should be at least 2 inches wide to prevent added injury to tissue when it is tightened. Once applied, the tourniquet should be released only under the supervision of a doctor.

A person with a tourniquet should have immediate medical attention. Be sure to indicate the tourniquet to the doctor, or make a note on the victim's forehead. The tourniquet may be hidden from view by clothing or some other covering.

Poisoning

If a poisoning victim is conscious, dilute the poison by giving the person a glass or two of water or milk to drink. Try to identify the poison before giving any other treatment. The label on the container will

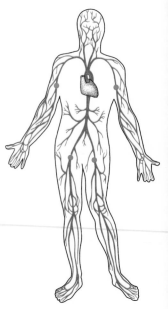

The large dots show points where pressure can be applied to arteries to stop bleeding from the limbs.

For a poisoning victim, immediately call a poison control center or a hospital.

probably tell you the name of the poison and an **antidote**. An antidote is a substance that works against the poison.

The safest thing to do, however, is to call a poison center and ask for specific instructions from a trained professional. The toll-free number for your state's Poison Control Center can probably be found in your local telephone book. Otherwise, call the emergency room of a nearby hospital.

If instructed to do so by the Poison Control Center, you should make the person vomit. Use 1 tablespoon of syrup of ipecac in a glass of water, or use a spoon to tickle the back of the throat. Sometimes, however, vomiting should not be induced. Vomiting a strong acid or alkali, for example, can cause further damage. If the poisoning victim is unconscious, keep the air passages open and do not induce vomiting. Do not give liquids to an unconscious person.

Gently get the victim to medical help as fast as you can. If possible, take along the poison container or a sample of the victim's vomit. Tell the specialist what poison has been taken, how much, and about how long ago.

Treatment of shock

Very serious injury, bleeding, or burns often cause **shock**. Shock is a serious condition and must be treated quickly. Shock means that a person's blood is not circulating as it should. A shock victim usually feels faint, weak, cold, and often nauseated. The victim's skin may look pale or blue. It will feel cold and clammy. Breathing is not regular, and the pulse is weak and fast.

An important factor in preventing and treating shock is to keep the victim's body temperature about normal. This usually means keeping a person covered, though under certain circumstances—in extreme heat

The shock victim should be covered only enough to keep the body temperature close to normal.

or sun, for instance—it may be necessary to keep the person shaded. Place the person flat on the back with the feet slightly raised. Control bleeding if any is present. Make sure the person's breathing passages are clear. Loosen all tight clothing. Do not move the person any more than is needed. Do not give the person anything by mouth. Reassure the victim, and get medical help as quickly as possible.

Fractures

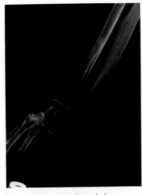

A break in a bone is called a **fracture**. Usually there is pain at the point of fracture. The victim resists moving the injured part. It may be bent out of shape, and swelling may occur very quickly. In a closed fracture, the skin is not broken. In an open fracture, the broken bone comes through the skin or a wound reaches from the surface of the skin to the break in the bone. There is danger that infection may enter the wound. When you think that someone may have a fractured bone, send for medical help. Make the injured person lie down. Give the treatment for shock. Control any bleeding. Fractures of the neck or the back can be made worse by moving the injured person. Wrong movements can lead to injury of the spinal cord. This can cause permanent paralysis or death.

Not even a physician can tell sometimes whether a fracture has occurred unless an X ray is taken.

Dislocations and sprains

A condition called **dislocation** occurs when a bone moves out of place at a joint. When the ligaments and tendons around a joint are torn or bruised, the condition is called a **sprain**. Swelling and pain occur very quickly. Without an X-ray examination, even a physician may not be able to tell whether the injury is a sprain, a dislocation, or a fracture.

The best first aid for a sprain is to quickly wrap the injured area firmly, apply ice to it, elevate it above the heart, and then rest it for about 24 hours. The tight wrap limits swelling, and ice shrinks the broken blood vessels. Elevating the injured area helps to drain the fluid from the damaged area, and rest will prevent further damage. If the victim of a sprain or a dislocation is in shock, treat the shock in the proper way. But remember, only a doctor should try to put a dislocated bone "back in place."

Strains

Strains are stretched or torn muscles. Strains occur from overworking muscles that are not used to much activity or are not properly "warmed up." Improper lifting and playing a sport you have not practiced in a long time, for example, strain the back and leg muscles.

First aid for a strain consists of stopping the activity and resting the body part as soon as pain is felt in the muscle. Apply ice wrapped in a cloth to ease the pain and muscle cramp. Rest is important.

Do *not* apply butter to a burn. *Do* apply cold water to first-degree burns.

Burns

Burns can be caused by fire, sunlight, electricity, and chemicals. In the case of fire burns, send for medical help immediately if the burned area is large. While waiting for help, treat the person for shock. If the burned area is small, some action can be taken. Cut away clothing from around the burned area. Do not pull at any cloth that is attached to the burned area. If there are blisters, be careful not to break them. Do not use any substance, such as grease, soda, or salve, on the burn.

First-degree burns. In a first-degree burn, the skin is not broken, but it may be reddened. Soaking the burned area in cool water for 15 minutes is soothing and will prevent the burn from getting worse. If needed, apply a dry dressing.

Second-degree burns. In a second-degree burn, the skin is blistered and red. Cover a *small* burn area completely with cold water for at least 15 minutes. A *large* area should *not* be treated with water. Instead, remove loose clothing, but do not try to remove material that sticks to the skin. Apply several layers of dry gauze or clean towels. Second-degree-burn victims sometimes suffer from shock. Treat the person for shock, and get medical help immediately.

Third-degree burns. Third-degree burns are deep, and the skin is charred or destroyed. Third-degree burns are always very serious. First-aid care should include treating the shock that usually follows such burns. Use a clean dressing, just as you would for second-degree burns. Do *not* apply water or any medicine. Get medical help quickly.

Chemical burns. When a burn is caused by a chemical, quickly flood the burned area with a large amount of water for at least 15 minutes. If more than a small area is affected, cut away all clothing with scissors. Then cover with gauze, treat for shock, and get medical help.

Give careful attention to eye burns caused by chemicals. Flood the eye with large amounts of water for at least 15 minutes. Do this even before calling for help. Cover both eyes to stop eye movement until the injured person can get to a physician.

Fire. Fast action may keep a person whose clothing is on fire from being badly burned. Place the person on the floor or ground, and smother the flames by rolling the person over. If possible, wrap the person in a heavy material, such as a rug, a coat, or a blanket.

Exposure to heat or cold

Too much heat or cold can cause the conditions known respectively as **heatstroke** and **hypothermia** (see Chapter 30). When a person suffers heatstroke, the skin becomes hot and dry and the pulse becomes fast and strong. Unconsciousness and convulsions may follow. Move the victim to a cool place. Then either apply wet cloths or ice to the victim's skin or place the victim in a tub of cold water. Get medical help as quickly as possible.

Heat exhaustion is the result of the body's loss of large amounts of water and salt in perspiration. The skin is cold, white, and clammy. Breathing is shallow and the pulse is weak. The victim may faint. To treat heat exhaustion, move the victim to a cool place. Then give the person salt water to sip. Use 1 teaspoon of salt in 1 quart of water.

Hypothermia can occur in anyone who has been exposed to cool temperatures, even the low 60s Fahrenheit, for a prolonged period. The first step in treating hypothermia is to prevent a further drop in the victim's temperature. Remove wet clothing, and keep the victim warm. If outdoors, wrap the person in a dry blanket or sleeping bag. Give the victim, if conscious, small amounts of a warm liquid to drink. Never give alcoholic drinks to the victim. Get medical help as soon as possible. If the victim is unconscious, keep the air passages open. If needed, give artificial respiration.

If you suspect that frostbite has occurred (see Chapter 30), carry the victim indoors. Warm the frostbitten area as gently as possible. Place the area in warm water, or apply cloths soaked in warm water. Do not use high heat.

Snakebite

Get medical help as soon as possible. Even if the bite is from a nonpoisonous snake, a tetanus shot may be needed.

Symptoms of a poisonous snakebite are one or two large puncture marks, swelling, and burning pain. The snake venom, or poison, spreads slowly through the body. Keep the victim as quiet as possible. Movement increases circulation and makes the venom spread more quickly. Keep the bitten limb still and at or below the level of the heart. If you will have medical help within an hour, apply a tight band about 2 inches above the bite. Do not cut off circulation. Leave enough slack so that a finger may be worked under the constriction band.

The venom injected by a snakebite can be fatal.

393

If breathing problems and shock develop and help is more than an hour away, apply the band and cut through the skin over the bite. Make cuts that are ¼ inch deep and long. The cuts should be up and down the limb, never sideways. Suck the venom out of the wound with a suction cup or with your mouth. Snake venom is not a stomach poison. But it can be dangerous to the person giving first aid if that person has an open sore in the mouth. Always rinse the mouth well.

Electric shock

Rescuing an unconscious person from a live electrical wire is always dangerous. The rescuer may be killed by electricity from touching the body of the victim. If the switch is near, turn off the current. Otherwise, use a dry stick, dry clothing, dry rope, or some other dry material—not metal—to move the victim from the wire. Start artificial respiration or cardiopulmonary resuscitation if needed. Send for help.

Convulsions

A **convulsion** involves strong contractions of involuntary muscles. Some causes of convulsion are epilepsy, serious head injuries, some kinds of poisoning, and various illnesses. In some types of convulsions, the person's body stiffens. In other types, the arms, legs, trunk, and neck have violent muscular contractions.

First-aid treatment for convulsions usually means protecting the victim, who may be thrashing about, from getting hurt. Do not restrict the person's movements. Put a folded blanket under the person's head, if possible. But be careful. The movements of a person having a convulsion can be very powerful. The person cannot control them. You may be hurt while trying to help. After the convulsion, place the victim on his or her side. Check to see if the air passage is open. Be sure that breathing is normal.

Children sometimes have convulsions when they have fevers. This may be the beginning of a serious illness. Call a physician at once.

Everyday emergencies

You may never have to take care of people who are seriously hurt. However, you may have to take care of yourself or someone else in a minor emergency. Remember that what looks like a small injury may turn out to be serious. It is wise, therefore, to look carefully for injuries, especially in the case of a fall or forceful blow to some part of the body. When the skin is broken even slightly, there is a danger of infection. All wounds should be cleaned and covered with a sterile bandage. Finally, never underestimate the potential for shock in an accident. Keep the victim quiet and the body temperature as close as possible to normal.

Bruises. When the skin is bruised but not broken, apply cold, wet cloths or ice to the area for 30 minutes or longer. This relieves pain and lessens swelling and black-and-blue marks. If a bruise is not treated until the next day, use warm, wet cloths. Bruise marks mean that blood vessels under the skin are broken. It may take days or even weeks for the blood to be reabsorbed into the blood vessels. A black eye is an example of such an injury.

Nosebleeds. Hold the bleeding nostril closed with slight pressure on one side of the nose. Apply continuous pressure for 10 minutes. Most nosebleeds can be stopped this way. A person with a nosebleed should sit with head tilted forward and not move about. If bleeding continues, get medical attention.

Fainting. An illness, bad news, or an unpleasant sight might lead to a person's passing out or fainting. Do *not* put the person's head between the legs. Instead, lay the person down and raise the legs to increase blood supply and oxygen to the brain. Loosen clothing around the neck. If vomiting occurs, roll the person onto the side. The person should remain lying down until he or she feels better and then gradually helped to a sitting or standing position.

Blisters. Cover a blister with a sterile dressing. In most cases, leave it alone and do not break it. The liquid will be absorbed into the surrounding body tissue. If the blister accidentally breaks, wash the area thoroughly with soap and water. Reapply a sterile dressing.

Animal bites. Because of the chance of infection, wash any animal bite thoroughly with soap and water. Call a physician. If possible, the animal should be caught immediately. Notify the police or the local health department. An expert should find out if the animal has rabies. A bite from a rabid animal can be fatal if untreated. If the animal is not rabid, the victim does not need antirabies vaccinations, though a tetanus shot may be needed.

Insect bites. When an individual is stung by a bee, wasp, hornet, or yellow jacket, first check the affected area carefully for any stinger that may need to be removed. In minor cases, apply cold cloths or ice to ease pain and lessen swelling. Then apply a soothing lotion, such as calamine. If the person has had an allergic reaction to an insect bite in the past or if breathing problems occur and swelling continues, get medical help right away.

Tick bites are treated in a different fashion. If the tick is attached to the skin, take the time to remove it carefully. Use tweezers if available. Otherwise, use fingers protected with a tissue or paper towel. Grasp the tick as close to the skin as possible. Pull up with a steady, even pressure. Avoid twisting or jerking the tick, since those movements are likely to break off pieces of the tick. After the tick is removed, wash the skin with soap and water. (It is also wise to wash your hands after

Insects that sting can be more than just a nuisance.

removing ticks from pets.) Remember that infection or disease may follow a tick bite. It is therefore important to report the bite to a doctor if any such signs occur within 10 days.

Eye injuries. A small object, such as a speck of dirt, may get into the eye and be irritating. Do not rub the eye, because you might scratch the surface. With clean hands, pull the lower eyelid down to see if the object lies on the inner surface. If it is there, lift it out with the corner of a clean, soft cloth. If you cannot see the object, look downward and gently grasp the lashes of the upper lid. Pull the upper lid downward over the lower eyelashes. This action may dislodge the object from the upper lid. Loosely cover both eyes, and get medical help if the object cannot be removed.

Puncturing of the eye is very serious and can cause blindness. Do not remove the object or wash the eye. Lay the person down, and cover both eyes loosely to stop the movement of the injured eye. Get medical help immediately.

Key Words

antidote	fracture	hypothermia
convulsion	heat exhaustion	shock
dislocation	heatstroke	sprain
emergency	hemorrhage	strains
first aid		tourniquet

- Proper first aid can prevent additional medical problems and may save a life.
- Certain emergency conditions must be recognized and treated at once. Such conditions are severe bleeding, failure to breathe, heart attack, and poisoning.
- When a person has taken poison, the safest thing to do is to call a poison center.
- An important part of first aid is preventing and treating shock.
- Whenever the skin is broken even slightly, there is a danger of infection.

1. Give four of the general rules to follow in any medical emergency.
2. Describe how to control bleeding.
3. Why is a tourniquet dangerous to use?
4. Describe how to make a poisoning victim vomit if you had been instructed to do so by the Poison Control Center.
5. If a poisoning victim is conscious, how can you help? How can you help an unconscious victim?
6. Explain how you can prevent and treat shock.
7. How are a closed fracture and an open fracture different?
8. How can you tell whether or not a person is suffering from heatstroke or from heat exhaustion? What is the treatment for each?
9. What are the symptoms of a poisonous snakebite? Describe the treatment.
10. How should you treat a tick bite? What should you do after the tick is removed?

1. Contact several ambulance services in your community by telephone. Question a representative of each service on the following subjects: (1) the amount of training their drivers undergo, (2) what kinds of first-aid procedures their staff is capable of carrying out, and (3) what is done about the transporting of minors when a legal guardian or parent is not able to give consent. Bring the results of your questionnaire to class for discussion.
2. Ask a member of your local chapter of the American Red Cross to come to your class to explain the procedures that lead to a first-aid certificate. Ask the Red Cross representative to bring brochures that might be left with the class for later discussion.

Chapter 32
CPR

After reading this chapter, you will be able to:

☐ Identify the early warning signals of a heart attack.

☐ Describe the steps involved in cardiopulmonary resuscitation.

☐ Tell how to prevent choking and how to assist a victim of choking.

☐ Explain how the Heimlich maneuver is performed.

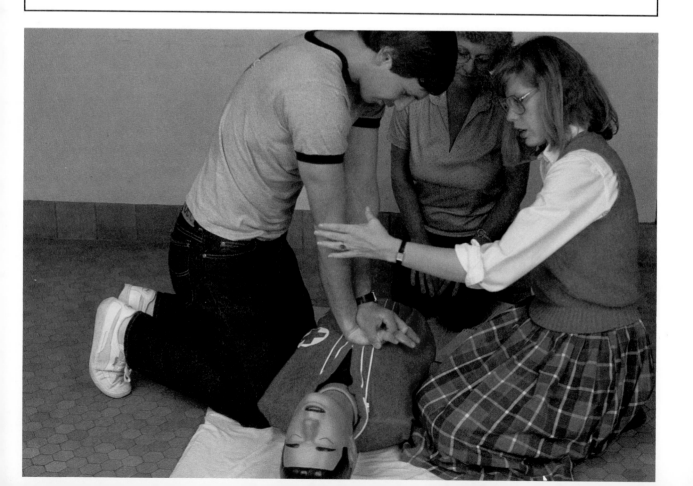

It was a mild, sunny afternoon in late May. School would be out for the summer in a few weeks, but that wasn't soon enough for some of the students in Mr. Selden's sophomore biology lab. They were trying to concentrate on the lesson when suddenly their teacher's words trailed off. The class looked up just in time to see Mr. Selden grab his chest and then slump to the floor.

Greg Molowski was on his feet in an instant. He had taken a course in the lifesaving technique known as CPR—short for *cardiopulmonary resuscitation*. Determining that Mr. Selden was not breathing and had no pulse, Greg immediately began the procedure.

Two weeks later, when Mr. Selden was released from the cardiac care unit of the hospital, he knew that he had Greg Molowski—and CPR—to thank for his life.

Every year, many thousands of Americans die suddenly. Heart attack is the number one cause of these deaths. In a recent year, more than 550,000 people died of heart attacks. Other causes of sudden death include choking, drowning, poisoning, suffocation, electrocution, and problems related to alcohol abuse, drug abuse, and smoke inhalation. Many sudden deaths could have been prevented. Since more than half the victims die before they reach the hospital, the person's life may be in the hands of those who happen to be nearby. A far greater number of lives would be saved if more people were trained in CPR.

Prevention of sudden death

Who can perform CPR? Only those who have successfully completed CPR training courses can. This includes passing tests of knowledge and performance. CPR courses are offered throughout the country by the American Heart Association and the American Red Cross.

Cardiopulmonary resuscitation combines artificial respiration with artificial circulation. The rescuer makes certain that the victim's airway is open and unblocked and gives the victim oxygen by breathing into her or his lungs. The air exhaled by the rescuer contains enough oxygen to keep life processes working in a person who is not breathing. The rescuer next forces the victim's heart to pump blood by applying pressure to the victim's chest. The heart lies behind the breastbone and against the backbone. Pressure on the breastbone squeezes the heart and forces blood out. Releasing the pressure allows the heart to fill with blood.

Since the most frequent cause of sudden death is heart attack, it is important to recognize the warning signs:

- uncomfortable pressure, fullness, squeezing, or pain in the center of the chest lasting 2 minutes or more—pain may spread to the shoulders, neck, jaw, or arms
- pale skin

- sweating
- nausea
- shortness of breath
- a feeling of weakness

Sometimes these symptoms seem to become less severe. Then they return again. They can occur in anyone, even a young person, at any time and in any place for no apparent reason.

The two types of life support

There are two important phases of emergency care—**basic life support** and **advanced life support**. A rescuer who provides basic life support has been trained to recognize (1) a blocked airway; (2) absence of breathing, or "respiratory arrest"; and (3) absence of a heartbeat or pulse, or **cardiac arrest**. Once the rescuer observes these symptoms, he or she is able to provide the correct method of CPR.

A rescuer who provides advanced life support has been trained to give basic life support. In addition, such a rescuer knows how to operate medical equipment and to use other techniques to keep the person

More lives could be saved if more people received training in the administration of CPR.

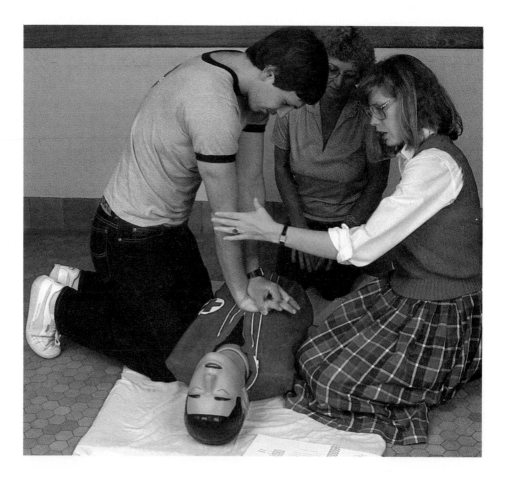

alive. Advanced life support includes the kinds of emergency care provided by an ambulance paramedic, a nurse, or a doctor.

Advanced life support can usually be obtained by calling a community's **emergency medical services (EMS)** system. You should know the telephone number to reach your community's EMS system. In most of the United States, the emergency number is 911. This number may be dialed at a pay phone without depositing money. In case the EMS system is not available, you should also know the location of the nearest hospital emergency room that provides 24-hour emergency care, or you can just dial "O" for your local operator's help.

A community's emergency care system might provide a fast response and expert service. Even so, the person who is with the victim at the beginning of the emergency can make the difference between life and death. If that person can provide basic life support, the victim will have a better chance of surviving.

The A-B-Cs of CPR

CPR is a simple procedure, as simple as A-B-C. In fact, the letters A, B, C can be used to identify the three steps in administering the life-saving technique: *A* = *A*irway, *B* = *B*reathing, *C* = *C*irculation.

Airway

If a person nearby collapses, determine first if the victim is conscious by shaking the person's shoulder and shouting, "Are you okay?" If there is no response, call out for help.

Next, a trained rescuer opens the victim's airway. If the victim is not already lying flat on the back, roll the victim over. Move the entire body at once as a total unit. To open the airway, the rescuer lifts the chin gently upward with one hand while pushing down on the forehead with the other to tilt the head back. Once the airway is open, the rescuer's ear is placed close to the victim's mouth. The rescuer must (1) *look* for the chest to rise and fall, (2) *listen* for sounds of breathing, and (3) *feel* for breath on her or his cheek. If none of these signs is present, the victim is not breathing. If opening the airway does not cause the victim to begin to breathe, **rescue breathing** must be provided.

Breathing

The best way to provide rescue breathing is to use the mouth-to-mouth technique. The trained rescuer puts the palm of one hand on the victim's forehead and pinches the victim's nose shut. The heel of the hand is kept on the forehead to maintain head tilt. The other hand should remain under the bony part of the lower jaw to lift the chin up. The rescuer's mouth is placed over the victim's mouth. Then the rescuer blows two slow, full breaths into the victim.

Circulation

The rescuer must next find out if the victim's heart is beating. This is done by feeling the carotid artery in the neck. The hand under the victim's chin moves to the voice box (Adam's apple). The tips of the index and middle fingers slide into the groove on the side of the neck beside the voice box to feel for the pulse. If there is a pulse (heartbeat) but no breathing, the rescuer should continue mouth-to-mouth resuscitation. Give one breath every 5 seconds for an adult. Covering the mouth and nose, give one breath every 3 seconds for a baby or child. If there is no breathing and no pulse in the carotid artery in the neck, the victim is suffering cardiac arrest.

If there is no pulse, artificial circulation must be attempted, along with rescue breathing. Artificial circulation is provided by external pressure on the breastbone. This is known as **external cardiac compression.** The rescuer kneels at the victim's side near the chest. Pressure is applied just above the notch at the lowest portion of the breastbone. The rescuer places the heel of one hand on the breastbone 1½ to 2 inches above the notch. The other hand is placed on top of the first. The fingers should be kept off the chest wall. This is easier to do if the fingers are interlocked.

As the hands press downward, the rescuer's shoulders move directly over the victim's chest. Arms must be kept straight. On an adult victim, the breastbone is pushed down about 1½ to 2 inches. Then the pressure is completely relaxed. This allows the victim's chest to return to its normal position. But the rescuer's hands are kept on the victim's chest, ready for the next push. Applying pressure and relaxing pressure should take equal lengths of time.

If the victim has possibly suffered a neck injury (in a diving or an automobile accident, for example), lift the chin alone without pressing on the forehead or lifting the neck. Do not move the victim's head.

CPR with one rescuer.   When there is only one rescuer, she or he must switch back and forth between cardiac compression and rescue breathing. The proper ratio is 15 chest presses to 2 slow full breaths. The rate for chest presses should be 80 to 100 times per minute. The rescuer counts quietly, "One and two and three…and fifteen" and then quickly moves to the head to give 2 slow full breaths. Within 5 seconds, the rescuer should return to doing chest presses.

CPR with two rescuers.   If a second person is available at the scene, he or she can take over CPR for the first rescuer, who may become tired. The second person should first activate the EMS system if it was not done and then say, "I know CPR! Can I help?" The first rescuer stops CPR after two ventilations. The second person kneels down on the other side of the victim and checks the pulse. If there is no pulse, the second person moves in, gives two breaths, and begins chest presses. The second person continues one-rescuer CPR by him or herself. The two people can (individually) take turns doing CPR until medical help arrives. Previously, it was recommended that two rescuers act at the same time — one doing cardiac compression and the other rescue breathing. This was changed in June, 1986.

CPR for infants and small children

Basic life support for infants and small children is similar to that for adults except for a few important differences.

Airway.   When handling an infant, it is easy to tilt the head back too far. Backward tilting that is forceful might block breathing passages instead of opening them. So gently tilt the head back by placing one hand on the infant's forehead. Use the fingertips under the bony part of the lower jaw to lift the chin up and open the mouth.

Breathing.   Instead of closing an infant's nose with the fingers, the rescuer covers both mouth and nose with his or her own mouth. Small breaths with less air are used to inflate the lungs — 1 small breath every 3 seconds.

Circulation.   The pulse of an infant or small child is checked by placing the tips of the fingers over the brachial artery on the upper arm. This pulse can be felt midway between the elbow and the shoulder on the inside of the arm. The technique for cardiac compression is also different for infants and small children. Only one hand is used for compression.

For infants, one hand must be slipped under the infant's shoulders to provide a firm support for the back. Only the tips of the ring and middle fingers of the other hand are used to compress the breastbone. Place the fingers slightly lower than the center of the breastbone (one finger width below an imaginary line between the nipples). Press the breastbone down ½ to 1 inch. The rate is faster — 100 presses per min-ute.

Ratio of Compressions to Breaths	Rate of Compressions
15:2	80 to 100 times/min

For small children, place the heel of one hand two finger widths above the lower end of the breastbone. Press the breastbone down 1 to 1½ inches, depending upon the size of the child. The rate should be 80 to 100 times per minute.

For children over 8 years, the method for adult CPR is used.

Monitoring the victim

The rescuer must check from time to time to see if the victim is bene-fiting from the breaths and presses. This can be determined by period-ically checking the pulse. Presses should be stopped and the neck checked for return of the victim's real pulse. If the victim has a pulse, give mouth-to-mouth breathing. If there is still no pulse, two breaths (one breath for infant and child) should be given and chest presses continued. If someone else checks the pulse while presses are being given, a faint artificial pulse will be felt from the presses. This means the presses are being done right. However, this is *not* the victim's real pulse. Continue CPR.

	Part of Hand	Hand Position	How Much to Push	Number of Presses
Infants	tips of ring and middle fingers	on breastbone one finger width below nipple line	½ to 1 inch	100 per minute
Children	heel of hand	lower half of breastbone	1 to 1½ inches	80 to 100 per minute

The pulse should be checked every 2 or 3 minutes. But *never* stop chest presses for more than 7 seconds. A rescuer should stop giving CPR only if: (1) a doctor says the victim is dead; (2) the victim has a return of his or her own heartbeat (pulse); (3) the rescuer is so tired that he or she cannot press any longer; or (4) medical services, such as an ambulance crew, take over care of the victim.

Complications, such as rib fractures or fractures of the breastbone, may result from putting external pressure on a victim during CPR. The risk may seem great, but the alternative to it might very well be death.

Choking

Choking on food or some other object causes many accidental deaths. Most of these deaths could be avoided if people took a few simple common-sense precautions in their day-to-day lives.

Adults. Since the majority of choking accidents occur during eating, learn to eat slowly. Cut meat and fish into small pieces, and be on the lookout for small bones, seeds, and pieces of shell in all your food. While mealtime should not be an unhappy occasion, try to avoid talking or laughing while you chew or swallow. Be aware also that alcoholic beverages decrease sensation in the mouth and lessen one's normal caution in eating. Thus, extra care ought to be taken by those having alcoholic drinks with their meals.

This procedure for saving a choking victim is recommended by both the American Red Cross and the American Heart Association.

Children.   Small children and infants are prime choking victims. Encourage children to remain seated and calm while eating. Food can easily become lodged in the throat if the child gets excited or trips while walking or running with food in the mouth. Make sure that bones and shells have been removed from food given to small children. Be certain that toys do not contain small parts (such as plastic eyes) that could be chewed or pulled off by a toddler. In general, keep all small, "swallowable" articles out of the reach of young children.

How to save a choking victim

Immediate recognition and treatment of choking are necessary if the victim is to survive. The "universal distress signal" for choking is clutching the neck. But not everyone knows about this signal. This emergency is often mistaken for a heart attack.

A choking victim will suddenly become quiet, and a look of alarm will come over the victim's face. A person having these signs must not be left alone. A choking victim cannot speak or breathe and will start to turn blue. The person is now just minutes away from a preventable death.

Dr. Henry Heimlich has developed a simple procedure to save a choking victim. The **Heimlich maneuver,** as it is called, can be performed by almost anyone. It takes only a few seconds. If you think that a person is choking, ask, "Are you choking?" Although a choking victim cannot speak, the person will usually be able to signal with a nod of the head.

Conscious victim.   If the victim is still conscious and either standing or sitting, do the following.

1. Stand or kneel behind the victim, and wrap your arms around the person's waist under his or her arms.
2. Make a fist with one hand. Place the thumb side of the fist against the victim's abdomen slightly above the navel. Stay clear of the ribs.
3. Grasp the fist tightly with your other hand.
4. Press your fist into the victim's abdomen with a quick upward thrust. Repeat these abdominal thrusts until the food or other object is forced out or the person becomes unconscious.

Unconscious victim.   The following procedure can also be used with a conscious victim. It is especially recommended if the rescuer is small or weak. While straddling the victim (placing one leg on either side of the victim's body), the weak or small rescuer can use his or her own body weight to get the necessary force for the thrust.

1. First, roll the unconscious victim onto his or her back with the face up.
2. Facing the victim, kneel and straddle the victim's legs.
3. Place the heel of one hand on the victim's abdomen slightly above the navel and below the rib cage.
4. Cover this hand with the other hand, and press into the victim's abdomen with a quick upward thrust.
5. If the victim does not expel the object, repeat the thrusts. BE PERSISTENT.

Infant victim.   Place the infant face down over your thigh. Deliver four back blows, forcefully, between the shoulder blades with the heel of your hand. Turn onto back with head lower than trunk. Deliver four thrusts using same hand position as for chest compressions in infant CPR procedure. Then check whether you can see and remove the object that

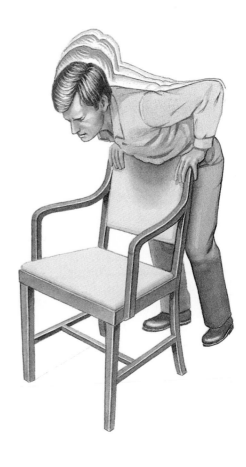

Two techniques are available to save yourself from choking.

is blocking the airway. If it cannot be seen, attempt to ventilate. If the airway is still blocked, repeat these steps until successful.

Yourself. If you choke while alone, press your own fist into your abdomen with a quick upward thrust. Several thrusts may be necessary.

An alternative method is to use the edge of a fixed object instead of your hands. Hit the abdomen firmly over the back of a chair or against the edge of a table, countertop, railing, or some other nearby object.

Key Words

advanced life support	cardiopulmonary resuscitation	external cardiac compression
basic life support	emergency medical services (EMS)	Heimlich maneuver
cardiac arrest		rescue breathing

- Many sudden deaths could be prevented if more people knew how to perform cardiopulmonary resuscitation (CPR).
- CPR is a combination of artificial respiration and artificial circulation.
- Common-sense measures can prevent many accidental deaths from choking.
- Separate procedures have been developed to save yourself, adults, infants, and children from choking.
- To save a choking victim, you must know how to recognize and treat the problem quickly.

1. Name five possible causes of sudden death.
2. Explain how CPR can save a person's life.
3. List four early warning signs of a heart attack.
4. Explain the difference between basic life support and advanced life support.
5. Once the victim's airway is open, what three things should someone performing CPR do?
6. State four preventive measures that should be used with children to avoid choking.
7. What is the universal distress signal for choking?
8. What are the signs that a person might be choking?
9. Describe the steps that can be taken to help a conscious choking victim.
10. Describe the procedure for saving yourself if you choke.

1. Invite a representative of the American Red Cross to class to demonstrate the life-saving measures detailed in this chapter for choking victims. Various members of the class should volunteer to try these techniques in front of the representative using other students as would-be victims. All members of the class should pay special attention to the most common errors the volunteers make in using these maneuvers.
2. Experts on life-saving techniques have noticed certain psychological problems related to performing CPR. These problems include (1) fear of taking responsibility for someone else's life, (2) having mouth-to-mouth contact with a dying or possibly dead person, and (3) the risk of "catching something". Contact an official at the American Heart Association or the American Red Cross, and find out what advice is given to students of CPR courses. Report your findings to the class.

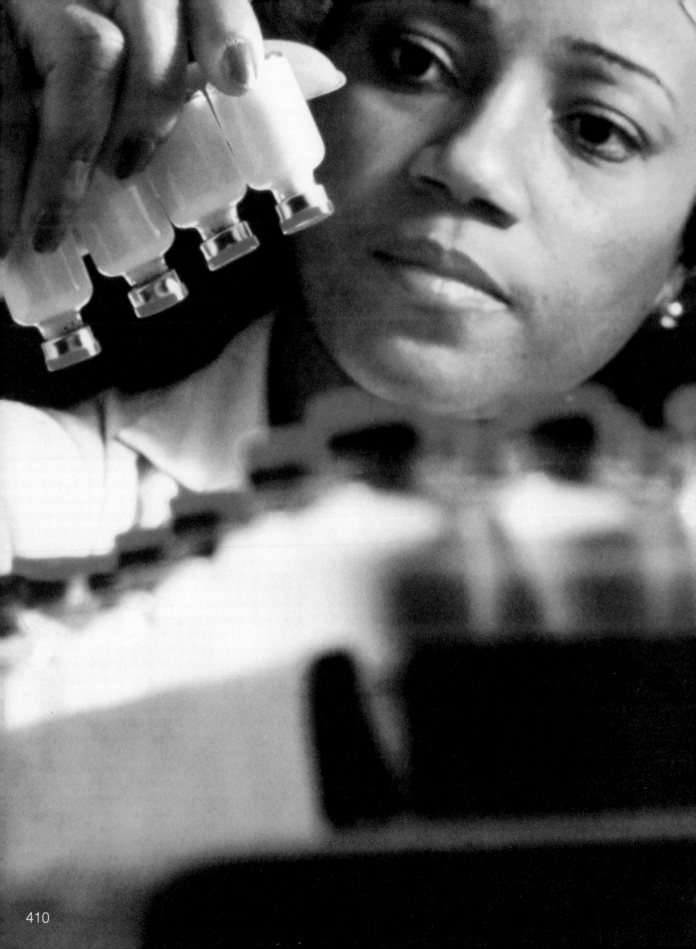

Unit 10
Health Careers and Services

Chapter 33

Selecting Health Care

After reading this chapter, you will be able to:

- ☐ Distinguish between the services performed by medical specialists and general practitioners.
- ☐ Determine when it is wise to consult a doctor about a health problem.
- ☐ Explain what takes place during a general examination.
- ☐ Describe the differences between traditional physicians and those who practice holistic medicine and biofeedback.

It is reassuring to know that medical care is available when you are ill. But good medical care is also important when you are in good health. You have to be able to trust your physician. Your health, after all, is at stake.

Physicians should have licenses to practice medicine in the states where they work. If a physician specializes in one field of medicine, certificates of training for that specialty should be on view in her or his office.

Doctors may be general practitioners or specialists.

Many family doctors are general practitioners. A person studying to become a general practitioner spends three or four years in college and four years in medical school. Up to three years is then spent as a resident in an approved hospital. This residency is a time of advanced training. After training, doctors must pass a state board examination before receiving a license to practice medicine.

Medical science has grown so quickly that it would be impossible for one person to learn enough to treat all illnesses. Instead, more and more doctors become **specialists**. Specialists spend years studying one system of the human body to learn the most advanced skills in diagnosis and treatment of that system. Special fields a doctor may choose include brain surgery, medical care for children, treatment of eye disorders, or treatment of skin disease. The list on pages 414–415 details a variety of medical specialties. Family doctors can recommend a medical specialist to you if they find that you need special attention.

Internists are another type of specialist. They are skilled in diagnosing, or finding out, what illnesses people have. They specialize in internal medicine (medical care for the inside of the human body). Internists must have three years of advanced training in diagnosis and in the care of internal disorders. After training, they must take a special examination to be certified.

When should you call your family doctor?

Jenny was looking forward to the district track meet. She was the top athlete in the 440-yard run and the 880-yard run. Two days before the track meet, she began to feel pains in her abdomen. She didn't pay much attention to them because she had felt pains like these during spring training. The pains got worse and worse. Jenny was nauseated and felt as though she was going to vomit. She took her temperature and found that she had a fever. Her father reminded her that the flu was going around and suggested that she rest in bed. Jenny's father then called the family doctor to ask what could be done to speed up recovery in time for the track meet. The doctor recommended an examination right away, and the examination showed that Jenny had

Medical Specialties	
Specialist	**Job**
Allergist	diagnoses and treats patients for asthma, hay fever, hives, and other allergies
Anesthesiologist	gives anesthetic (drugs that ease pain) during surgery; checks the condition of the patients before and after surgery
Cardiologist	diagnoses and treats heart diseases
Dermatologist	diagnoses and treats all forms of skin disease
Endocrinologist	diagnoses and treats problems having to do with the endocrine glands
Gastroenterologist	treats gastrointestinal (stomach and intestine) disorders
Gynecologist	diagnoses and treats problems having to do with the reproductive organs of women
Neurologist	diagnoses and treats problems of the central and peripheral nervous systems
Obstetrician	specializes in all aspects of childbirth—care of the mother before, during, and after delivery
Ophthalmologist	cares for and corrects eye problems
Orthopedic surgeon	performs surgery on bones and joints
Otolaryngologist	treats nose, ear, and throat disorders
Otologist	treats ear problems
Pathologist	carries out laboratory tests of body tissues and fluids; studies the causes of death
Pediatrician	specializes in the medical care of children
Plastic surgeon	treats skin and soft-tissue deformities; performs surgery to improve external features
Psychiatrist	specializes in mental and emotional disorders
Radiologist	examines and treats patients using X-ray and radium therapy

Continued

Medical Specialties	
Specialist	**Job**
Thoracic surgeon	performs surgery on the chest and lungs
Vascular surgeon	performs surgery on the heart and blood vessels
Urologist	treats disorders of the urinary tract (kidneys, ureters, urethra); also specializes in treatment of male reproductive organs

appendicitis. The very next day her swollen appendix was taken out by a surgeon.

Jenny missed the track meet, but she was lucky to have received quick medical care. If her father had put off calling the doctor and had given her remedies for the flu, Jenny's appendix might have burst. Infection would then have spread throughout her abdomen. The result could have been a long, serious illness or even death.

Jenny's case illustrates a decision that people must often make—at what point should a doctor be called?

Most parents call the family doctor when their child has a fever over 102°F. They usually don't call a doctor if the child has only a runny nose, headache, or scraped knee. The decision is probably based on past experience and common sense.

Be aware of the most important warning signals. You should call a doctor at once if you or someone around you shows these signs:

■ Pain is very bad and does not go away.
■ Blood is coughed up or appears in the stool or urine.
■ Diarrhea or vomiting does not stop.

The type of checkup you receive depends on the health problems you are experiencing.

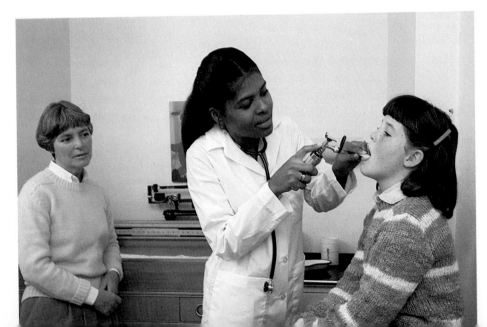

Don't be afraid to ask your doctor about medical terms you don't understand.

- Fever is high—102°F or above.
- Breathing is uneven, fast, or short.
- Heartbeat is very fast or not regular.
- The person is unconscious.
- There are injuries, such as broken bones, cuts, or wounds.
- The person is confused or in a dazed state.
- The person has been bitten by a stray animal.

How to talk with your doctor

When you visit a doctor, you should explain as clearly as possible just what is bothering you. Doctors want you to tell them specifically about your problems. They will ask questions such as these:

- **What is the major problem?** The doctor is trying to find out what bothers you the most. Let's imagine that your main problem is ringing in the ear.
- **How long have you had the problem?** The doctor wants to know when you first heard the ringing in your ear. Try to be exact and, if possible, to give a date. You should expect this question and know the answer before you go to the doctor's office.
- **Have you ever had the problem before?** The doctor wants to know about your past medical history. It is important to know if you have allergies, what medicines you might be taking, and what illnesses you have had. This kind of information may provide a clue to the cause of the ringing in your ear.
- **Have you had problems with your eyes, nose, glands, digestion, lungs, and so on?** The doctor is going over the systems of your body to make sure no information has been overlooked.
- **How do you like school? Do you smoke cigarettes or drink alcohol? Do you take part in sports or other school activities?** These questions are about your environment and day-to-day life. Important clues to an illness may be found by asking questions about

your social history. For example, the doctor may learn that you play in the school band and sit right in front of a trumpet player. This may have affected your ear. The doctor can then give specific tests or examine certain parts of the ear to find out the cause of your problem.

Next step: physical examination

After learning your medical history, the doctor may give you a complete physical examination. This head-to-foot examination is very thorough. The doctor will use different kinds of equipment during the examination. A **tongue depressor** is a flat wooden stick used to press down the tongue to get a better view of the tonsils and throat. An instrument called an **otoscope** shines a light into the outer-ear canal and onto the eardrum. In order to see the retina of the inner eye, the doctor uses an **ophthalmoscope**, an instrument especially designed for this purpose. The doctor listens to the sounds made by the heart and lungs with a **stethoscope**. The **sphygmomanometer** measures blood pressure. To test reflexes, the doctor strikes the muscle tendons near the patella (kneecap) with a triangular rubber mallet.

The doctor will feel your thyroid and lymph glands, located under the jaw and in the armpits and groin region. The abdominal cavity will be checked for unnatural lumps and swollen organs. The reproductive organs and rectum may also be examined.

Laboratory analysis

The third stage of a medical checkup often includes a chest X ray, blood count, and urinalysis. There are many kinds of blood tests and other laboratory tests. Some special tests include the following:

- Analysis of cerebrospinal fluid (fluid in the spinal cord).
- Analysis of a throat culture for strep (a bacterial infection).
- Analysis of a cervical smear in a Pap test (test for cervical cancer).
- Analysis of amniotic fluid in amniocentesis (test before birth to find out whether any of a baby's chromosomes are abnormal).

You will not be given all the tests described here. The type of examination will differ, depending upon your needs and requirements.

Patients' rights

Regardless of the length or type of checkup, always ask questions when you do not understand the medical terms used by your doctor. You have the right to ask, too, about the methods of treatment the doctor uses and whether they will be painful. If you must have an operation, you will want to ask what the risks are and how much time you will spend recovering.

Before you decide to have a particular treatment, you might want to ask the opinion of a second doctor. This is especially true if the problem is very serious or the treatment very risky.

When to get treatment for mental health problems

Psychiatrists, psychologists, and psychiatric social workers are specialists in the treatment of mental health problems. Many people still think these specialists only treat individuals who are "crazy." Such people would be embarrassed to be treated for mental health problems. But attitudes toward these specialists and people's ideas about mental health are changing rapidly. Did you know that mental health experts today are helping large numbers of "normal" people?

Sometimes a crisis—breakup of a relationship, death of a close friend or family member, personal failure, overwork—can upset a normal person for a period of time. The person might even be unable to carry out daily activities for a while. Such a person may need the guidance of a counselor in order to manage the crisis better. At other times, a person might want the advice of a counselor to help cope with problems before they become crises. If you decide to seek the help of a counselor, don't be embarrassed. Try to relax, and be as truthful as possible in answering the questions you are asked.

Doctors of dental surgery

In addition to doctors of medicine, another group of practitioners is important to our health: doctors of dental surgery. A doctor of dental

Dental Specialties	
Specialist	**Job**
Oral surgeon	performs surgery on the jaws and other parts of the mouth if they do not work properly or are injured
Oral pathologist	studies diseases of the oral cavity
Orthodontist	diagnoses and treats deformities of the teeth
Endodontist	diagnoses and treats diseases of the pulp chamber and root canals inside the teeth
Periodontist	diagnoses and treats problems of the gums and bones that support the teeth; uses braces to straighten crooked teeth
Prosthodontist	specializes in making supporting structures and artificial replacements, or dentures, for missing natural teeth

surgery (D.D.S.), or dentist, is qualified to treat diseases of the gums, teeth, and jaws. Some dentists have advanced training and specialize in a certain area. The list on page 418 explains the jobs of some dental specialists.

Most people in this society have an image of a doctor as someone who wears a white coat and prescribes medication. But not all physicians work this way. Other societies and cultures have long had different approaches to health care. Lately, some of these alternatives to traditional medicine have gained acceptance in our country. These new approaches are being used as a replacement for or a supplement to more conventional treatment.

Holistic medicine

Practitioners of **holistic medicine** are concerned with the body, mind, and spirit of a patient, or the "whole" person. Patients are encouraged to take control of their own health by combining older healing methods with recent advances in medicine. The holistic practitioner works with patients to help them remain healthy and to minimize the need for treatment. Unfortunately, many people who advertise that they are holistic practitioners use methods of treatment that border on quackery. Be a smart health consumer. Select health and medical professionals who will help you with your wellness goals.

Biofeedback

Can high blood pressure, migraines, stress, and menstrual cramps be controlled by the mind without using any medicine or treatment? According to certified **biofeedback** therapists, you can be trained to monitor heart rate, skin temperature, and muscle tension through the use of a biofeedback machine. The training increases your ability to control problem signals given by the body. Select a therapist who is affiliated with a medical school.

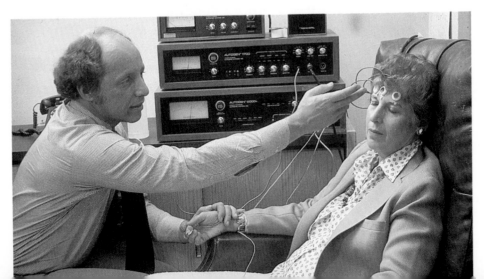

Biofeedback helps the mind to control problems of the body. Dr. Eliot Greenspan is a foremost practitioner of biofeedback.

Key Words	
	biofeedback ophthalmo- specialists holistic scope sphygmomanometer medicine otoscope stethoscope internists tongue depressor

Main Ideas

- Doctors are either general practitioners or specialists.
- It is important to know the warning signals that tell you to call your doctor.
- It is wise to be able to answer your doctor's questions clearly to ensure the best diagnosis and treatment.
- A number of alternatives to conventional medicine have emerged in this society.

Understand the Reading

1. How do internists differ from family doctors?
2. How is the job of a gynecologist related to the job of an obstetrician?
3. List ten warning signals that mean you should call a doctor.
4. Describe what happens during the three stages of a medical checkup.
5. What is an otoscope? An ophthalmoscope?
6. Name three laboratory tests a doctor might use as part of an examination.
7. What does the abbreviation D.D.S. stand for?
8. What is holistic medicine?
9. According to the list on page 415, what kinds of disorders does a urologist treat?
10. What are some of the medical conditions biofeedback has been used to treat?

Apply Your Knowledge

1. Write the names of products advertised on TV that claim to treat health problems. These should include diet aids and treatments for such irreversible conditions as hair loss. Bring these to class, and attach them to a bulletin board. After a month, examine the materials that have been collected. Consult a physician or other health specialist, and discuss the advantages and disadvantages of using these products.
2. With the help of a librarian, locate an account of life on the frontier by an early settler of America. In particular, find passages that describe health problems that arose, as well as the ways in which these were treated. Discuss your account with the class. Give attention to how modern medicine deals with the problems you have singled out.

420

Chapter 34

Self-Care and the Consumer

After reading this chapter, you will be able to:

☐ Explain the importance of health insurance coverage and describe the types of plans that exist in this country.

☐ State the differences in primary, secondary, and tertiary health care.

☐ Recognize which medicines and combinations of medicines are personally harmful to you.

☐ Explain how to guard against receiving treatment from a "quack."

☐ Explain the function of the labels on prescription and nonprescription medications.

When you own something valuable, it is your responsibility to care for it—to keep it in the best working order possible. This is especially true of your most valuable possession—your health. *Self-care* does not mean self-treatment or self-medication. It means, rather, that you know enough to be responsible for your own health.

You don't need a family doctor to remind you that exercise is important for your heart. A specialist doesn't have to tell you that a proper diet must be followed if you want to stay in shape. And everyone knows smoking is harmful to both lungs and heart. Self-care is simply a commonsense way of reducing risks. Part of the wellness goal you set for yourself should be self-care.

The health consumer

Being an intelligent **health consumer** is the key to self-care. Choosing the right medical-treatment center, buying medicines, knowing the cost of health care, and investing in a medical insurance plan make up a total health-care program.

Health insurance

If you had to stay in the hospital for a week, the cost of your visit could easily be over $2,000. Visits to a doctor's office can also be quite expensive. Because the cost of medical care can be so high, many people in this country have health insurance plans that help to pay the cost of medical bills.

Private plans bought by the individual are called **voluntary insurance** plans. **Group insurance** plans are available to a great many people through their jobs. If you become enrolled in either a private or a group insurance plan, be sure you fully understand the cost of the insurance policy and the benefits you can receive from it. You will also need to know exactly what kinds of health services the insurance will pay for. These features differ from policy to policy. A smart health consumer will "shop around" to determine which health plan suits his or her needs.

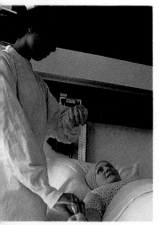

Health insurance helps reduce the high cost of medical care to the individual.

Medicare and Medicaid

People with low incomes and older people on social security are able to get government aid to pay for health care. **Medicare** is a program of health insurance available to certain disabled people and people who are 65 or older. **Medicaid** is available to people of all ages who cannot afford private health insurance and are not insured through a group health plan.

Some countries have standardized national health insurance programs. These programs are similar to Medicaid and Medicare, except that they cover all citizens. The rising cost of health care and the inadequacy of many insurance policies have created political pressure for a national health plan in the United States. Those in favor of such a program stress that it would make proper health care available to everyone, rich or poor. People who are against it feel that a national health insurance plan would be costly to taxpayers. They also feel that medical care would not be as good as it is now.

Health maintenance organizations

In the last decade, a lower-cost approach to health care has become available through Health Maintenance Organizations (**HMOs**). Instead of making unexpected, high-cost payments for care when they are sick, many people in the United States are joining HMOs. An HMO is made up of doctors, nurses, and technicians who provide complete health-care services. For some HMO members, there is a fixed monthly fee. For others, membership is paid in part or in full by their employers. This replaces traditional medical insurance.

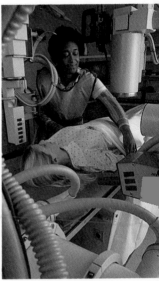

For no additional charge, tests such as these are provided to HMO members.

Physical examinations, including X rays, blood tests, cardiograms, and other specialized diagnostic tests, are available to HMO members at no additional cost. Care during illnesses or medical emergencies, including surgery and hospitalization, is also covered by the regular monthly payments. These payments, along with government support, create a fund that helps cover the costs of establishing and running a Health Maintenance Organization. The cost of treating patients is paid out of the fund. HMOs attempt to keep medical costs low by promoting health measures and practicing preventive medicine.

HMOs keep medical costs down in other ways. Doctors always treat patients. But nurse specialists and physician's assistants administer routine health care. Also, prepayment for medical services encourages people to seek care early in the development of illnesses. With early medical care, possibly serious conditions can be detected when they are less difficult and less expensive to cure. Finally, HMOs eliminate the nuisance of health insurance claim forms and medical bills.

Of course, HMOs are not for everyone. Many patients prefer the freedom of choosing their own physicians and health-care specialists. Patients who are undergoing treatment for a chronic (ongoing) condition by a doctor may prefer to stay under the care of that doctor. As with other decisions that are part of a self-care program, the decision to join or not join an HMO must be weighed carefully.

Every health care center is different.

As a consumer, you should be careful to choose a family doctor who will send you to a good specialist when necessary. Your doctor should be associated with the best medical center in your area. You should know the following terms when choosing a medical center.

Primary care. Treatment given by a doctor at a clinic, emergency room, or doctor's office is called **primary care**. This care is also called "ambulatory" or "outpatient" care.

Secondary care. Treatment given by specialists at a private or community hospital is called **secondary care**. This care is also referred to as "hospital" or "inpatient" care.

Tertiary care. Treatment given by specialists at a hospital that is part of a university is called **tertiary care**. Some types of operations, such as experimental heart surgery and organ transplants, can be done in these hospitals.

Medical centers have improved.

Less than a century ago, many people refused to go to a hospital for care. Sanitary conditions were not good. Many attendants, if they had any training at all, were poorly trained. Patients with mental illness or contagious diseases often were confined without good care. Many patients died in hospitals. Some died of the diseases they had when they entered the hospital. Others died of infections they got in the hospital.

Today's hospitals give good and total medical services. They also make the patient as comfortable as possible. Many kinds of medical treatment can be given only in a hospital. Laboratories, X-ray equipment, and operating rooms are important tools in the hospital for diagnosing and treating disease. A new development, the modern X-ray machine unit

Medical conditions in hospitals today have improved over those in hospitals a century ago.

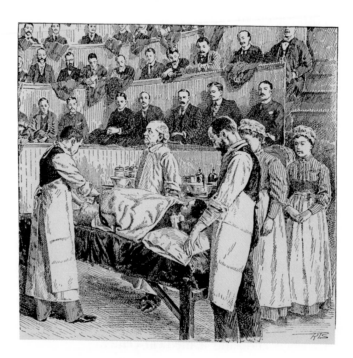

called the **Computerized Tomographic Scanner (CTS)**, is found in hospitals. It can take tens of thousands of X-ray readings in less than 5 seconds. The scanner takes cross-sectional views of any part of the head or body. With this new tool, physicians are able to locate tumors and other internal problems. Now surgery is not always needed to discover such problems.

Greater resources in the hospital

In a medical center such as a hospital, the family doctor and the medical specialist can work as a team. Trained registered and practical nurses, technicians, and many other hospital staff members are also part of the team.

Every year, people in the United States spend billions of dollars for drugs without the advice of a good doctor. Many of the drugs bought for self-treatment are of little or no value. Others may be harmful.

When you are ill, your family doctor uses tests and questions to decide what kind of medication is best for you. Let your doctor know if you are taking medication of any kind. If you are taking over-the-counter drugs, or **OTC drugs**, and your doctor prescribes a different drug, the mixing of the two could be dangerous.

Combinations of medicine and certain foods can sometimes have a bad effect. For example, when you take an antibiotic called erythromycin with orange juice, the vitamin C in the juice makes the antibiotic less effective.

Let your doctor know if you have any allergies. Also let the doctor know if you have ever been allergic to an antibiotic. If antibiotics or other drugs are prescribed for you to treat an illness, throw away leftover medications after you are well. Do not use them for another illness without seeing a doctor. Repeated taking of antibiotics can make you resistant to their effects. But do make sure you take all the doctor prescribes. Not taking an antibiotic for as long as you should may cure symptoms, but not the disease. The symptoms could return again later.

Can some medicines be harmful to you?

Many years ago, there were more traveling medicine shows than medical doctors. The traveling medicine shows were popular. They entertained people with songs and comedy. And they convinced many people that sickness, aging, and insomnia could be cured quickly and simply with one of "nature's elixirs" (cure-alls).

Medicine shows were convincing because people were "planted" in the audience to tell how a certain elixir cured their illness. These people were paid by the shows. They often staged their stories with dramatic

Medical quackery

action. The sales pitch made many listeners think that the "plants," or storytellers, really felt better after taking the elixir. In modern medicine, the effectiveness of high expectations is called the **placebo effect**. In medical experiments, the placebo used looks the same as the medicine that is being tested. The placebo itself has no medicine in it. It is given to patients to see how they react when they believe that they are taking the medicine. The patient and even the physician may not know which is the real medicine and which is the placebo. Researchers have found that one-third of the patients taking a placebo will show improvement. This shows that "mind over matter" can sometimes be more effective than the chemical in the medicine.

Medicine shows are still around today, but they don't travel on wagons pulled by horses from city to city. Instead, printed advertising has taken over. About 200 million people spend $2 billion each year to buy "miracle cures" for cancer, lifelong cures for arthritis, instant weight reducers, breast enlargers, so-called health foods, and unnecessary vitamins. The audience is larger than ever, but the pitch remains the same.

Why quackery works

There are many reasons why some people think they are helped by devices and products that really have limited value. Just like the make-believe healers of years past, modern quacks use our deepest fears of disease, illness, pain, and death to sell their products. When family doctors and specialists cannot cure us or ease our pain, we sometimes become frightened. Worried people may be easily swayed by overstated claims because they want so much to find hope somewhere.

Many illnesses are cured by the body itself because the human body has many defense systems that fight illness. That means most people recover from illness in time, whether or not they get proper treatment. A person may think a "miracle treatment" has brought about a cure when, in fact, the disease has simply run its course.

Other diseases are chronic. A person may seem to improve at times and then become worse at other times. Arthritis, stomach ulcers, epilepsy, asthma, and some types of cancer are examples of chronic illnesses. A reliable doctor will tell the patient that there will be ups and downs. A good doctor will also explain that the patient can be helped but probably not cured. But a person or organization selling a miracle cure may take advantage of the situation. Treatment may be given and a cure claimed when improvement comes. When a relapse occurs, the patient is told that treatment was stopped too soon. More treatment is then prescribed.

Sometimes illness is caused by emotional problems. Because of the placebo effect, the patient may get better with any kind of treatment that takes the mind off the problems. Such improvement is only short-lived. But this may not have been explained in advance. When the

Use common sense to protect yourself against quackery.

symptoms appear again, the patient may lose faith in the treatment. Then she or he may go from one kind of "sure cure" to another, hoping for a magical cure. Another kind of deception occurs when cures are claimed for diseases that a person may not even have.

How to guard against medical quackery

We live amid an information explosion. Radio, television, newspapers, and magazines give up-to-the-minute reports on almost everything. But reports may be conflicting, and news may be inaccurate. It is imperative that we learn to evaluate news about drugs, medical procedures, health claims, and claims of consumer safety that may be critically important to our well-being. How can such news be evaluated? The following questions may be helpful:

■ **What is the source of the report?** A national health institute, medical school, or major medical center is likely to release more significant and truthful news on a health topic than a private concern or a single practitioner. When, for example, a major tobacco company

427

Medications must undergo testing before they are dispensed in large quantities to the public.

disputes the findings of numerous nonprofit health organizations linking cigarette smoking to heart disease and lung cancer, consider *who* would be more likely to distort the truth.

- **What stage of research is reported?** Is the drug being tested in test tubes, on animals, or on human subjects? Clinical research involving human subjects will yield more meaningful results about drugs intended for human use.

- **How valid were the clinical testing procedures?** Drug research may be influenced by the subject's desire to get well and the investigator's desire to have positive results. Medical research has found that about one-third of all patients respond positively to any substance that they believe is medication. In **double-blind testing**, one group of patients receives the drug being tested. A second, similar group receives placebos. The two substances are coded by an independent person so that the patients, the people administering the substances, and the observers recording the results of the experiment do not know who received the real drug. The random selection of patients involved in such testing is also important.

- **How extensive was the testing?** Tests using large sample populations and made over fairly long periods of time are likely to reveal results that are valid in general practice. Follow-up studies on the effects of prolonged use or possible later side effects are also important.

- **How completely are the results of the study reported?** An evaluation of the seriousness of the side effects and a comparison of the new drug or treatment with drugs or medical practices currently used are important elements in medical reporting.*

What a prescription says

A prescription is a written note from a doctor to a pharmacist. It tells the pharmacist what kind of medicine is needed and how often it should be taken.

A prescription should have the following information: name of the medication, amount, **dose** (amount to be taken), the time between doses, specific instructions, and the patient's name. Specific information, such as "refrigerate," "take only on full stomach," or "shake well before using," is important to help the medicine work well.

Doctors and pharmacists can make mistakes when writing or preparing prescriptions. It is your responsibility as a consumer to read the prescription and understand what you are taking. Don't be afraid to ask your doctor or pharmacist about your prescription.

The list of common abbreviations on page 429 will help you understand the information on a prescription.

*Adapted from "How to Evaluate News About Miracles," *The Medicine Show,* Consumers Union of the U.S., Inc., Mt. Vernon, New York.

Special Abbreviations Used by Your Doctor

ad lib.	as needed	q.2h	every 2 hours
agit. a. us.	shake before using	q.3h	every 3 hours
a.c.	before meals	q.4h	every 4 hours
b.i.d.	twice per day	q.i.d.	4 times per day
dieb. alt.	every other day	q.s.	as much as is needed
o.d.	every day	stat.	immediately
p.c.	after meals	t.i.d.	three times per day
q.h.	every hour	p.r.n.	when needed

Nonprescription, or over-the-counter, drugs

Labels and warnings on OTC drugs help to protect you against using them in the wrong way. They also protect you against possible harmful side effects. A federal law requires all OTC drugs to have the following information on the labels:

- Name of the product.
- Name and address of the manufacturer, packer, or distributor.
- Net content of the package.
- Active ingredients and the amount of certain ingredients.
- Name of any habit-forming drug contained in the prescription.
- Warnings and cautions needed for the protection of the user.
- Proper directions for safe and effective use.

Before buying any OTC drug, check to make sure that the package has not been opened. Most drugs now come in special tamperproof packaging. Do not buy any drug with a broken seal or wrap.

Labels and warnings on over-the-counter drugs are there for your protection.

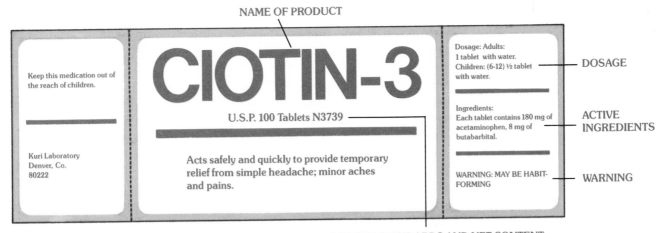

NAME OF PRODUCT

Keep this medication out of the reach of children.

Kuri Laboratory
Denver, Co.
80222

CIOTIN-3

U.S.P. 100 Tablets N3739

Acts safely and quickly to provide temporary relief from simple headache; minor aches and pains.

Dosage: Adults:
1 tablet with water.
Children: (6-12) ½ tablet with water.

DOSAGE

Ingredients:
Each tablet contains 180 mg of acetaminophen, 8 mg of butabarbital.

ACTIVE INGREDIENTS

WARNING: MAY BE HABIT-FORMING

WARNING

ACCEPTED STANDARDS AND NET CONTENT

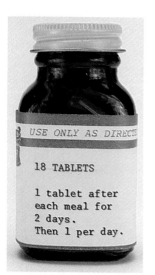

Read the label on your medicine bottle. Make sure you understand how much you are supposed to take and how often you are supposed to take it.

What do you have in your medicine cabinet?

If you checked your medicine cabinet, how many different kinds of drugs would you find? The medicine cabinet in an average home holds an assortment of cold remedies and health aids, including some kind of antiseptic, decongestant, cough syrup, pain reliever, and antacid. Here are some important things you should know about the following common OTC medications.

Antiseptics. Antiseptics such as hydrogen peroxide may be good for cleaning wounds and for killing bacteria. Three percent hydrogen peroxide is good as a cleaning agent. But the peroxide used for bleaching hair is too strong. Remove all embedded dirt with soap and warm water or hydrogen peroxide from wounds that are small and can be treated at home. If the dirt cannot be removed, see a doctor.

Decongestants. These are drugs used primarily to ease congestion. The drugs cause the membrane in the nose to "shrink" in order to stop excess secretion. Two common decongestants are ephedrine and phenylephrine. These drugs work only for several hours each time they are taken. When they are used for several days, the membranes of the nose will again produce more secretion. See your doctor to find out the cause of an allergy or congestion. If antihistamines must be used, use only a small amount. Since some antihistamines cause drowsiness, do not take them if you must drive. Carefully follow the directions on the label.

Cough syrups. These drugs can make you cough to help remove anything that is irritating the trachea. They can also help stop your cough. Cough syrups that help you get rid of phlegm contain an expectorant, an ingredient that makes you cough more. Cough syrups that help to quiet the cough center contain an ingredient called an antitussive. Sometimes a dry, hacking cough may prevent sleep. In those cases, a cough syrup with dextromethorphan, an antitussive, may help. Most cough syrup labels suggest that you stop taking a cough syrup and contact your doctor if the cough does not go away in three days.

Pain relievers. Many people use aspirin to lower fever and ease pain. We now know that aspirin, once thought to be a safe pain reliever, can cause serious health problems for some people, especially children. It can also interfere with the action of other drugs. If a bottle of aspirin has a vinegary odor, throw it away. It has been kept too long.

Antacids. These decrease acid in the stomach. One major type of antacid is called a systemic antacid. These popular and widely advertised antacids contain sodium bicarbonate that can neutralize or decrease hydrochloric acid quickly. However, it does not have a long-term neutralizing effect. The disadvantage of systemic antacids is that they dissolve and are absorbed into the bloodstream. Then the kidneys must work hard to keep the right amount of acid in the body.

The second major type of antacid is called a nonsystemic antacid. These antacids are not absorbed into the bloodstream. Some contain magnesium and make the feces soft. Others contain aluminum and make the feces hard. If you have stomach pains, *don't* take any antacids before seeing your doctor to find out the cause of the pain.

Clean your medicine cabinet.

How long have you had the drugs in your medicine cabinet? Do you still have the medicine from your last cold? Many OTC drugs have an expiration date. This date tells when the drug may no longer be useful. Most antibiotics lose their effectiveness over a period of time. The antibiotic tetracycline may even become poisonous after the expiration date.

If you leave the medicine cabinet open, the drugs inside will be exposed to light. This may make the drugs lose their strength, or potency. If you do not tightly screw the caps on medicine bottles, the moisture and warmth of the bathroom may make pills crumble. Other medications may decompose, or break down, into their chemical elements. Some medicines, such as iodine and cough syrups, are mixed with alcohol. If bottles are not properly closed or if they are old, the alcohol will evaporate, leaving harmful substances. Medications that must remain sterile, such as eye drops, may become contaminated through careless storage. Bacteria will grow in the solution. Medications that have sugar may also grow bacteria if they are kept too long.

Key Words

Computerized Tomographic Scanner (CTS)	group insurance	primary care
	health consumer	secondary care
	HMOs	self-care
dose	Medicaid	tertiary care
double-blind testing	Medicare	voluntary insurance
	OTC drugs	
	placebo effect	

Main Ideas

- Health insurance helps cover the high cost of medical expenses.
- Different types of care are available through different types of health-care centers.
- It is important to know which medicines and combinations of medicines might be harmful to you.

Continued

- It is important to know how to recognize a medical quack and how to determine the trustworthiness of a medical news report.
- The wise health consumer will learn to read the labels on both prescribed and OTC drugs.
- Your medicine cabinet may contain outdated medicine that can be harmful to you.

Understand the Reading

1. What is the difference between voluntary insurance and group insurance?
2. Explain the difference between Medicare and Medicaid.
3. Discuss the advantages and disadvantages of HMOs.
4. How does primary care differ from secondary care? From tertiary care?
5. List three differences between today's hospitals and hospitals a century ago.
6. Why is it important to let your doctor know during treatment if you are taking any medication?
7. What is the placebo effect? How are placebos used in medical testing?
8. What is a chronic disease?
9. Explain double-blind testing.
10. Why should your medicine cabinet not be left open?

Apply Your Knowledge

1. Interview a pharmacist. Determine what medications the average family medicine cabinet should have. Also learn which products need to be replaced periodically because they lose their effectiveness over time. Report your findings to the class.
2. Ask a local representative of a company that sells health insurance policies to speak to your class. Request that the representative bring samples of group insurance policies that highlight the different types of coverage available. Discuss with the representative the differences and similarities between the various policies.
3. Read up on the government programs of Medicare and Medicaid. Find out when these programs began and the qualifications one needs to take advantage of either program. Describe your findings in a paper for class.
4. Write to the Food and Drug Administration. Ask them: (1) how they go about testing a drug before it is released for sale, (2) how long testing takes, and (3) what percentage of drugs so tested are eventually sold to the public. Also determine what facts lead to some prescription drugs eventually being sold as OTC drugs. Summarize your findings in a class report.

Chapter 35

Health in the United States

After reading this chapter, you will be able to:

☐ Describe the health services provided at the community, state, and federal levels.

☐ List the jobs done by the Public Health Service.

☐ Describe the goals of various volunteer health agencies.

☐ Name some of the tasks performed by the World Health Organization (WHO).

El Camino North
Dialysis
Patient Accounts
Health Services Eng.
Management Eng.

Have you ever noticed the blue stamp on large pieces of meat in the supermarket? The stamp is placed there by the United States Department of Agriculture (U.S.D.A.). Through the stamp, the U.S.D.A. tells us what quality we can expect from that particular piece of meat. But the U.S.D.A. does more than judge the grade of meat. The agency also makes sure that every food product that reaches our dinner tables has passed government safety and health standards.

The U.S.D.A. is just one link in a nationwide chain of health agencies. Working together, these agencies help us—both as individuals and as a nation—to achieve our wellness goals.

Standards of health

Experts believe that by the year 2000 people can expect their average life span to be 80 years. How healthy we will be then will depend a great deal on our present wellness goals. Our life span will also depend on preventive medicine, health-care methods, and the state of our environment.

Today, we take it for granted that standards have been established for pure water, clean air, safe food, and proper medications. We think that these standards ensure that the quality of the environment, of food, and of medicine is the same everywhere in the United States. However, these set standards can protect us only as long as they stay in effect. New problems keep arising. Lack of technology and government red tape can prevent us from solving these problems quickly.

The average life span increases with each advance in medical science.

Beginnings of public health services

People organized governments when they began to live in villages, towns, and cities. They made laws to control things that were important to them as a group. No one person could deal with these matters alone. Governments took care of police and fire protection, water supplies, disposal of wastes, and protection and improvement of **public health**. Public health means the health of everyone, not just certain individuals.

In the past, communicable, or contagious, diseases were the greatest health problem. Preventing the spread of these illnesses was the biggest health concern of governments. Quarantine is an example of an early method that was used to help stop the spread of communicable diseases. Later, it was discovered that communicable diseases were caused by microorganisms. Organized ways to kill these microorganisms were developed. They included purifying drinking water, disposing of sewage, and pasteurizing milk. Inspecting food supplies and killing insects that spread disease are some other methods of destroying these organisms. Modern cities could not exist without such services.

You read in Chapter 1 how new sanitation laws, the development of effective vaccines, and mass immunization helped the United States win the battle against such infectious diseases as pneumonia, influenza, and tuberculosis. You have also learned ways in which you can make preventive health choices to help protect yourself against today's killers—heart disease, cancer, high blood pressure, and stroke. The theme of the Surgeon General's report on health promotion and disease prevention entitled *Healthy People* is that the health of Americans today can be significantly improved through actions people can take themselves. The report lists the following simple measures to enhance the prospect of good health:

- Elimination of cigarette smoking.
- Attention to alcohol misuse.
- Moderate dietary changes to reduce intake of excess calories, fat, salt, and sugar.
- Moderate exercise.
- Periodic screening for major disorders at intervals determined by age and sex.
- Obeying speed laws and using seat belts.

Health and Safety for You is more than the name of a book—it is a goal for all Americans.

Something to think about

Healthy People

Health services

Little by little, many other health services have been added to the responsibilities of government. However, the government is not alone in providing health services. Business and labor organizations and voluntary health associations also help to fight disease and to improve health.

Health in the community

Depending on the area in which you live, the health department of your city, county, or town is responsible for a variety of health services. The following are some of these services.

Keeping stray animals off the street. Local health departments help to keep stray animals off the street. Dogs that have been abandoned by their owners can be a menace to a community. A person bitten by a stray dog may contract a painful and dangerous infection called rabies.

Strays may tip over trash cans while looking for food, thus creating a sanitation problem.

Inspecting kitchens in restaurants and hotels. Have you ever had stomach pains after eating out? If so, you may have had a minor case of food poisoning. Your local health department checks the cleanliness of eating places. It tries to make sure that the food is prepared in a safe and clean way.

Removing wastes. In our nation, everything from paper diapers to plastic spoons is thrown away. Your local health board supervises the collection and elimination of wastes.

Examining the water supply. Clean water is essential to the survival of a community. Your local health department makes sure that minimum water-purity standards set by the federal health agencies are enforced.

Inspecting hotels, motels, and public buildings. Are bedbugs, lice, and other such pests a thing of the past? The answer in some localities, unfortunately, is no. It is the responsibility of the local health department to check public buildings to make sure that they are kept sanitary.

Coordinating neighborhood health centers. Many communities have health centers or clinics that give medical care to those who cannot afford it elsewhere. These clinics are run by the local health department. They usually deal with problems related to unwanted pregnancies, drug abuse, mental illness, and sexually transmitted diseases.

Collecting and analyzing vital data. Can you imagine a city the size of New York not keeping records of the marriages, births, and health status of its people? All communities keep such **vital data** (needed information). The information is used to plan for future needs and to control such health problems as epidemics.

The state department of health

Every state has a department of health. State and local health departments have similar jobs. The state department of health usually deals with problems too large for local departments. Special health services, such as running large centers for mentally and physically handicapped people and licensing medical personnel, are usually funded by state governments.

What you can expect from federal health services

The federal government is responsible for public health services that involve more than one state. It gives a great deal of money to such

City water supplies must be checked often for pollution.

state and local health services to carry out their programs. They must, however, meet government standards before receiving such help.

The **Public Health Service**, a division of the **Department of Health and Human Services**, is concerned with all aspects of health in the United States. Its many branches include the Food and Drug Administration; the National Institutes of Health; the Centers for Disease Control; the Health Resources and Services Administration; the Alcohol, Drug Abuse, and Mental Health Administration; and the Agency for Toxic Substances and Disease Registry. The following services are provided by the various branches of the Public Health Service:

■ Supports research programs in all areas of health and disease to be carried out in universities, hospitals, and research institutes.
■ Investigates and controls serious outbreaks of communicable diseases anywhere in the United States.
■ Prevents communicable diseases from entering the United States from other countries.
■ Certifies the safety, quality, and usefulness of vaccines.
■ Gives information about the prevention and treatment of disease.

437

The Centers for Disease Control (CDC) in Atlanta, Georgia, is a branch of the Public Health Service. Some activities the CDC is concerned with are the control of communicable diseases, setting standards for the treatment of communicable diseases, establishing immunization schedules, and health promotion. The CDC provides its services to people all over the world.

Epidemiologists, or "disease detectives," at the CDC track down the source of infection when an outbreak of infectious disease occurs. Health officials then try to stop the disease from spreading. CDC officials have found the sources of epidemics of typhoid, malaria, hepatitis, and sexually transmitted diseases throughout the United States. These diseases can sometimes still be serious health hazards.

Nongovernmental voluntary health agencies

Voluntary agencies do important work in medical research and health education. The American Heart Association, the Arthritis Foundation, the March of Dimes Birth Defects Foundation, and the National Association for Mental Health are examples of such voluntary agencies. They sometimes show a community what can or should be done and then turn the work over to local agencies.

The American National Red Cross and the American Heart Association teach large numbers of people methods of saving lives. Other agencies are interested in the needs of special groups. These agencies work to help such groups as crippled children, the blind, the deaf, the mentally retarded, and veterans. There are visiting-nurse associations that provide health instruction and nursing care for patients in their own homes. Safety councils work to promote accident prevention.

Professional associations, such as the American Medical Association, the American Public Health Association, the American Dental Association, and the American Nurses Association, have added much to the knowledge of disease. These groups also work to inform the public about ways to prevent disease and injury.

Classes like this, sponsored by the American Red Cross, instruct people in life-saving techniques.

Volunteers play an important part in protecting and improving the health of people in the United States.

An important function of voluntary health agencies is the sharing of their information and expertise. On request, some of them provide free pamphlets, newsletters, and posters. You can write for this free information. (See the Resource Guide in the appendix of this book for addresses.)

A special health organization

A special agency of the United Nations, the **World Health Organization (WHO)**, has the goal of improving the level of physical and mental health of all the world's people. This is a goal that can be reached only by worldwide cooperation.

The major activities of WHO include giving new information about medical and health matters (such as epidemics and research results), stopping illegal drug traffic, preventing the spread of communicable disease, and giving aid to countries that must deal with epidemics.

Toward better health for everyone

Health services are an important part of every community. Taxes support public health agencies that care about the health of all citizens. There are laws to protect your health. Different agencies work on special health problems, and millions of dollars are spent for medical research and for health care.

Still more information is needed about how to keep people healthy. It is also important to make full use of the knowledge we already have. Each person has the responsibility to keep as strong and healthy as possible. Everyone should work with the governmental and voluntary organizations that have been set up to protect and improve health.

Key Words

Main Ideas

- Health services in the United States are carried out at the local, state, and federal levels.
- The Public Health Service is an important federal health agency that is concerned with all aspects of health in the United States. It supports research in all areas of health and disease.
- Much important health work is done by a number of volunteer health agencies.
- The World Health Organization (WHO), a branch of the United Nations, promotes good health all over the world.

Understand the Reading

1. List five jobs your local health department does.
2. Why is it necessary for local health departments to pick up stray dogs?
3. Why are vital data important to a city?
4. Which division of the Department of Health and Human Services is concerned with health in the United States?
5. Name three of the services provided by the Public Health Service.
6. List four activities that the Centers for Disease Control is concerned with.
7. What are epidemiologists? Describe some of the work they have done.
8. Name four voluntary health agencies.
9. Describe some of the work of voluntary health agencies.
10. What does WHO stand for? What is the main goal of WHO?

Apply Your Knowledge

1. Arrange to interview an official in your community health department. Determine (1) the types of health care available to individuals who are unable to pay and (2) how your community cares for its handicapped members. Share your findings with the class by writing a report.
2. Using the Resource Guide in the appendix, select three voluntary health agencies. Write to these agencies and request any materials on public health that they furnish free of charge. Attach the materials you receive to a class bulletin board so that the information can be shared with your classmates.

Chapter 36
Health Careers

After reading this chapter, you will be able to:

- [ ] Describe some of the advantages of a career in the health field.
- [ ] Explain the major differences between entry-level, intermediate-level, and higher-level health careers.
- [ ] List various careers at the entry, intermediate, and higher levels.
- [ ] Describe the training involved in many health fields.

Because of the expanding health-care needs of a growing population with increasing numbers of elderly people, employment in medical-care services will greatly increase in the years to come. The Bureau of Labor Statistics has revised its labor-force projections for the 1990s. Listed among the fastest-growing occupations are a number of health-related careers.

A career in health

When most people think of big industry, they think of car manufacturing, transportation, steel, food production, or banking. People do not often think of health as a big industry. Actually, the health industry is one of the largest in the United States.

The advantages of health careers

Unlike some other large industries, the health industry is not limited to just a few areas of the country. Large cities, where many people live, need large numbers of health workers. But small towns and rural areas need health workers, too. Because of the need for good health services in all parts of the world, health workers can find jobs almost any place they choose.

Opportunities in health careers

The health-care industry has hundreds of different kinds of job openings. Some jobs call for many years of special training, while others require little special training. Still other jobs let you learn while you are working. There are some careers in which you can set up your own business. In other careers, you can work for someone else. Some jobs are very technical and call for a solid scientific background. Other jobs do not demand such high-level knowledge, but do call for people who work well with their hands or who can get along well with other people.

Help in getting started

One of the biggest advantages of choosing and following a career in health services is the possibility of getting monetary help to start. Because of the great need for good health care, government and nongovernment groups sponsor programs that make it easier to begin a career in the health field. Several ways exist for students to get loans or grants. Scholarships and part-time employment opportunities are possible as well. The federal government sponsors numerous programs to support training in the area of health. Hospitals, private industry, labor unions, and other organizations offer more help.

Technological advancements and new jobs

Jobs in the field of health change all the time. Some jobs today didn't exist a few years ago. For example, many jobs have resulted from the discovery of the X ray. Today, there are even more advanced uses for X rays. Computerized **tomographic scanners** are providing new jobs. These scanners are X-ray machines that can take pictures of a section of the inside of the body without shadows from other sections interfering. Since computers are being used to study and interpret information from laboratories, people who know about them are also needed in the health field.

A variety of opportunities

Some health jobs involve scientific skills. The work is done in a university or laboratory. Other health jobs are not technical at all. Many of these call for people who can get along well with others and who can work in places where there is a great deal of activity. Being a receptionist in a clinic is one example of such a job.

There are also opportunities for those who like to teach. What is known about health must be passed on to others if society is to get the most good from that knowledge.

Preparing for a health career

How should you prepare for a health career? There is no single answer to this question because there are so many different careers. Since there is a wide choice of careers, the length of time needed and the place of preparation vary.

There are some jobs in which a person can work and learn at the same time. This is called **on-the-job training**. Other jobs have a training period that begins after high school and lasts for several weeks or months. Still others require several years of professional training. Being a physician requires a college degree in addition to years of specialized training.

Entry-level careers

The health careers that require the least amount of formal education are called **entry-level careers**. Some entry-level health careers are those of surgical technician, EEG technologist, EKG technologist, respiratory-therapy technician, clinical laboratory assistant, dietetic technician, and medical assistant. The last of these is described here.

Medical assistant. The duties of medical assistants can be either clinical or administrative. Clinical duties involve taking and recording a patient's temperature, weight and height, blood pressure, and medical history.

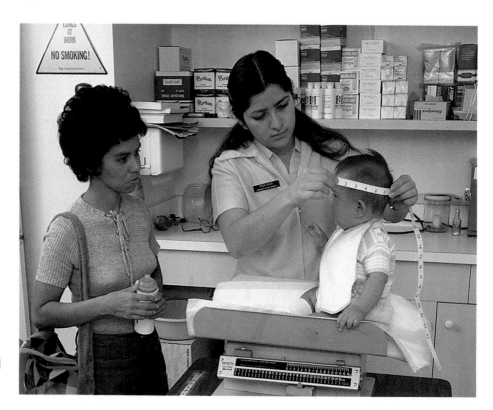

The paramedic is trained to do many of the jobs once performed only by physicians and nurses.

Medical assistants also perform basic laboratory tests, prepare patients for examination, assist the physician in examining patients, and sterilize instruments. Administrative duties may include answering the phone, greeting patients, recording and filing patient data, filling out medical reports and insurance forms, and handling bookkeeping and billing. Medical assistants should have a high school diploma and are trained on the job. Recommended high school subjects are mathematics, health, biology, typing, computers, and office skills. You can also attend a

Food-service workers (*left*) see to it that everyone in the hospital receives a properly balanced meal.

Lab technicians (*right*) provide important behind-the-scenes support for other health professionals.

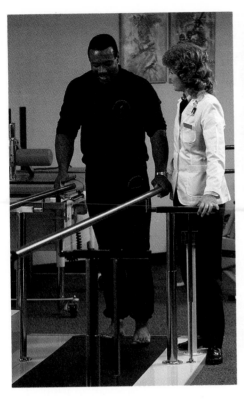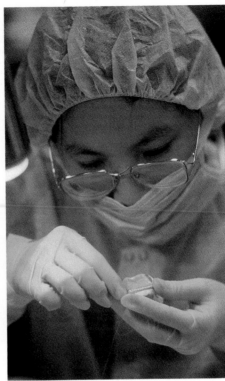

It is the job of the physical therapist (*left*) to help the patient regain use of an injured body part.

The technician at the right is adjusting a heart valve that will later be used to save a life.

community college and work toward an associate degree. Communication skills are important. For further information, write to The American Association of Medical Assistants, 20 North Wacker Dr., Suite 1575, Chicago, IL 60606.

Intermediate-level careers

Intermediate-level careers in health require an associate degree, which can be earned in two years of college. Since more preparation and training are necessary, intermediate-level jobs usually pay better than entry-level jobs. Some of the intermediate-level health careers are cyto-technologist, dental hygienist, pediatric assistant, radiation-therapy technologist, licensed practical nurse, and physical-therapy assistant. The last two of these are described here.

Licensed practical nurse. Licensed practical nurses (LPNs) care for the physically or mentally ill. They do not have the professional education and training of registered nurses, but can provide nursing care that requires some technical knowledge. They take and record temperature and blood pressure, change dressings, and give prescribed medications to patients. Some LPNs work in such specialized units as intensive care or recovery rooms. They also assist in the delivery, care, and feeding of infants. All LPNs must be licensed by completing a state-approved

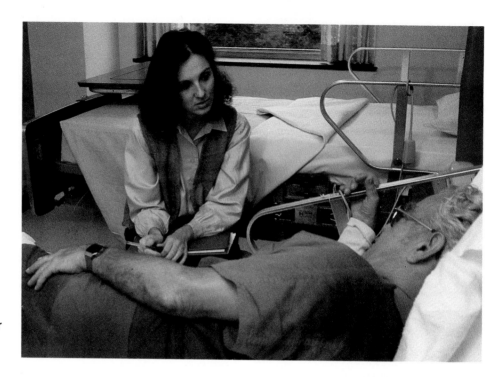

The hospital social worker discusses with patients problems they can expect to encounter after leaving the hospital.

program in practical nursing and passing a written examination. Job opportunities are excellent in nursing homes, home-health agencies, and private-duty nursing. For more information, write to The National Federation of Licensed Practical Nurses, Inc., P. O. Box 11038, Durham, NC 27703.

Pediatricians must be able to meet the needs of patients who are often too young to express their needs.

Physical-therapy assistant. A physical-therapy assistant is a skilled technical health worker who, under the supervision of a physical therapist, assists with patients' treatment programs. Some of the duties include training patients to do exercises, administering treatments that use special equipment, assisting patients in performing tests, and reporting patients' responses. The course of study includes physical, biological, and social sciences; technical courses in physical therapy; and clinical experience. For more information about licensing and registration, write to The American Physical Therapy Association, 111 North Fairfax St., Alexandria, VA 22314.

Nurses perform a wide range of functions, from assisting during surgery to administering medication.

Higher-level careers

Higher-level careers in health usually require a four-year college degree, although several of these professions require additional years of education, training, and experience. Some higher-level health careers include medical technologist, speech pathologist, health educator, veterinarian, occupational therapist, registered nurse, physical therapist, and physician. The last four of these careers are examined here.

Occupational therapist. An occupational therapist works as a member of a medical team that helps patients who are mentally or physically disabled. The patients are taught skills that allow them to live independent and productive lives. They are taught how to use such equipment as wheelchairs, splints, and aids for eating and dressing. Therapists work in school systems, schools for handicapped children, outpatient

Pharmacists must know how medications are to be taken and must be able to pass that information along to the consumer.

447

clinics, nursing homes, and community mental health centers. Preparation for this career includes a bachelor's degree in occupational therapy from a four-year college. For more information, write to The American Occupational Therapy Association, 1383 Piccard Dr., Rockville, MD 20850.

Surgeons receive training in specialized procedures that save countless lives each year.

Registered nurse. The work setting usually determines the role of the registered nurse's responsibilities. A registered nurse can work in a hospital, a nursing home, a physician's office, a student health facility, a school of nursing, or a private home. Nurses must graduate from an approved school of nursing and pass a national examination. There are three different programs for nurse's training—associate (a two-year college program), diploma (a three-year program sponsored by a hospital), and bachelor's degree (a four-year college program). If you are planning to work in a public health agency or in a supervisory or administrative position, you must have a bachelor's degree. For further information, write to The American Nurses Association, 2420 Pershing Rd., Kansas City, MO 64108.

Physical therapist. Physical therapists, or PTs, provide treatment that restores bodily functions, relieves pain, and prevents further disability in patients suffering from injury or disease. They are also responsible for instructing patients, supervising physical-therapy assistants, physical-therapy aides, and other health workers in carrying out the rehabilitation program. A physical therapist performs tests and evaluations that provide information about joint motion, strength and endurance of muscles, and whether braces or artificial limbs are needed.

High school courses that are useful include health, chemistry, biology, mathematics, and physics. Some of the physical-therapy curriculum includes anatomy, physiology, neuroanatomy, neurophysiology, and biomechanics of motion. Therapists work in rehabilitation centers, schools, hospitals, nursing homes, and outpatient clinics. All states require a license to practice physical therapy. Applicants must have a degree or certificate from an accredited program in physical therapy and pass a state examination. For further information, write to The American Physical Therapy Association, 1111 North Fairfax St., Alexandria, VA 22314.

Physician. A physician generally uses knowledge and skills to cure diseases of the human body and mind. Refer to Chapter 33 for a brief description of medical specialists. The requirements include three to four years of college in a premedical course, four years of medical school, one year of residency, and two to five years of extended residency in a special area of medicine. For further information, write to The American Medical Women's Association, 465 Grand St., New York, NY 10002 or The American Medical Association, 535 N. Dearborn St., Chicago, IL 60610.

Some Other Careers in the Health Field

Career	Description of work	Preparation required
Biomedical-equipment technician	services, operates, and maintains medical machinery used in health-care facilities	1 to 2 years of training after high school
Computer programmer	writes programs (instructions) for computers to analyze results of laboratory tests and other information	3 to 4 years of college
Dental laboratory technician	makes and repairs dentures and other dental devices	1 to 3 years of training after high school
Dentist	general practice or one of the dental specialties, such as orthodontics or dental surgery	3 to 4 years of college; 4 years dental school
Dietitian (nutritionist)	plans special diets; conducts research in foods; supervises food preparation in institutions	4 years of college
Dietetic technician	plans meals and supervises food-service staff in institutions	1 to 2 years of training after high school
Emergency medical technician	gives first aid in emergencies; drives ambulance or attends the patient in the ambulance	several weeks to 6 months of training after high school
Food technologist	develops practical processing methods to produce new foods in commercial quantities and test new foods; designs new packing techniques	4 years of college and graduate work
Health educator	health teaching in schools, colleges, public-health departments, special programs for the handicapped, and so on	4 to 5 years of college
Histologic technician	prepares sections of body tissues for microscopic examination by freezing, cutting, mounting, and staining	12-month hospital course and graduate of AMA-accredited histologic technician program, plus Board of Registry examination
Industrial hygienist	protects personnel from industrial health hazards, such as vibration, toxic chemicals, dust, gas, poor lighting, infectious diseases, and fatigue	4 years college and graduate work
Inhalation-therapy technician	assists physicians in operating equipment to supply oxygen to patients	1 to 3 years of training after high school
Medical laboratory technician	makes special laboratory tests in hospitals, clinics, and physicians' offices	2 to 4 years of college
Medical librarian	supervises medical libraries and medical records in hospitals	4 to 5 years of college

Continued

Career	Description of work	Preparation required
Medical-record technician	prepares, codes, and preserves patients' records in clinics and hospitals	1 to 2 years of training after high school
Medical social worker	assists families with economic and other problems related to medical care	4 years of college, 2 years of graduate work
Noise technician	devises noise-control programs for today and for the future	2–7 years of study; both on-the-job training and formal college education
Nurse, registered (RN)	nursing care of the physically and mentally ill; public health; teaching and supervision	2 to 4 years of college or 3 years in a school of nursing
Nurse practitioner	expanded nursing role, including some health-care services that traditionally have been the responsibility of the physician	training as a registered nurse plus advanced formal study
Nursing aide	nonmedical duties to assist professional nurse	a few weeks of training in hospital (varies)
Optician	makes eyeglasses or contact lenses from an ophthalmologist's prescription	1 to 3 years of training after high school
Optometric technician	assists the optometrist	1 to 2 years of training
Optometrist	tests vision; prescribes glasses	3 to 4 years of college, 4 years of optometric school
Osteopath	general medical care with emphasis on manipulation and massage	2 years of college, 4 years of osteopathic college, 1 or more years of internship
Pharmacist	preparation of drugs for treatment of illness; filling of prescriptions	4 to 5 years of college
Podiatrist (chiropodist)	treats foot disorders; prescribes correct shoes	1 to 2 years of college, 4 years of school of podiatry
Prosthetist and orthotist	designs, makes, and fits artificial limbs or braces	2 or more years of college
Psychologist, clinical	mental testing; diagnosis and treatment of mental and emotional disorders	4 years of college, 3 or 4 years of graduate work in psychology, 1 or more years of internship
Public health engineer	specializes in environmental health	4 to 5 years of college

entry-level careers higher-level careers	intermediate- level careers	on-the-job training tomographic scanners

- Jobs for health workers are available in both rural and urban areas throughout the United States and the world.
- Financial assistance is available to train for a health career.
- Entry-level health careers allow you to start working soon after high school. Intermediate-level careers require some college study. Higher-level careers usually require a college degree.
- The amount of education and training needed for a health career will determine the responsibilities.

1. Describe some of the advantages and opportunities in a health career.
2. What is the difference between entry-level and intermediate-level health careers?
3. List five entry-level careers.
4. What are some of the clinical duties of a medical assistant?
5. Describe the requirements for a career as a licensed practical nurse.
6. Describe the course of study for a career as an optician.
7. Name the three different programs in nurse's training. Which is necessary for a job with a public health agency?
8. Describe the kind of treatment a physical therapist provides.
9. What sort of job settings are available to a person with training as a physical therapist?
10. How many years of schooling are needed for a career as a health educator? As an optometrist?

1. Contact an employment agency in your community, and investigate local health-career opportunities. Determine what conditions lead to changes in the types and number of jobs in a given specialty. Report your findings to the class.
2. Interview your family doctor. Ask which schools the doctor attended and when. Find out what publications the doctor reads to keep up with current events in medicine. Determine if any changes have taken place in the course of study leading to an M.D. degree since she or he attended school. Discuss with class members what you have learned in this interview.

Resource Guide

This resource guide was developed to assist you in obtaining information and materials on topics covered in the text.

Action on Smoking and Health (ASH)
2013 H Street, N.W.
Washington, D.C. 20006

Al-Anon World Service Headquarters
1 Park Avenue, Second Floor
New York, New York 10016

*Alcoholics Anonymous
General Service Office
P.O. Box 459
Grand Central Station
New York, New York 10163

*American Cancer Society
19 West 56th Street
New York, New York 10019

American Dental Association
211 East Chicago Avenue
Chicago, Illinois 60611

*American Diabetes Association
2 Park Avenue
New York, New York 10020

American Dietetic Association
430 North Michigan Avenue
Chicago, Illinois 60611

*American Heart Association
7320 Greenville Avenue
Dallas, Texas 75231

*American Lung Association
1740 Broadway
New York, New York 10019

American Medical Association
535 North Dearborn Street
Chicago, Illinois 60610

*American National Red Cross
2025 E Street, N.W.
Washington, D.C. 20006

Arthritis Foundation
115 East 18th Street
New York, New York 10003

*Contact local chapter.

*Better Business Bureau of Metropolitan New York
257 Park Avenue South
New York, New York 10010

*Cystic Fibrosis Foundation
60 East 42nd Street
New York, New York 10017

*Epilepsy Foundation of America
4351 Garden City Drive
Landover, Maryland 20784

Family Service Association of America
44 East 23rd Street
New York, New York 10017

Group Against Smoker's Pollution (GASP)
9811 Lanham-Severn Road
College Park, Maryland 20740

*Mothers Against Drunk Drivers
5330 Primrose Drive, Suite 146
Fair Oaks, California 95628

National Coalition Against Domestic Violence
2401 Virginia Avenue, N.W.
Suite 306
Washington, D.C. 20037

National Council on Alcoholism, Inc.
Batterymarch Park
Quincy, Massachusetts 02269

*National Dairy Council
6300 River Road
Rosemont, Illinois 60018

National Fire Protection Association
470 Atlantic Avenue
Boston, Massachusetts 02210

*The National Foundation— March of Dimes
1275 Mamaroneck Avenue
White Plains, New York 10602

National Hemophilia Foundation
110 Greene Street
New York, New York 10012

National Hot Line on Youth Suicide
1-800-621-4000

National Institute of Mental Health—Mental Health Emergencies Section
5600 Fishers Lane
Rockville, Maryland 20852
301-443-4515

*National Kidney Foundation
2 Park Avenue
New York, New York 10016

*National Multiple Sclerosis Society
205 East 42nd Street
New York, New York 10017

National Safety Council
444 North Michigan Avenue
Chicago, Illinois 60611

National Society for the Prevention of Blindness, Inc.
79 Madison Avenue
New York, New York 10016

*Students Against Driving Drunk
W. T. Woodson High School
9525 Main Street
Fairfax, Virginia 22032

U.S. Consumer Product Safety Commission
Washington, D.C. 20207

U.S. Department of Agriculture
Washington, D.C. 20250

U.S. Department of Health and Human Services

Clearinghouse on Child Abuse and Neglect Information
P.O. Box 1182
Washington, D.C. 20013

Consumer Information Center
Pueblo, Colorado 81009

Food and Drug Administration
Office of Consumer Affairs, Public Inquiries
5600 Fishers Lane (HFE-88)
Rockville, Maryland 20857

National Clearinghouse for
  Alcohol Information
  P.O. Box 2345
  Rockville, Maryland 20852

National Clearinghouse for Drug
  Abuse Information
  P.O. Box 416
  Kensington, Maryland 20795

National Clearinghouse for
  Family Planning Information
  1700 North Moore Street
  Arlington, Virginia 22209

National Clearinghouse for
  Mental Health Information,
  Public Inquiries
  Room 15C-05
  5600 Fishers Lane
  Rockville, Maryland 20857

National Institute on Aging
  9000 Rockville Pike
  Bldg. 31, Room 5C-35
  Bethesda, Maryland 20892

Office on Smoking and Health
  Technical Information Center
  Park Bldg., Rm. 116
  5600 Fishers Lane
  Rockville, Maryland 20857

U.S. Department of Transportation
  National Highway Safety
  Administration
  Washington, D.C. 20590

Youth Suicide National Center
  1825 I Street, N.W., Suite 400
  Washington, D.C. 20006
  202-429-2016

Glossary

abortion Ending of a pregnancy.

acid rain Condition in which rainwater has an unusually high level of acid.

acquired immunity (ih MYOO nuh tee) Immunity the body builds up after having a disease.

ACTH Hormone produced by the pituitary gland. It causes the adrenal glands to produce their hormones.

active immunity Ability to form antibodies against pathogens before they can cause disease.

addiction Condition in which a drug user must either have regular doses of the drug or suffer painful and even fatal withdrawal symptoms.

adrenal (uh DREE nul) **glands** Two endocrine glands that lie above the kidneys. They produce adrenalin and cortisone.

adrenalin (uh DREN uh len) Hormone produced by the inner portion of the adrenal glands. It increases muscle tone in the skeletal muscles and slows down activity in the digestive tract.

advanced life support Emergency care that includes both basic life-support techniques and the use of medical equipment and therapy.

AIDS (acquired immune deficiency syndrome) (uh KWYRD ih MYOON dih FISH un see SIN drum) Infectious disease that destroys the body's natural ability to fight off infection.

alcoholism Illness characterized by regular, heavy drinking of alcoholic beverages.

alimentary (AL uh MEN tuh ree) **canal** Series of organs that move food through the body.

alveoli (al VEE uh LY); singular: **alveolus** (al VEE uh lus) Tiny air sacs that make up the greater part of the lungs.

Alzheimer's (ALZ hy murz) **disease** Disease that causes mental decline in the elderly.

amblyopia (AM blee OH pee uh) Dim vision.

amino (uh MEE noh) **acids** The building blocks from which protein is made; the end products of the digestion of proteins.

amniocentesis (AM nee oh sen TEE sis) Test performed before birth to find possible defects in the fetus by examining amniotic fluid.

amphetamine (am FET un MEEN) Synthetic drug that is used to treat depression, overweight, and excessive sleeping.

amylase (AM uh LAYS) Enzyme in saliva that breaks down starch into sugar.

analgesic (AN ul JEE zik) Drug used to relieve pain.

anemia (uh NE mee uh) Disease in which the blood lacks either hemoglobin or red blood cells or both.

anesthetic (AN es THET ik) Drug that causes insensitivity to pain.

angina pectoris (an JY nuh PEK tuh ris) Chest pain that occurs when the heart muscle does not get as much blood as it needs.

antibiotic (ANT ih by AH tik) Drug that can kill organisms that infect the body.

antidote (ANT ih DOHT) Substance that works against a poison.

antiseptic Any substance that prevents the growth of bacteria.

antisocial (AN ty SOH shul) Working against other people, groups, or society.

antitoxins (ANT ih TAHK sinz) Substances produced by body to destroy poisons produced by pathogens.

anxiety (ang ZY uh tee) Sense of uneasiness or stress about the future.

aorta (a OR tuh) Largest artery in the body. The aorta and its branches carry blood to the body.

aqueous humor (A kwee us HYOO mur) Fluid between the cornea and lens of the eye.

arteriosclerosis (ahr TIR ee oh skluh ROH sis) Condition in which walls of the arteries harden and become thick, making it hard for blood to circulate.

artery Blood vessel that carries blood away from the heart.

arthritis Condition in which joints become swollen and painful.

ascorbic (uh SKOR bik) **acid** Vitamin C.

association (uh soh see AY shun) **neurons** Neurons that connect sensory neurons to motor neurons.

asthma (AZ muh) Condition in which the muscles in the walls of the bronchi contract, making it hard to breathe.

astigmatism (uh STIG muh TIZ um) Faulty vision caused by irregularities in the curved surfaces of the cornea or lens.

atherosclerosis (ATH uh roh skluh RO sis) Condition in which coronary arteries are narrowed by deposits of fatty material on the inner walls.

atrium (A tree um) Upper chamber of each side of the heart.

audiometer (awd ee OM ih tur) Instrument used to measure a person's ability to hear.

autonomic (AW tuh NAHM ik) **nervous system** Nerves that control involuntary body action, such as heartbeat, breathing, and digestion.

axon (AKS on) Nerve fiber that carries impulse away from the cell.

barbiturate (bahr BICH ur it) Drug that is used to relieve anxiety, but can be dangerous if used without proper medical supervision.

basal metabolic rate Measure of the amount of energy a person uses per hour while resting.

basic life support Emergency care that uses the techniques of cardiopulmonary resuscitation (CPR) to restore heartbeat or breathing.

benign (bih NYN) **tumor** Tumor that is not harmful and does not spread.

bile duct Tube through which bile passes from the gall bladder to the duodenum. Bile helps the body digest fats.

biofeedback (BY oh FEED bak) Medical procedure in which the mind is trained to monitor certain physical responses of the body.

biological (BY oh LOJ ih kul) **age** Degree of change in a person as body grows older.

biopsy (BY AHP see) Method of cancer detection in which body tissue is removed and examined under a microscope.

blepharitis (BLEF uh RY tis) Swelling of the eyelid.

blood alcohol concentration (BAC) Amount of alcohol in a person's blood.

blood pressure Pressure of the blood against the walls of the arteries. **Systolic** (sis TAH lik) **pressure** is the blood pressure at the time of the heartbeat (systole). **Diastolic** (DY uh STAH lik) **pressure** is the blood pressure between heartbeats (diastole).

bolus (BOH lus) "Ball" of food that has been chewed and is ready to be swallowed.

bone marrow Soft tissue found in the hollow area inside bones.

botulinum (BAHCH uh LY num) Bacterium that causes **botulism,** a severe form of food poisoning.

bronchi (BRAHN KY); singular: **bronchus** (BRAHN kus) Two large tubes that lead from the trachea to the lungs.

bronchitis (brahn KY tis) Swelling of the bronchi, usually caused by viral infection.

caffeine Mildly stimulating drug contained in tea, coffee, cocoa, chocolate, and cola drinks.

calcium Mineral that is needed for proper development of bones and teeth.

calculus (KAL kyuh lus) Hard, limelike layer that forms on the teeth when plaque is not removed.

calories Units in which energy is measured. Calories are used to measure the energy value of foods.

cancer Uncontrolled and irregular growth of abnormal cells.

capillary (KAP uh LEH ree) Tiny blood vessel. Capillaries connect arteries to veins.

carbohydrate (KAHR boh HY DRAYT) Nutrient that is the main source of energy for the body. Sugars and starches are carbohydrates.

carcinogen (kahr SIN uh jen) Substance that causes cancer.

carcinogenic (kahr SIN uh JEN ik) Able to cause cancer.

cardiac arrest Absence of a heartbeat or pulse.

cardiac muscle Heart muscle.

cardiopulmonary resuscitation (KAHR dee oh PUL muh ner ee ree SUSS uh TA shun) Lifesaving technique that combines artificial respiration and artificial circulation; also called CPR.

cartilage (KAHR tuh lij) Tough connective tissue that is softer than bone.

cataract (KAT uh RAKT) Cloudiness of an eye lens causing blurred vision.

cell differentiation (dif ur en shee AY shun) Process by which dividing cells in a growing organism follow shape patterns to reflect the jobs they will do.

central loss Hearing disorder caused by damage to the auditory nerve that leads from the cochlea to the brain or by damage to the brain center for hearing.

central nervous system Brain and spinal cord.

cerebellum (SER uh BEL um) "Little brain," located beneath the back part of the cerebrum. Its activities are below the level of consciousness.

cerebrum (suh REE brum) Large, upper part of the brain considered center of conscious mental activity.

cervix (SUR viks) Neck of the uterus.

chancre (SHANK ur) Painless open sore on the genital organs that occurs during the primary stage of syphilis.

charley horse Injury to the front part of the thigh in which the muscle, blood vessels, nerves, and other soft tissues are damaged.

chemotherapy (KEE moh THER uh pee) Treatment of disease, such as cancer, with chemicals.

chewing tobacco A form of ground tobacco that is placed between the cheek and gum.

child abuse Emotional and physical abuse of a child by adults.

cholesterol (kuh LES tur ol) A fatty substance produced by the body that aids in the production of hormones and cell membranes.

chromosomes (KROH muh SOHMZ) Threadlike bodies found in the nuclei of cells. They contain the substances that pass along inherited characteristics.

chyme (KYM) Thin, soupy liquid that food becomes in the stomach when it mixes with gastric juices.

ciliary (SIL ee EHR ee) **muscle** Muscle in the eye that helps to change shape of the lens in order to focus.

cocaine Dangerous drug that is both a stimulant and a painkiller.

cochlea (KOHK lee uh) Organ of the inner ear that is filled with liquid and transmits impulses from the middle ear to the brain.

codeine (KOH DEEN) Narcotic made from opium that is used for relief of pain and congestion, particularly in cough medicines.

coma (KOH muh) State of unconsciousness.

communicable (kuh MYOO nih kuh bul) **disease** Disease that spreads when conditions are favorable for bacteria and viruses to grow.

conception Uniting of an ovum and a sperm to form a zygote.

conditioning Planned program of exercise, rest, and eating that is followed in order to reach and stay in top physical condition.

conductive loss Hearing disorder caused by any block to the passage of sound waves through the outer or middle ear.

congenital (kahn JEN uh tul) **heart disease** Heart defect present at birth.

conjunctivitis (kun JUNK ti VY tis) Infection that causes swelling, redness, and itchiness of the mucous membrane covering the front part of the eyeball and the inside surface of the eyelid.

contraception Prevention of conception. Contraception is one form of **birth control.**

contraceptives Medications and devices that prevent conception.

convulsion Strong attack of involuntary muscle contractions.

cornea (KOR nee uh)   Clear covering over the front part of the eyeball through which light enters the eye.

coronary arteries   Vessels that carry blood to the heart muscle.

cortisone (KOR tuh ZOHN)   Secretion from the outer part of the adrenal glands that helps the body react to stress.

CPR   See **cardiopulmonary resuscitation.**

cranium (KRAY nee um)   Eight flat bones of the head excluding the bones of the face and the lower jaw.

cretinism (KREE tun IZ um)   Condition that occurs when the body does not produce enough thyroxin; can lead to physical and mental retardation.

cystic fibrosis (SISS tik fy BROH sis)   Inherited disease that affects mucous and sweat glands of children.

Daily Food Guide   Chart recommended by the U.S. Department of Agriculture for planning nutritious meals and snacks. It classifies foods into groups based on the nutrients they contain.

decalcification (dee KAL suh fuh KAY shun)   Loss of calcium, which causes bones to weaken.

decibel (DESS uh BEL)   Unit for measuring the loudness of sound.

defense mechanisms   Ways of behaving that help a person maintain a sense of security when experiencing certain kinds of emotional conflict.

dendrite (DEN dryt)   Impulses picked up by nerve fibers.

dental caries (KAR eez)   Tooth decay.

dentin (DEN tin)   Bone tissue inside teeth.

depressant   Drug that causes the activity of certain areas of the brain and spinal cord to slow down.

dermatitis (DER muh TY tis)   Inflammation of the skin.

dermis (DER mis)   Under layer of the skin.

detoxification (dee TAHKS uh fuh KAY shun)   Removal of a possible poison, such as alcohol, from the body.

diabetes (DY uh BEE teez) **mellitus**   Disease in which the body cannot use sugar properly.

diaphragm (DY uh FRAM)   Wall of muscle and connective tissue that separates the chest cavity from the abdominal cavity.

diastole (dy ASS tuh lee)   Period of rest or relaxation of the heart.

diphtheria (dif THIR ee uh)   Serious infectious illness caused by bacteria. The main symptoms are sore throat and difficulty in breathing and swallowing.

diplopia (di PLOH pee uh)   Double vision.

dislocation   Displacement of one or both bones at a joint.

DNA   Abbreviation for deoxyribonucleic acid, a molecule that is basic in cell production and heredity.

dominant gene (JEEN)   Gene that determines which trait will appear in someone.

dominant inheritance   Process of receiving at least one dominant gene for a trait from one parent.

Down's syndrome   Inherited disease in which a child receives 47 chromosomes instead of 46; also called trisomy 21.

ductless glands   See **endocrine glands.**

duodenum (DOO uh DEE num)   First section of the small intestine. Most of the digestive process occurs in the duodenum.

eardrum   Membrane that separates the outer ear from the middle ear.

elderly abuse   Emotional or physical abuse of the elderly by younger people.

embryo (EM bree OH)   In human reproduction, the cluster of dividing cells during the first two months of development in the uterus.

emergency medical services (EMS) system   System set up within a local community to provide fast action when emergencies take place.

emphysema (EM fuh ZEE muh)   Condition of the lungs in which the alveoli become enlarged and inflexible, making it very hard for a person to breathe.

endocrine (EN duh krin) **glands**   Glands that produce hormones and release them directly into the bloodstream; also called glands of internal secretion or ductless glands.

endometrium (EN doh MEE tree um)   Lining of the uterus, shed in menstruation.

enriched   Having added vitamins and minerals.

enuresis (EN yoo REE sis)   Bedwetting, or the involuntary discharge of urine.

enzymes (EN ZYMZ)   Chemicals in digestive juices that break down food into simpler substances so that they can be absorbed into the bloodstream.

epidermis (EP uh DER mis)   Protective outer layer of the skin.

epididymis (EP uh DID uh mis)   Structure in the male connecting the testis with the vas deferens.

epiglottis (ep ih GLOT tis)   Thin piece of cartilage that covers the opening to the trachea.

epilepsy (EP uh LEP see)   Nervous disorder that may cause a person to lose consciousness briefly or to go into convulsions.

equilibrium   Balance.

esophagus (ih SAHF uh gus)   Tube that connects the mouth to the stomach.

essential amino acid   One of the nine amino acids that cannot be produced by the human body and must be obtained in food.

estrogen (ESS truh jin)   Hormone that stimulates development of secondary sex characteristics in females.

eustachian (yoo STAY shun) **tube**   Tube that connects the middle ear with the back of the nose and throat.

expiration   Process of forcing air out of the lungs.

extended nuclear (eks TEN did NOO klee ur) **family**   Family unit formed through divorce consisting of more than two parents, stepbrothers, stepsisters, and so forth.

external auditory canal (eks TURN ul AW dih toh ree kuh NAL)   S-shaped channel through which sound passes from outer ear into middle ear.

fallopian (ful LOH pee un) **tubes**   Two tubes in the human female through which ova pass from the ovaries to the uterus.

family therapy   Counseling process through which problems among members of a family are resolved.

FAS (fetal alcohol syndrome) (FEE tul, SIN drum)   Birth defects caused by a pregnant mother's use of alcohol.

fasciculus (fah SIK yuh lus)   Bundle of connected muscle fibers. A single muscle is made up of many fasciculi.

fat   Nutrient in food that provides energy and helps the body absorb vitamins.

FDA   The Food and Drug Administration, a U.S. government agency that makes sure that food and drug products meet safety and health standards.

fetus (FEE tus)   In human reproduction, the developing individual after the second month in the uterus.

fiber   Rough part of plant foods—the cell walls of leaves, fruits, seeds, bulbs, and flowers. Also known as roughage.

fight response   Positive, constructive use of the energy created by stress.

flatus (FLAY tus)   Gas produced in the stomach or intestine.

flight response   Response to stress that consists of destructive action or avoidance.

fluoride (FLOOR EYED)   Salt of fluorine that is helpful in preventing tooth decay, often added to drinking water.

follicle (FOL ih kul)   Tissue surrounding a hair.

fracture   Break in a bone.

frostbite   Injury to body tissues caused by extreme cold.

fungus (FUNG gus)   Form of plant life that lives best in dark, warm, moist areas.

gamma rays   Most dangerous type of radiation. Gamma rays can penetrate body tissues.

gastric juices   Liquids secreted by glands in the stomach; mix with food and aid in digestion.

genes   Small units of DNA in chromosomes that pass inherited characteristics from parent to child.

genetic code   Order in which certain chemical compounds are arranged in DNA molecules; the "instructions" that tell the cells of the body what to do.

genital herpes (JEN uh tul HUR peez)   Viral infection in the genital area.

genitals   The external sexual organs.

gerontologist (jer un TOL uh jist)   Person who studies the elderly.

gingivitis (JIN juh VY tis)   Condition in which the gums become dark red, soft and swollen, and bleed easily.

glaucoma (glau KOH muh)   Disease of the eye in which fluid is trapped between the cornea and the iris.

gonads (GOH NADZ)   Sex glands; the organs that produce ova or sperm and sex hormones. In females, the gonads are the ovaries. In males, the gonads are the testes.

gonorrhea (GAHN uh REE uh)   Common sexually transmitted disease caused by rod-shaped bacteria called gonococci.

grief (GREEF)   Strong reaction to the loss of someone cared deeply about.

group therapy (THAIR uh pee)   Psychotherapy practiced on a group of individuals with similar problems.

halitosis (HAL uh TOH sis)   Bad breath.

hallucinogen (huh LOO sin uh jen)   Drug that causes visions and distortions of the other senses.

hashish   Powerful resin produced in the tops of the marijuana plant.

HDL (high-density lipoprotein) (lip oh PROH teen)   Proteins that travel through the blood removing cholesterol and fatty deposits.

heart attack   Condition that occurs when the heart muscle does not receive enough blood. Usually a person feels severe chest pain with nausea and sweating.

heart murmur   Blowing or swishing noise caused by blood passing through a defective heart valve.

heat exhaustion   Illness that occurs when the body loses large amounts of water and salt through sweating after exposure to heat.

Heimlich maneuver (HYM lik muh NOO vur)   Technique developed to save victim of choking.

hemoglobin (HEE muh GLOH bin)   Substance in red blood cells that carries oxygen from the lungs to all parts of the body.

hemophilia (HEE muh FIL ee uh)   Condition in which the blood clots slowly or not at all.

hemorrhage (HEM uh rij)   Very heavy bleeding.

hepatitis (HEP uh TY tis)   Condition in which the liver becomes swollen and inflamed.

hernia (HER nee uh)   Condition that occurs when any organ or part of an organ is pushed through the wall around it; also called a rupture.

heroin   Dangerous, habit-forming narcotic drug made from opium.

heterosexual (HET uh roh SEK shoo wal)   Attracted to members of the other sex.

HMO (health maintenance organization)   A low-cost approach to health insurance where members visit approved clinics for medical treatment.

holistic (ho LIS tik)   Medicine that treats the body, mind, and spirit as a "whole."

homosexual (HOH muh SEK shoo wal)   Attracted to members of one's own sex.

hormone   Chemical produced by the endocrine glands and carried in the bloodstream. Hormones regulate the body's many systems so that they work together.

hospice (HOS pis)   Care facility for the terminally ill; a program of care for such individuals.

hydrocephalic (HY droh suh FAL ik)   Having fluid trapped inside the brain, which causes the brain to enlarge and push against the skull.

hyperopia (HY puh ROH pee uh)   Farsightedness; difficulty in seeing things that are close because the eyeball is too short from front to back.

hypertension (HY pur TEN shun)   Chronic high blood pressure.

hyperthermia (HY pur THUR mee uh)   Use of heat to kill cancer cells.

hyperventilation (HY pur VEN tuh LAY shun)
Breathing in too much oxygen, causing dizziness or
fainting.

hypothalamus (HY poh THAL uh mus)   Part
of the brain located above the pituitary gland. Some
scientists believe the hypothalamus helps the pituitary
gland regulate body temperature.

immunization (IM yuh nuh ZAY shun)   Injecting
a substance into the body that helps it resist a disease.

impetigo (IM puh TEE goh)   Skin infection caused by
bacteria.

incubation (ING kyuh BAY shun) **period**   Time
between the entrance of disease organisms into the
body and the appearance of symptoms.

incus (ING kus)   Tiny bone between the malleus and
stapes in the middle ear. It is shaped like an anvil and
helps amplify sound waves as they travel from eardrum to inner ear.

influenza (IN floo EN zuh)   Highly contagious respiratory disease caused by a virus.

inspiration   Taking air into the lungs.

insulin (IN suh lin)   Hormone secreted by the islets of
Langerhans that enables sugar to enter the body cells
to be used for energy.

involuntary muscles   Muscles that are not under a
person's conscious control, such as stomach and heart
muscles.

involuntary smoking   Unwilling inhalation of smoke
from someone else's burning cigarette, cigar, or pipe.

iodine (EYE uh DYN)   Mineral needed for proper
working of the thyroid gland.

iris (EYE ris)   Round, colored muscle behind the cornea that controls the amount of light entering the eye.

iron   Mineral that is important for proper muscle contraction. It is found in hemoglobin.

iron-deficiency anemia   Condition in which a person
feels tired because not enough iron is being taken
into the body.

islets of Langerhans (LAHN gur HAHNZ)   Tiny
clusters of gland tissue in the pancreas that produce
the hormone insulin.

joint   Place where two or more bones are connected.

lactase (LAK tayz)   Enzyme produced by the body to
break down milk sugar.

lactic acid   Chemical that forms in muscles as they
contract.

lacto-ovo-vegetarian (LAK toh OH voh vej uh TER ee
un)   Person who eats no meat, but does include eggs
and milk in the diet.

lactose (LAK tohs)   Milk sugar found in milk products.

lacto-vegetarian (LAK toh vej un TER ee un)   Person
who eats no meats or eggs, but does include milk,
cheese, and butter in the diet.

larynx (LAR inks)   Organ in the upper part of the
respiratory tract that contains the vocal cords. Also
called the voice box or Adam's apple.

LDL (low-density lipoprotein) (lip oh PROH teen)
Protein that travels through blood and deposits cholesterol along artery walls.

lens   Oval, clear structure behind the pupil of the eye
that bends light rays so that they focus on the retina.

lethal gene   Gene that causes the death of the organism that inherits it.

leukemia (loo KEE mee uh)   Cancer in which there is
a great increase in the number of white blood cells
(leukocytes).

leukocytes (LOO kuh SYTS)   White blood cells. Leukocytes surround and eat organisms that enter the
body.

ligament (LIG uh munt)   Tissue that connects two or
more bones to each other at a joint.

LSD   Lysergic acid diethylamide, a synthetic drug that
causes unpredictable changes in sensations.

lymph (LIMF)   Clear fluid that washes all the cells of
the body.

lymph nodes (LIMPF NOHDZ)   Small structures along
the lymph vessels that make some white blood cells
and that kill pathogens.

M.A.D.D. (Mothers Against Drunk Drivers)
Organization to combat the threat of drunk drivers
to young people.

mainstream smoke   Smoke inhaled and exhaled by a
smoker.

malignant melanoma (muh LIG nunt   MEL uh NOH
muh)   Rare type of skin cancer.

malignant tumor   Tumor that is made up of abnormal
cells and grows in an irregular pattern; a cancer.

malleus (MAL ee us)   Tiny hammer-shaped bone in
the middle ear that helps amplify sound waves as they
travel from eardrum to inner ear.

malocclusion (MAL uh KLOO zhun)   Failure
of the teeth to bite together properly due to irregular
spacing or to the shape of the jaw.

marijuana   Plant whose dried tops and leaves produce
changes in mood and sense perceptions when smoked
or eaten.

measles   Serious childhood disease that begins with a
cough, fever, and red rash.

Medicaid   Program of health insurance provided by
the U.S. government to people who cannot afford private health insurance.

Medicare   A program of health insurance provided by
the U.S. government to persons over 65 years of age.

medulla oblongata (muh DUL uh   ob lon GOT uh)
Lowest part of the brain; regulates breathing, heart
action, and blood circulation.

melanin (MEL uh nin)   Pigment that gives color to the
hair, skin, and eyes.

melanoma (mel uh NOH muh)   Tumor of the skin containing dark pigment.

meningitis (MEN in JY tis)   Inflammation of the
membranes that surround the brain and spinal cord;
usually caused by a viral or bacterial infection.

menopause (MEN uh PAWZ)   In the female, the stage
of life when the ovaries stop producing ova, usually
around age 50.

menstruation (MEN stroo AY shun) Discharge of the endometrium from the uterus.

metabolism (muh TAB uh LIZ um) Chemical change that goes on in cells to support life.

metastasis (muh TAS tuh sis) Spreading of a disease, such as cancer, to another part of the body.

methadone (METH uh DOHN) Synthetic drug used as a painkiller and as a heroin substitute.

microcephalic (MY kroh suh FAL ik) Having a head much smaller than normal size.

midbrain Area of brain that, with pons, controls eye and facial movement and hearing.

minerals Nutrients needed to control the body's chemical processes.

miscarriage Birth of a fetus before it has developed enough to live outside the uterus.

mononucleosis (MAH noh NOO klee oh sis) Common viral infection among young adults.

morphine (MOR FEEN) Narcotic drug made from opium that is used primarily for the relief of pain.

motor neurons Neurons that transfer impulses from the brain to muscles and glands.

multifactorial inheritance (mul tee fak TOR ee ul in HEH rih tuns) Genetic traits influenced by many factors.

multi-infarct dementia (MUL tee IN farkt dih MEN shuh) Series of minor strokes that causes damage to the brain.

multiple sclerosis (skluh ROH sis) Disease in which the covering surrounding the nerves is destroyed.

mumps Contagious disease that produces fever and painful swollen glands under the jawbone.

muscle lameness Tearing of tiny muscle fibers that occurs when muscles are overused.

mutation Change in a gene.

myoglobin (MY uh GLOH bin) Red-colored protein that supplies oxygen to muscle cells and is very much like hemoglobin.

myopia (my OH pee uh) Nearsightedness; difficulty in seeing things that are far away because the eyeball is too long from front to back.

narcotic (nahr KAH tik) Any of a group of drugs that relieve pain and bring on sleep.

nerve loss Hearing disorder caused by damage to the special sensory cells in the cochlea.

neurosis (noo ROH sis) Form of mental illness characterized by poor development of skills needed to meet basic emotional needs.

niacin (NY uh sin) Important B vitamin that is needed for healthy skin and for proper functioning of the nervous and digestive systems.

nicotine (NIK uh TEEN) Powerful, colorless poison in tobacco smoke.

nitrites (NY TRYTS) Chemical preservatives added to some foods to prevent growth of deadly botulinum.

nocturnal emission (nahk TURN ul ee MISH un) Normal, involuntary discharge of semen during sleep; also called a wet dream.

nutrients Substances in food that provide energy, build and repair cells, and regulate body processes.

OAA (Older Americans Act) Act under which states receive funds to be used by agencies to help the aging.

open dating Practice by which food manufacturers stamp packages with dates that help the consumer identify fresh foods.

optic (AHP tik) **nerve** Nerve that carries impulses from the retina to the brain.

orthodontics (OR thuh DAHN tiks) Treatment of malocclusion.

osteoporosis (OS tee oh puh ROH sis) Condition in which the bones become gradually weak and brittle.

OTC drugs Over-the-counter drugs; drugs that can be bought without a doctor's prescription.

otosclerosis (OH toh sklih RO sis) Condition in which too much bone forms where the stapes connects to the inner ear.

ovaries (OH vuh reez) Two organs in the lower part of the abdomen in the female. They produce ova (eggs) and hormones that cause the female secondary sexual characteristics to develop.

ovulation (ov yuh LAY shun) Monthly release, ejection, and movement of a mature ovum from the ovary.

ovum (OH vum); plural: **ova** (OH vah) Female reproductive cell made in the ovaries.

oxidation (oks uh DAY shun) Process of producing energy from food with the help of oxygen.

ozone (OH ZOHN) Very active form of oxygen produced by the action of sunlight on impurities in the atmosphere.

papillae (puh PIL EE) Tiny projections on the tongue that contain taste receptors and help the tongue "hold onto" food.

paralysis Inability to move all or some parts of the body.

parathyroid (PAR uh THY ROID) **glands** Small endocrine glands in the neck. Their secretions control the body's use of calcium and phosphorus.

parent abuse Physical and emotional abuse of parents by their children.

particulates (par TIK yuh lits) Tiny, harmful particles of dust and ash, especially those given off by burning fuels.

passive immunity Resistance to disease that lasts only a short time.

pathogen (PATH uh jin) Disease-causing microorganism.

pediculosis (puh dik yoo LOH sis) Skin disorder caused by lice.

penis (PEE nis) Reproductive organ of the male.

periodontal (PER ee oh DAHNT ul) **membrane** Tissue that surrounds each tooth in the gum and holds it in place.

peripheral (puh RIF uh rul) **nervous system** Nerves that carry messages to the brain and spinal cord from other parts of the body.

peristaltic (PER uh STAWL tik) **waves** Series of contractions of the muscles making up the esophagus that push food down to the stomach.

pertussis (pur TUSS is)   Highly contagious disease marked by very bad coughing spells. Also called whooping cough.

phosphorus (FAHS fuh rus)   Mineral needed for proper development of bones and teeth.

pigment   Matter in the cells of the epidermis that produces skin coloring.

pineal (PY nee ul) **gland**   Endocrine gland located in the center of the brain that produces substances that help to regulate the body's daily rhythms.

pituitary (pi TYOO uh TER ee) **gland**   Endocrine gland located deep inside the brain that regulates growth and influences the other endocrine glands.

placebo (plah SEE boh) **effect**   Improvement in patients who have taken an inactive substance that is believed to have a medicine in it.

placenta (pluh SEN tuh)   Organ by which the fetus is attached to the uterus and through which it is nourished.

plaque (PLAK)   Sticky, colorless layer of bacteria that constantly forms on the teeth.

plasma (PLAZ muh)   Pale yellow liquid part of the blood as distinguished from the blood cells.

platelet (PLATE lit)   Cell in the blood that helps clots to form.

pleura (PLOOR uh)   Smooth, moist membranes that cover the lungs and the inside of the chest cavity.

pleurisy (PLOOR uh see)   Condition in which the pleura become rough and sticky and make breathing difficult and painful.

plug tobacco   Chewing tobacco sold in block form.

PMS (premenstrual syndrome) (pree MEN stru ul SIN drum)   State of physical discomfort preceding menstrual period in some women.

pneumonia (noo MOH nyuh)   Inflammation of the lungs.

poliomyelitis (PO lee oh MY uh LY tis)   Contagious viral disease that can cause nerve damage and result in permanent paralysis of muscles.

polyunsaturated (polee un SATCH uh ray tud) **fats**   Group of nonbonding fat molecules found in corn oil, sunflower oil, and cottonseed oil.

pons (PONZ)   Area of brain that, with the midbrain, controls eye and facial movements and hearing.

postpolio syndrome (POHST pol ee oh SIN drum)   Disease in which symptoms of poliomyelitis reappear in former victims of the disease.

prenatal care   Doctor's care of a pregnant woman.

primary care   Treatment that is given by a doctor at a clinic, an emergency room, or a doctor's office.

progesterone (proh JES tuh rohn)   Hormone responsible for beginning of menstruation.

prophylaxis (PROH fuh LAK sis)   Thorough cleaning of the teeth by a dentist or a dental hygienist.

protein   Nutrient needed for building and replacing cells.

protein complementarity   Combining foods to get the most protein value from them.

psychoactive (SY koh AK tiv) **drug**   Drug used to change a person's mood or behavior.

psychoanalysis (SY koh un NAL uh sis)   Method of treating emotional and mental disorders in which patients are made aware of their psychological makeup.

psychosis (sy KOH sis)   Mental disorder in which a person is out of touch with reality part of the time.

psychosomatic (SY koh suh MA tik) **disorder**   Form of mental illness in which a real physical illness or symptom occurs as a result of an emotional disturbance.

psychotherapy (SY koh THER uh pee)   Treatment of mental and emotional disturbances.

puberty (PYOO bur tee)   Stage of life when a person's reproductive system begins to work.

pulled muscle   Condition where a large muscle bundle or tendon is torn or separated from the bone.

pulmonary (PUL muh ner ee) **artery**   Blood vessel that carries blood from the heart to the lungs.

pulmonary vein   Blood vessel that carries blood from the lungs to the heart.

pulp cavity   Space in the dentin of the tooth that holds nerves, lymph vessels, and blood vessels.

pupil   Round opening of the eye through which light enters.

radiation   Invisible form of energy that comes from the splitting of atoms.

radioactive substances   Materials that give off radiation.

rape   Forced sexual intercourse.

recessive (ri SESS iv) **gene**   Gene or trait that has no effect when a dominant gene is present.

recessive inheritance   Process of receiving two recessive genes for a trait, one from each parent.

red blood cells   Oxygen carriers in blood.

reflex   Automatic muscle action directed by the spinal cord rather than by the brain.

reflex (REE flex) **arc**   Pathway from the senses to the spinal cord and back.

resistance   Body's ability to fight infection.

respiration   Exchange of oxygen and carbon dioxide; includes both outer and inner respiration.

respiratory center   Area of the brain that controls breathing.

retina (RET in uh)   Lining of the back of the eyeball on which light rays focus.

Rh factor   Substance in red blood cells that becomes important during transfusions or pregnancy.

rheumatic (roo MA tik) **fever**   Infectious disease that affects the joints and often damages the heart.

rheumatic heart disease   Lifelong damage that results from rheumatic fever.

riboflavin (RY buh FLAY vin)   Important B vitamin needed for healthy skin and for proper functioning of the nervous and digestive systems.

ringworm   Common fungal infection that causes itching and sores of the scalp.

root (of tooth)   Part of the tooth that is set within the gum and jawbone.

rubella (roo BEL uh)   Mild form of measles that is dangerous to the fetus of an infected pregnant woman. Also called German measles or three-day measles.

S.A.D.D. (Students Against Driving Drunk)
Organization whose aim it is to eliminate alcohol-related traffic deaths among young people.

salivary (SAL uh VER ee) **glands** Three pairs of glands that secrete saliva, the liquid that pours into the mouth to moisten and soften food.

saturated (SATCH uh RAY tud) **fats** Solid fats found in meat, butter, coconut oil, and palm oil.

scabies (SKAY bees) Infection of the skin caused by mites.

sclera (SKLER uh) Tough, white part of the eye that gives the eye its shape.

scrotum (SKROH tum) Pouch that holds the testes.

sebum (SEE bum) Oily secretion of the skin.

secondary care Treatment that is given by specialists at a private or community hospital.

secondary sexual characteristics Different characteristics that develop at puberty in the two sexes.

self-care Act of using common sense to prevent illness and injury and to avoid harming one's health.

semen (SEE mun) Fluid containing sperm that is made and discharged by the male reproductive organs.

semicircular (SEM ih SUR kyuh lur) **canals** Three small tubes in the inner ear that control the sense of balance.

senility (sih NIL uh tee) Memory disease of the elderly.

sensory neurons (SEN suh ree NOOR onz) Neurons that transfer impulses from the sense organs to the spinal cord or brain.

sex-linked inheritance Process of receiving traits carried on the sex chromosomes.

sexuality Condition of being male or female; the sum of the feelings, thoughts, behavior, and structure that make up males and females.

sexually transmitted disease Communicable disease spread from an infected person to others through sexual contact; also called an STD.

shinsplints Pain in the lower leg in front of the shin, usually caused by running on a hard surface.

shock Condition that often follows an injury in which a person's blood is not circulating properly.

sickle-cell anemia Disease caused by an inherited gene; affects the shape of red blood cells and their ability to carry oxygen.

sickle-cell trait Condition in which a person carries one gene for sickle-cell anemia but does not suffer from the disease itself.

sidestream smoke Smoke that goes directly into the air from the burning end of a cigarette, cigar, or pipe.

specialist Doctor who has spent years studying one system of the human body to learn the most advanced skills in diagnosis and treatment for that field.

speed Ability to move the whole body or parts of the body quickly from one place to another.

sperm Male reproductive cell.

sphygmomanometer (SFIG moh muh NAHM uh tur) Instrument used to measure blood pressure.

spinal cord Part of the nervous system contained within the backbone.

spirochetes (SPY ruh KEETS) Spiral-shaped bacteria that cause syphilis.

spouse abuse Emotional or physical abuse by a husband or wife directed at the other.

sprain Painful injury to ligaments, tendons, or muscles near a joint.

stapes (STAY PEEZ) Tiny, stirrup-shaped bone in the ear that helps amplify sound waves as they travel from the eardrum to the inner ear.

STD See **sexually transmitted disease**.

steroids (STEER oydz) Anti-inflammatory drug abused by some athletes to stimulate muscle bulk.

stethoscope (STETH uh SKOHP) Instrument used to listen to the sounds made by the heart and lungs.

stimulant Drug that speeds up the body's processes.

strabismus (struh BIZ mus) Abnormality of the eyes in which the two eyes do not focus on the same point.

stress Effect on the human body of physical and mental demands and pressures.

stressor Something that makes a demand on the body.

stroke Sudden blocking of blood flow to an area of the brain, usually caused by the formation of a blood clot in a small blood vessel.

sty Infection of glands along the edge of the eyelid.

sutures (SOO churz) Spaces between bones in the skull.

synovial (su NOH vee ul) **fluid** Fluid surrounding the ends of bones that keeps the joints moistened so bones can move freely.

syphilis (SIF uh lis) Sexually transmitted disease caused by spirochetes.

systole (SIS tuh lee) Contraction of the heart.

Tay-Sachs (TAY SAKS) Fatal brain damage caused by a certain inherited gene found mostly in infants of East European Jewish ancestry.

temperature inversion Unusual situation in which warm air high above the earth's surface traps cool air closer to the ground and prevents it from rising.

tendon Tissue that joins muscles to bones.

terminally (TER muh nuh ly) **ill** In the final stages of a life-ending disease.

tertiary (TUR shee EHR ee) **care** Treatment that is given by specialists at a university hospital.

testes (TES TEEZ); singular: **testis** (TES tis) Two glands in a pouch lying outside the abdomen in the male. They produce sperm and make hormones that influence the development of the male secondary sexual characteristics.

testosterone (tes TAHS tuh ROHN) Hormone that stimulates the development of secondary sexual characteristics in males.

tetanus (TET in us) Disease usually caused by bacteria that enter the body through a break in the skin.

therapist Person trained in methods of helping a mentally ill person to recover.

thermal (THUR mul) **pollution** Contamination of water by heat.

thiamine (THY uh min)   Important B vitamin that is needed by the nerves, the muscles, and the digestive system.

throat culture   Test used to detect infection. A sterile cotton swab is rubbed on the throat and then onto a special plate to see what bacteria are present.

thymus (THY mus) **gland**   Endocrine gland located in the upper chest that is believed to produce substances that help fight infection.

thyroid (THY roid) **gland**   Endocrine gland in the neck that influences metabolism.

thyroid-stimulating hormone   Hormone produced by the pituitary gland that causes the thyroid to produce its hormone.

thyroxine (thy RAHK SEEN)   Hormone produced by the thyroid gland.

tobacco tar   Black, sticky substance obtained from the burning of tobacco.

tolerance   Ability of the body to take in a drug without feeling the expected effects.

tomographic (TOME uh GRAF ik) **scanners**   X-ray machines that take pictures of the inside of the body without producing shadows.

tourniquet (TOOR nih kit)   Band of cloth or other material pulled tightly around an arm or a leg to stop bleeding.

toxic (TAHK sik) **shock syndrome (TSS)**   Life-threatening disease probably caused by toxins released by bacterium on the skin.

toxic (TAHK sik) **wastes**   Waste products produced by industry.

toxin (TAHK sin)   Poisonous substance.

toxoid (TAHK soid)   Type of vaccine made from poisonous waste products of disease-causing microorganisms.

trachea (TRAY kee uh)   Tube in the upper part of the chest; the windpipe.

tranquilizer   Drug that is used to calm a person's emotions without interfering with alertness.

trick riding   Unsafe driving practice sometimes used by motorcyclists in which the driver carries out stunts for pleasure.

tumor   Group of cells forming a mass or lump.

umbilical (UM BIL ih kul) **cord**   The cord that connects the fetus to the placenta, passing oxygen, water, and other nutrients from the mother to the fetus.

umbilicus (UM bu LY kus)   Navel; the small depression in the abdomen where the umbilical cord was attached to the fetus.

unit pricing   Practice by which food merchants post signs that tell the cost of foods per unit of weight.

U.S. RDA   U.S. Recommended Daily Allowance, a list that tells the amount of nutrients and calories needed daily by most people in the United States.

uterus (YOO tuh rus)   Organ in the female in which the fetus develops; womb.

uvula (YOO vyuh luh)   Small, fleshy organ at the back of the roof of the mouth that helps to close off the nasal opening when food is swallowed.

vaccine (vak SEEN)   Substance used to increase the body's immunity to a certain disease.

vagina (vuh JY nuh)   Tube that connects the uterus to the outside of the body.

vas deferens (VAS DEF uh runz)   Two sperm ducts in the male that lead from the epididymis to the urethra.

vegetarian   Person who does not eat meat.

vein   Vessel that carries blood to the heart.

ventricle (VEN tri kul)   Lower chamber of each side of the heart.

vesicle (VES ih kul)   Small, blisterlike elevation on the skin that is a symptom of genital herpes.

vestibule   Structure between the cochlea and semicircular canals in the inner ear that helps one know about the position of the head in relation to gravity.

villi (VIL EYE); singular: **villus** (VIL us)   Tiny, fingerlike projections in the inner lining of the small intestine that contain blood vessels for absorption of nutrients into the blood and lymph vessels.

vitamins   Nutrients that help regulate body processes.

vitreous (VIT tree us) **humor**   Jellylike substance responsible for maintaining eyeball's round shape.

voluntary muscles   Muscles that can be purposely controlled. These muscles are attached to bones and are also called skeletal muscles or striated muscles.

withdrawal symptoms   Undesirable side effects that occur when an individual stops taking certain drugs; include trembling, hallucinations, nausea, and vomiting.

World Health Organization (WHO)   Special agency of the United Nations that works to improve the physical and mental health of all the world's people.

Index

Picture Credits

Title Page: Lawrence Migdale

Table of Contents: vi: Ken Lax/The Stock Shop; vii: Michel Heron; viii: Russell Dian; ix: Chris Jones/The Stock Market

Unit Openers: Unit 1: Peter Frank/Click, Chicago; Unit 2: Mieke Maas/The Image Bank; Unit 3: William Hubbell/Woodfin Camp; Unit 4: Howard Sochurek/Woodfin Camp; Unit 5: Howard Sochurek/Woodfin Camp; Unit 6: Gary Milburn/Tom Stack & Associates; Unit 7: (*left to right*) Manfred Kage/Peter Arnold, Inc., Evelyn Tronca/Tom Stack & Associates, Manfred Kage/Peter Arnold, Inc., Centers for Disease Control; Unit 8: Chris Jones/The Stock Market; Unit 9: Tom Tracy/MediChrome/The Stock Shop; Unit 10: Dick Luria/MediChrome/The Stock Shop

2: Clyde Smith/Peter Arnold, Inc.; 5: Sybil Shackman/Monkmeyer; 6: Michael Renner/Bruce Coleman, Inc.; 7: American Dental Association; 9: Ted Tsumura; 11: Bill Ross/Woodfin Camp; 18: Steve Powell/All-Sport/West Light; 19: (*left*) Steve Ross/PhotoUnique, (*right*) David Madison/Bruce Coleman, Inc.; 20: Zao-Longfield/The Image Bank; 21: Ken Levinson/Monkmeyer; 24: Russell Dian; 25: Bill Stanton/ISP; 28: Glyn Cloyd/Taurus; 29: (*both*) Russell Dian/McGraw-Hill; 30: (*top*) Russell Dian/McGraw-Hill, (*middle and bottom*) Ted Tsumura; 31: (*top and middle*) Ted Tsumura, (*bottom*) Russell Dian/McGraw-Hill; 32: Bob McKeever/Tom Stack & Associates; 33: Stanley Rice/Monkmeyer; 34: James Karales/Peter Arnold, Inc.; 36: Hugh Rogers/Monkmeyer; 40: Donald Smetzer/Click, Chicago; 42: Wayne Miller/Magnum; 43: Blair Seitz; 44: Robert Maxham/The Stock Shop; 46: Donald Smetzer/ Click, Chicago; 49: (*top*) Blair Seitz, (*bottom*) Tsuva/DPI; 52: Co Rentmeester/The Image Bank; 55: Harry Wilks/Stock, Boston; 56: Tony Duffy/All-Sport/West Light; 60: Kay Chernush/Wheeler Pictures; 61: Erika Stone/Peter Arnold, Inc.; 63: John Lei/Omni-Photo Communications; 65: Joe McNally/Wheeler Pictures; 66: Gabe Palmer/The Image Bank; 69: L. H. Jawitz/The Image Bank; 70: Blair Seitz; 75: Kelly Langley/DPI; 80: James Karales/Peter Arnold, Inc.; 83: (*both*) Manfred Kage/Peter Arnold, Inc.; 87: Kenneth Garrett/Woodfin Camp; 91: UPI/Bettmann Newsphotos; 93: American Cancer Society; 95: William Hubbell/Woodfin Camp; 98: Jerry Howard/Stock, Boston; 100: Paul Conklin/Monkmeyer; 102: Click, Chicago; 103: John McGrail/Wheeler Pictures; 104: Richard